MW01232996

MAIN EXHIBITION OF LOTS

Orange County Convention Center • North/South Building • Room 220 D, E, F
9860 Universal Blvd • Orlando, FL 32819

Monday, January 1st	9 AM-7 PM ET	Thursday, January 4th	8 AM-7 PM ET
Tuesday, January 2nd	8 AM-7 PM ET	Friday, January 5th	8 AM-7 PM ET
Wednesday, January 3rd	8 AM-7 PM ET	Saturday, January 6th	8 AM-5 PM ET

PUBLIC, INTERNET AND MAIL BID AUCTION #422

Orange County Convention Center • North/South Building; Room 230 A, B
9860 Universal Blvd • Orlando, FL 32819

Session 1 .... Wednesday, January 3 .... 2 PM ET
Session 2 .... (Platinum Night I) .... Wednesday, January 3 .... Dinner @ 5 PM ET; Auction @ 6 PM ET
Session 3 ...... (Patterns)................................. Wednesday, January 3 .... Approx 8:30 PM ET
Session 4 .... Thursday, January 4 .... 9:30 AM ET
Session 5 .... Thursday, January 4 .... 2 PM ET
Session 6 ...... (Dr. Loewinger Collection) ...... Thursday, January 4 .... Dinner @ 6 PM ET; Auction @ 7 PM ET
Session 7 .... (Kutasi Collection).................... Thursday, January 4 .... Approx 8 PM ET

Session 8 .... (Platinum Night II) .... Thursday, January 4 .... Approx 9 PM ET .... Lots 3350-3906

Session 9 .... Friday, January 5 .... 9 AM ET
Session 10 .... Friday, January 5 .... 2 PM ET
Session 11 .... Friday, January 5 .... 5 PM ET
Session 12 .... Saturday, January 6 .... 9:30 AM ET
Session 13 .... Saturday, January 6 .... 1 PM ET
Session 14 .... Saturday, January 6 .... 5 PM ET

Lots are generally sold at the approximate rate of 200 per hour, but it is not uncommon to sell 150 lots or 300 lots in any given hour. Please plan accordingly so that you don't miss the items you are bidding on.

This auction is subject to a 15% Buyer's Premium.

The World's #1 Numismatic Auctioneer

HERITAGE HA.com
Auction Galleries

3500 Maple Avenue, 17th Floor, Dallas, Texas 75219-3941
214-528-3500 • 800-US COINS (872-6467)

LOT SETTLEMENT AND PICKUP:

Thurs.-Sat., Jan. 4-6..... 10 AM – 1 PM
Sun., Jan. 7 .... 9 AM – 12 PM
(By appointment only)

Direct Client Service Line: Toll Free 1-866-835-3243 • e-mail: **Bid@HA.com**

View full-color images at **HA.com/Coins**

Auctioneer: Samuel W. Foose AU3244
Auction presented by:
Heritage Numismatic Auctions, Inc.: AB0000665

Cataloged by Mark Van Winkle, Chief Cataloger;
Brian Koller, Catalog Production Manager; Mark Borckardt, Senior Cataloger;
Jon Amato, John Beety, Bill Fivaz, Stewart Huckaby, Greg Lauderdale, Bruce Lorich, David W. Perkins, John Salyer

Photography and Imaging by Jody Garver, Chief Photographer;
Leticia Crawford, Piper Crawley, Lucas Garritson, Thea Klaas, Lori McKay,
Deign Rook, Tony Webb, Jason Young,

Production and design by Cindy Brenner, Cathy Hadd, Michael Puttonen, Marsha Taylor

FAX BIDS TO:
214-443-8425

FAX DEADLINE:
Tues., Jan. 2, Noon CT

INTERNET BIDDING:
Closes at 10 PM CT
before the session
on sale

Auction
Results

Available Immediately
at our website:
HA.com/Coins

AUCTION #422

Dear Platinum Nights Bidder,

Welcome to Heritage's F.U.N. 2007 Platinum Night sessions. Platinum Nights features some of the very finest coins that Heritage Auction Galleries is auctioning at the 2007 annual Orlando convention of the Florida United Numismatists, as their Official Auctioneer. Quite simply, this is the most amazing "Platinum Night" ever held. First off, you will notice that we are offering so many incredible, wonderful, desirable coins that we had to hold two Platinum Night sessions, so Platinum Nights is the new standard! So many national numismatic treasures that it takes five catalogs (don't miss the Pattern, Loewinger and Kutasi volumes) to present all of Platinum Nights on Wednesday and Thursday!

Bringing together the "rarest of the rare," Platinum Night has become a legendary part of the numismatic scene in America. The growth of the concept has been so significant that we need to remind ourselves that our inaugural event was held only three years ago at F.U.N. This year's coins certainly follow in that tradition of importance, and are some of the most magnificent items that we have ever offered on the auction block.

In fact, there are so many important rarities that it is impossible to list even a small portion of the highlights selected out of the consignments of more than 500 numismatists who entrusted Heritage with their treasures. Among the stellar rarities from America's numismatic heritage: an 1855 Kellogg & Co. $50, certified as PR64 by PCGS; Kellogg's personal 1852/1 Humbert $20, PCGS PR65; an 1839 $10, NGC PR67 Ultra Cameo; an MCMVII Ultra High Relief $20, PR68 PCGS; five Willow Tree pieces (two sixpence and three shillings); an incredibly rare complete, cased 16-coin proof set of 1868 coinage designs struck in aluminum; more than 150 gold proofs; or 458 patterns! Many of these featured coins were contributed by our anchor consignors, and I invite you to read more about them in the main F.U.N. catalogs. What a great time to be a coin collector!

If you are coming to Orlando to participate in this exciting, historic event, please take a moment to visit with me in lot viewing or at the Heritage tables. I always enjoy making new friends at F.U.N., and catching up with old ones. If your schedule doesn't allow you to join us, we still welcome your participation through the Internet at HA.com. With 250,000+ registered bidder-members in our online community, you are always among friends and fellow collectors. Good luck with your bidding!

Sincerely,

Greg Rohan
President

TERMS AND CONDITIONS OF AUCTION

Auctioneer and Auction:

1. This Auction is presented by Heritage Auction Galleries, a d/b/a/ of Heritage Auctions, Inc., or their affiliates Heritage Numismatic Auctions, Inc. or Currency Auctions of America, Inc., d/b/a as identified with the applicable licensing information on the title page of the catalog or on the HA.com Internet site (the "Auctioneer"). The Auction is conducted under these Terms and Conditions of Auction and applicable state and local law. Announcements and corrections from the podium and those made through the Terms and Conditions of Auctions appearing on the Internet at HA.com supersede those in the printed catalog.

Buyer's Premium:

2. On bids placed through Heritage, a Buyer's Premium of fifteen percent (15%) will be added to the successful hammer price bid on lots in Coin and Currency auctions, or nineteen and one-half percent (19.5%) on lots in all other auctions. If your bid is placed through eBay Live, a Buyer's Premium equal to the normal Buyer's Premium plus an additional five percent (5%) of the hammer price will be added to the successful bid up to a maximum Buyer's Premium of Twenty Two and one-half percent (22.5%). There is a minimum Buyer's Premium of $9.00 per lot. In Gallery Auctions only, a ten percent (10%) handling fee is applied to all lots based upon the total of the hammer price plus the 15% Buyer's Premium.

Auction Venues:

3. The following Auctions are conducted solely on the Internet: Heritage Weekly Internet Coin, Currency, Comics, and Vintage Movie Poster Auctions; Heritage Monthly Internet Sports and Marketplace Auctions; OnLine Sessions. Signature Auctions and Grand Format Auctions accept bids on the Internet first, followed by a floor bidding session; bids may be placed prior to the floor bidding session by Internet, telephone, fax, or mail.

Bidders:

4. Any person participating or registering for the Auction agrees to be bound by and accepts these Terms and Conditions of Auction ("Bidder(s)").

5. All Bidders must meet Auctioneer's qualifications to bid. Any Bidder who is not a customer in good standing of the Auctioneer may be disqualified at Auctioneer's sole option and will not be awarded lots. Such determination may be made by Auctioneer in its sole and unlimited discretion, at any time prior to, during, or even after the close of the Auction. Auctioneer reserves the right to exclude any person it deems in its sole opinion is disruptive to the Auction or is otherwise commercially unsuitable.

6. If an entity places a bid, then the person executing the bid on behalf of the entity agrees to personally guarantee payment for any successful bid.

Credit References:

7. Bidders who have not established credit with the Auctioneer must either furnish satisfactory credit information (including two collectibles-related business references) well in advance of the Auction or supply valid credit card information. Bids placed through our Interactive Internet program will only be accepted from pre-registered Bidders; Bidders who are not members of HA.com or affiliates should pre-register at least two business days before the first session to allow adequate time to contact references.

Bidding Options:

8. Bids in Signature Auctions or Grand Format Auctions may be placed as set forth in the printed catalog section entitled "Choose your bidding method." For auctions held solely on the Internet, see the alternatives on HA.com. Review at HA.com/common/howtobid.php.

9. Presentment of Bids: Non-Internet bids (including but not limited to podium, fax, phone and mail bids) are treated similar to floor bids in that they must be on-increment or at a half increment (called a cut bid). Any podium, fax, phone, or mail bids that do not conform to a full or half increment will be rounded up or down to the nearest full or half increment and this revised amount will be considered your high bid.

10. Auctioneer's Execution of Certain Bids. Auctioneer cannot be responsible for your errors in bidding, so carefully check that every bid is entered correctly. When identical mail or FAX bids are submitted, preference is given to the first received. To ensure the greatest accuracy, your written bids should be entered on the standard printed bid sheet and be received at Auctioneer's place of business at least two business days before the Auction start. Auctioneer is not responsible for executing mail bids or FAX bids received on or after the day the first lot is sold, nor Internet bids submitted after the published closing time; nor is Auctioneer responsible for proper execution of bids submitted by telephone, mail, FAX, e-mail, Internet, or in person once the Auction begins. Internet bids may not be withdrawn until your written request is received and acknowledged by Auctioneer (FAX: 214-443-8425); such requests must state the reason, and may constitute grounds for withdrawal of bidding privileges. Lots won by mail Bidders will not be delivered at the Auction unless prearranged.

11. Caveat as to Bid Increments. Bid increments (over the current bid level) determine the lowest amount you may bid on a particular lot. Bids greater than one increment over the current bid can be any whole dollar amount. It is possible under several circumstances for winning bids to be between increments, sometimes only $1 above the previous increment. Please see: "How can I lose by less than an increment?" on our website.

The following chart governs current bidding increments.

Current Bid	Bid Increment	Current Bid	Bid Increment
< $10	$1	$3,000 - $4,999	$250
$10 - $29	$2	$5,000 - $9,999	$500
$30 - $59	$3	$10,000 - $19,999	$1,000
$60 - $99	$5	$20,000 - $29,999	$2,000
$100 - $199	$10	$30,000 - $49,999	$2,500
$200 - $299	$20	$50,000 - $99,999	$5,000
$300 - $499	$25	$100,000 - $249,999	$10,000
$500 - $999	$50	$250,000 - $499,999	$25,000
$1,000 - $1,999	$100	$500,000 - $1,499,999	$50,000
$2,000 - $2,999	$200	> $1,500,000	$100,000

12. If Auctioneer calls for a full increment, a floor/phone bidder may request Auctioneer to accept a bid at half of the increment ("Cut Bid") which will be that bidders final bid; if the Auctioneer solicits bids other the expected increment, they will not be considered Cut Bids, and bidders accepting such increments may continue to participate.

Conducting the Auction:

13. Notice of the consignor's liberty to place reserve bids on his lots in the Auction is hereby made in accordance with Article 2 of the Texas Uniform Commercial Code. A reserve is an amount below which the lot will not sell. THE CONSIGNOR OF PROPERTY MAY PLACE WRITTEN RESERVE BIDS ON HIS LOTS IN ADVANCE OF THE AUCTION; ON SUCH LOTS, IF THE HAMMER PRICE DOES NOT MEET THE RESERVE, THE CONSIGNOR MAY PAY A REDUCED COMMISSION ON THOSE LOTS. Reserves are generally posted online several days prior to the Auction closing. Any successful bid placed by a consignor on his Property on the Auction floor or by telephone during the live session, or after the reserves for an Auction have been posted, will be considered an Unqualified Bid, and in such instances the consignor agrees to pay full Buyer's Premium and Seller's Commissions on any lot so repurchased.

14. The highest qualified Bidder shall be the buyer. In the event of any dispute between floor Bidders at a Signature Auction, Auctioneer may at his sole discretion reoffer the lot. Auctioneer's decision and declaration of the winning Bidder shall be final and binding upon all Bidders.

15. Auctioneer reserves the right to refuse to honor any bid or to limit the amount of any bid which, in his sole discretion, is not submitted in "Good Faith", or is not supported by satisfactory credit, numismatic references, or otherwise. A bid is considered not made in "Good Faith" when an insolvent or irresponsible person, or a person under the age of eighteen makes it. Regardless of the disclosure of his identity, any bid by a consignor or his agent on a lot consigned by him is deemed to be made in "Good Faith".

16. Nominal Bids. The Auctioneer in its sole discretion may reject nominal bids, small opening bids, or very nominal advances. If a lot bearing estimates fails to open for 40–60% of the low estimate, the Auctioneer may pass the item or may place a protective bid on behalf of the consignor.

17. Lots bearing bidding estimates shall open at Auctioneer's discretion (approximately 50% of the low estimate). In the event that no bid meets or exceeds that opening amount, the lot shall pass as unsold.

18. All items are to be purchased per lot as numerically indicated and no lots will be broken. Bids will be accepted in whole dollar amounts only. No "buy" or "unlimited" bids will be accepted. Off-increment bids may be accepted by the Auctioneer at Signature Auctions and Grand Format Auctions. Auctioneer reserves the right to withdraw, prior to the close, any lots from the Auction.

19. Auctioneer reserves the right to rescind the sale in the event of nonpayment, breach of a warranty, disputed ownership, auctioneer's clerical error or omission in exercising bids and reserves, or otherwise.

20. Auctioneer occasionally experiences Internet and/or Server service outages during which Bidders cannot participate or place bids. If such outage occurs, we may at our discretion extend bidding for the auction. This policy applies only to widespread outages and not to isolated problems that occur in various parts of the country from time to time. Auctioneer periodically schedules system downtime for maintenance and other purposes, which may be covered by the Outage Policy. Bidders unable to place their Bids through the Internet are directed to bid through Client Services at 1-800-872-6467.

21. The Auctioneer or its affiliates may consign items to be sold in the Auction, and may bid on those lots or any other lots. Auctioneer or affiliates expressly reserve the right to modify any such bids at any time prior to the hammer based upon data made known to the Auctioneer or its affiliates. The Auctioneer may extend advances, guarantees, or loans to certain consignors, and may extend financing or other credits at varying rates to certain Bidders in the auction.

22. The Auctioneer has the right to sell certain unsold items after the close of the Auction; Such lots shall be considered sold during the Auction and all these Terms and Conditions shall apply to such sales including but not limited to the Buyer's Premium, return rights, and disclaimers.

Payment:

23. All sales are strictly for cash in United States dollars. Cash includes: U.S. currency, bank wire, cashier checks, travelers checks, and bank money orders, all subject to reporting requirements. Checks may be subject to clearing before delivery of the purchases. Credit Card (Visa or Master Card only) and PayPal payments may be accepted up to $10,000 from non-dealers at the sole discretion of the auctioneer, subject to the following limitations: a) sales are only to the cardholder, b) purchases are shipped to the cardholder's registered and verified address, c) Auctioneer may pre-approve the cardholder's credit line, d) a credit card transaction may not be used in conjunction with any other financing or extended terms offered by the Auctioneer, and must transact immediately upon invoice presentation, e) rights of return are governed by these Terms and Conditions, which supersede those conditions promulgated by the card issuer, f) floor Bidders must present their card.

24. Payment is due upon closing of the Auction session, or upon presentment of an invoice. Auctioneer reserves the right to void an invoice if payment in full is not received within 7 days after the close of the Auction.

25. Lots delivered in the States of Texas, California, or other states where the Auction may be held, are subject to all applicable state and local taxes, unless appropriate permits are on file with us. Bidder agrees to pay Auctioneer the actual amount of tax due in the event that sales tax is not properly collected due to: 1) an expired, inaccurate, inappropriate tax certificate or declaration, 2) an incorrect interpretation of the applicable statute, 3) or any other reason. Lots from different Auctions may not be aggregated for sales tax purposes.

26. In the event that a Bidder's payment is dishonored upon presentment(s), Bidder shall pay the maximum statutory processing fee set by applicable state law.

27. If any Auction invoice submitted by Auctioneer is not paid in full when due, the unpaid balance will bear interest at the highest rate permitted by law from the date of invoice until paid. If the Auctioneer refers any invoice to an attorney for collection, the buyer agrees to pay attorney's fees, court costs, and other collection costs incurred by Auctioneer. If Auctioneer assigns collection to its in-house legal staff, such attorney's time expended on the matter shall be compensated at a rate comparable to the hourly rate of independent attorneys.

28. In the event a successful Bidder fails to pay all amounts due, Auctioneer reserves the right to resell the merchandise, and such Bidder agrees to pay for the reasonable costs of resale, including a 10% seller's commission, and also to pay any difference between the resale price and the price of the previously successful bid.

29. Auctioneer reserves the right to require payment in full in good funds before delivery of the merchandise.

30. Auctioneer shall have a lien against the merchandise purchased by the buyer to secure payment of the Auction invoice. Auctioneer is further granted a lien and the right to retain possession of any other property of the buyer then held by the Auctioneer or its affiliates to secure payment of any Auction invoice or any other amounts due the Auctioneer or affiliates from the buyer. With respect to these lien rights, Auctioneer shall have all the rights of a secured creditor under Article 9 of the Texas Uniform Commercial Code, including but not limited to the right of sale. In addition, with respect to payment of the Auction invoice(s), the buyer waives any and all rights of offset he might otherwise have against the Auctioneer and the consignor of the merchandise included on the invoice. If a Bidder owes Auctioneer or its affiliates on any account, Auctioneer and its affiliates shall have the right to offset such unpaid account by any credit balance due Bidder, and it may secure by possessory lien any unpaid amount by any of the Bidder's property in their possession.

31. Title shall not pass to the successful Bidder until all invoices are paid in full. It is the responsibility of the buyer to provide adequate insurance coverage for the items once they have been delivered.

Delivery; Shipping and Handling Charges:

32. Shipping and handling charges will be added to invoices. Please refer to Auctioneer's website www.HA.com/common/shipping.php for the latest charges or call Auctioneer. Auctioneer is unable to combine purchases from other auctions or affiliates into one package for shipping purposes.

33. Successful overseas Bidders shall provide written shipping instructions, including specified customs declarations, to the Auctioneer for any lots to be delivered outside of the United States. NOTE: Declaration value shall be the item(s) hammer price together with its buyer's premium.

34. All shipping charges will be borne by the successful Bidder. Any risk of loss during shipment will be borne by the buyer following Auctioneer's delivery to the designated common carrier or third-party shipper, regardless of domestic or foreign shipment.

35. Due to the nature of some items sold, it shall be the responsibility for the successful bidder to arrange pick-up and shipping through third-parties; as to such items Auctioneer shall have no liability.

36. Any request for shipping verification for undelivered packages must be made within 30 days of shipment by Auctioneer.

Cataloging, Warranties and Disclaimers:

37. NO WARRANTY, WHETHER EXPRESSED OR IMPLIED, IS MADE WITH RESPECT TO ANY DESCRIPTION OR CONDITION REPORT CONTAINED IN THIS AUCTION OR ANY SECOND OPINE. Any description of the items or second opine contained in this Auction is for the sole purpose of identifying the items for those Bidders who do not have the opportunity to view the lots prior to bidding, and no description of items has been made part of the basis of the bargain or has created any express warranty that the goods would conform to any description made by Auctioneer.

38. Auctioneer is selling only such right or title to the items being sold as Auctioneer may have by virtue of consignment agreements on the date of auction and disclaims any warranty of title to the Property. Auctioneer disclaims any warranty of merchantability or fitness for any particular purposes.

39. Translations of foreign language documents may be provided as a convenience to interested parties. Heritage makes no representation as to the accuracy of those translations and will not be held responsible for errors in bidding arising from inaccuracies in translation.

40. Auctioneer disclaims all liability for damages, consequential or otherwise, arising out of or in connection with the sale of any Property by Auctioneer to Bidder. No third party may rely on any benefit of these Terms and Conditions and any rights, if any, established hereunder are personal to the Bidder and may not be assigned. Any statement made by the Auctioneer is an opinion and does not constitute a warranty or representation. No employee of Auctioneer may alter these Terms and Conditions, and, unless signed by a principal of Auctioneer, any such alteration is null and void.

41. Auctioneer shall not be liable for breakage of glass or damage to frames (patent or latent); such defects, in any event, shall not be a basis for any claim for return or reduction in purchase price.

Release:

42. In consideration of participation in the Auction and the placing of a bid, Bidder expressly releases Auctioneer, its officers, directors and employees, its affiliates, and its outside experts that provide second opines, from any and all claims, cause of action, chose of action, whether at law or equity or any arbitration or mediation rights existing under

the rules of any professional society or affiliation based upon the assigned description, or a derivative theory, breach of warranty express or implied, representation or other matter set forth within these Terms and Conditions of Auction or otherwise. In the event of a claim, Bidder agrees that such rights and privileges conferred therein are strictly construed as specifically declared herein; e.g., authenticity, typographical error, etc. and are the exclusive remedy. Bidder, by non-compliance to these express terms of a granted remedy, shall waive any claim against Auctioneer.

Dispute Resolution and Arbitration Provision:

43. By placing a bid or otherwise participating in the auction, Bidder accepts these Terms and Conditions of Auction, and specifically agrees to the alternative dispute resolution provided herein. Arbitration replaces the right to go to court, including the right to a jury trial.

44. Auctioneer in no event shall be responsible for consequential damages, incidental damages, compensatory damages, or other damages arising from the auction of any lot. In the event that Auctioneer cannot deliver the lot or subsequently it is established that the lot lacks title, provenance, authenticity, or other transfer or condition issue is claimed, Auctioneer's liability shall be limited to rescission of sale and refund of purchase price; in no case shall Auctioneer's maximum liability exceed the high bid on that lot, which bid shall be deemed for all purposes the value of the lot. After one year has elapsed, Auctioneer's maximum liability shall be limited to any commissions and fees Auctioneer earned on that lot.

45. In the event of an attribution error, Auctioneer may at its sole discretion, correct the error on the Internet, or, if discovered at a later date, to refund the buyer's purchase price without further obligation.

46. If any dispute arises regarding payment, authenticity, grading, description, provenance, or any other matter pertaining to the Auction, the Bidder or a participant in the Auction and/or the Auctioneer agree that the dispute shall be submitted, if otherwise mutually unresolved, to binding arbitration in accordance with the commercial rules of the American Arbitration Association (A.A.A.). A.A.A. arbitration shall be conducted under the provisions of the Federal Arbitration Act with locale in Dallas, Texas. Any claim made by a Bidder has to be presented within one (1) year or it is barred. The prevailing party may be awarded his reasonable attorney's fees and costs. An award granted in arbitration is enforceable in any court of competent jurisdiction. No claims of any kind (except for reasons of authenticity) can be considered after the settlements have been made with the consignors. Any dispute after the settlement date is strictly between the Bidder and consignor without involvement or responsibility of the Auctioneer.

47. In consideration of their participation in or application for the Auction, a person or entity (whether the successful Bidder, a Bidder, a purchaser and/or other Auction participant or registrant) agrees that all disputes in any way relating to, arising under, connected with, or incidental to these Terms and Conditions and purchases, or default in payment thereof, shall be arbitrated pursuant to the arbitration provision. In the event that any matter including actions to compel arbitration, construe the agreement, actions in aid or arbitration or otherwise needs to be litigated, such litigation shall be exclusively in the Courts of the State of Texas, in Dallas County, Texas, and if necessary the corresponding appellate courts. The successful Bidder, purchaser, or Auction participant also expressly submits himself to the personal jurisdiction of the State of Texas.

48. These Terms & Conditions provide specific remedies for occurrences in the auction and delivery process. Where such remedies are afforded, they shall be interpreted strictly. Bidder agrees that any claim shall utilize such remedies; Bidder making a claim in excess of those remedies provided in these Terms and Conditions agrees that in no case whatsoever shall Auctioneer's maximum liability exceed the high bid on that lot, which bid shall be deemed for all purposes the value of the lot..

Miscellaneous:

49. Agreements between Bidders and consignors to effectuate a non-sale of an item at Auction, inhibit bidding on a consigned item to enter into a private sale agreement for said item, or to utilize the Auctioneer's Auction to obtain sales for non-selling consigned items subsequent to the Auction, are strictly prohibited. If a subsequent sale of a previously consigned item occurs in violation of this provision, Auctioneer reserves the right to charge Bidder the applicable Buyer's Premium and consignor a Seller's Commission as determined for each auction venue and by the terms of the seller's agreement.

50. Acceptance of these Terms and Conditions qualifies Bidder as a Heritage customer who has consented to be contacted by Heritage in the future. In conformity with "do-not-call" regulations promulgated by the Federal or State regulatory agencies, participation by the Bidder is affirmative consent to being contacted at the phone number shown in his application and this consent shall remain in effect until it is revoked in writing. Heritage may from time to time contact Bidder concerning sale, purchase, and auction opportunities available through Heritage and its affiliates and subsidiaries.

State Notices:

Notice as to an Auction in California. Auctioneer has in compliance with Title 2.95 of the California Civil Code as amended October 11, 1993 Sec. 1812.600, posted with the California Secretary of State its bonds for it and its employees, and the auction is being conducted in compliance with Sec. 2338 of the Commercial Code and Sec. 535 of the Penal Code.

Notice as to an Auction in New York City. These Terms and Conditions are designed to conform to the applicable sections of the New York City Department of Consumer Affairs Rules and Regulations as Amended. This is a Public Auction Sale conducted by Auctioneer. The New York City licensed Auctioneers are Kathleen Guzman, No.0762165-Day, and Samuel W. Foose, No.0952360-Day, No.0952361-Night, who will conduct the Auction on behalf of Heritage Auctions, Inc. ("Auctioneer"). All lots are subject to: the consignor's right to bid thereon in accord with these Terms and Conditions of Auction, consignor's option to receive advances on their consignments, and Auctioneer, in its sole discretion, may offer limited extended financing to registered bidders, in accord with Auctioneer's internal credit standards. A registered bidder may inquire whether a lot is subject to an advance or reserve. Auctioneer has made advances to various consignors in this sale.

Rev. 10_6_06

ADDITIONAL TERMS AND CONDITIONS OF AUCTION

COINS and CURRENCY TERM A: Signature Auctions are not on approval. No certified material may be returned because of possible differences of opinion with respect to the grade offered by any third-party organization, dealer, or service. No guarantee of grade is offered for uncertified Property sold and subsequently submitted to a third-party grading service. There are absolutely no exceptions to this policy. Under extremely limited circumstances, (e.g. gross cataloging error) a purchaser, who did not bid from the floor, may request Auctioneer to evaluate voiding a sale: such request must be made in writing detailing the alleged gross error; submission of the lot to the Auctioneer must be pre-approved by the Auctioneer; and bidder must notify Ron Brackemyre (1-800-872-6467 ext. 312) in writing of such request within three (3) days of the non-floor bidder's receipt of the lot. Any lot that is to be evaluated must be in our offices within 30 days after Auction. Grading or method of manufacture do not qualify for this evaluation process nor do such complaints constitute a basis to challenge the authenticity of a lot. AFTER THAT 30-DAY PERIOD, NO LOTS MAY BE RETURNED FOR REASONS OTHER THAN AUTHENTICITY. Lots returned must be housed intact in their original holder. No lots purchased by floor Bidders may be returned (including those Bidders acting as agents for others) except for authenticity. Late remittance for purchases may be considered just cause to revoke all return privileges.

COINS and CURRENCY TERM B: Auctions conducted solely on the Internet THREE (3) DAY RETURN POLICY: Certified Coin and Uncertified Currency lots paid for within seven days of the Auction closing are sold with a three (3) day return privilege. Third party graded notes are not returnable for any reason whatsoever. You may return lots under the following conditions: Within three days of receipt of the lot, you must first notify Auctioneer by contacting Client Service by phone (1-800-872-6467) or e-mail (Bid@HA.com), and immediately ship the lot(s) fully insured to the attention of Returns, Heritage, 3500 Maple Avenue, 17th Floor, Dallas TX 75219-3941. Lots must be housed intact in their original holder and condition. You are responsible for the insured, safe delivery of any lots. A non-negotiable return fee of 5% of the purchase price ($10 per lot minimum) will be deducted from the refund for each returned lot or billed directly. Postage and handling fees are not refunded. After the three-day period (from receipt), no items may be returned for any reason. Late remittance for purchases revokes these Return privileges.

COINS and CURRENCY TERM C: Bidders who have inspected the lots prior to any Auction will not be granted any return privileges, except for reasons of authenticity.

COINS and CURRENCY TERM D: Coins sold referencing a third-party grading service are sold "as is" without any express or implied warranty, except for a guarantee by Auctioneer that they are genuine. Certain warranties may be available from the grading services and the Bidder is referred to them for further details: ANACS, P.O. Box 182141, Columbus, Ohio 43218-2141; Numismatic Guaranty Corporation (NGC), P.O. Box 4776, Sarasota, FL 34230; Professional Coin Grading Service (PCGS), PO Box 9458, Newport Beach, CA 92658; and Independent Coin Grading Co. (ICG), 7901 East Belleview Ave., Suite 50, Englewood, CO 80111.

COINS and CURRENCY TERM E: Notes sold referencing a third-party grading service are sold "as is" without any express or implied warranty, except for guarantee by Auctioneer that they are genuine. Grading, condition or other attributes of any lot may have a material effect on its value, and the opinion of others, including third-party grading services such as PCGS Currency, PMG, and CGA may differ with that of Auctioneer. Auctioneer shall not be bound by any prior or subsequent opinion, determination, or certification by any grading service. Bidder specifically waives any claim to right of return of any item because of the opinion, determination, or certification, or lack thereof, by any grading service. Certain warranties may be available from the grading services and the Bidder is referred to them for further details: Paper Money Guaranty (PMG), PO Box 4711, Sarasota FL 34230; PCGS Currency, PO Box 9458, Newport Beach, CA 92658; Currency Grading & Authentication (CGA), PO Box 418, Three Bridges, NJ 08887. Third party graded notes are not returnable for any reason whatsoever.

COINS and CURRENCY TERM F: Since we cannot examine encapsulated coins or notes, they are sold "as is" without our grading opinion, and may not be returned for any reason. Auctioneer shall not be liable for any patent or latent defect or controversy pertaining to or arising from any encapsulated collectible. In any such instance, purchaser's remedy, if any, shall be solely against the service certifying the collectible.

COINS and CURRENCY TERM G: Due to changing grading standards over time, differing interpretations, and to possible mishandling of items by subsequent owners, Auctioneer reserves the right to grade items differently than shown on certificates from any grading service that accompany the items. Auctioneer also reserves the right to grade items differently than the grades shown in the prior catalog should such items be reconsigned to any future auction.

COINS and CURRENCY TERM H: Although consensus grading is employed by most grading services, it should be noted as aforesaid that grading is not an exact science. In fact, it is entirely possible that if a lot is broken out of a plastic holder and resubmitted to another grading service or even to the same service, the lot could come back with a different grade assigned.

COINS and CURRENCY TERM I: Certification does not guarantee protection against the normal risks associated with potentially volatile markets. The degree of liquidity for certified coins and collectibles will vary according to general market conditions and the particular lot involved. For some lots there may be no active market at all at certain points in time.

COINS and CURRENCY TERM J: All non-certified coins and currency are guaranteed genuine, but are not guaranteed as to grade, since grading is a matter of opinion, an art and not a science, and therefore the opinion rendered by the Auctioneer or any third party grading service may not agree with the opinion of others (including trained experts), and the same expert may not grade the same item with the same grade at two different times. Auctioneer has graded the non-certified numismatic items, in the Auctioneer's opinion, to their current interpretation of the American Numismatic Association's standards as of the date the catalog was prepared. There is no guarantee or warranty implied or expressed that the grading standards utilized by the Auctioneer will meet the standards of any grading service at any time in the future.

COINS and CURRENCY TERM K: Storage of purchased coins and currency: Purchasers are advised that certain types of plastic may react with a coin's metal or transfer plasticizer to notes and may cause damage. Caution should be used to avoid storage in materials that are not inert.

COINS and CURRENCY TERM L: NOTE: Purchasers of rare coins or currency through Heritage have available the option of arbitration by the Professional Numismatists Guild (PNG); if an election is not made within ten (10) days of an unresolved dispute, Auctioneer may elect either PNG or A.A.A. Arbitration.

Mail Bidding at Auction

Mail bidding at auction is fun and easy and only requires a few simple steps.

1. Look through the catalog, and determine the lots of interest.

2. Research their market value by checking price lists and other price guidelines.

3. Fill out your bid sheet, entering your maximum bid on each lot using your price research and your desire to own the lot.

4. Verify your bids!

5. Mail Early. Preference is given to the first bids received in case of a tie. When bidding by mail, you frequently purchase items at less than your maximum bid.

Bidding is opened at the published increment above the second highest mail or Internet bid; we act on your behalf as the highest mail bidder. If bidding proceeds, we act as your agent, bidding in increments over the previous bid. This process is continued until you are awarded the lot or you are outbid.

An example of this procedure: You submit a bid of $100, and the second highest mail bid is at $50. Bidding starts at $51 on your behalf. If no other bids are placed, you purchase the lot for $51. If other bids are placed, we bid for you in the posted increments until we reach your maximum bid of $100. If bidding passes your maximum: if you are bidding through the Internet, we will contact you by e-mail; if you bid by mail, we take no other action. Bidding continues until the final bidder wins.

Mail Bidding Instructions

1. **Name, Address, City, State, Zip**
   Your address is needed to mail your purchases. We need your telephone number to communicate any problems or changes that may affect your bids.

2. **References**
   If you have not established credit with us from previous auctions, you must send a 25% deposit, or list dealers with whom you have credit established.

3. **Lot Numbers and Bids**
   List all lots you desire to purchase. On the reverse are additional columns; you may also use another sheet. Under "Amount" enter the maximum you would pay for that lot (whole dollar amounts only). We will purchase the lot(s) for you as much below your bids as possible.

4. **Total Bid Sheet**
   Add up all bids and list that total in the appropriate box.

5. **Sign Your Bid Sheet**
   By signing the bid sheet, you have agreed to abide by the Terms of Auction listed in the auction catalog.

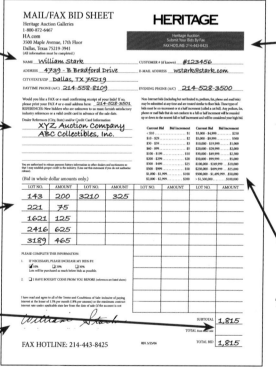

The official prices realized list that accompanies our auction catalogs is reserved for bidders and consignors only. We are happy to mail one to others upon receipt of $1.00. Written requests should be directed to Customer Service.

6. **Fax Your Bid Sheet**
   When time is short submit a Mail Bid Sheet on our exclusive Fax Hotline. There's no faster method to get your bids to us *instantly*. Simply use the **Heritage Fax Hotline number: 214-443-8425.**

   When you send us your original after faxing, mark it "Confirmation of Fax" (preferably in red!)

7. **Bidding Increments**
   To facilitate bidding, please consult the following chart. Bids will be accepted on the increments or on the half increments.

Interactive Internet™ Bidding

You can now bid with Heritage's exclusive *Interactive Internet™* program, available only at our web site: HA.com. It's fun, and it's easy!

1. Register online at:
   HA.com

2. View the full-color photography of every single lot in the online catalog!

3. Construct your own personal catalog for preview.

4. View the current opening bids on lots you want; review the prices realized archive.

5. Bid and receive immediate notification if you are the top bidder; later, if someone else bids higher, you will be notified automatically by e-mail.

6. The *Interactive Internet™* program opens the lot on the floor at one increment over the second highest bid. As the high bidder, your secret maximum bid will compete for you during the floor auction, and it is possible that you may be outbid on the floor after Internet bidding closes. Bid early, as the earliest bird wins in the event of a tie bid.

7. After the sale, you will be notified of your success. It's that easy!

Interactive Internet™ Bidding Instructions

1. Log Onto Website
Log onto **HA.com** and choose the portal you're interested in (i.e., coins, comics, movie posters, fine arts, etc.).

2. Search for Lots
Search or browse for the lot you are interested in. You can do this from the home page, from the Auctions home page, or from the home page for the particular auction in which you wish to participate.

3. Select Lots
Click on the link or the photo icon for the lot you want to bid on.

4. Enter Bid
At the top of the page, next to a small picture of the item, is a box outlining the current bid. Enter the amount of your secret maximum bid in the textbox next to "Secret Maximum Bid." The secret maximum bid is the maximum amount you are willing to pay for the item you are bidding on (for more information about bidding and bid increments, please see the section labeled "Bidding Increments" elsewhere in this catalog). Click on the button marked "Place Absentee Bid." A new area on the same page will open up for you to enter your username (or e-mail address) and password. Enter these, then click "Place Absentee Bid" again.

5. Confirm Absentee Bid
You are taken to a page labeled, "Please Confirm Your Bid." This page shows you the name of the item you're bidding on, the current bid, and the maximum bid. When you are satisfied that all the information shown is correct, click on the button labeled, "Confirm Bid."

6. Bidding Status Notification
One of two pages is now displayed.

a. If your bid is the current high bid, you will be notified and given additional information as to what might happen to affect your high bidder status over the course of the remainder of the auction. You will also receive a Bid Confirmation notice via email.

b. If your bid is not the current high bid, you will be notified of that fact and given the opportunity to increase your bid.

Heritage Auction Galleries Numismatic Staff

Steve Ivy - Co-Chairman and CEO

Mr. Ivy's interest in rare coins began about forty-eight years ago, when as a youth, he began collecting and studying rare coins. In 1963 he began advertising coins for sale in national publications and seven years later at the age of twenty, opened Steve Ivy Rare Coins in downtown Dallas. The company grew rapidly, and in 1972, was incorporated as Steve Ivy Rare Coin Co., Inc. In June, 1976, Steve Ivy Numismatic Auctions was incorporated as a wholly owned subsidiary. Throughout this time, Ivy managed the business as well as serving as chief numismatist, buying and selling millions of dollars worth of coins during the 1970s and early 1980s. In early 1983, James Halperin, founder and former president of New England Rare Coin Galleries, was brought in as a full partner with Mr. Ivy, and the name of the parent corporation was changed to Heritage Rare Coin Galleries. The names of subsidiaries were similarly changed to reflect the Heritage name. Since the addition of Halperin, Mr. Ivy's primary responsibilities include the management of the selling efforts of the company in all markets — wholesale, retail, investment and auction — and the formation of corporate policy for long term growth. Mr. Ivy is also responsible for the day-to- day management of the administrative, accounting, data processing and marketing departments of the company as they relate to each subsidiary or affiliate, and corporate relations with financial institutions, as well as outside legal and accounting firms. Mr. Ivy remains intimately involved in numismatics, attending all major national shows and engaging in daily discourse with industry leaders on all aspects of the business of numismatics. His views on grading, market trends and hobby developments are respected throughout the industry. He serves on the Board of Directors of the Professional Numismatists Guild (PNG) as immediate past president, an organization whose members are elected and who must abide by a strict code of ethics and conduct. Mr. Ivy is also the current Chairman of Industry Council Tangible Assets. Mr. Ivy is a member of most leading numismatic organizations, including the American Numismatic Association, Florida United Numismatists, Texas Numismatic Association and numerous others. In addition, Mr. Ivy's keen appreciation of history is reflected in his activity in non-numismatic organizations as well, including past or present board positions on the Texas Historical Foundation and the Dallas Historical Society, the latter of which he also served as Exhibits Chairman. Mr. Ivy is an avid collector of Texas books, manuscripts and National Currency, and owns one of the largest and finest collections in private hands.

James Halperin - Co-Chairman

James Halperin is probably the most successful professional numismatist of all time. Jim and traders under his supervision have transacted billions in coin business, and have outsold all other numismatic firms every year for over 20 years. An astonishing percentage of America's more prominent coin dealers learned their craft by working for Jim at one time or another. Born in Boston, Massachusetts in 1952, Jim attended Middlesex School in Concord, Mass. from 1966 to 1970. At the age of 15, he formed a part-time rare coin (numismatic) business, and discovered that he had a knack — and a nearly photographic memory — for coins. Shortly thereafter, Jim scored a perfect 800 on his math SATs and received early acceptance to Harvard College. After attending three semesters during 1970-1971, he took a permanent leave of absence to pursue a full-time numismatic career. In 1975, Jim personally supervised the protocols for the first mainframe computer system in the numismatic business, which, in less than four years, would catapult his firm to the top of the industry. Later in 1975 (at age 22), he founded the first rare coin investment partnership. Coins purchased by Jim in 1976 and 1977 for less than $360,000 were liquidated at auction in April, 1980 for over $2.15 million, whereupon each $7,500 investor received slightly over $34,700 after all commissions, incentive fees and expenses. Fidelity Investments CEO Ned Johnson was one of the limited partners, as were numerous other individuals, at least two of whom used the proceeds to save their businesses during the recession of 1980-81. In 1983 he merged his company with that of his friend and then-arch-rival, Steve Ivy, whom Jim had long admired. Their partnership, has become the world's largest and most successful numismatic company, as well as the third largest auctioneer in America based on annual sales volume. Jim remains arguably the best "eye" in the coin business today (he won the professional division of the PCGS World Series of Grading in August 2004), and may know more about evaluating the condition and value of coins than anyone alive. In the mid-1980s, he authored "How to Grade U.S. Coins" (also posted on the web for free at www.CoinGrading.com), a highly-acclaimed, landmark text upon which the NGC and PCGS grading standards in effect today were ultimately based. He is a bit of a renaissance man, too. A well-known futurist, Jim is also an active collector of EC comics and early-20th century American art among other things (see some highlights on view at www.jhalpe.com), venture capital investor, philanthropist (he endows a multimillion-dollar health education foundation), and part-time novelist. "The Truth Machine," his first attempt at fiction, was published in 1996, became an international science fiction bestseller (300,000 copies sold to date), and was optioned for development as a major motion picture by Warner Brothers. Jim's second novel, titled "The First Immortal," was published in early 1998 and immediately optioned as a Hallmark Hall of Fame television miniseries. Jim has been married to Gayle Ziaks (MFA, Fmr. TWU Asst. Professor of Dance, Chairwoman of The Dance Council) since 1984. In 1996, with funding from Jim and Gayle's foundation, Gayle founded Dance for the Planet, which has grown to become the largest free dance festival in the world. Gayle and Jim have two sons, David (b.1991) and Michael (b.1995). P.S. If you buy any of Jim's books, you will be supporting a good cause. Jim donates all royalties and other book-related income to charity.

Greg Rohan - President

Mr. Rohan's interest in both rare coins and business began at the age of eight when he not only started collecting coins, but also began buying them for resale to his schoolmates. In 1971 at the age of ten, he was already buying and selling coins from a dealer's table at trade shows in his hometown of Seattle. His business grew rapidly, and by 1985 he had offices in both Seattle and Minneapolis. He joined Heritage in 1987 as Executive Vice-President and Manager of the firm's rare coin business. Today, as an owner and as President of Heritage, his responsibilities include overseeing the firm's private client group and working with top collectors in every field in which Heritage is active. Mr. Rohan is involved with many of the rarest and most important collections handled by the firm, including the purchase of the Ed Trompeter Collection (the world's largest numismatic purchase according to the "Guinness Book of World Records"). The purchases and sales of the legendary 1894 San Francisco Dime, 1838 New Orleans Half Dollar, and 1804 Silver Dollar were personally handled by Mr. Rohan. He has been instrumental in working with collectors, consignors and their advisors regarding significant collection in the fields of books, manuscripts, comics, currency, jewelry, vintage movie posters, sports and entertainment memorabilia, decorative arts and fine art. In addition, Mr. Rohan is Chapter Chairman for North Texas of the Young Presidents' Organization (YPO), a Sage Society member of the American Numismatic Society (ANS), member of the Professional Numismatists Guild (PNG), and a life member of the American Numismatic Association. He also is a member of most leading numismatic organizations including Early American Coppers Club (EAC), Florida United Numismatists (FUN), Central States Numismatic Society (CSNS), and the Texas Numismatic Association (TNA). He is an active supporter of the arts. During his career, Mr. Rohan has handled more than $1 billion worth of rare coins, collectibles and art and provided expert consultation concerning the authenticity and condition (grade) of coins for the Professional Coin Grading Service (PCGS). He has provided expert testimony for the United States Attorneys in San Francisco, Dallas and Philadelphia and for the Federal Trade Commission (FTC). Additionally, he evaluated and handled the deaccession of properties held by the State of Connecticut for the Museum of Connecticut History. Mr. Rohan co-authored "The Collectors Estate Handbook" (ISBN 0-9651041-2-5), winner of The Robert Friedberg Award for numismatic book of the year. Mr. Rohan currently serves on the seven-person Advisory Board to the Federal Reserve Bank of Dallas where he is in his second appointed term. He and his wife, Lysa, are avid collectors of rare wine, Native American artifacts, and American art.

Paul Minshull - Chief Operating Officer

As Chief Operating Officer, Paul's hard work, dedication and tireless efforts have helped Heritage grow and refine its various ventures. Paul's managerial responsibilities include integrating all aspects of sales, personnel, inventory, security and MIS for Heritage Rare Coin Galleries and Heritage Numismatic Auctions, Inc., Heritage Comics and Currency Auctions of America along with other affiliates. His major accomplishments have included: Overseeing the hardware migration from mainframe to PC network and software migration of all inventory and sales systems. Supervising the implementation and growth of a major internet presence. Management of a successful employee-suggestion program that generates 200 or more ideas each month - a program that started in 1995 and has helped increase employee productivity, expand business, and has improved employee retention. One of Paul's important management responsibilities is overseeing the company's highly-regarded IT department. Paul has been the driving force behind all of Heritage's Web development. From the start of Heritage's first web site in 1997 to the addition of the tremendously successful Internet Auctions, IT and web development have become a significant portion of Heritage's future plans and expansion opportunities. As the only numismatic auction house that combines traditional floor sales with active Internet bidding, the totally interactive system has catapulted Heritage to the top Rare Coin web site (according to Forbes Magazine "Best of the Web" in the fall of 1999 and 2001). Web sales and auctions now average over seven figures each month and are a significant profit center for Heritage. Paul was born in Michigan and came to Heritage in 1984 after 12 years as the General Manager of a plastics manufacturing company in Ann Arbor. He began as a general partner in Heritage Capital Properties, a $2,000,000-equity real estate partnership. In this capacity he managed all aspects of purchase, sale and rental of residential real estate. The partnership liquidated and closed in 1996. Concurrent with his work in the real estate division, Paul assumed increasing responsibilities with Heritage Capital Corporation. Since 1987, he has been the Sales Manager, Vice President of Operations and since 1996, Chief Operating Officer for all Heritage companies and affiliates. Paul maintains an active interest in sports and physical fitness. He and his wife have three children.

Todd Imhof - Vice President

Unlike most of today's professional numismatists, Todd did not start off as a collector. A twist of fate shortly after graduating college in 1987 led Todd to decline an offer from a prestigious Wall Street bank to join a former high school classmate who operated a small rare coin company in the Seattle area, Hertzberg Rare Coins. At that time, the rare coin industry was undergoing huge changes from the advent of NGC & PCGS grading and the growing computer technology that businesses were adapting to. Being new to the industry, Todd had an easier time than most embracing the new dynamics and soon discovered a personal passion for rare coins - and for working with high-level collectors. Todd has already accomplished more than the vast majority of dealers will in a lifetime and he enjoys a reputation that is envied by the entire numismatic community. During his tenure with Hertzberg, it was named by Inc. magazine one of the nation's fastest growing private companies three years in a row (1989, 1990 & 1991). In 1991, he co-founded Pinnacle Rarities, Inc., a boutique-styled firm that specialized in servicing the rare coin industry's savviest and most prominent collectors, where he served as President until his decision to join us here at Heritage in May, 2006. At 25, he was among the youngest people ever accepted to the Professional Numismatists Guild, and currently serves on its Consumer Protection Committee. In 1992, he was invited to join the Board of Directors for the Industry Council for Tangible Assets, serving as its Chairman between 2002-2005. In last November's Morse Sale, he became the only person in history to purchase two separate $1mm+ coins during a single auction session! Before joining Heritage, Todd was no stranger to a great many of Heritage's Legacy clients who had already sought his counsel and found his expertise and integrity to be of great value. Over the years, our Consignment Directors had noted that so many of the finest and best performing coins being sold in Heritage auctions were linked to the same dealer . . . Todd Imhof. We made it a priority to recruit Todd and were delighted he accepted our invitation to join us here in Dallas. He really understands what a collector is trying to accomplish and has an uncanny ability to identify the perfect coins at the right prices. He really impresses clients and colleagues by his ability to navigate complex and difficult deals with unsurpassed professionalism. We are very proud to welcome Todd to our executive team and we're confident you'll benefit tremendously from his knowledge and integrity.

Norma L. Gonzalez - VP of Operations - Numismatic Auctions

Born July 12, 1975, in Dallas, Texas. She began pursuing her career as a young adult when making the decision to join the U.S. Navy in August of 1993 after graduating from High School. During her five-year enlistment she received her Bachelor's Degree in Resource Management and traveled to Japan, Singapore, Thailand and lived in Cuba for three years. Once her enlistment was over she moved back to Dallas where her family resides. Norma joined Heritage Galleries & Auctioneers in 1998. With her experience from the United States Navy she has made a big impact on the Heritage team. Always ready for a challenge, she spent her days at Heritage and her nights at school aspiring to receive her Master's degree. She was promoted to Vice President in 2003 and received her Master's Degree in Business Administration in August. She currently manages the operation's departments, including but not limited to Coins, Currency, World & Ancient Coins, Sportscards & Memorabilia, Comics, Movie Posters, Pop Culture and Political Memorabilia. Outside of work Norma enjoys running, biking and spending time with her family. In February 2004 she ran a 26.2-mile marathon in Austin, Texas and later, in March she accomplished a 100-mile bike ride in California.

Cathy Hadd - VP - Marketing

A native of Illinois, Cathy Hadd graduated from the University of Iowa with a BFA in Fine Arts, where she studied printmaking and lithography under Maurice Lasansky and Virginia Meyers. She then worked toward her MBA in Management/Arbitration from the same institution. Cathy married in moved to Dallas in 1984. In 1987, Cathy joined Heritage as part of the marketing department on a contract basis, working primarily in production and design. Eight months later, she became the Marketing-Service Manager, and shortly thereafter, was named Vice-President of Marketing, a position she holds to this day. Under Cathy's guidance and leadership, the Marketing Department, which is responsible for all advertising, promotion, and public relations efforts for the entire company, has been honored with over one hundred Graphic, Design, and Promotional awards, on both a regional and a national level. In addition, Cathy has been instrumental in obtaining three Guinness World Records on behalf of Heritage, and is working on number four. During her tenure at Heritage, Cathy has definitely been bitten by the collecting bug; over the last several years she has obtained an eclectic assortment of collectible material such as vintage jewelry, movie props, pop culture memorabilia, and fine art. More than anything, however, Cathy enjoys the incredible variety of people her job has brought her into contact with, including Spider-Man co-creator Stan Lee, GI Joe creator Don Levine, and a number of fascinating numismatists and celebrities. Cathy is very involved in the community and volunteers her time and services to the Leukemia Association, the Kidney Foundation, Dallas Challenge, and Dance for the Planet. She is a member of several numismatic and professional organizations, but still finds time to relax at home with her husband of more than 21 years and her two children, daughter Paige, a competitive cheerleader, and son Andrew, who received an academic chemistry scholarship at the University of Colorado, and is on the bike team at CU.

Steven R. Roach - Director, Trusts and Estates

Steven R. Roach, Director of Trusts & Estates, received his JD from The Ohio State University Moritz College of Law. He was a senior editor on Ohio State's Journal of Law & Policy where he published a note on laws affecting financial privacy and was a national-level moot court competitor. He served as a judicial extern to United States District Court Judge Gregory Frost, and was a summer research fellow for the American Bar Association (ABA) Section on Dispute Resolution in Washington, D.C. He was a managing editor for the Pro Bono Research Group (PBRG) and was named a Public Service Fellow with Dean's Special Recognition.

Steve is admitted to practice law in the state of Texas and is a member of the American Bar Association, the Dallas Bar Association, and the Dallas Estate Planning Council. Steve received his BA with high honors from the University of Michigan with a dual degree in the History of Art and Organizational Studies. He received the Tappan award for outstanding performance in the History of Art program and studied in Florence, Italy. While at Michigan, he was a member of the Pi Kappa Alpha fraternity, president of Michigan's History of Art Association, and secretary of Mortar Board. Prior to starting law school, Steve worked at Heritage as a numismatist and senior grader. He was a grader at ANACS for several years, and has worked with Christie's and Spink-America in New York, and PCGS in Los Angeles. His articles have received two prestigious Numismatic Literary Guild (NLG) awards and his numismatic exhibits have captured numerous Best of Show awards. In 2000, Michigan Governor John Engler appointed Steve to his home state's 50 State Quarter Design Commission. Steve has been actively involved in numismatics for more than 15 years and the American Numismatic Association (ANA) named him its Outstanding Young Numismatist of the Year in 1997. Starting in January, 2007, Steve will be authoring the "Inside Collecting" column in Coin World, the world's largest coin hobby publication.

John Petty - Director - Media Relations

John joined Heritage in June, 2001 as the first employee of the newly-formed Heritage Comics division. A passionate collector, comics historian, and Overstreet advisor, John had a life-long interest in comics and was anxious to join such an exciting industry. John's collecting interests are broad, encompassing everything from Golden Age comics to presently published titles. His consuming interest, however, is in original comic art (he proudly owns the world's largest collection of art featuring Jack Kirby's Mister Miracle), which he's been collecting since 1984. In addition to comics and art, John collects lobby cards, movie posters (with a special emphasis on Japanese dai kaiju titles such as Godzilla, Mothra and Rodan), Captain Action figures, first edition books (particularly Arkham House titles) and dabbles in antique pocket watches. In 2004, John became the Director of Media

Relations, and now handles Public Relations, copywriting and media affairs for the entire company as part of Heritage's award-winning Marketing Department. He also works on special assignments such as magazine articles, special book projects and TV productions from time to time. Originally from the New York area, John now lives in Irving, TX with Judy, his significant other, two dogs and three cats. He holds a Bachelor of Music degree in Voice from Baldwin-Wallace College in Berea, OH, and has worked as a professional magician and escape artist, as well as a radio talk show host, a wine tasting instructor and a comedy defensive driving teacher. In his spare time, John enjoys leather carving, silent movies, and Celtic music. As Director of Media Relations, John writes Press and Media Releases for all of Heritage's many divisions. He works with external media consultants, and is frequently called upon to give interviews on behalf of Heritage for TV, radio, and print media. He is Chief Copywriter and Copy Reviewer for all Advertising and Marketing Projects, and writes special projects, including book and magazine articles, on a variety of Heritage-related subjects. He was the lead scriptwriter for the newly-produced HNAI DVD, and is currently working on a similar DVD project for several other divisions. John is also one of Heritage's leading auctioneers, and can frequently be seen calling Movie Poster, Entertainment, and Fine & Decorative art auctions. Currently, John co-writes monthly columns for both The Comics Buyers Guide and Big Reel Magazine.

Marti Korver - Manager - Credits/Collections

Marti has been working in numismatics for more than three decades. She was recruited out of the banking profession by Jim Ruddy, and she worked with Paul Rynearson, Karl Stephens, and Judy Cahn on ancients and world coins at Bowers & Ruddy Galleries, in Hollywood, CA. She migrated into the coin auction business, running the bid books for such memorable sales as the Garrett Collection and representing bidders as agent at B&R auctions for 10 years. She also worked as a research assistant for Q. David Bowers for several years. Memorable events included such clients (and friends) as Richard Lobel, John Ford, Harry Bass, and John J. Pittman. She is married to noted professional numismatist and writer, Robert Korver, (who is sometimes seen auctioneering at coin shows) and they migrated to Heritage in Dallas in 1996. She has an RN daughter (who worked her way through college showing lots for Heritage) and a son who is currently a college student and sometimes a Heritage employee) and a type set of dogs (one black and one white). She currently collects kitschy English teapots and compliments.

Leo Frese - Executive VP - Numismatic Auctions

Leo has been involved in numismatics for nearly 40 years. He has been a professional numismatist since 1971 and has been with Heritage for over 20 years. He literally worked his way up the Heritage "ladder" through dedication, hard work, and a belief that the client is the most important asset Heritage has. He worked hand-in-hand with Bob Merrill for nearly 15 years and today he is the Director of Consignments for Heritage Numismatic Auctions. Leo has been actively involved in assisting clients sell nearly $500,000,000 in numismatic material. Leo was recently accepted as a member of PNG and is a life member of the ANA and holds membership in FUN, CSNS, and other numismatic organizations. He believes education is the foremost building block to numismatics and encourages all collectors to broaden their horizons and get actively involved in the hobby. Donate freely to YN organizations both locally and on the national level. Leo's outside interests include collecting Minnesota pottery and elegant depression glass. Although travel is an important element of his job, he relishes time at home with his family. His wife Wendy, children Alicen and Adam, and son-in-law Jeff are his personal treasures.

David Mayfield - Consignment Director

David has been collecting and trading rare coins and currency for over 35 years. A chance encounter with his father's coin collection at the age of nine led to his lifetime interest. David has been buying and selling at coin shows since the age of 10. He became a full time coin & currency dealer in the mid-80s. David's main collecting interest is in all things Texas, specializing in currency and documents from the Republic of Texas. Being a sixth generation Texan whose family fought for Texas' independence has only increased the value and meaning of these historical artifacts for him. After more than two decades of marriage, David and Tammy have two wonderful sons, Brian and Michael.

Jim Jelinski - Consignment Director

A collector since age 8, Jim has been involved in numismatics over 5 decades, progressing from humble beginnings to professional dealer and educator. He is a Life member of the American Numismatic Association, the American Numismatic Society and other state and national numismatic organizations. Starting as Numismatic Buyer for Paramount International Coin Corporation in 1972, he went on to open Essex Numismatic Properties, in 1975 in Portsmouth, New Hampshire, acting as President and CEO. Later, positions at M.B. Simmons & Associates, of Narberth, Pennsylvania, included, Director of Sales, Director of Marketing and Advertising, and Executive Vice President. In 1979, he reorganized Essex in Connecticut and, as Essex Numismatics, Inc., worked as COO., and partner. Later in the mid 1980's, Jim became a majority stockholder and CFO. His involvement with Essex Numismatics, Inc. remained a constant until his recent move to Dallas to join the staff at Heritage Capital Corporation as Senior Numismatist, and Consignment Coordinator. "I am a father of two sons, and am actively involved in both my church and my community. I have just completed my 20th season of coaching youth athletics, I am involved in Boy Scouting as a troop leader and as a merit badge counselor. I have been a fund raiser for Paul Newman's "Hole in the Wall Gang" camp for terminally ill children, and for Boy Scouts. My personal diversions include fly fishing, sky diving, cooking, and wine collecting," adds Jim.

Sam Foose - Consignment Director and Auctioneer

Sam's professional career at Heritage divides neatly into two parts. Sam joined Heritage Numismatic Auctions, Inc. in 1993 as an Auction Coordinator. Over the next five years, Sam ran the day-to-day auction operations, ultimately rising to Assistant Auction Director. He also first started calling auctions during these years. After serving as a Senior Manager and Consignment Director in other collectible fields outside of numismatics, Sam returned to Heritage in 2002 as a Consignment Director in time to help Heritage's expansion into other collectible areas. In this important role, Sam travels the country assisting clients who wish to liquidate their collections of coins, paper money, decorative arts, and sports collectibles. To Sam, helping consignors make the best decisions to maximize their returns from the auctioning of their properties is the most rewarding part of his job. Sam also holds auction licenses in several jurisdictions, and has hammered in excess of $150 million in collectibles as one of Heritage's primary auctioneers. During his elusive (but much appreciated) free time, Sam really enjoys spending time with his wife (Heather) and two children (Jackson and Caroline). His personal interests include gardening, golf, grilling, and sports.

David Lisot - Consignment Director

David Lisot has over three decades of experience in coins and collectibles as a researcher, newsletter publisher, auction cataloger, and website creator. He has attended collector conventions throughout the United States and world since 1971. His expertise encompasses U.S. and world coins and paper money, as well as other areas of collectibles such as post cards, cigar label art, antique advertising, jewelry, pocket watches, stamps and more. He is Director of the Heritage Coin Club Outreach program as well as a Director of Consignments. His background includes radio and television exposure. His achievements include being featured in the Public Television series, Money Moves, with Jack Gallagher, as on-air talent and segment producer for coins and collectibles. He was the reporter for Financial News Network, (now CNBC), bringing the message of numismatics to viewers on Wall Street with his live news program, Coin Report, that aired daily for almost five years. He founded the website Cointelevision.com, a free news and programming service about coin collecting on the Internet. As a videographer he has produced the award winning documentaries, Money, History in Your Hands, with veteran film star James Earl Jones that aired on Public Television as well as, Era of Hometown Bank Notes, for the Higgins Money Museum. A recent achievement is the Heritage Auctions corporate video, Selling Your Coins and Currency at Auction, hosted by Jay Johnson, 36th Director of the United States Mint, which won awards in the International Film and Television and Telly competitions. Since the 1980's he has videotaped over 750 lectures and presentations about coins and collecting as seen on Coinvideo.com. Lisot served as a Governor of the American Numismatic Association from 1994-95, and was twice awarded the coveted Glenn Smedley Award. He has worked on numerous committees as well as contributing his videotaping services to collector clubs to help increase their membership and promote overall interest in the different hobbies. He is an associate member in the Professional Numismatists Guild for his video production as well as a long-time or life member in the American Numismatic Association, American Israel Numismatic Association, California State Numismatic Association, Central States Numismatic Society, Numismatics International, Florida United Numismatists, Numismatic Association of Southern California, Society of International Numismatists, Sociedad de Numismatica de Mexico, and the Texas Numismatic Association. Lisot is a graduate of University of Colorado in Boulder, with a bachelor's degree in philosophy. He continued his education at UCLA in Los Angeles, California. He earned the title, Graduate Gemologist, studying at the Gemological Institute of America in California. He has attended classes for television and videography at various schools in Colorado, California and Texas. He is currently enrolled in a Master of Liberal Studies program at Southern Methodist University (SMU) in Dallas, Texas. David is married with two children. He enjoys travel, history, exercise, and religious studies.

Bob Marino - Consignment Director & Senior Numismatist
Bob joined the Heritage staff in 1999 as a Senior Numismatist buying and selling coins, managing the company's auctions on Ebay and Yahoo and working with auction consignors. He moved to Dallas from the Bitterroot Valley in western Montana where he was self employed selling coins on the Internet. In spare time, he enjoys building furniture and collecting GSA Morgan dollars. Bob and his wife have one child.

Charles Clifford - Consignment Director
Charles has been involved with collectibles for over 35 years. His first venture with coins began in the 1970's when he drove to banks all over North Texas buying bags of half dollars to search for the 40% silver clad coins. He has broad experience having worked as a bullion trader, a rare coin buyer, worked in both wholesale and retail sales, served as a cataloger for the auction company, and has traveled to hundreds of coin and sports card conventions across the country. He also has the distinction of working with Steve Ivy/Heritage over four decades - spanning the 1970's to the 2000's. Currently he is involved in assisting clients obtain top dollar for the items they have for sale, either by direct purchase or by placing their material in auction. He recently returned to Heritage after a 13-year absence. He cited Heritage's total commitment to "World Class Customer Service" and the "Can Do - Nothing is Impossible" attitude of management and each and every employee as the driving force in his decision to return. He enjoys collecting hand-blown Depression glass and antique aquarium statues.

Matt Orsini - Consignment Director
A coin collector for most of his life, Matt's relationship with Heritage began as an intern with the cataloging staff, and then his responsibilities were broadened to answering client e-mails (including tele-commuting from Trinity). Matt graduated from Trinity University with a BS in Business Administration in 2005, concentrating in Finance and Marketing. As a Consignment Director, Matt turned his passion for coins into a profession, and now often travels picking up consignments. He is an avid sports fan, probably stemming from his own athletic talents in basketball, baseball, soccer, and track.

Mike Sadler - Consignment Director
Mike Sadler joined the Heritage team in September 2003. Mike's career roots however, are not from the coin collecting industry. After high school Mike attended the United States Air Force Academy earning a degree in civil engineering. Air Force pilot training followed, and Mike pinned on his silver wings in June 1985. After seven years flying various Air Force aircraft, he went to work for American Airlines where he still works today. More than once, Mike has surprised other Heritage employees serving as their pilot while they flew to shows, conventions, and to visit our clients throughout the country. Like so many of our clients, Mike started putting together sets of coins from circulation when he was a small boy. Of course that collection grew and grew, and ultimately, it went to the auction blocks with Heritage in January 2004. Before coming to Heritage, his unlimited access to air travel enabled him to attend coin shows all around the country whenever he wanted. He gained a tremendous knowledge of rare coins and developed an outstanding eye for quality. He is a trusted friend and colleague to many of today's most active collectors. Having been a collector for so long, and a Heritage consignor himself, Mike understands the needs of the collector and what Heritage can offer. Mike is married, has three children, and enjoys coaching and playing lacrosse

David Lewis - Consignment Director
David Lewis joined Heritage in 2005 as a numismatist, with an extensive numismatic background in wholesale, retail, and internet sales. David's current duties are focused on Heritage's website features, especially "Ask an Expert" and "Coins and Currency Questions", as well as telephone consignments and purchases of rare coins and collections. David is a 22-year veteran of the United States Air Force, and has more than 5000 hours of flight-time as an Airborne Mission Supervisor and Hebrew linguist. David is the winner of the Numismatic Guarantee Corporation's 2004 and 2005 Best Presented Registry Set Awards, and is an avid collector of Washington Quarters and quarter varieties. He holds membership in the ANA, CSNS, and the Barber Coin Collectors Society, among other organizations. David's interests include flying, world travel, history, and collecting Art Deco ceramics and antiques.

Katherine Kurachek - Consignment Director
Katherine graduated from the University of Mississippi in 1993, and then resided in Colorado before moving to Dallas. Acting on a suggestion from her father, an avid coin collector, Katherine came to work for Heritage in January 2003. She has worked alongside Leo Frese for several years, honing her experience in dealing with the numismatic wholesale trade. In her spare time she enjoys gardening, golf, and walking her two Akitas.

Mark Van Winkle - Cataloger

Chief Cataloger Mark Van Winkle has worked for Heritage (and previously Steve Ivy) since 1979. He has been Chief Cataloger of Heritage Auction Galleries since 1990, and as such has handled some of the premier numismatic rarities that have been sold at public auction since that time. Mark's literary achievements are considerable also. He was editor of Legacy magazine, won the 1989 NLG award for Best U.S. Commercial Magazine, and the next year won another NLG award for Best Article with his "Interview With John Ford." In 1996 he was awarded the NLG's Best Numismatic Article "Changing Concepts of Liberty," and was accorded a third place Heath Literary Award that same year. He has also done extensive research and published his findings on Branch Mint Proof Morgan Dollars, in addition to writing numerous articles for Coin World and Numismatic News, Mark has also contributed to past editions of the Red Book, and helped with the Standard Silver series in Andrew Pollock's United States Patterns and Related Issues. He was also a contributor to The Guide Book of Double Eagle Gold Coins.

Mark Borckardt - Cataloger

Senior Cataloger Mark Borckardt started attending coin shows and conventions as a dealer in 1970, and has been a full-time professional numismatist since 1980. He received the Early American Coppers Literary Award, and the Numismatic Literary Guild's Book of the Year Award, for the Encyclopedia of Early United States Cents, 1793-1814, published in 2000. He serves as a contributor to A Guide Book of United States Coins, and has contributed to many references, including the Harry W. Bass, Jr. Sylloge, and the Encyclopedia of Silver Dollars and Trade Dollars of the United States. Most recently, he was Senior Numismatist with Bowers and Merena Galleries, serving as a major contributor to all of that firm's landmark auctions, as well as the Rare Coin Review. Mark is a life member of the American Numismatic Association, and an active member of numerous numismatic organizations. He is an avid collector of numismatic literature, holding several thousand volumes in his library, as well as numismatic related postcards and ephemera. When not immersed in numismatics, he is an avid bowler, carrying an average just over 200, and with seven perfect 300 games. Mark is a graduate of the University of Findlay (Ohio) with a Bachelors Degree in Mathematics. Mark and his wife have a 20-something year old son, and twin daughters who are enrolled at Baylor.

Brian Koller - Cataloger

Catalog Production Manager Brian Koller's attention to detail ensures that every catalog, printed and on-line, is as error free as technology and human activity allows. In addition to his coin cataloging duties, he also helps with consignor promises and customer service issues. Brian has been a Heritage Auctions cataloger since 2001, and before that he worked as a telecom software engineer for 16 years. He is a graduate of Iowa State University with a Bachelor's degree in Computer Engineering, and is an avid collector of U.S. gold coins. Brian's numismatic footnote is as discoverer of a 1944-D half dollar variety that has the designer's monogram engraved by hand onto a working die. In addition to describing many thousands of coins in Heritage catalogs, Brian has written more than one thousand reviews of classic movies, which can be found on his website, filmsgraded.com.

John Salyer - Cataloger

Cataloger John Salyer has been a numismatist and coin cataloger with Heritage since October of 2002. John began collecting Lincoln Cents, Jefferson Nickels, Mercury and Roosevelt Dimes, and Franklin Halves at the age of eleven, as a sixth-grader in Fort Worth; his best friend was also a collector, and his dad would drive them to coin shops and flea markets in search of numismatic treasures. The two youngsters even mowed lawns together in order to purchase their coins, which were always transferred into Whitman folders. John graduated from the University of Texas with a bachelor's degree in English. Prior to his numismatic employment, he worked primarily within the federal government and for several major airlines. His hobbies include playing guitar and collecting antique postcards; as an avid golfer, he also enjoys spending time on the links. John has enjoyed making his former hobby his current occupation, and he still actively collects coins.

Jon Amato - Cataloger

Cataloger Jon Amato has been with Heritage since March 2004. He was previously a Program Manager in the New York State Department of Economic Development, and an Adjunct Professor at the State University of New York at Albany, where he taught economic geography, natural disasters assessment, and environmental management. Jon is currently writing a monograph on the numismatic history and rarity of the draped bust, small eagle half dollars of 1796-1797. His research included surveying more than 4,000 auction catalogs, recording the descriptions, grades, and photos of 1796-1797 halves. He published an article entitled "Surviving 1796-1797 Draped Bust Half Dollars and their Grade Distribution," in the John Reich Journal, February 2005, Vol. 16, Issue 2, and also wrote "An Analysis of 1796-1797 Draped Bust Half Dollars," in The Numismatist, Sept. 2001, Vol. 114, No. 9. Jon belongs to many numismatic organizations, including the ANA, ANS, John Reich Collectors Society, and the Liberty Seated Collectors Club, and has made several presentations at ANA Numismatic Theaters. He earned a bachelor's degree from Arizona State University, an M.A. from the State University of New York at Buffalo, and a Ph. D. from the University of Toronto.

Greg Lauderdale - Cataloger

Cataloger Greg Lauderdale grew up in Dallas, and he began working in a coin shop there in 1979. His interest in numismatics and his trading skills blossomed, and he became a Life Member of the ANA only two years later in 1981. During the 1980s, he conducted several coin auctions in the Dallas Area, including several for the Dallas Coin Club show. He first contracted with Heritage Auction Galleries to help write the 1985 Baltimore ANA auction catalog. He joined Heritage full-time in September of 1985, working as a cataloger and a coin buyer. Greg "left" Heritage in 1988 to develop his personal rare coin company, but has continued to split his time between cataloging for Heritage and trading on eBay from his new home in Maui. In addition to his numismatic sales, Greg has developed into quite a 'presence' in the world of rare and early Hawaiian postcards. For those bidders who attend Heritage's auctions in person, Greg can often be seen working at the front table – one of the few catalogers in America who is actively involved in the selling process!

John Beety - Cataloger

Cataloger John Dale Beety grew up in Logansport, Indiana, a small town associated with several numismatic luminaries. Highlights as a Young Numismatist include attending Pittman III, four ANA Summer Seminars (thanks to various YN scholarships), and placing third in the 2001 World Series of Numismatics with Eric Li Cheung. He accepted a position with Heritage as a cataloger immediately after graduation from Rose-Hulman Institute of Technology after serving an internship at Heritage during the summer of 2004. In addition to his numismatic interests, he enjoys many types of games, with two state junior titles in chess and an appearance in the Top 20 Juniors list of the World Blitz Chess Association.

DENOMINATION INDEX

GOLD DOLLARS

Conditionally Scarce 1852-C
Gold Dollar MS64

Superb Gem 1851 Liberty Gold Dollar

3350 **1851 MS67 NGC.** This fully struck and highly lustrous Superb Gem has frosty yellow-gold color with tending toward light green. It is a well-made example with exceptional aesthetic appeal. A tiny die bulge near the forecurl attests to the late die state, as do minor die cracks at the lower left part of the obverse. Nearly vertical striae cover the fields on both sides, and this feature is only visible on sharply struck coins, and then only with the help of magnification. Struck during the height of the California gold rush with a strong possibility that this piece was actually coined from gold mined in that region. Census: 4 in 67, 4 finer (11/06). (#7513)

3351 **1852-C MS64 NGC.** Variety 7-H. The 18 in the date is lightly repunched south, and clash marks are noted near the coronet tip and the left wreath stem. Well struck for a Southern branch mint product, particularly on the curls near Liberty's ear. As seen on many gold dollars, the peripheries display cartwheel luster, while the open fields are moderately prooflike. Strike-throughs are noted beneath Liberty's chin and between the LA in DOLLAR, but the surfaces are remarkably void of contact. Although the Charlotte Mint struck 72,574 half eagles in 1852, their emission of gold dollars was substantially smaller. A mere 9,434 pieces were struck, and of that amount probably only 80-85 pieces are extant today in all grades. This is one of the finer examples known of this Type One Charlotte issue. Census: 6 in 64, 5 finer (11/06). (#7518)

Near-Gem 1854 Type Two Gold Dollar

3352   1854 Type Two MS64 PCGS. The Type Two or Small Indi-an Head gold dollars are always in demand by date and type collectors, as well as advanced specialists. Although an attractive design in the eye of most collectors, James Barton Longacre did not think this one through, and problems with the strike plague most survivors. This piece is an exception to that rule, as the reverse has a full and complete date, and all other design features are similarly well defined. It is a highly lustrous yellow-gold example with traces of olive coloration on the reverse. A lint mark on the obverse curves over ICA and through the top of the final letter. (#7531)

Scarce Near-Gem 1854 Gold Dollar

3353   1854 Type Two MS64 NGC. The relatively small quantity of Mint State pieces of this issue are most often limited in grade by striking deficiencies, certainly not the case with this sharply detailed example. The luster and overall surfaces of this piece are truly impressive. The fields are nearly mark-free, the only ripple in the fabric of the piece being moderate die clashing, as seen on almost every Type Two gold dollar known. Both sides exhibit a fresh, original, highly lustrous appearance. A significant type coin in this grade as most Type Two dollars are AU or lower. (#7531)

Scarce Near-Gem 1855
Type Two Gold Dollar

3354   1855 MS64 NGC. In 1854 it was decided by Mint officials that the gold dollar was too small and thick for its weight. James Longacre adapted his three dollar gold design in creating a slightly broader and thinner coin. The Type Two gold dollar features Liberty wearing a headdress rather than a coronet, as on the Type One; and Liberty is encircled by the legend UNITED STATES OF AMERICA, rather than thirteen peripheral stars. This near-Gem example is highly lustrous and features pleasing shades of peach and honeygold. Both sides show prominent die clashing, which is not unusual, but the coin's striking details are definitely better than average for the issue, especially on DOLLAR and on the date.
From The Freedom Collection. (#7532)

Fabulous 1855 Type Two Dollar Gem

3355   1855 MS65 PCGS. Several hundred 1855 gold dollars have been certified by PCGS and NGC through MS64. A significant drop in the population occurs at the Gem and finer levels of preservation, where fewer than 100 coins have been seen. This fabulous MS65 specimen displays outstanding luster and a mix of yellow-gold, mint-green, and light tan coloration. The design features are well brought up, except for minor softness in the top of the 8, which is typical for the issue. Well preserved surfaces exhibit light clash marks on each side. Population: 36 in 65, 17 finer (11/06). (#7532)

Stunning MS66 1855
Type Two Gold Dollar

3356   1855 MS66 PCGS. Both the 1854 and 1855 Type Two gold dollars were minted to the extent of a tad more than three-quarters of a million pieces each, and yet both are quite elusive in the higher Mint State grades. Their scarcity is largely due to the inappropriate design placement, putting the high-points of each side in opposition. Type Two dollars are in demand chiefly from type collectors who desire to complete a U.S. type set, or a gold type set. Statistically, from the current combined NGC/PCGS population data, the 1855 shows a few more certified survivors in MS66 and finer grades than the 1854. Those services combined have certified 25 pieces of the 1855 in MS66, with seven pieces finer, while they have graded 17 examples of the 1854 in MS66, with five coins finer (11/06).

From any technical or aesthetic point of view, this is a lovely and appealing coin, one that is instantly appealing. First Foremost, one must mention the lustrous and radiant surfaces, which are delightfully patinated in hues of orange-gold and green-gold, with glints of lilac and apricot predominating on the reverse. While the clash marks that are ubiquitous in the Type Two gold dollars are present here (and they do not affect the grade anyway), the surfaces are stunningly pristine and un-encumbered by obvious signs of contact, large or small. The almost universal strike weakness of this type is here limited to trifling softness on Liberty's highpoint hair and the 8 in the date and LL in the denomination. Nonetheless a stunning and delightful example of this rare type. Population: 14 in 66, 3 finer (11/06).

From The James Paul Collection. (#7532)

Low Mintage 1855-C Gold Dollar AU55

3357   1855-C AU55 NGC. Unlisted Variety. Although Doug Winter's reference only discusses a single variety for this Charlotte issue, there are actually two different reverse dies identified from the small 9,803 coin mintage. Here the final 5 of the date is situated just to the right of center under the A. Bright yellow-gold surfaces show typical deficiency in strike and rather heavy die clashing about the portrait on the obverse. The 1855-C is desirable as the only C-mint issued of the Type Two design and is obviously challenging in AU grades. *From The Twin Hollows Collection.* (#7533)

Type Two 1855-C Gold Dollar AU58

3358   1855-C AU58 NGC. Unlisted Variety. In his reference *Gold Coins of the Charlotte Mint: 1838-1861* (1988), Douglas Winter states, "One die variety is known to exist." However, the present piece is from a different reverse die than his plate coin. The date is entered further right, with the second 5 beneath the right half of the A in DOLLAR. This is the preferable reverse die, since DOLLAR and 1855 are well struck compared to examples of Variety 9-K. The 1855-C is essential to a Charlotte Mint type set, since it is the sole Type Two issue. Only 9,803 pieces were struck, and demand for survivors is formidable. This bold and partly lustrous straw-gold representative displays mint-made clash marks and minor strike-throughs, but post-strike distractions are trivial. Census: 41 in 58, 13 finer (11/06). (#7533)

Rare, Bold 1855-D Type Two
Gold Dollar AU55

3359   1855-D AU55 NGC. Variety 7-I. The only Type Two gold dollar produced at the Dahlonega Mint, and one of the rarest of all gold dollars. As the skimpy mintage of 1,811 examples would imply, the issue is rare in all grades, and particularly elusive in Mint State or nearly so. Both services combined have certified less than a dozen examples (including resubmissions) in Mint State. Akers comments of this issue, "Most specimens have an extremely weak 8 in the date, and exhibit severe clash marks on both obverse and reverse. However, some specimens do have full dates, but they are extremely rare." This is one such piece, with all digits, including the 8, in the date bold. The generous strike has also fully brought up Liberty's hair. The inevitable clash marks are seen on each side, and most of the mint luster still remains. The lemon-yellow obverse deepens to yellow-gold with tinges of magenta on the reverse. Rare so fine, and an extremely attractive example of this rare D-mint gold dollar. Census: 6 in 55, 19 finer (11/06).
From The Twin Hollows Collection. (#7534)

Conditionally Elite 1859-C Gold Dollar MS62

3360   1859-C MS62 PCGS. Variety 11-M. Generally poorly struck and produced from inferior planchet stock, the '59-C has become a real challenge for collectors to locate in problem-free condition in any grade. The center of the reverse is weakly defined on this piece as are the hair curls on Liberty. However, the satiny surfaces are remarkably free from any large or distracting abrasions. Mint State pieces are genuinely scarce, and MS63 is the top grade level that a mere three examples have achieved, all three at PCGS. This MS62 offering represents a conditionally elite group. Population: 7 in 62, 3 finer (11/06). (#7552)

Rare Superb Gem 1861 Gold Dollar

3361   1861 MS67 NGC. Coined at the beginning of the Civil War, this piece is one of the most plentiful Type Three Gold Dollars. The mintage, slightly exceeding 500,000 coins, is the third highest of the design type. Although CA of AMERICA is slightly weak, every other design detail is boldly defined. The surfaces of this Superb Gem display frosty luster with vibrant orange-gold color. Since 1993, we have offered more than 200 examples of this date, but just three MS66 grade coins represent the former high water mark for quality in all of our offerings. Census: 2 in 67, 0 finer (11/06). (#7558)

1861-D Gold Dollar, MS64
A Great Rarity and Tied for
Second Finest Known

3362 1861-D MS64 NGC. Variety 12-Q, the only known die marriage. With an unknown, but tiny mintage that is estimated in the range of 1,000 to 1,500 pieces, the 1861-D gold dollar is a great rarity and easily the rarest Dahlonega gold dollar. It is also the rarest and most in-demand of the Type Three gold dollars, whether in circulated or Mint State grades. NGC and PCGS list 79 examples in all grades. Additionally, it is the *second-rarest of all gold dollars,* surpassed only by the near-unobtainable 1849-C Open Wreath issue. Only 55-65 pieces are believed known today of the 1861-D with an estimated 10-12 coins in mint condition. This piece is certainly at the top of the Condition Census, and in fact may be tied for finest known with the "Alabama Collection" PCGS MS64. Green Pond and Duke's Creek both had an MS63, but this does not appear to be either of those pieces.

The unrecorded mintage of 1861-D gold dollars was struck by the Confederate States of America after it took over the Dahlonega Mint in April 1861. Mint Director George Kellogg resigned, and the 1861-D dollars were struck by "amateur minters," as Winter terms them, in May 1861. Winter says the coins were produced from an obverse die left over from the 1860-D dollar, despite the fact that Breen reports that "two pairs of dies" were shipped on Dec. 10, 1860, from the Mother Mint in Philadelphia, arriving on Jan. 7, 1861, before Georgia seceded from the Union in April. This issue is the only coin emission manufactured solely and exclusively under the auspices of the CSA.

Winter notes that on all known examples, the U and N in UNITED are weak, and sometimes the IC in AMERICA also show weakness (as seen on this coin). Unlike most known 1861-D gold dollars, this piece shows smooth surfaces that are free from most of the planchet distractions usually encountered. The only areas that show any (barely) visible signs of planchet problems are a couple of shallow swipes of granularity in the central to upper portion of the reverse. The surfaces are frosted and the coin displays rich orange-gold coloration. This near-Gem example is one of three so graded at NGC and PCGS combined, with a single example graded finer at NGC (10/06).

From The Freedom Collection. (#7559)

Superb Prooflike 1866 Gold Dollar

3363   1866 MS68 Prooflike NGC. Relatively few 1866 gold dollars are though to have survived out of an original mintage of 7,100 business strikes. Approximately 120 examples have been certified in Mint State grades by NGC and PCGS, mostly in the MS63 to MS65 grade levels; many of these are likely resubmissions. Prooflike specimens are available, mostly in the lower to middle grades of Uncirculated. Only four Prooflike coins have been seen in the lofty grade of MS68. The example offered here displays nearly gold-on-black contrast when the piece is viewed from a direct overhead angle. Yellow-gold surfaces are impeccably preserved, and exhibit sharply struck design elements. The gold specialist will not want to miss out on the opportunity to acquire such a magnificent coin. Census: 1 in 68, 0 finer (11/06). (#77565)

Elusive Gem Proof 1856 Gold Dollar

3364   1856 Slanted 5 PR65 PCGS. The year 1856 was in many ways a transitional year at the nation's mints. Preparations were under way to do away with the filthy and unpopular "old copper" half cents and cents, and accordingly the Philadelphia Mint struck a large number of pattern Flying Eagle cents made of copper-nickel, in a new, small-size format. The arrows at the date from 1853-1855 on minor silver coinage, signifying a reduced silver content, were removed in this year. The newly opened San Francisco Mint struck its first dimes and quarter eagles, along with the only Indian Princess, Small Head (Type Two) gold dollars produced in 1856. Meanwhile, the newly designed Indian Princess, Large Head (Type Three) gold dollars were produced at the Philadelphia and Dahlonega mints.

The Philadelphia Mint manufactured more than 1.76 million business strike gold dollars during 1856, in two styles, with the 5 in the date either upright or slanted. An unknown but small number of proofs was also produced, usually estimated at 10 to 15 pieces. Most other coin denominations, with a couple of exceptions, from 1850 to 1856 show slanted 5s, while they disappear altogether by 1857. A popular numismatic chestnut holds that Mint Engraver James B. Longacre preferred his 5s slanted, while other mint personnel favored the upright 5s. For much more on the phenomenon of slanted or italic 5s, see the article "A New Slant on Coins of 1850-56" by Craig Krueger and John W. Dannreuther in *The Numismatist,* June 2002. Krueger and Dannreuther draw a distinction between "slanting" and "italic" numerals, and note that they are mutually exclusive: "Slanting" numerals can be non-italic, and some upright numerals show italic characteristics.

Although Walter Breen believed that the Upright 5 gold dollar in the Floyd T. Starr sale (Stack's, 10/1992) was a proof, Jeff Garrett and Ron Guth's recently released *Gold Encyclopedia* states categorically that the piece was a prooflike business strike, and that all proofs are of the "Slant 5" style. The current specimen shows the date low and slanting upward to the right, a diagnostic for genuine proofs, but beyond that it shows the unmistakable characteristics of proof coinage.

The surfaces exhibit rich reddish-gold coloration. The fields show the deep mirrors one would expect from a proof, and the devices are nicely frosted and give the coin a two-toned appearance. One interesting aspect seen on this piece is light die clashing in the reverse fields. This was a common problem on Type Two gold dollars, and it appears that mint personnel continued to consider a planchet optional before striking even in the first year of Type Three production. Population: 2 in 65, 0 finer (11/06). (#7606)

Rare 1857 Gold Dollar, PR64

3365 1857 PR64 PCGS. The 1857 is rare in proof format, struck the year before larger production proof mintages began for other U.S. coins. The exact mintage of proof 1857 proof gold dollars is unknown, but it is presumably very small, as pre-1858 proof coins were distributed as singles not as sets, as in later years. It is believed that 8-10 separate proofs are known today. This is a deeply reflective example that shows significant (but unacknowledged) cameo contrast against the frosted devices. Indeed, a pronounced gold-on-black appearance is evident, especially on the obverse, when the coin is viewed from directly overhead. Pedigree identifiers include a slight streak of granularity in the lower left obverse field, a U-shaped lint mark below the T in UNITED, and a few other small lint marks in the right obverse field. A few wispy handling marks prevent the achievement of an even higher grade. This is a rare and important proof striking, as well as a rare opportunity for the specialist to acquire this seldom-seen gold dollar. Population: 4 in 64, 1 finer (10/06). (#7607)

Conditionally Rare 1860 Gold Dollar PR64 Cameo

3366 1860 PR64 Cameo PCGS. From a relatively high proof mintage for the era of 154 pieces, Garrett and Guth (2006) estimate that probably 25 to 30 coins still survive "in collector's hands." This example has a remarkably fine appearance that instantly highlights the contrasting fields and devices on either side. The striking details are unimpeachable, as one would hope for a proof. Shallow marks on Liberty's jaw and in the left obverse field seemingly limit the grade of this otherwise pleasing specimen. A patch of interesting roller marks (as struck) is noted near the center of the reverse, extending through the LL in DOLLAR. Population: 1 in 64 Cameo, 2 finer (11/06). (#87610)

Finest Certified 1860
Gold Dollar PR66 Cameo

3367   1860 PR66 Cameo NGC. According to Mint records, 154 proof gold dollars were produced at Philadelphia in 1860, although it is believed that fewer than 50 pieces have survived into the 21st century. This specimen is certainly among the finest of those extant. The mirrored fields are colored an even orange-gold, but surrounding the frosted head of Liberty is a thin line of light yellow-gold, highlighting the cameo effect. There is one small area of brilliance just below the ear of the frosted head, giving the appearance of a sparkling gem earring. The reverse is equally attractive from the standpoint of color, but there is some light porosity at the O in DOLLAR, and a minute lintmark above the A. These minor imperfections are only mentioned for future identification purposes. Rest assured that this will be a very popular item in the sale. Census: 1 in 66, 0 finer (11/06). (#87610)

Gorgeous, Finest Certified 1863
PR67 Cameo Gold Dollar

3368   1863 PR67 Cameo NGC. Jeff Garrett and Ron Guth, in their book entitled *Encyclopedia of U.S. Gold Coins, 1795-1933*, estimate that less than one-half of the reported mintage of 50 coins is still known. The major grading services have certified about 25 pieces, but this certainly includes some resubmissions. This gorgeous PR67 Cameo, the finest seen by either NGC or PCGS, exhibits great contrast, that takes on a gold-on-black appearance when it is viewed from directly overhead. Orange-gold surfaces display crisply struck motifs, and are devoid of significant marks. Census: 1 in 67 Cameo, 0 finer (11/06). (#87613)

1866 Gold Dollar PR66 Cameo PCGS

3369   1866 PR66 Cameo PCGS. The Breen proof *Encyclopedia* says of this issue, "Date from the half dime logotype, heavy, nearer to ribbon bows than to DOLLAR, and level. ... Heavy low date, wreath tops joined. Almost R-7." This visually compelling Premium Gem is among the four highest-graded examples at NGC and PCGS combined, and is the single finest-known Cameo specimen at PCGS (three others are designated by PCGS as Deep Cameo). Sharply struck throughout, with essentially pristine surfaces and just a touch of haze noted on each side. The frosted devices create a lovely cameo contrast with the deeply reflective fields. Population: 1 in 66, 0 finer (11/06). (#87616)

Outstanding 1866 Gold Dollar PR67 Ultra Cameo

3370   1866 PR67 Ultra Cameo NGC. Proof 1866 gold dollars are very rare, and it is estimated that fewer than 20 specimens of the original 30 pieces minted still remain. 16 coins have been graded by NGC and PCGS, 14 have been assigned the Cameo designation, and 12 have been labeled Deep or Ultra Cameo. Obviously, some of these are resubmissions. At any rate, the Superb Ultra Cameo in this lot displays a rich orange-gold patina and outstanding contrast between the frosted, boldly struck design elements and highly reflective fields. Both faces are impeccably well preserved. Census: 3 in 67 Ultra Cameo, 0 finer (11/06). (#97616)

Rare Gem Proof 1872 Gold Dollar

3371   1872 PR65 PCGS. Even business strikes of this date, with a mintage of 3,500 pieces, are seldom seen, although when encountered they are quite lovely, and a few extremely high grade pieces are seen infrequently in the marketplace, most of them at least partially prooflike. The Harry W. Bass, Jr., Collection contained three examples. The proof mintage was 30 coins, although more proof examples appear to have survived than for other dates with comparable mintages. In Gem condition PCGS has certified only five pieces, with none finer, and none at NGC (11/06). The present example features deep, mellow orange-gold surfaces with considerable contrast, and a couple of tiny, undistracting dark toning spots visible under a lens, one on the 7 in the date, a second on the lower hair curls. Nonetheless attractive, and quite rare. (#7622)

Elusive 1872 Gold Dollar
PR65 Deep Cameo

3372   1872 PR65 Deep Cameo PCGS. Although generally not given any notoriety within the series, the 1872 gold dollar is a significant rarity both as a high grade business strike and as a proof. The mintage of the latter and the focus of our attention here originated at just 30 pieces, with attrition diminishing the total extant to less than 20 coins. Both sides exhibit an exactness of strike and beautiful orange-gold color that quickly identify it as a proof. There is a small lamination by the U in UNITED and a paper-thin disturbance on the cheek is debatably mint-caused. Population: 1 in 65, 0 finer, 5 finer at NGC (11/06). (#97622)

Astonishing 1872 Gold Dollar
PR67 Ultra Cameo

3373   1872 PR67 Ultra Cameo NGC. The 1872 One dollar proof shows a mintage of 30 pieces. Jeff Garrett and Ron Guth, in their *Encyclopedia of U.S. Gold Coins, 1795-1933,* write: "More 1872 coins have been offered for sale that others of the series with mintages of less than 50. The 1872 gold dollar is another date that appears to have a survival rate greater than the original mintage. When studying the rarity of any gold coin, the population date can be very misleading. It is very common for a rare coin to have been resubmitted multiple times in search of a higher grade. this can mean thousands of dollars on some coins, and dealers and collectors can be persistent."

Garrett and Guth suggest that no more than 20 1872 dollar proofs have survived; Walter Breen, writing in his *Complete Encyclopedia of U.S. and Colonial Coins,* estimates 13 to 17 pieces are extant. PCGS and NGC have seen a total of 10 proofs to date, seven Cameo proofs, and seven "Deep/Ultra Cameo" examples.

The brass-gold surfaces of the current PR67 Ultra Cameo display astonishing gold-on-black contrast. The design elements are exquisitely brought up, and impart bold definition to the bonnet, the letters of LIBERTY, the hair, and to the intricacies of the reverse wreath. Some die polish lines are noted in the fields of each side, and a minor planchet defect to the upper right of the first S in STATES may help to identify the coin. A couple of faint linear marks at the upper part of Liberty's head are mentioned for accuracy. Census: 3 in 67 Ultra Cameo, 0 finer (11/06). (#97622)

The Garrett 1873 Gold Dollar
PR65 Cameo

3374   1873 Closed 3 PR65 Cameo NGC. *Garrett Collection.*
The 1873 gold dollar is a major rarity among 19th century U.S. gold
coins. It is also one that has been infrequently offered over the decades, and one that lacked any solid scholarship until Harry X Boo-
sel discovered that all proofs of this year are of the Closed 3 variant.
In the Garrett catalog in November 1979, Bowers was careful to
state his uncertainty about this coin's status as a proof or first-strike
prooflike, even though he did state that this piece showed a "conspicuous unfinished feather in the headdress located below the A in
STATES." Nine years later Walter Breen published this as the sole diagnostic of genuine proofs in his *Complete Encyclopedia*.

Each side shows a number of lint marks from the dies being
wiped with a cloth. The lint adhering to the dies then was stamped
on the finished coin. The proof 1873 is one of the rarest coins in the
entire gold dollar series. Only 25 proofs were struck. It is unlikely
if half that number exist today as recognizable proof strikings. The
fields are nicely mirrored but lack the depth that one might expect
of a proof from this period. Even orange-gold coloration covers each
side. An extremely rare opportunity for the gold dollar collector or
aficionado of 19th century proof gold. Census: 1 in 65 Cameo, 0
finer (11/06). (#7623)

Splendid 1881 Gold Dollar
PR66 Ultra Cameo

3375   1881 PR66 Ultra Cameo NGC. A mere 87 proofs were produced this year from an enticingly low total mintage of 7,707 pieces, but the comparatively large number of hoarded prooflike survivors that were actually struck from the same dies has long-skewed the actual rarity of 1881 proof gold dollars. The instantly appealing yellow-gold specimen offered here is struck with pinpoint sharpness and boasts dramatic field-to-device contrast. Simply put, an awe-inspiring proof that sells for little more than the more available issues from 1882 forward. Census: 6 in 66, 2 finer (11/06). (#97631)

Flashy 1884 Gold Dollar PR66 Cameo

3376   1884 PR66 Cameo PCGS. Doubled Date. Breen-6107. This rather dramatic doubling is found on all proofs from this year. Although the proof mintage for the 1884 gold dollar was dramatically increased from previous years (officially 1,006 pieces), the limited number of surviving examples suggests that many were subsequently melted. This outstanding specimen benefits from rich orange-gold color and appealing contrast between the fields and devices. For pedigree purposes, a small lintmark is located under the portrait to the left of the A in AMERICA. Population: 4 in 66, 2 finer (11/06). (#87634)

Stunning 1886 Premium Gem Cameo Gold Dollar

3377   1886 PR66 Cameo NGC. NGC and PCGS have certified a total of about 80 1886 proof gold dollars, that had a mintage of 1,016 pieces. Jeff Garrett and Ron Guth (2006) mention that: "Evidence exists that coins from this period were handled very carelessly by Mint employees. Impaired proofs are not uncommon...." Approximately 60 coins have been designated as cameos. The Premium Gem Cameo offered in this lot exhibits rich brass-gold surfaces that assume a stunning gold-on-black contrast when viewed from a direct angle. A well executed strike shows on the design features, and both sides are devoid of mentionable marks. Census: 18 in 66, 3 finer (11/06). *From The RNB Collection.* (#87636)

Desirable 1796 No Stars Quarter Eagle, XF Details

3378   1796 No Stars—Obverse Repaired, Improperly Cleaned—NCS. XF Details. Breen-1, Breen-6113, Bass-3002, BD-2, High R.4. The key identifier of this variety is that the arrowheads extend just about to the end of N of UNITED. This coin has three distinctions. It is the first precious-metal coin without stars issued for circulation by the United States prior to 1836; it is the first to show the heraldic eagle; and is the earliest made showing 16 reverse stars, apparently honoring Tennessee's admission to the Union.

Peach-gold surfaces are imbued with wisps of orange and light green, and reveal fine inoffensive hairlines, especially on the obverse. The design elements retain fairly nice detail; most of E PLURIBUS UNUM is strong, as are the eagle's wing feathers. A repair appears to have been made at the lower left obverse rim. All in all, a decent one-year type coin, despite the NCS disclaimer. (#7645)

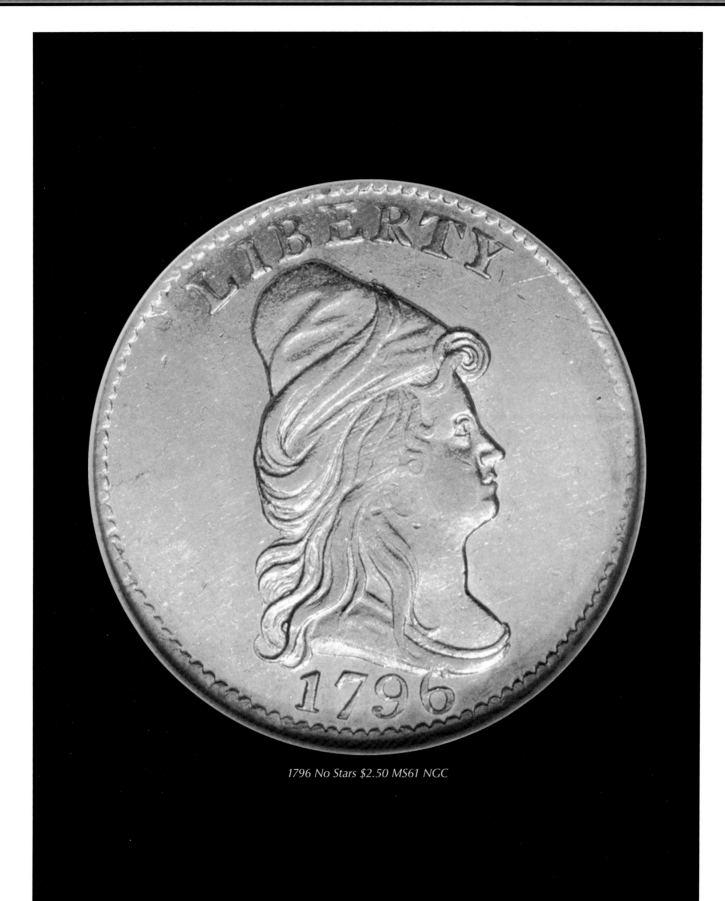

1796 No Stars $2.50 MS61 NGC

1796 No Stars $2.50 MS61 NGC

Beautiful Mint State 1796 No Stars Quarter Eagle

3379   1796 No Stars MS61 NGC. Breen-1, Breen-6113, Bass-3002, BD-2, R.4. BD Obverse State c/Reverse State b. A one-year type coin; the only No Stars quarter eagle (or early gold or silver coin); the first date of the denomination; a 210-year-old coin with an estimated original mintage of only 963 pieces; the first coin struck with 16 stars to commemorate Tennessee's admission into the Union; the rarest gold type coin; likely the second-rarest type coin, inclusive of all metals—how many other U.S. coins have so many claims to fame and desirability? (Answer: none.)

Jeff Garrett and Ron Guth's *United States Coinage—A Study by Type* (2005) says concerning this transcendent type rarity, "The quarter eagle denomination debuted in 1796, and the first type appeared without any stars on the obverse, making it the only 'star-less' early U.S. silver or gold coin. All examples of this type were struck at the Philadelphia Mint, and only in a limited quantity of 963 pieces. This design presents a real challenge to the type collector because of its great rarity. Nevertheless, a surprising number of high-grade circulated examples exist. In fact, it is easier to find a nice About Uncirculated example of this type than it is to find one in Very Fine. **In Mint State, this type is virtually unobtainable and extremely expensive.**" [Emphasis ours.]

This BD-2 variety, also known as "Normal Arrows," is the collectible variant of the year. (John Dannreuther, in the new Bass-Dannreuther early U.S. gold reference, pegs the estimated mintage at 897 pieces, subtracting the estimated 66 pieces of the BD-1 "Extended Arrows" variety.) On the reverse the arrowheads end nearly beneath the right upright of the N in UNITED. The D in UNITED is near a wing feather. On the single obverse die, the 1 in the date is bolder than 796, and fairly close to, but not touching, the hair curls. The 6 in the date is jammed up against the bottom of the drapery.

This piece appears to be in the BD Obverse/Reverse States b/c. Slight traces remain, after lapping, of the previous die crack joining the bottoms of LIBER, here visible as a threadlike connection from B to E and a small remnant connecting the right side of the bottom serif of R with the diagonal stroke. The reverse shows a lumpish die break at the tip of the eagle's right (facing) wing. The BD reference comments, "This popular one-year type coin trades, no matter what the die state, mainly on eye appeal and the absence of problems, whether Mint-caused, circulation related, or jewelry related." If that is so, then the successful bidder on this delightful—and delightfully rare—gold type coin will rejoice. The surfaces are a consistent orange-gold, with considerable reflectivity present on each side, and few mentionable distractions. Scrutiny beneath a lens reveals a few obverse adjustment marks through the hair and cap, and a bit of strike weakness through the center—but no surface distractions or impairments remotely worthy of singling out. A lovely coin, one of the utmost rarity, beauty, and historic importance. Census (as 1796 No Stars): 4 in 61, 5 finer (11/06). (#7645)

1796 No Stars $2.50 MS63 NGC

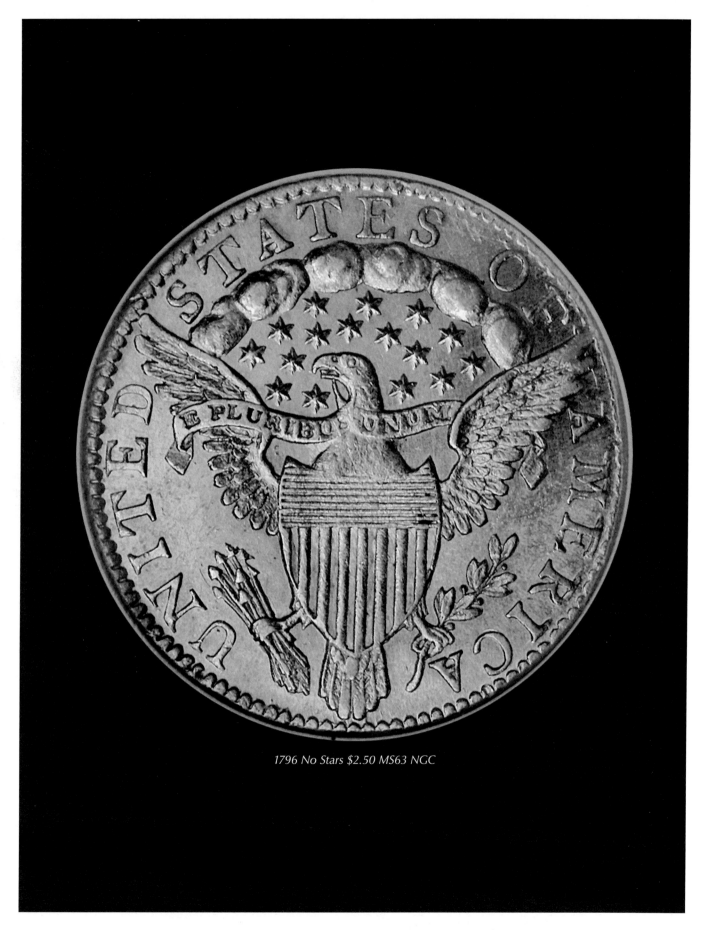

1796 No Stars $2.50 MS63 NGC

Amazing Select Mint State 1796 No Stars Quarter Eagle

3380 **1796 No Stars MS63 NGC.** Breen-1, Breen-6113, Bass-3002, BD-2, High R.4. Among the early quarter eagles produced from 1796 to 1834 are several important type coins, including two distinct single-year designs and several important subtypes of these basic designs. There is little doubt that the 1796 No Stars quarter eagle and the 1808 Capped Bust quarter eagle are two of the most important type coins in the entire panorama of American numismatics.

After the Mint Act of April 2, 1792, was passed by Congress, steps were taken to proceed with a physical Mint facility in Philadelphia, then the nation's capital. The cornerstone for the new building, the first official government structure in the United States, was placed on July 31, 1792, and construction continued until early 1793. It was March 1 of that year that the first coins were produced within the physical Mint building, those coins being the 1793 Chain cents, specifically the famous "Chain Ameri" pieces.

Although the capability to produce silver and gold coinage existed at that same time, there was a delay in production of the precious metals. The original 1792 coinage Act specified that the Mint treasurer, assayer, and chief coiner shall each post a bond in the amount of $10,000 to ensure their proper handling of gold and silver deposits. While this doesn't seem to be a large amount today, it was substantial for the time. The annual salary for the assayer and chief coiner in 1795 was $1,200, thus the required bond was more than eight years' salary. Congressional approval was then required to lower the necessary bond to $5,000, a more reasonable requirement. Once these bonds were posted, silver dollars were coined in 1794, and gold coins beginning in 1795.

The first quarter eagles were struck on September 21, 1796, with a delivery of just 66 pieces. It is believed that all of these pieces were the extremely rare variety now known as BD-1 (BD for Bass-Dannreuther), that a further delivery of 897 pieces dated December 8, 1796, were all examples of this BD-2 variety, and finally a delivery of 432 quarter eagles dated January 14, 1797, were all the BD-3 variety of the 1796 With Stars design. Although an exact correlation of varieties and original Mint delivery records is guesswork at best, these quantities are clearly supported by the number of known specimens of each die marriage. There are six known examples of BD-1, approximately 80 to 100 examples of BD-2, and 40 to 50 examples of BD-3. Each of these current estimated populations represent about 10% of the proposed original mintage.

For those who are not well versed in numismatic terminology, we present a brief explanation of the term "delivery" or "delivery date." In the early Mint, individuals (persons or firms) brought their silver or gold to the Mint where it was received by the Mint treasurer. After being refined by the assayer to the proper purity, the deposit would be received by the chief coiner for production into actual coins. These coins would then be delivered back to the Mint treasurer with an associated document known as a "delivery warrant" with a specific quantity of coins produced and the date that they were received by the treasurer. It was these dated "delivery warrants" that now give us the term "delivery" or "delivery date."

These first quarter eagles featured the Draped Bust obverse design in a plain field with LIBERTY above and the date below. The reverse was the Heraldic Eagle design adapted from the Great Seal. A shield covered the eagle's breast with a row of clouds and a constellation of 16 stars above. The legend UNITED STATES OF AMERICA follows the border, and the eagle holds an olive branch and eight (more or less) arrows in its claws. Today, it is fascinating to think of the possibility suggested by James Ross Snowden in 1860, the possibility that a 1796 quarter eagle exists with a Small Eagle reverse. In his *Description of Ancient and Modern Coins, in the Cabinet Collection at the Mint of the United States* Snowden commented: "1796. The gold coins of this year have sixteen stars upon the obverse, eight upon each side of the effigy. The first coinage of quarter eagles took place this year. The first issue, which was made on the twenty first of September, was of the same type as the eagle."

This example is a remarkable piece. It is an intermediate die state, based on descriptions in the Bass-Dannreuther reference. There is only slight evidence of obverse die lapping, with the lower hair curls behind the shoulder still mostly complete. A faint die crack is visible from the obverse border at 9 o'clock, curving up into the field toward the back of the cap. Another faint crack can be seen from the lower right corner of E to the front edge of the cap. Additional die cracks have actually disappeared due to lapping of the obverse die. The reverse has a tiny die lump between the wing tip and the upper serif of F. Both sides have lightly reflective fields with bright yellow-gold luster. Faint hairlines are evident in addition to tiny abrasions, yet there are no significant marks on either side. Peripheral rose and lilac toning can be seen on the obverse with honey-gold toning along the borders on the reverse. Although it is not the finest known example of the 1796 No Stars quarter eagle, this piece is clearly among the top half dozen, a Condition Census specimen.

From The Freedom Collection. (#7645)

Lot 3381: 1796 Stars $2.50 MS61 NGC

Lustrous Mint State 1796 With Stars Quarter Eagle

3381   1796 Stars MS61 NGC. Breen-6114, Bass-3003, BD-3, R.5. BD Die State b. Few of the With Stars quarter eagles were produced with significant numbers of varieties and/or die states. The surface reason for this is quite straightforward: Since so few early quarter eagles were minted, few dies were needed. Because mintages were small, the dies were not employed for long, accounting for the lack of die cracks, die breaks, cuds, lapping, clashing, and other factors that create a new die state.

The reasons *why* so few quarter eagles were coined in the first place requires a bit more explanation, but *convenience* seems to be the key. Walter Breen's monumental *Encyclopedia of U.S. and Colonial Coins* suggests that most were held in local banks, subject to the infrequent requests from depositors for the denomination: "During this whole decade [1796-1807], quarter eagles were coined only in isolated driblets of a few hundred or at most a few thousand pieces. In most of these years, each date represented a new design modification—creating instant rarities and type coins. The problem is less why the coins are rare, why so few were made to begin with, but why any were struck at all! To judge from available Archives records, they were ordered on whim by a few local banks (principally the Bank of Pennsylvania and the Bank of the United States); to judge from the condition of survivors, they spent most of their time in vaults. Between 1803 and 1833, the Mint's major output consisted of cents, half dollars, and half eagles; all other denominations had a kind of poor-relative status—seldom called for, few made, little welcome." From 1795 through 1804, more than 140,000 eagles totaling $1.4 million were coined. From 1804, when eagle coinage was discontinued, until 1838, when it was reinstated, the half eagle was produced in quantities of about 2.1 million pieces, or $10.5 million in face value. In contrast, the lowly quarter eagle was produced to the extent of only about 64,000 pieces totaling $160,000 from 1796 through 1834, when the Classic Head type premiered.

Kentucky became the 15th state to join the Union in 1792, and accordingly the early U.S. gold and silver coins of 1794 and 1795, generally speaking, featured 15 stars on new dies. When Tennessee was admitted to the Union on June 1, 1796, coinage designs accommodated a 16th star on new dies, but Mint Director Elias Boudinot became aware that the burgeoning Union's stars would eventually crowd other design features off of the nation's coins. He accordingly ordered Engraver Robert Scot to limit the number of stars on new dies to the original 13.

The 16 stars are arranged 8 x 8 on this With Stars quarter eagle, which Breen calls "very rare," noting that the 432 pieces of the issue were delivered on Jan. 14, 1797. The recently published Garrett-Guth *Gold Encyclopedia* says, "This subtype is somewhat rarer than the 1796 No Stars quarter eagle, yet it generally sells for much less in comparable grades. Most examples are in circulated condition, with a cluster at the About Uncirculated level that may represent some unreported resubmissions. Mint State examples are extremely rare; included among them is a single gem example. Late states of the dies show heavy lapping to remove clash marks."

The present specimen appears to be from early in the BD Die State b. It shows light cracks from star 1 through 8, and a light crack from the 6 right into the field. Other cracks from that die state are not yet seen. The R in LIBERTY is quite weak, and light adjustment marks are noted on the reverse above TAT in STATES and through the eagle's tail feathers. Brilliant yellow-gold coloration is present on both sides, with good luster and light field chatter. For the early gold specialist, the significance of this incredible and historic early U.S. gold coin needs no further elaboration. Census: 2 in 61, 9 finer (11/06). (#7647)

Lot 3382: 1796 Stars $2.50 MS65 NGC

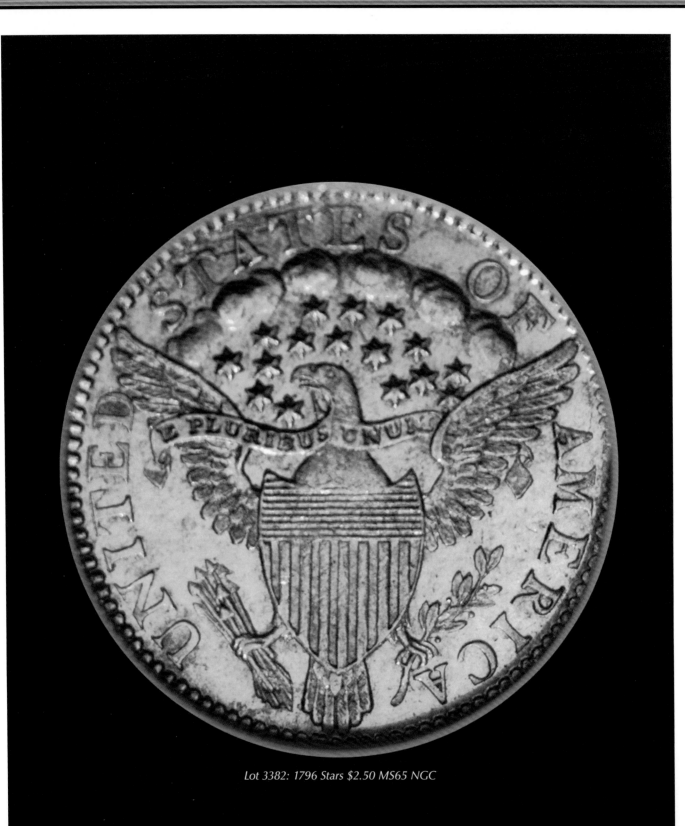

Lot 3382: 1796 Stars $2.50 MS65 NGC

Impressive Gem 1796 With Stars Quarter Eagle
An Extraordinary Rarity

3382   **1796 Stars MS65 NGC.** Breen-6114, Bass-3003, BD-3, R.5. BD Die State b. This is the only Gem quality 1796 With Stars quarter eagle certified. The next finest examples grade MS63, and the population goes downward from there. NGC and PCGS have combined to grade just 14 pieces in all Mint State grades, and that total undoubtedly includes several resubmissions. There are certainly less than 10 true Mint State examples of this issue still in existence today. In all grades, the total estimated population is only 40 to 45 coins from a mintage generally believed to be 432 coins.

Historical Commentary

The Mint Act of 1792 authorized all of the gold and silver coins that would eventually be struck by the young Philadelphia Mint. After property was acquired, construction of the actual buildings was completed, and all was ready to produce the Nation's first coinage, copper, silver, and gold. Despite completion of the physical components and acquisition of the necessary equipment, coinage of gold and silver could still not be accomplished as the bonding requirement for key employees was too strict. These employees were unable to meet the original requirement of $10,000 bond to insure against possible loss.

Rittenhouse approached Congress with a request to reduce this amount, which they eventually did. The new requirement was $5,000 bond, a more reasonable figure for the time. It was understood that steps would be put in place for these bonded employees to only have access to a limited amount of gold and silver at any one time, further reducing the risk to the government. Finally, all was set for production of precious metals coinage. Silver dollars and half dollars were coined for the first time late in 1794, followed by other silver denominations. Half eagles and eagles came next, with the first gold coins struck in July 1795, and finally the quarter eagles were produced beginning in September 1796 with the No Stars issue. Even after all was set for production of gold coins, few quarter eagles were produced. The denomination of choice for depositors were the larger half eagles and eagles.

The Design

Creation of the early quarter eagle design is generally attributed to Robert Scot, the first Chief Engraver of the Philadelphia Mint.

A bust of Liberty faces right, draped and capped, with the 1796 date below and LIBERTY above. A total of 16 stars are arranged with eight to the left and eight to the right, each oriented point-to-point. Only a few early U.S. coins have stars oriented in this manner as the usual orientation has a single point toward the border.

The reverse has a large, Heraldic eagle patterned after the Great Seal of the United States. A ribbon in the eagle's beak extends left and right, bearing the inscription E PLURIBUS UNUM. The eagle holds a bundle of arrows (eight are visible) in its dexter claw and an olive branch in its sinister claw. A shield on the eagle's breast consists of eight vertical stripes and nine horizontal crossbars. Above the eagle's head is a row of clouds (seven or eight, depending on the viewer's perspective) and 16 stars in a seemingly random placement. The statutory legend UNITED STATES OF AMERICA follows the border clockwise, from 7:30 to 5:30.

Individual Die Characteristics

Notable features of this die pair include the digit 6 overlapping the bottom edge of the drapery on the obverse and the raised die file lines through TATE on the reverse. The 8x8 star arrangement on the obverse is somewhat inconsistent with a wide space between star 1 and the hair curl, enough to permit a ninth star on the left, which would have eliminated the crowded appearance of the stars on the right.

This Coin

The Gem 1796 With Stars quarter eagle that we are pleased to present is from the famous Byron Reed Collection. Both sides are sharply detailed with bright yellow-gold color displaying greenish tendencies. The fields are fully prooflike, suggesting the possibility that this may have been a special strike, although we hesitate to declare it a specimen strike or presentation piece. A few faint abrasions on each side are hardly significant, and obviously did not concern the graders at NGC.

This is an early die state, although a light bulge appears in the left obverse field, usually seen on later die state pieces of various coins. A faint die crack extends right from the digit 6 and another crack connects the stars on the left. The lower hair curls are mostly complete, indicating that this example was struck prior to die lapping.

Roster of Mint State Pieces

The eight pieces listed in this roster is by no means complete as pedigree research in early gold coinage is seriously lacking. The Harry Bass coin, considered AU58 by some observers, is almost certainly a full Mint State example, thus included here. The other Mint State example offered in the present sale is almost certainly one of the following, although we have not been able to make a conclusive match.

MS65 NGC. This coin. Byron Reed Collection; Durham Western Heritage Museum; Christie's and Spink America (10/1996), lot 41.

MS63 NGC. John Whitney Walter (Stack's, 5/1999), lot 1790; Bowers and Merena (11/2002), lot 3063; Bowers and Merena (3/2004), lot 2512.

MS63. Stack's (2/1974), lot 495; Jimmy Hayes Collection; Auction '84, lot 1365; Auction '89, lot 1356.

MS63. Smithsonian Institution.

MS62 NGC. Heritage (11/2005), lot 2363.

MS61. John Whitney Walter (Stack's, 5/1999), lot 1791.

MS61 PCGS. Charles T. Steigerwalt (5/1907); John H. Clapp; Clapp Estate; Louis E. Eliasberg, Sr.; Eliasberg Estate (Bowers and Ruddy, 10/1982), lot 80; Long Beach Connoisseur (Bowers and Merena, 8/1999), lot 337; Cincinnati Collection (Heritage, 1/2005), lot 8761.

AU58 prooflike. Fred Sweeney (10/24/1972); Harry W. Bass, Jr. Bass Sylloge number 3003 and now on display at the American Numismatic Association.

Walter Breen recorded three different pieces as "presentation pieces" in his *Proof Encyclopedia*. These included lot 2496 in the June 1912 Henry Chapman sale of the George Earle Collection, a coin that appeared in the 1875 sale of the M.I. Cohen Collection, an example that appeared as lot 12 in the 1886 sale of the Dr. Edward Maris Collection, and a piece sold in the 1974 "Winter Sale." (#7647)

Lightly Circulated 1802/1 Quarter Eagle

3383   1802/1 AU58 NGC. Breen-6118, BD-2, High R.5. The rarest of three die marriages for the year. The ES in STATES is widely spaced, and the upright of the E is centered between a pair of clouds. The eagle's lower beak is extended due to a minor engraving blunder. Ample satin luster emerges when this pale-gold example is rotated beneath a light. The centers show some softness of strike, as usual for this early gold type. Light friction on the obverse highpoints prevents a Mint State grade. A small planchet flaw (as made) beneath the chin will identify the present piece. While all 1802 quarter eagles are traditionally referred to as overdates, no examples are known that display an irrefutable underdigit, and many numismatists regard the final digit as merely repunched. Despite a stingy mintage of 3,035 pieces, three die marriages are known for the 1802, all of which share a common obverse. (#7650)

Challenging 1802/1 Two and a Half MS61

3384   1802/1 MS61 PCGS. Breen-6118, BD-1, R.4. 1802 quarter eagles are traditionally referred to as 1802/1 overdates, although researchers concluded several years ago that a defective 2 punch is the source of the line that connects the ball of the 2 to its curve. The 1802/1, or 1802/'1' as it is sometimes referred to, has three die marriages. BD-1 is identified by a repunched left pendant on the T in UNITED. This canary-gold example has its quotient of bright luster, and the surfaces are unmarked aside from a trivial obverse rim nick at 3 o'clock. The strike is bold except for localized softness in the centers. Mint-made features include a clash mark within the shield, a thin strike-though on the cap, and a pair of faint, parallel adjustment marks near the neck. Population: 6 in 61, 10 finer (10/06). (#7650)

MS63 1802/1 BD-1 Quarter Eagle

3385   1802/1 MS63 NGC. Breen-6118, BD-1, R.4. The top of the 1 in the date is about level with the lowest hair curl, and the small so-called "overdate" 2 is evenly spaced between the bust and the dentils. On the reverse the left serif of the T in UNITED is recut, and a short metal spike runs from the left (facing) shield corner to the eagle's left wing. The I in AMERI-CA touches a leaf, and the last A in AMERICA is closer to the claw than to the leaf.

This quarter eagle issue is commonly and traditionally called an overdate, although most numismatists have concluded that a defective digit punch is the source of the anomalous 2 in the date. This terminology is, at least in part, likely due to the existence of the true (and obvious) overdate 1802/1 half eagle. The obverse of this variety was married successively with three different reverses, producing the BD-1 through BD-3 varieties. The reverse was also used to strike the 1802 JR-3 dime, which also shows the shield spike quite strongly.

This Select Mint State specimen offers good luster, with alternating areas of green-gold and apricot-gold on each side, an unusual but captivating effect. As on the dimes produced with this reverse, the motto is somewhat (but not notably) weak, and the eagle's neck feathers are essentially nonexistent. Although no clash marks are visible on the obverse, the reverse appears to be early Reverse State c as outlined in the Bass-Dannreuther *Early U.S. Gold Coin Varieties.* The "die line" or "graver's mark" is visible from the second wing feather to the A in AMERICA, and the early stage of a die crack shows from the rim to the last A in AMERICA, although not yet invading the curve of the C. Light adjustment marks are seen on the obverse rim from 8 to 9:30, but this piece is a nonetheless desirable and collectible example of early American gold. Census: 14 in 63, 5 finer (12/06). (#7650)

1802/1 $2.50 MS65 NGC

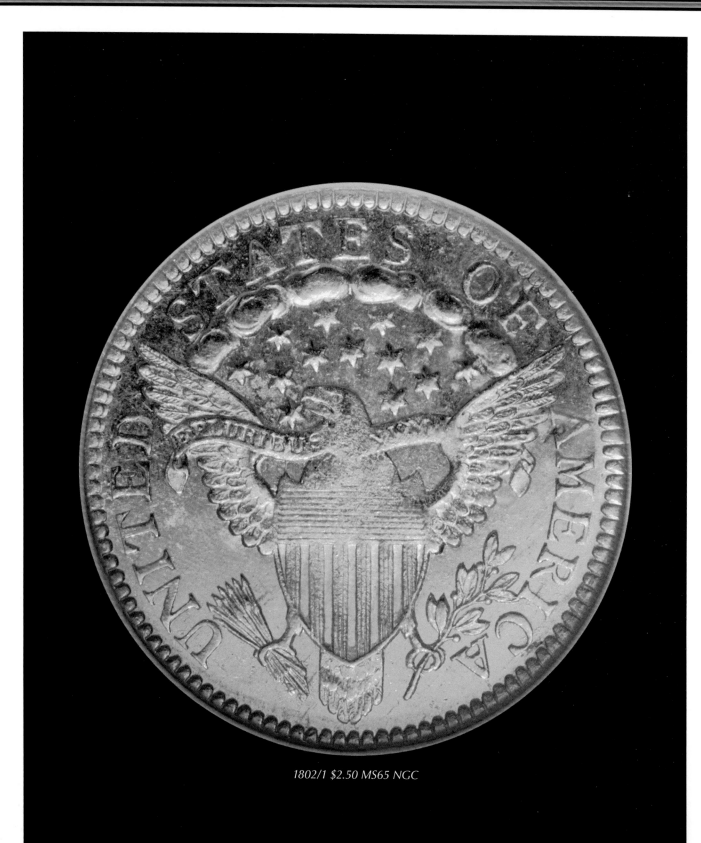

1802/1 $2.50 MS65 NGC

Gem Mint State 1802/1 Quarter Eagle, BD-3

3386   1802/1 MS65 NGC. Breen-4, Breen-6118, Bass-3009, BD-3, R.5. There exist three known die combinations for the quarter eagles of 1802, and all share a common obverse die that is routinely called an overdate. However, its status as an overdated die is highly questionable. As John Dannreuther notes in *Early U.S. Gold Coin Varieties:* "The fact that there were no quarter eagles dated 1799, 1800, or 1801 should lend credence to the overdate status of the 1802, but most researchers have come to the conclusion that whatever is under the 2 is not the vestiges of a 1." Dannreuther continues: "Some have suggested the calling of this quarter eagle an overdate is due to the obvious 1802/1 half eagle—an analogy easily seen. A defective 2 punch or break is now considered the likely culprit for the '1' below the 2 in the date."

Among the three varieties of 1802 quarter eagles, the BD-3 variety is seen less often than BD-1, but much more often than BD-2. The reverse is easily recognized by two constant features, a vertical spike from the left corner of the shield to the ribbon above, intersecting the ribbon below the space between B and U in PLURIBUS, and also by clear recutting of star 1 in the constellation that shows nine distinct points, rather than the usual six points.

Like many of the Draped Bust quarter eagles, the reverse die used for this variety was also used to coin Draped Bust dimes, in this case both 1802 and 1803 dimes. This interdenominational use of reverse dies was a situation unique to the dimes and quarter eagles. There are no documented instances of eagles and half dollars sharing reverse dies, and of course, quarter dollars had the denomination incorporated as part of the design, thus could not be used for production of half eagles. In addition to its use for the BD-3 quarter eagles of 1802, this reverse was also used to produce 1802 JR-1 dimes and 1803 JR-1 dimes.

This example represents the usually seen die state with a short die crack from the right reverse border at 2 o'clock to the wing tip. The vertical die defect from the left corner of the shield is also described by Dannreuther as a die crack, although it appears to remain constant throughout the life of the reverse die for both quarter eagles and dimes, and may actually be a die scratch created by the engraver. The 1802 JR-1 dime is unique (or nearly so) with the crack at 2 o'clock evident on those known examples, while the 1803 JR-1 dime (also extremely rare) apparently has additional reverse cracks. A single 1802 BD-3 quarter eagle in the Smithsonian Institution does not have this die crack, according to Dannreuther, thus represents the initial use of this reverse die. Thus the emission sequence appears to be 1802 BD-3 quarter eagles first, 1802 JR-1 dimes second, and 1803 JR-1 dimes third, with the possibility of additional quarter eagles struck between the production of the 1802 and 1803 dimes.

Although all quarter eagles from 1796 (With Stars) through 1807 are considered a single design type, Draped Bust With Stars, with the Heraldic Eagle reverse, there are actually six different subtypes, highly unusual with only 13 known die marriages for this series. The subtypes include: the 1804 14 Stars reverse; 1796 with eight obverse stars on each side; 1797 with obverse stars arranged seven by six and with 16 reverse stars; 1798 with obverse stars arranged six by seven; 1802, 1804, and 1806/4, all with obverse stars arranged eight by five; and 1805, 1806/5, and 1807, all with seven by six obverse stars.

Current population data from NGC and PCGS indicate that this particular 1802 quarter eagle is one of just two MS65 examples certified, with none finer, and this assumes that the two pieces certified by NGC are different coins. Otherwise, this piece is the sole Gem example of the date that survives. It is fully lustrous with brilliant green-gold surfaces and deeply reflective mirrored fields. Both sides have a few insignificant abrasions that are of virtually no concern, given the age and beauty of this specimen. The central obverse and reverse have considerable weakness that is typical of the variety, although some specimens are more sharply struck. A trace of old lacquer remains on the reverse, just above the right wing tip. Coating a coin with lacquer was an old-time preservation method, and it can still be successfully removed with the proper procedures, although this should best be done by a specialist in numismatic conservation. The overall aesthetic appeal of this Gem is extremely high, and it is one of the finest pieces, if not the best, that still exists today. *From The Freedom Collection.* (#7650)

Radiant Choice AU 1805 Quarter Eagle

3387   1805 AU55 PCGS. Breen-6121, BD-1, R.4. A band of bright luster connects the stars and legends. The devices also display substantial luster. A few mint-made roller marks cross Liberty's hair, but the surfaces are uncommonly smooth for the grade save for light vertical hairlines on the right obverse field. Rich apricot toning graces open areas, while the radiant margins are yellow. Light friction on the cheek and clothing is all that prevents a finer grade. The 1805 has a tiny reported mintage of 1,781 pieces, most of which were melted long ago. Many survivors have problems, unlike the present piece, which deserves placement within a quality early gold type set. Encapsulated in an old green label holder. (#7653)

Pleasing 1805 Quarter Eagle, AU58

3388   1805 AU58 NGC. Breen-6121, BD-1, R.4. This is the only known die marriage. Jeff Garrett and Ron Guth write in their book *Encyclopedia of U.S. Gold Coins* that: "Later the die was annealed (softened), a 6 was punched over the 5, and more quarter eagles were struck. Such economies were common in the early days of the Philadelphia Mint, but it was quite unusual to reuse a die in this manner (most other overdates involve dies that had never been hardened or used to strike coins before)."

This high-end AU specimen displays bright yellow-gold surfaces with a few speckles of deeper orange-gold in limited areas of the obverse. The design features are well defined, save for weakness in portions of the motto on the ribbon and on the adjacent neck and breast of the eagle. A few obverse adjustment marks are noted. Census: 13 in 58, 9 finer (11/06). (#7653)

Rare Mint State 1805 Quarter Eagle

3389   1805 MS61 PCGS. Breen-6121, BD-1, R.4. The only dies for the date, and perhaps worthy of an R.5 rating, since Heritage auction appearances average fewer than one per year. Survivors are concentrated in AU grades, and only a single MS64 PCGS piece exceeds the MS62 level. The present lovely example is mildly proof-like. The highpoints offer a hint of powder-blue patina. The strike is sharp. A few parallel roller marks cross the reverse center, but the surfaces are surprisingly void of identifying abrasions. Encapsulated in a prior generation PCGS holder. Population: 2 in 61, 4 finer (9/06). (#7653)

Elusive Uncirculated 1807 Capped Bust Right Quarter Eagle

3390   1807 MS61 PCGS. Breen-6124, BD-1, R.3. In the ultra-challenging Capped Bust Right series of the quarter eagles, the final year 1807 is the date that is most often available to collectors for type purposes. It seems that from the beginning the quarter eagle denomination has played second fiddle to its larger half eagle counterpart. The mintage of this issue, a tiny 6,812 pieces, is nevertheless more than double the production of its closest competitor in the series. In addition to the already low mintage, many of the gold coins struck during this period succumbed to the mass meltings of the pre-1834 period. Only decades later when greater gold reserves were discovered in the hills of northern Georgia, gold content was reduced, and Federal legislation eased the pressure on the price of gold did production increase and gold coinage begin to circulate freely.

The typical Mint State 1807 quarter eagle is ill-defined in the centers and hampered by numerous adjustment marks. This attractive representative boasts a pleasing mixture of green-gold alloy and reddish patina. The strike is considerably above-average for the issue and, while certainly present, adjustment marks are almost exclusively confined to the center of the reverse. Overall, we could hardly imagine a more desirable representative at such a modest Mint State grade level and, as such, an ideal Capped Bust Right type candidate. Population: 6 in 61, 20 finer (12/06). (#7656)

Rare 1808 Quarter Eagle, XF40 Details

3391   1808—Ex-Jewelry, Cleaned—ANACS. XF40 Details.
Breen-6125, Bass-3017, BD-1, R.4. Jeff Garrett and Ron Guth (2006) write that: "The 1808 quarter eagle enjoys heightened demand because it is the only date of its type, making it a 'must have' coin for anyone putting together a United States gold type set. The number of survivors is few, consistent with the low mintage (2,710 pieces)."

Semi-bright yellow-gold surfaces display traces of reddish-tan, and some fine hairlines. Sharp definition is noted on the design elements, that are well centered on the planchet. A repair has been made on the shield. (#7660)

1808 $2.50 MS63 NGC

1808 $2.50 MS63 NGC

Select Mint State 1808 Quarter Eagle Rarity

3392   1808 MS63 NGC. Breen-6125, Bass-3017, BD-1, R.4. Johann Matthias (John) Reich joined the Mint engraving staff on April 1, 1807, and served a 10-year tenure until March 31, 1817. He was responsible for the Capped Bust coinage so familiar today. Reich set about redesigning every denomination from the half cent through the half eagle. In 1807, his Capped Bust design appeared for the first time on half dollars, and a similar design also appeared on the half eagles in 1807. Early the next year, a modification of this design, known today as the Classic Head, appeared on large cents and followed on the half cents in 1809. For silver coins, the Capped Bust design was utilized for dimes in 1809, quarter dollars in 1815, and half dimes in 1829. Silver dollars and eagles were not in production, thus the Reich designs never appeared on those denominations. Perhaps the single most important entry in the Reich parade of designs is the quarter eagle of 1808.

John Reich was a native of Bavaria who learned the engraving trade from his father, Johann Christian Reich. According to L. Forrer in the *Biographical Dictionary of Medalists:* the elder Reich was "born at Eisenberg (Saxe-Altenburg) about 1740, settled at Furth in 1758, and died in 1814. He probably began as an assistant to a Counter-manufacturer, but started business on his own account about 1770, as shown by various counters bearing his name, some of which refer to the famine of 1771/1772. He had a factory of organs, clocks, mathematical instruments, musical boxes, and other objects. Of that period is a series of medals by him dated 1771 and 1772, and commemorating also that famine." The younger Reich, according to Forrer, collaborated with his father from about 1789 to 1800. Johann Matthias was born in Furth in 1768. Many of the medals issued during those years with the signature of Reich were the work of both father and son together. John Reich immigrated to America in 1800, settling in Philadelphia. Apparently he came at the suggestion of Henry Voigt, and quickly gained the attention of Mint Director Elias Boudinot. In a June 16, 1801 letter to President Thomas Jefferson, Boudinot commented that "I have been waited on by Mr. Reich and was much pleased with his work." Jefferson, in turn, agreed to have Reich prepare the design for his own Indian Peace medal.

Robert Patterson replaced Boudinot as director of the Mint, and then hired John Reich as assistant engraver. A short time later, another engraver arrived from Europe. Moritz Furst came to Philadelphia and "was firmly convinced that he was to assume the office of chief engraver, according to representations which had been made to him by Thomas Appleton, the American consul at Leghorn," according to Georgia S. Chamberlain in the March 1955 issue of *The Numismatist.* Eventually, both Reich and Furst worked on designs for various medals at the Mint. Reich left his post at the Mint in 1817, and spent his remaining 16 years in Albany, New York.

The 1808 quarter eagle is the only issue of this denomination to display Reich's handiwork. Only 2,710 pieces were minted during the year, and it is likely that all were from this single pair of dies. Only one variety is known with approximately 150 surviving pieces. The combination of a low survival and high demand from type, date, and variety collectors ensures that examples are infrequently offered and hotly contested when they are made available. In Walter Breen's *Complete Encyclopedia,* the author states: "No archives documentation explains the small mintage, abandonment of the design, or noncoinage of quarter eagles for the dozen years to follow. All we have is conjectures; mine follow." Essentially, Breen suggested that the banks, who made regular deposits of gold to be converted to coin, preferred the half eagle coins: "over 90% of the time they wanted most or all their gold deposits coined into half eagles." This same reason is usually quoted for large production of half eagles throughout the early 19th century, but it fails to explain why the largest gold coin of that time, the eagle, had not been produced since 1804, not to appear again until 1838.

The example that we offer represents the usual die state with an obverse die crack through the rear peak of the cap, continuing over the cap to the left, and through all stars on the right. There is no evidence of die lapping or any other cracks on either side. It is believed that the obverse die actually cracked as it was being made, and that no perfect die coins exist. As always, the border dentils are weak, and almost nonexistent on the obverse. The surfaces are lightly abraded as always, with faint adjustment marks visible through ES OF on the reverse. The central obverse and reverse design detail is bold and the overall eye appeal is excellent. Both sides are fully lustrous with slightly reflective fields and rich orange-gold color. Hints of rose patina complete the picture.
From The Freedom Collection. (#7660)

Mint State 1821 Quarter Eagle

3393   1821 MS62 NGC. Breen-6126, Bass-3018, BD-1, R.5. It had been 13 years since the last quarter eagles were coined until this denomination was resumed again. Production remained low with 6,448 quarter eagles produced in 1821, and this mintage was more than one-third the total output for the entire design from 1821 through 1827. Based on mintage figures alone, the rarity of the entire type can be seen, with just 17,042 pieces struck during that period. But the mintage was not everything, as John Dannreuther points out: "Besides the usual factors that remove coins from circulation—wear, loss, and so on—the early gold issues faced another factor that doomed many of them. Pre-1834 old coins were melted after the June 28, 1834 passage of the act reducing the weight of gold coins."

After John Reich left the Mint, Robert Scot was the only engraver that remained, and it is he who is given credit for this design, actually a modification of Reich's earlier design. Scot is a mysterious figure among the various chief engravers who served the Mint over the years. He received his appointment to the Mint staff on November 23, 1793, and remained until his death in late 1823. Many years earlier, at about the time John Reich joined the Mint, Scot's future potential had been discussed by Mint Director Patterson who stated that he was "so advanced in life, that he cannot very long be expected to continue his labors." At the time, Robert Scot was 62 years old, and Patterson was 64!

The 1821 quarter eagle is the first issue of this design, and the entire mintage is from a single die pair. The first examples were proofs, struck from polished dies. Because so few business strikes were coined after the proofs, nearly all have reflective surfaces as on this coin. Both sides are lightly abraded as expected for the grade. A few faint hairlines are also evident. The central design motifs are boldly defined, and the stars near the obverse border are fully detailed. The surfaces have fully brilliant green-gold color with satin luster.

From The Freedom Collection. (#7662)

Rare Near-Mint 1824/1 Quarter Eagle

3394 **1824/1 AU58 PCGS.** Breen-6127, BD-1, R.5. The BD-1 is the only known variety for the year. The left edge of the 1 is over the left edge of a dentil, and the 8 is centered over a dentil. The numerator and denominator in the fraction are distant from each other and from the integer. Although this issue is recorded as an overdate, that feature fades with time and is not much visible on the present example. An unused 1821 obverse die was used in 1824, since there were no quarter eagle coinages in the intervening two years. This piece offers still-lustrous lemon-yellow surfaces, with just a touch of highpoint wear and light field chatter. A bit of strike softness shows on the left (facing) wing of the eagle. Rare so fine. Population: 2 in 58, 8 finer (11/06). (#7663)

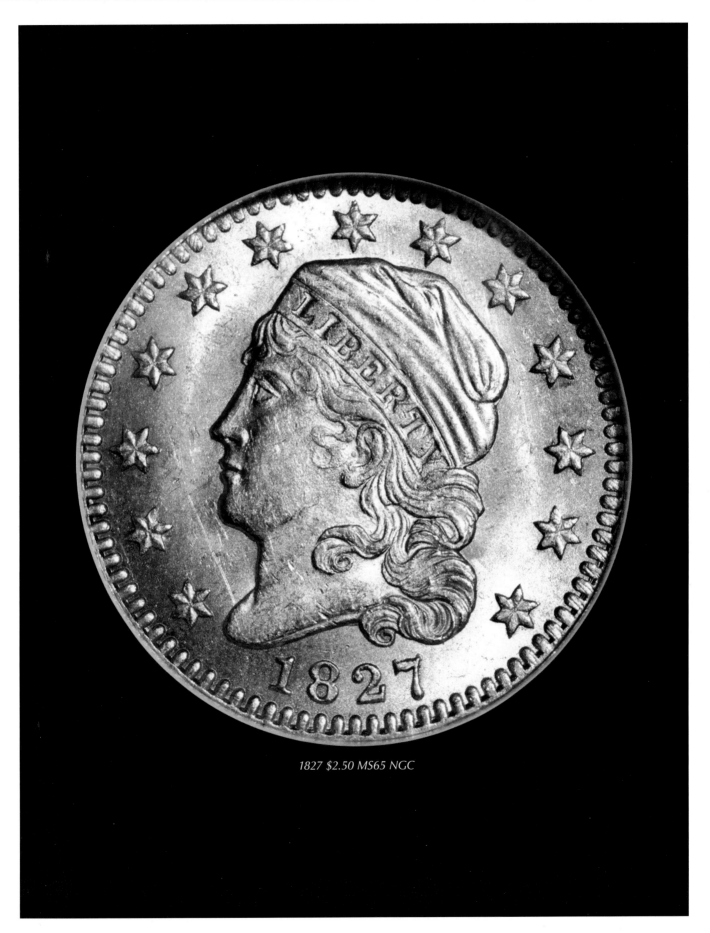

1827 $2.50 MS65 NGC

1827 $2.50 MS65 NGC

Exceptionally Rare Gem 1827 Quarter Eagle

3395   1827 MS65 NGC. Breen-6131, Bass-3025, BD-1, R.5. The only known dies, with the close fraction reverse having previously served in both 1825 and 1826. In the outstanding new book *Early U.S. Gold Coin Varieties - A Study of Die States 1795-1834* by John Dannreuther and Harry Bass, the authors state that the reverse was produced from reverse State c, "lapped to remove clashing that occurred when it was paired with the 1826/6 obverse *(possibly exists in State a/b before lapping... and conceivably in a later state with some injury to either die.)*" Dannreuther further notes that the single Bass Collection example was struck with this lapped die, with the angled clashmarks noted between the left end of the scroll and the wing on reverse State b removed.

It is therefore significant that examination of this coin shows faint but undeniable angled clash marks, again below the left side of the scroll and near the eagle's beak. These marks are not as strong as the clashmarks that appear on reverse State b, where the mark makes contact with the wing. Rather, the marks on this piece are a bit more subdued, most noticeable at the angle. The Bass *Sylloge* states that the dies for Mr. Bass' example were perfect, "the reverse now lapped to remove clash marks." However, the Childs specimen, an MS62 coin sold by Bowers and Merena in 1999, was noted as having similar marks to the present coin. A selection of other recent appearances made by Mint State specimens of the date reveals no other mentions of clashmarks at all, and photographic evidence is inconclusive as to how often these marks appear, thanks in no small part to the small size of the coin.

Another feature of the reverse deserves mention, as well. Notable on the right side of the scroll, and as struck, is some unevenness around the letters NUM. We believe that this may be a sign of die crumbling, which would mean that this could be the late die state Dannreuther speculates about. There is no question that the dies used to strike this piece have been lapped, but it remains open to question whether they were lapped incompletely or this is a new die clash. Further numismatic research will need to be done in order to answer this question.

Of course, what makes research on this piece difficult is the fact that this is quite a rare coin in an absolute sense and even more so in high grades. This is thanks in large part to a tiny mintage of 2,800 pieces, and in even larger part to the wholesale melting of all gold coins that took place in the early 1830s when the intrinsic value of the gold in U.S. coinage exceeded the face value. Not more than 50 pieces are believed to exist in all grades. The major services have combined to certify 57 pieces, but this figure includes resubmissions.

The coin itself is uniformly pale green-gold in color and well struck for the issue, a little blunt in the centers, but with no trace of weakness on the stars. It is a bright, frosty piece, enormously attractive both at a glance and upon closer examination. The few trivial surface blemishes that are present affect neither the grade nor the eye appeal, with perhaps the most important for pedigree purposes being a tiny tick between the right end of the scroll and the eagle's neck. Significantly, this is also one of only two pieces to have ever received a Gem grade from either of the major services, and it is the sole example in such a lofty grade—and one of a mere fifteen pieces overall—that Heritage has ever had the privilege to offer. Indeed, according to our records, this is the first time either Gem-certified example of the date has been offered at public auction. This is an opportunity for the connoisseur of both rarity and quality, and as such, an opportunity that may not arise again for many years. Census: 1 in 65, 0 finer (11/06). (#7666)

Pleasing 1829 Quarter Eagle, AU58

3396   1829 AU58 PCGS. Breen-6132, BD-1, High R.4. Although sometimes lumped together with the quarter eagle type from 1821 to 1827, issues from 1829 to 1834 are a distinct type. In 1829, new technology used to produce the quarter eagle included a close collar that provided for uniform and smaller diameters. Also, the borders are beaded and the head of Liberty has been modified.

This lightly circulated example displays attractive yellow-gold surfaces that show a subtle greenish tint. The design features are nicely defined, including excellent detail in all of the star centers. Both sides are remarkably clean. A small alloy spot above the 8 in the date may help to identify the coin. (#7669)

Noteworthy 1830 Quarter Eagle MS61

3397   1830 MS61 PCGS. Breen-6133, Type of Bass-3027, R.4. As with all dates in the reduced size Capped Head Left series, only a single die pairing was used to strike the 1830 quarter eagle. Here the dies can be identified by a repunched I in AMERICA combined with a final star distant from the border. This desirable Mint State representative, while a trifle scuffy in the fields, exhibits a generally strong strike and flashy semi-reflective luster. A solitary hairline scratch can be detected on the obverse from Liberty's lower curls to star 2. Noteworthy quality for this seldom-offered early type. Population: 5 in 61, 28 finer (11/06). (#7670)

Lovely MS64 1831 Quarter Eagle

3398   1831 MS64 PCGS. Breen-6134, BD-1, R.4. While there is only one generally acknowledged die pairing for this issue, the proof specimen write-up in the Harry W. Bass, Jr. *Museum Sylloge,* by Q. David Bowers offers this tantalizing note: "In addition to the standard die for this variety, there *may* be another, not known to modern students of the series, a mention located by QDB in 1997 when perusing old catalogues... In his April 1886 sale of the J.S. Twining Collection, W. Elliot Woodward offered Lot 950, a Proof 1831, followed by Lot 951 described as: '1831 Different die; nearly equal to the last, scarce.' * To complete the record it is necessary to mention the 1859 note by Dr. Montroville W. Dickeson, *American Numismatical Manual:* 'One type and two varieties. Rare.' However, most of Dickeson's die notes on early gold coins are erratic, and as such they cannot be used by modern student[s] of the series (nor did Harry W. Bass, Jr., use them)."

Discovery of new errors, or long-forgotten varieties, is part of what makes numismatics such a rich and enduring passion for so many numismatists and *numismaphiles*. As Bowers quotes Harry Bass, Jr., in the prefatory material of the Bass *Sylloge:*

> *"The opportunity to do this in my area of specialty has heightened for me the charm and excitement of collecting."*

While this lovely coin is not a proof, it was struck from the same dies. The same reverse die was used with different obverse dies for the years 1830 through 1834. The engraver, perhaps William Kneass, blundered the U in UNITED, along with the last A and the I in AMERICA. Each letter was first punched too far to the left, then corrected. Recutting also shows on the R in AMERICA, and the lowest arrowhead is blunted. The first 2 in the denomination is broken midway and has a curled base, while the second 2, in the denominator, has a flat base. On the obverse the date is well formed, with all digits level, and stars 8, 11, and 13 show signs of recutting.

The prooflike fields on this piece are highly attractive, and they are nearly complete with the exception of a thin ring of mint luster just inside the denticles on each side. The striking details are strong throughout with the exception of the juncture of the left (facing) wing of the eagle and the left side of the shield. Light, even, reddish-tinted patina is seen over both obverse and reverse. Population: 11 coins in 64, with eight pieces finer (10/06). (#7671)

Sharply Defined 1832 Quarter Eagle, AU55

3399   1832 AU55 PCGS. Breen-6135, BD-1, R.4. One die pair was used to strike the 4,400 quarter eagles in 1832. Jeff Garrett and Ron Guth (2006) say: "In 1832, the relief on Liberty's head was made higher, resulting in generally weaker strikes and few fully struck examples." The Choice AU piece offered in the current lot exhibits above-average detail for the issue. The star centers are sharp, as is most of Liberty's hair and the eagle's plumage. Just a touch of softness is noted in the hair above Liberty's ear. Bright yellow-gold surfaces exhibit ample luster in the areas around the design elements. *From The Hill Country Collection.* (#7672)

Choice Mint State 1833 Quarter Eagle

3400   1833 MS64 NGC. Breen-6136, Bass-3030, BD-1, R.5. A new design modification made its first appearance on the quarter eagles and half eagles in 1829. The occasion for this new design was incorporation of new technology at the Mint—the closed or close collar that imparted a "mathematical equality" to the diameter of struck coinage, according to Mint Director Samuel Moore. William Kneass had been hired to replace Robert Scot as the chief engraver, and it is he who is credited with this design. Actually, the design is essentially the same as the previous design, although the hair has a more luxurious appearance, and the borders now consist of beads rather than dentils. The reverse is nearly identical to the previous design. In fact, only two reverse dies were used for the entire design type issued from 1829 to 1834. The 1829 reverse has a square-based large 2 in the denomination, while the reverse used from 1830 through 1834 has a curve-based large 2 and also has the letter U in UNITED repunched.

This example is from the constant die state of the variety. Faint cracks connecting the upper and lower knobs of each 3 in the date are the result of a defective punch, and not actual cracks in the physical coinage die. Dannreuther discusses this at some length in his reference, noting: "the duplication of the exact *crack* on the 3 of the dimes indicates a defective punch, not a die that cracked."

This is a splendid near-Gem example of the date, second rarest of this design type behind the 1834 With Motto issue. Only about 60 to 80 examples of this date are known, according to Dannreuther, although this cataloger believes that the total may be closer to 100 pieces. Regardless, the entire design type is rare, with well under 1,000 surviving examples of all dates from 1829 to 1834. In fact, the true number of survivors is probably closer to 500 than to 1,000 coins. Both sides exhibit the usual grade-consistent abrasions. The surfaces have brilliant yellow luster with reflective fields. The usual minor design weakness is evident at the centers, just like nearly every other non-proof example of this date.
From The Freedom Collection. (#7673)

Amazing Gem 1838 Classic Head Quarter Eagle

Appealing Near-Gem McCloskey-B 1837 Quarter Eagle

3401   1837 MS64 PCGS. McCloskey-B, R.3. The most available die pairing for the 1837, recognizable by a wide left border and three lines per vertical stripe on the shield. An arrowhead touches the right foot of the final A in AMERICA. As a date, the 1837 is somewhat overlooked in the Classic Head quarter eagle series, although only a few dozen Uncirculated examples survive. That number dwindles to a handful of coins in Choice and better grades. This ultra-frosty representative is boldly struck in all areas and has an especially vibrant, satiny sheen. Were it not for a few paper-thin scrapes in the reverse field, this lovely quarter eagle would almost certainly qualify as a Gem. Even so, the eye appeal is extremely high. Population: 3 in 64, 1 finer (10/06).
From The Stone 1837 Collection. (#7695)

3402   1838 MS65 NGC. Just one die marriage is known for the 1838 Classic Head quarter eagle. Although this issue has a tendency to be grouped with the more obtainable issues in the Classic series such as the 1834 and 1835, few people have been witness to a sufficient number of Mint State pieces to pass judgment on its rarity above AU. Most high grade examples appear to range from AU 58 to MS 62 and, at the Gem level, the 1838 is extremely rare with less than 10 distinct specimens known. This piece shows a strong strike and exceptional luster characteristics beneath rich reddish-gold color. Field marks are generally very light and the only abrasions of note are a pair of small ones above the eagle's right wing that we mention for pedigree purposes, not because of their distracting nature.
Ex: Heritage (1/2000), lot 7609.
From The Freedom Collection. (#7696)

Pleasing 1839-C Quarter Eagle, AU58

3403   1839-C AU58 NGC. Recut 39. Winter 3-C, McCloskey-C, R.3. Only 165-175 1839-C quarter eagles are believed extant today out of an original mintage of 18,140 pieces. AU pieces are very popular with collectors because of the Classic design and obverse mintmark. The devices on this piece are generally well defined, except for minor softness on the star centers. There are surprisingly few abrasions on either side; for pedigree purposes, we mention a tiny indention near star 6, and a couple of round abrasions under the E and R of AMERICA. A die crack travels from the upper left corner of the shield through the eagle's beak. Census: 62 in 58, 14 finer (11/06). (#7699)

Rare Mint State 1839-C Quarter Eagle, MS62

3404   1839-C MS62 ICG. Overdate Variety 2-A. Struck from the first set of obverse and reverse dies, with the familiar die crack from the rim through the E in STATES. This piece combines its natural green-gold alloy with an overlay of reddish patina. The devices are well defined in the centers, with characteristic bluntness only on a few of the obverse stars. There is a large shallow planchet lamination (as struck) on the cheek. High grade (pieces grading AU or better) examples of this popular Charlotte issue are generally available for a price, but the appearance of an MS62 1839-C is most unusual, indeed Condition Census for the issue. (#7699)

Impressive 1840-C Quarter Eagle
MS63 NGC

3405   1840-C MS63 NGC. Variety 1-A. At the MS63 level, this piece is tied with seven others at the top of the list of currently graded examples at NGC and PCGS combined. This is a very impressive coin. The striking details are well brought up on each side with no obvious areas of weakness. The flashy green-gold surfaces exhibit a strong semi-prooflike sheen in the fields with satiny mint luster intermixed. Fortunately (or unfortunately, depending upon one's point of view), there are no singular marks on either side that can be pointed to as a reliable pedigree identifier. Census: 3 in 63, 0 finer (11/06). (#7718)

Choice About Uncirculated
1842-D Quarter Eagle

3406   1842-D AU55 NGC. Variety 3-F. The 1842-D quarter eagle is widely acknowledged as one of the most difficult pieces of Dahlonega gold to acquire. Of the original mintage of 4,643 pieces, it is estimated by Winter that only 75 to 85 exist in all grades, with About Uncirculated examples a small fraction of that. Although NGC records five Mint State examples, PCGS has graded none, and it is impossible to know exactly how many of those pieces represent resubmissions. On this Choice AU piece, the wheat-gold surfaces retain soft but significant peripheral luster. The devices, which have minor but distinct wear and a handful of long, thin abrasions, possess above-average detail nonetheless. A handful of flaws and handling marks affect the fields as well. Still, this is an important opportunity to acquire a high-grade circulated example of this often-elusive issue. (#7725)

Mint State 1842-D Quarter Eagle

3407 1842-D MS61 NGC. Variety 3-F. Only one die marriage is known for the issue, hardly a surprise since a mere 4,643 pieces were struck. This example was an early emission from the dies, since repunching is apparent beneath the bases of the 18 in the date. The strike is pleasantly sharp, with only unimportant softness noted on the shield lines and the curl beneath the ear. Minor, shallow, and mint-made planchet flaws are present near star 12, above the eagle's left (facing) shoulder and head, and beside the R in AMERICA. The borders display bright cartwheel luster, while the fields are mildly prooflike. The surfaces are remarkably free of identifiable marks. Census: 4 in 61, 1 finer (8/06). (#7725)

Challenging 1842-O Quarter Eagle MS62

3408 1842-O MS62 NGC. The '42-O has an impressively low mintage of only 19,800 pieces, and it is one of the rarest issues in the series of New Orleans Mint quarter eagles. The fields are bright and prooflike, giving the coin a special appearance that is most likely missing from many of the other high grade survivors. It is also better struck than most, with no weakness apparent on Liberty's hair curls and just the slightest softness on the eagle's left (facing) leg. Lightly abraded over each side, as the grade would indicate, the only surface flaw that is significant enough to use as a pedigree identifier is a small planchet void next to star 12. Census: 2 in 62, 4 finer (12/06). (#7726)

Possible Finest Known 1843-D
Large D Quarter Eagle

3409   1843-D Large D MS62 NGC. Variety 4-H, the less-common Large D variety. Although this issue is generally available due to its large emission—by the standards of the mint and the era—of 36,209 business strikes, most examples encountered today are well circulated. D-mint gold pundit Doug Winter writes, "It is believed that 3,537 quarter eagles using this reverse were struck on October 7, 1843. ... This variety is quite rare and it should sell for a substantial premium over the common [Small Mintmark] varieties." PCGS now recognizes this variety, which should give it another boost. The present MS62 example is one of the finest Mint State pieces of the issue that Heritage has ever offered, save for two MS63 specimens, in the last dozen-plus years, and it *may possibly be the finest certified of this rare variety.* Both sides offer distraction-free surfaces, with beaming luster and attractive green-gold coloration. A well-struck, lovely, and rare piece. (#97730)

Unsurpassed 1847-C
Quarter Eagle MS64 NGC

3410   1847-C MS64 NGC. Ex: North Georgia Collection. Variety 8-F. This Choice Uncirculated example is well struck, with bright, pleasing lime-gold toning and shimmering luster. The fields have a faintly prooflike sheen, especially on the obverse, which is facilitated by the presence of some wispy die striations. A few trivial marks are noted in the fields, as well as on Liberty's neck, but none of these are large enough to distract. This issue had the highest mintage of any Charlotte Mint quarter eagle, and is one of the most available. Mint State survivors are scarce, however, and just nine pieces have been graded at MS64 by NGC and PCGS combined, with none finer (11/06). (#7745)

Brilliant Near-Mint 1848
CAL. Quarter Eagle

3411   **1848 CAL. AU58 NGC.** The 1848 CAL. quarter eagle is always popular as a reminder of the historic, rough-and-tumble California Gold Rush era in the American West. Many collectors including the present cataloger consider this coin to be the United States' first commemorative coin, although it is not a coin with an entirely new design conceived specifically to commemorate a person or event. The CAL. stamped onto the dies to commemorate the first shipment of California gold to the U.S. Mint in Philadelphia appears to be, rather, an expedient, one calculated to both observe the event and yet produce coins from the new source of gold as quickly as possible. Since only 1,389 quarter eagles were manufactured, the issue far overshadows the 1848 (no CAL.) quarter eagle, also a low mintage issue that is (understandably, since the special nature of the CAL. pieces ensured that many more would be carefully preserved) far more elusive in Mint State—if hardly as popular and in demand.

The current combined NGC/PCGS population data suggest that the 1848 CAL. coins were indeed recognized early on as something special, as the average grade for certified pieces is in the range of AU55 to AU58. In AU55 both services combined have certified 10 coins, with 11 in AU58. There are 44 coins (or grading events) certified in Mint State, including three pieces in MS68! The current specimen offers brilliant orange-gold surfaces with much luster remaining. The well-struck example shows light evidence of a short stay in circulation, but no singular distractions. Census: 6 in 58, 21 finer (12/06).
From The Twin Hollows Collection. (#7749)

1848 $2.50 CAL. MS64 NGC

1848 $2.50 CAL. MS64 NGC

Remarkable Choice 1848 'CAL.' Quarter Eagle

3412   1848 CAL. MS64 NGC. The classic commemorative series of 1892 and later had their roots in a particular event more than 40 years earlier, according to a variety of numismatic scholars. The coins produced, the "CAL." quarter eagles of 1848, were commemoratives in a slightly different sense from the pieces that came later. Rather than bearing a completely different design from circulating pieces (and, in fact, it seems some examples went into circulation, judging from the wear on them), these first pieces coined from California gold had the notation "CAL." stamped into the field above the eagle. The modification may have been simple, but enough correspondence exists between the Mint and various individuals that the commemorative intent of the pieces was clear.

The surfaces of this immensely appealing and Choice quarter eagle are yellow-gold with glints of emerald in the fields and an area of greenish-gold above the eagle's head, a shift in color that would appear on more and more coins as California gold became the Mint's largest source of the metal. Well struck overall, though slight weakness is noted in the centers, and a thin, shallow abrasion is noted to the left of Liberty's lips. The highly lustrous fields are partially prooflike, a trait shared by most of the near-Mint and Mint State examples known today. The FUN sales of 2004 and 2006 saw Heritage offer MS67 and MS68 ★ examples, respectively, of this fascinating issue, and while this piece is not in so lofty a grade as either of those fantastic coins, this Choice representative is the finest Heritage has offered aside from them. Census: 3 in 64, 7 finer (11/06). *Ex: Superior, 2/98, lot 3343; Bowers and Merena's August 1998 roster of high-grade examples prepared by Mark Borckardt links this piece to the Kern specimen, which is Ex: B. Max Mehl, 5/50, lot 37 (described as "Proof"); Stack's, 5/65, lot 1130; Stack's, 10/68, lot 142; Stack's, 11/72, lot 780.* (#7749)

Elusive Mint State 1848-D Quarter Eagle

3413   1848-D MS62 PCGS. Variety 10-N, the Low Mintmark variety. While specimens of this issue appear with some regularity in the marketplace, most generally grade in the range of Extremely Fine to About Uncirculated. Mint State coins are quite rare and elusive. The Low Mintmark variety is considerably scarcer than the High Mintmark variety. It is distinguished by the arrow feathers which pass halfway through the mintmark, and the lower serif of the D which nearly joins the 1 in the fraction. This elusive piece offers lustrous green-gold surfaces. A couple of mint-made die irregularities show on the obverse—a small planchet lamination and two dotlike die bumps near star 3, along with some die crumbling at star 5—but considerable eye appeal is present. (#7751)

Rare Mint State 1849-D Quarter Eagle

3414   1849-D MS62 NGC. Variety 11-M. The 1849-D (10,945 coins produced) is similar in overall rarity to the 1848-D (13,771 pieces produced). The former issue, however, is rarer in high (AU-Mint State) grades. The two major grading services report 16 coins in Mint State (11/06), but when one allows for resubmissions, we still cannot overstate the high grade rarity of this issue. While this issue is not as well produced as the 1846-1848 quarter eagles from the Dahlonega Mint, the present example displays overall sharp definition. In fact, there are really no ill-defined features, and the yellow-gold surfaces show appreciable brightness in the fields. Scattered abrasions are consistent with the MS62 grade level, and the only noteworthy pedigree marker is a pinscratch in the lower right reverse field at the tip of the olive branch. (#7754)

Historic Gem 1850 Quarter Eagle
Finest at PCGS

3415   1850 MS65 PCGS. After the California Gold Rush began in 1848, the amounts of gold making their way to the Philadelphia Mint increased dramatically. While that institution produced more than 23,000 quarter eagles in 1849, in 1850 it increased the amount more than tenfold. Despite the high mintage for the era of more than a quarter of a million pieces, the 1850 issue is quite elusive in the higher reaches of Mint State. While NGC and PCGS combined have certified more than 138 *grading events* (not coins) from MS60 through MS64, only this single piece has been graded MS65, that at PCGS, although NGC has graded two pieces finer, both MS66 Star examples.

The surfaces are pretty yellow-gold and distraction-free, although light die rust shows on the obverse under a lens, creating a pebbly appearance. The strike is well executed except for light softness on the Y of LIBERTY and the lower beads of the hair cord nearby. A nice and attractive example of this historic early gold coinage. (#7755)

Scarce Mint State 1850-C Quarter Eagle

3416   1850-C MS60 PCGS. Variety 12-G. The mintmark is centered over the 1 in the fraction, and is immediately between the left (facing) claw and the fletchings. This example is very attractive and seems conservatively graded. The fine satin luster highlights lovely lime-gold and peach coloration. The prominent, wavy die clash marks on each side are entirely expected, for the issue. The striking details are definitely better than average for the Charlotte Mint, and careful examination is required in order to detect slight weakness on the obverse stars, Liberty's hair, and the lower parts of the eagle. A shallow abrasion above TA in STATES is the only noteworthy surface anomaly. This issue is scarce in Mint State, and, according to Doug Winter (1998): "This date is nearly impossible to locate without very heavily abraded surfaces." This coin must be an exception to the rule, as surface marks are absolutely minimal. Population: 1 in 60, 3 finer (11/06). (#7756)

Conditionally Scarce 1850-C Quarter Eagle MS61 NGC

3417 1850-C MS61 NGC. Variety 12-G. The mintage of the 1850-C was limited to 9,148 pieces, although it is actually seen with slightly greater frequency than some higher mintage C-mint issues. It is ranked 15th in overall rarity and 12th in high grade rarity by Winter. The elusive Uncirculated example offered here is a bright and fully lustrous with tinges of reddish patina. Both sides enjoy sharper definition than is normally encountered on the issue and multiple clash marks are seen about the central devices, a hallmark of this die pairing. Census: 13 in 61, 3 finer (11/06). (#7756)

Scarce Mint State 1850-C Quarter Eagle

3418 1850-C MS61 NGC. Variety 12-G. A more available Charlotte quarter eagle that becomes exceedingly scarce in Mint State. In this grade there are few measurably better, with just four pieces currently graded finer by the two major services. Well struck on both sides. The only noticeable weakness is on some of the obverse stars, and on the eagle's left (facing) leg, talons, and arrow fletchings. Lustrous with pleasing lime-gold toning, substantial semi-prooflikeness in the fields, and marks on each side that are numerous but mainly small and superficial, leaving the luster essentially undisturbed. Only 9,148 quarter eagles of this date were struck at the Charlotte Mint. Census: 13 in 61, 3 finer (11/06). (#7756)

Rare Mint State 1854-C Quarter Eagle

3419   1854-C MS61 NGC. Variety 15-I. Well struck for the issue, with typical softness noted on the eagle's neck and lower parts. The luster is somewhat muted, but faint semi-prooflikeness is observed in the fields. Only superficial marks exist on either side of the coin. According to Garrett and Guth (2006): "The 1854-C Liberty Head quarter eagle is a scarce and popular coin in all grades. Most of the coins offered are well circulated, and Mint State examples are very rare. Coins of this date are frequently found to have been harshly cleaned or damaged. A pleasing 1854-C quarter eagle is quite the prize." Census: 5 in 61, 7 finer (11/06). (#7770)

Elusive 1855-C Quarter Eagle MS60 NGC

3420   1855-C MS60 NGC. Winter 16-I. The elusive 1855-C quarter eagle is tied for first in overall rarity among Charlotte issues. Its mintage figure of 3,677 pieces is second-lowest in the series among C-mints behind only the 1843-C Small Date, and it has also gained the reputation as being one of the worst produced issues from the Charlotte Mint. All in all, the strike on this bright yellow-gold example is much above average, although being noticeably deficient on the lower portion of the eagle. Numerous shallow abrasions in the fields are the most obvious deterrent to a higher Mint State rating. Census: 2 in 60, 8 finer (11/06). (#7775)

Rare Mint State 1857-D Quarter Eagle

3421   1857-D MS61 NGC. Variety 20-M, the only known dies. A thin die line connects the right tip of the digit 5 to the bust truncation, a diagnostic of this obverse die. The reverse has a large D mintmark centered above the tip of the fraction bar, and joined to the branch stem. Although not as rare as the 1855-D or 1856-D quarter eagles, the 1857-D is a low-mintage issue that is rare in Mint State grades. This issue was produced in much higher quality than the previous two years. It has sharp design features on both sides with frosty luster and attractive lemon-gold color. Mint State examples of this date are seldom encountered, with estimates suggesting that only 10 to 12 examples survive today. (#7783)

Wonderful 1857-D Quarter Eagle, MS62

3422   1857-D MS62 PCGS. Variety 20-M, the only known dies. Only 2,364 pieces were struck of the 1857 Dahlonega issue. Douglas Winter, in the second edition of his book *Gold Coins of the Dahlonega Mint,* estimates that only 110 to 130 specimens exist in all states of preservation. Of these, eight to ten are estimated to be in Mint State condition. This MS62 example displays peach-gold surfaces with faint traces of light green, and the design elements are sharply impressed. A few wispy marks are noted over each side. Population: 6 in 62, 1 finer (11/06). (#7783)

Pretty MS64 1857-O Quarter Eagle
One of the Finest Certified

3423 **1857-O MS64 NGC.** This issue, from the last year of quarter eagle production at the New Orleans Mint, is scarce in AU and rare in Mint State. Only 34,000 coins were manufactured, about 20% of the emission in some previous years. As Garrett and Guth point out, collecting of coins by mintmark was all but unknown, and the existence of any Mint State example is nearly miraculous. If that is so, then this near-Gem coin is quite a miracle, boasting as it does pretty, pristine surfaces with considerable reflectivity and good eye appeal. The fields have prooflike tendencies. A bit of strike weakness can be seen on the lower beads in the hair cord and the curls below the ear, as well as on the eagle's left (facing) leg and right wing bottom, but this distraction is trivial, as the coin is essentially unimprovable. Census: 2 in 64, 0 finer (11/06). (#7784)

Sharp Uncirculated 1858-C Quarter Eagle

3424 **1858-C MS62 PCGS.** Variety 18-J. The 1858-C is the only C-mint quarter eagle produced between 1856 and 1860. Apparently the smaller gold denomination had almost been eliminated in favor of the continually produced half eagle. A mere 9,056 pieces were struck. Despite this small mintage, the 1858-C is actually the most available quarter eagle produced at the Charlotte facility during the decade and, according to Doug Winter, in high grade rarity it ranks 18th out of the 20 C-mint quarter eagles. From a population of perhaps 25-35 Mint State survivors, almost exclusively MS60-62 quality, comes this well detailed example. Both sides are overlaid in attractive reddish patina and show modest scuffiness in the fields. A pair of paper-thin blemishes that curve down Liberty's jaw and neck are the most obvious distraction. Population: 13 in 62, 3 finer (12/06). (#7787)

Conditionally Scarce 1860-C
Quarter Eagle MS61

3425   1860-C MS61 NGC. Variety 19-J. The strike is above average. The eagle's talons and leg feathers are not completely brought up, but display decent sharpness. A couple of shallow mint-made strike-thrus on the reverse field do not distract. The luster is both satiny and mildly reflective. The obverse is moderately abraded for the grade. A scant 7,469 pieces were struck for the 1860-C, the last quarter eagle issue from the Charlotte Mint. Mint State examples are scarce, and coveted by Southern gold specialists. Census: 6 in 61, 5 finer (11/06). (#7792)

Gem Prooflike Mint State 1887
Quarter Eagle Rarity

3426   1887 MS65 Prooflike NGC. Liberty Head quarter eagles minted during the decade of the 1880s were all low-mintage affairs, ranging from a low of 640 coins produced in 1881 to a high of 17,600 coins struck in 1889. Apparently there was little demand for the quarter eagles during this period. In 1887, just 6,160 of these quarter eagles were coined, and it is considered a scarce date in all grades. This MS65 Prooflike coin and another certified as MS66 are the two finest coins graded by NGC, and PCGS has not graded a single Gem representative (11/06). Both sides are sharply struck with virtually full design details as they appeared in the dies. The surfaces have deeply mirrored fields that are nearly equal to some proof examples. This is a rich orange-gold example with exceptional aesthetic appeal. (#77839)

Rare 1862 PR66
Ultra Cameo Quarter Eagle

3427   1862 PR66 Ultra Cameo NGC. The Garrett-Guth *Gold Encyclopedia* comments tellingly of this rare issue, "The reported and accepted mintage of just 35 coins is probably accurate for this rare issue. Although the mintage is much lower for the 1862 Proof Liberty Head quarter eagle, it is not as rare as the higher-mintage 1861 Proof quarter eagle. The population reports indicate that as many as 32 coins have been graded. This number is likely inflated by resubmissions. There are probably fewer than 15 coins of this date in Proof, including examples in the permanent collections of the Smithsonian and the ANS. The 1862 quarter eagle is just as rare as the famous 1863 quarter eagle, but it has been overshadowed by the latter date as it was a Proof-only issue." Of course, this is high praise from two of the most noted and prominent commentators on the American numismatic scene today, as the 1863 Liberty Head quarter eagle is a fabulous and legendary rarity, made to the extent of only 30 pieces.

Walter Breen's *Proof Encyclopedia* (1977) actually puts the 1862 in the same rarity class as the 1861 (Garrett-Guth notwithstanding), adding further, "probably a trifle rarer. The number of survivors may be as low as a dozen." The date is low in the exergue, punched somewhat delicately into the die. The leftover reverse die from 1860-61 was reused here, showing thinness in vertical stripes 2, 3, and 4 of the shield.

Scrutiny of the NGC and PCGS population reports confirms the rarity and desirability: Both services combined show a total of only 17 proof examples graded, an extremely low number completely in line with Breen's estimate when a reasonable factor is removed for resubmissions and crossovers. (In fact, Breen's estimate of a dozen pieces might be a bit on the high side.) This is the finest Gem and the only Ultra Cameo Gem at NGC, while PCGS has graded a single PR66 Deep Cameo (12/06). The expected and delectable black-on-gold contrast is prominent, and the coin is expectedly pristine. The only pedigree markers noted are two tiny, loupe-visible dark toning dots, one directly below star 9, another on the reverse in line with the tip of the olive branch. Ultra-rare, and ultra-nice. (#97888)

Scarce Proof 1867
Quarter Eagle PR64 PCGS

3428   1867 PR64 PCGS. An opportunity to acquire an example of this rare proof quarter eagle issue does not occur often. This near-Gem specimen possesses immense eye appeal for the grade. The striking details are unimpeachable and razor-sharp on all of the obverse and reverse design elements, including the denticles. The fields are watery and deeply reflective, and the frosted devices achieve a cameo-like effect on both sides. A splash of deep rose patina adorns the central reverse, and traces of orange color appear on Liberty's face and neck. A grade-limiting pinscratch extends from just left of the date well up onto Liberty's bust. A small red-orange alloy spot is noted along the obverse border, between stars 12 and 13. Population: 5 in 64, 2 finer (11/06).
From The RNB Collection. (#7893)

Luscious PR64 Ultra Cameo 1871
Quarter Eagle, Tied for Finest

3429   1871 PR64 Ultra Cameo NGC. The recorded proof mintage of 30 examples attests to the rarity of this issue. PCGS has graded only a single Deep Cameo piece, a PR63 specimen, while this piece is one of two PR64 Ultra Cameo pieces at NGC, with none finer (11/06). In fact, neither service has certified a Gem proof of this date, regardless of the degree of contrast, and there are only 13 pieces at both services, less the inevitable resubmissions. The lump on the neck below the lovelock is a diagnostic of genuine proofs (per the Breen *Proof Encyclopedia*), and the date is quite high and close to the bust. The luscious, deeply contrasting yellow-gold fields yield to a glint of magenta near the obverse rim.
From The RNB Collection. (#97897)

PR67 Cameo 1877 Quarter Eagle
Ex: Pittman

3430 **1877 PR67 Cameo NGC.** Ex: Pittman. Light original honey patina graces the portrait and fields on this exquisitely struck and flashy Superb Gem. The surfaces are virtually pristine, as expected from the grade. A trio of tiny curly lintmarks, as struck, on the lower right reverse identifies this exemplary specimen. Just 20 proof 1877 quarter eagles were struck. NGC and PCGS have certified 11 pieces in all grades, likely including resubmissions. While proof double eagles command numismatic headlines, pre-1880 proof quarter eagles are also extremely rare and can be acquired for significantly less, despite their infrequent auction appearances.
Ex: 2004 ANA Signature Auction (Heritage, 8/04), lot 7184; John Jay Pittman Collection, Part Two (David Akers, 5/98), lot 1836, which realized $26,800. Pittman bought the piece from Abe Kosoff's 1956 Thomas Melish sale (lot 1289) for $130.
From The RNB Collection. (#87903)

Deep Orange Toned Proof 1880
Quarter Eagle, PR63 Cameo

3431 **1880 PR63 Cameo NGC.** Only about a dozen proofs are known for this scarce date, representing about one-third of the original 36 coin mintage. Among known examples are the Smithsonian, Western Heritage Museum (Byron Reed), and American Numismatic Society coins held in institutional collections. Other specimens include the Eliasberg, Bass, and Trompeter Gems, and Choice proof pieces in the Garrett, Pittman, and Childs Collections. A thin hairline scratch is visible in the upper reverse field, an ideal marker for the pedigree of this lovely piece. This piece is a glittering yellow-gold representative with sharply detailed obverse and reverse devices. The Cameo contrast is created by frosty devices that are surrounded by deeply mirrored fields. (#87906)

Well Struck 1890 Gem Proof Deep Cameo Quarter Eagle

3432   1890 PR65 Deep Cameo PCGS. Jeff Garrett and Ron Guth (2006) write: "The mintage for the quarter eagle increased again in 1890 to the levels of production seen in the late 1880s. The demand for Proof gold coinage must have increased about this time as well because the number of surviving examples is dramatic. There are probably more than 50 specimens of the 1890 Liberty Head quarter eagle known. This includes two choice examples in the Smithsonian." Slightly over 30 proof 1890 quarter eagles have been seen by PCGS and NGC, along with nearly 20 Cameos, and a little over 20 Deep/Ultra Cameos.

This Gem Deep Cameo specimen displays lovely brass-gold color and crisply impressed design elements. Frosted motifs stand out against spectacular deep mirrored fields, and both sides are devoid of mentionable marks. Population: 2 in 65 Deep Cameo, 4 finer (11/06). (#97916)

PR64 Ultra Cameo 1892 Quarter Eagle

3433   1892 PR64 Ultra Cameo NGC. The proof mintage of 105 pieces for this issue complements the business strike emission of only 2,440 pieces, providing extra pressure for the proof from date collectors. Many business strikes are understandably prooflike, deceptively so, according to Garrett and Guth. The authors also note that many proof examples are impaired or damaged. Not so the present specimen, with excellently contrasting surfaces, pretty lemon-yellow coloration, and a bold, problem-free strike that brings up all the fine detail well. Census: 2 in 64 Ultra Cameo, 7 finer (11/06). *From The RNB Collection.* (#97918)

Gem Ultra Cameo 1894 Quarter Eagle

3434   1894 PR65 Ultra Cameo NGC. A sparkling, problem-free Gem example of this more-available proof issue, the present piece boasts attractive lemon-yellow coloration and a noteworthy absence of mentionable distractions. In the Gem Ultra Cameo grade NGC has certified three pieces, with 13 finer, while PCGS has also certified three Gem Deep Cameo pieces, with two finer (11/06). The reverse is essentially pristine, even under a glass, but the obverse reveals a few small, dotlike indentations, likely of Mint origin. The strike is boldly executed, with no apparent weakness on either side. (#97920)

1894 Liberty Quarter Eagle
PR66 Ultra Cameo

3435   1894 PR66 Ultra Cameo NGC. The official mintage for 1894 proof quarter eagles of 122 pieces is tied for the highest recorded up to this point in time, but it doesn't necessarily correlate into greater availability. While out-of-date estimates often quoted by book-conscious catalogers have placed the number of survivors in the 40-45 range, a more reasonable figure would probably be in the neighborhood of 65-75 survivors. Like most high grade pieces, this Premium Gem specimen sports dramatic contrast between fields and devices. An unfinished area between stars 9 and 10 culminates in tiny depression at its center. These mint-caused disturbances along the obverse border seem to show up on a number of 1894 proof quarter eagles. Census: 6 in 66, 7 finer (11/06). (#97920)

Outstanding 1897 Quarter Eagle
PR66 Deep Cameo

3436   1897 PR66 Deep Cameo PCGS. Only 136 proof quarter eagles were struck in 1897, and it is estimated that today approximately 45-50 pieces remain in all grades, although that number may be a bit on the low side. This is one of the finest known examples. The fields are dark pools of illimitable reflectivity, and hairline-free. The devices are richly frosted and provide a stark cameo contrast against the watery depths in the fields. The piece seems virtually perfect, with the only mentionable "defect" being a faint diagonal toning streak across Liberty's face. A slight degree of orange-gold toning occurs on the obverse, but the reverse displays a nearly full coating of lovely, deep rose and orange-gold coloration. Outstanding technical quality and eye appeal. Population: 4 in 66 Deep Cameo, 1 finer (11/06).
From The James Paul Collection. (#97923)

1898 PR64 Deep Cameo Quarter Eagle

3437   1898 PR64 Deep Cameo PCGS. Just 165 quarter eagle proofs were coined in 1898, with about 80 or so thought to exist today. This PR64 Deep Cameo specimen displays outstanding motif-field contrast, which takes on a gold-on-black appearance at all angles. The design elements are exquisitely brought up, with no areas revealing hints of softness. A few wispy handling marks are all that keeps this piece from attaining an even higher grade. This is a truly awe-inspiring coin that is sure to draw the interest of connoisseurs of gold coinage. Population: 2 in 64 Deep Cameo, 9 finer (11/06). (#97924)

Superb Deep Cameo Proof
1898 Quarter Eagle

3438   1898 PR67 Deep Cameo PCGS. This phenomenal and glittering Superb Gem proof has deeply mirrored fields around highly lustrous and frosty devices. The design elements are intricately detailed and the surfaces display brilliant and rich yellow-gold color. Like all proof gold coins from this era, the fields have a wavy or watery appearance. Such a look does not immediately verify the proof status of a gold piece, but the lack of this characteristic generally discounts the proof status of otherwise proof coins. Of course, one glance at this beauty and its true status as one of the 165 proofs coined is immediately evident.

While it is currently estimated that about half of the original mintage still survives, or about 80 coins, few can qualify as a Gem or finer. The present example is one of about a dozen such pieces, and probably ranks among the top four or five known examples. Current population reports show that one coin has been graded PR69 Ultra Cameo, and the Pittman coin (also offered in the present sale) is certified as PR68 Ultra Cameo. NGC has certified a few other submissions as PR68 Ultra Cameo or PR68 Cameo, although we suspect that some of those submission numbers represent attempts at an upgrade, finally culminating in the PR69 grade for the finest piece. Auction records reveal that only two or three top grade coins exist.

This example is the highest quality piece graded by PCGS, one of four submissions to receive the PR67 Deep Cameo grade from that service. Again, we suspect that the current PCGS population (11/06) represents just one or two coins. An extensive Census of proof gold coins is currently in progress, and will undoubtedly show the true rarity of these coins in the highest grades. (#97924)

The John Jay Pittman 1898 Quarter Eagle, PR68 Ultra Cameo Among the Finest Known

3439   1898 PR68 Ultra Cameo NGC. Ex: Pittman. With this lot, Heritage is pleased to begin our offering of a complete 1898 gold proof set, from the quarter eagle through the double eagle, all to be auctioned individually and each graded from PR66 to PR68 by NGC with the Ultra Cameo designation. The legendary John Jay Pittman is one of numismatics' foremost success stories. His tale is an instructive one that bears repeating. Pittman was for many years a chemical engineer at Eastman Kodak Company in Rochester, New York. Pittman managed to raise a family on a salary of from $10,000 to $15,000 per year. He took half of his salary to buy coins, concentrating mostly on what few others desired at the time. Proof U.S. gold coins were one of his specialties, but he was equally fond of foreign coins, including those of Canada, Cuba, Great Britain, Japan, Mexico, Russia, South Africa, and Sweden. Unafraid to take a gamble, Pittman, realizing that the coins in the 1954 auction of the deposed Egyptian King Farouk's collection would likely go for quite reasonable prices, is said to have taken a second mortgage on his home to make the trip to Cairo and bid on the coins, which turned out to be among his most significant acquisitions. A perfect demonstration of "buying straw hats in winter," Pittman invested about $100,000 during his lifetime on coins. He always bought the highest-graded, most historically significant coins he could—proof gold before 1858 was a particular favorite—and he held what he bought for many years, leaving the rest up to a free-market economy and the law of supply and demand. Pittman passed away in 1996, and David Akers oversaw the sale of his collection in two parts in 1997 and 1998. *John Jay Pittman's collection, in total, fetched upwards of $30 million.* One coin alone—an 1833 half eagle for which Pittman paid $635 in the King Farouk auction—brought $467,500.

Regarding this specific piece, the Garrett-Guth *Gold Encyclopedia* records, "A single 1898 quarter eagle has the distinction of receiving a PF-69 grade, which is the highest-graded Proof gold coin in the 19th century. Also among the finest examples seen is the John Jay Pittman coin, which was sold for $46,750 in 1998. That coin was sold uncertified, and it is very possible that [it] was later graded PF-69. Pittman purchased the coin in 1956 for $54. That is nearly 1,000 times the original purchase price!"

The phenomenal PR68 Ultra Cameo piece certified by NGC in the present lot, formerly in the Pittman collection, is one of six PR68 pieces at NGC, which has also graded one PR68 ★ piece and one PR69, all Ultra Cameo (11/06). The latter is apparently a different coin from the present piece, despite Garrett and Guth's conjecture. However, they are absolutely correct in their assertion that this example is among the finest specimens known. The pristine surfaces on either side offer the desirable black-on-gold contrast so admired in high grade proof gold, with thickly frosted devices providing a stark contrast to the profoundly mirrored, orange peel fields. (#97924)

Scarce Gem Proof 1903 Quarter Eagle

3440   1903 PR65 PCGS. The sharply delineated design elements and denticles leave little doubt about this coin's proof status. From a mintage of 197 pieces, of which perhaps half or a few more still survive, this glittering Gem displays deep watery reflectivity in the fields, which is only partially diminished by a touch of milkiness over each side. A heavy die chip (as struck) is attached to the left side of the upright of the 1 in the denomination. This lovely specimen is free of troublesome hairlines or contact marks. Population: 22 in 65, 6 finer (11/06).
From The RNB Collection. (#7929)

Splendid 1904 Quarter Eagle PR66

3441   1904 PR66 PCGS. Mint records indicate a modest production of just 170 proof quarter eagles in 1904. Mintages of Liberty quarter eagles generally declined from year to year through the first seven years of the 20th century, and with the exception of 1905 which had the lowest proof production, each year had a smaller coinage than the preceding year. It is unlikely that even half of the original production survives today as a recognizable proof. This specimen ranks among the finest that we have handled in recent years. Both sides exhibit rich orange-gold color and unfathomably deep, glassy mirrors. While not awarded a cameo designation, contrast is such that it could easily have gone the other way. The only visible disturbance under magnification is a series of mint-caused die file marks on the portrait. Population: 4 in 66, 1 finer (11/06). (#7930)

Gem Proof 1906 Quarter Eagle

3442   1906 PR65 PCGS. A glittering, brightly mirrored specimen with appreciable contrast for an early 20th century proof striking. Bits of lilac and orange patina lightly accent each side. While it seems obvious that the population data for this rare issue of 160 proofs is bloated by resubmissions (over 160 pieces have been certified), the number of surviving specimens may also have been understated in the past. In any case, only a small percentage qualifies in Gem and finer grades and this solidly graded specimen is among the nicest we have offered. Population: 12 in 65, 31 finer (11/06). (#7932)

Matched Set of Indian Quarter Eagles, MS62 NGC

3433   Indian Quarter Eagle Set. MS62 NGC. This is a complete, uniformly matched set of Indian quarter eagles from 1908 to 1929, including every date and mintmark issue. Each coin is certified as MS62 by NGC. Each individual coin is fully lustrous and sharply struck with colors ranging from medium honey-gold to brilliant yellow gold. The key-date 1911-D issue has darker yellow color with subdued luster and a bold mintmark. (Total: 15 coins) (#7939)

Key Date 1911-D Quarter Eagle, MS62

3444   1911-D MS62 NGC. The 1911-D is the key to the Indian Head quarter eagle series in all grades. Its 55,680-piece mintage is the lowest of the series, and few examples were saved at the time of issue. Most of the survivors are in the AU to lower Mint State range. High-end Uncirculated examples are scarce to rare.

The MS62 coin presented in the current lot displays bright brassy-gold surfaces, and the design elements are generally well defined, including the D mintmark. A few wispy handling marks are noted on each side, none of which are serious. All in all, this piece exhibits nice eye appeal for the grade. (#7943)

Mint State 1911-D Quarter Eagle

3445   1911-D MS62 PCGS. Like all of the most desirable Mint State 1911-D quarter eagles, this piece has a bold mintmark, although the plastic insert of the holder mostly covers the tiny D, making it hard to see. Tilting the holder at an extreme angle will reveal that the mintmark is boldly defined and complete. This piece is a pleasing light yellow example with frosty luster across both sides. The surfaces are typical for the grade with tiny abrasions, but none of any significance. As is often the case in our sales, a number of these desirable coins are offered in a variety of grades, providing collectors with quite a choice of different pieces. (#7943)

Key Date 1911-D Indian Head Quarter Eagle MS63

3446   1911-D MS63 PCGS. Gorgeous brassy copper-red coloration covers each side, while attractive gold and steel-gray accents are noticeable on the highpoints. The striking details are uniformly bold, including the headdress and the eagle's shoulder and talons. A tiny mark beneath Y in LIBERTY, and a couple of faint pinscratches on the reverse seem minimal as the only surface damage that might have limited the grade of the piece. The 1911-D is well known as the key date in the Indian quarter eagle series, and this Select Mint State example seems solidly graded and highly desirable as such. (#7943)

Important Select Mint State 1911-D Quarter Eagle

3447   1911-D MS63 PCGS. A pronounced wire rim on the upper right obverse helps to confirm that this Select Mint State specimen is a genuine example of the key date 1911-D quarter eagle. Boldly struck and satiny, the coin displays lovely reddish honey-gold toning which is brightly illuminated by effulgent luster. Unlike most MS63 pieces, this one is near-pristine and seems to lack even the smallest of surface blemishes on either side. For the sake of accuracy, we note a small prooflike area below TRUST, near the lower right reverse rim. We hasten to add that this feature is not overly detracting, and that it should not have influenced the technical grade of the piece. Housed in a green label holder. (#7943)

Select 1911-D Indian Two and a Half

3448   1911-D MS63 NGC. The Denver mintmark is bold on this shimmering key date quarter eagle. The fields are surprisingly un-abraded for the MS63 level, and the strike on the headdress is sharp for the type. A wire rim is present on the obverse between 10 and 5 o'clock. A reverse wire rim is even more prominent, between 3 and 11 o'clock. The low mintage 1911-D is the number one item on the want lists of most Indian quarter eagle collectors, and there are many of these, since the series is affordably obtained by date and mintmark relative to the other 20th century gold denominations. Most collectors end up with a circulated example, but here is an op-portunity to secure a lustrous problem-free Mint State piece. (#7943)

Exceptional MS63 1911-D
Key-Date Quarter Eagle

3449   1911-D MS63 NGC. Jeff Garrett and Ron Guth, writing in their *Encyclopedia of U.S. Gold Coins, 1795-1933,* say of the key-date 1911-D Indian Head quarter eagle: "...few examples were saved at the time of issue. Most of the survivors are in lower Mint State grades...." The population figures bear this out, as several hundred specimens fall into the MS61 to MS64 grade range.

The MS63 example that we present in this lot displays pret-ty peach-gold color that resides on well preserved surfaces that yield soft luster. Excellent definition is apparent on the feathers of the headdress and on most of the eagle's plumage, though we note some softness on the eagle's shoulder. Close examination reveals fewer marks than what might be expected for the grade. (#7943)

Lustrous MS63 1911-D Quarter Eagle

3450   1911-D MS63 NGC. This example has a bold mintmark, making it all the more desirable to collectors. Both sides are fully lustrous with rich yellow-gold luster and a certain lack of imperfections. Only the slightest abrasions are visible with magnification. It is well known that this is the key-date to the Indian quarter eagle series. For any collector considering the formation of a set of these coins, our recommendation is to acquire this date first, then carefully select matching pieces from the much larger populations of all other issues. (#7943)

Popular 1911-D Quarter Eagle MS63

3451   1911-D MS63 PCGS. The 1911-D boasts the lowest mintage among 20th century quarter eagle issues and has long been regarded as the undisputed key of the Indian Head series. Much of its popularity is also derived from collectors that are not necessarily assembling a set of Indian quarter eagles, but wish to own some of the best-known key issues from the last century. Other candidates might include the 1909-S VDB Lincoln cent, 1916-D Mercury dime, or 1916 Standing Liberty quarter. This Select example displays attractive reddish overtones and minimal surface marks. The mintmark, while not fully defined, certainly falls under the bold category. (#7943)

PROOF INDIAN QUARTER EAGLES

Lovely 1912 Gem Quarter Eagle

3452   1912 MS65 PCGS. True to most issues in the series, the 1912 can be located without too much cost or difficulty in average Uncirculated condition, with a quick check of census data from the two major services revealing that over 4,000 pieces have been certified in Mint State grades. Of course, the availability of Gem examples nearly drops off the radar screen.

This lovely representative exhibits bright satin-like surfaces and is accented in delicate copper-golden patina. Both sides exhibit a sharp strike with good detailing even on the lower feathers of the headdress. A couple of small marks are noted above the feathers in the obverse field, however, these hardly detract. Population: 48 in 65, 5 finer (11/06). (#7944)

Pristine Matte PR67 1908 Quarter Eagle

3453   1908 PR67 NGC. The heavy matte texture used by the Mint in this year is prominent on this piece, with the deep sandblast texture on deep olive-gold surfaces that is characteristic. Although this issue is the most frequently offered of the proof type, auction appearances are still quite infrequent, especially in high grades. PCGS and NGC combined have certified 24 pieces in PR67, with none finer (11/06), a figure that undoubtedly includes resubmissions. This piece is absolutely pristine and nearly quibble-free (save for a couple of tiny dark toning flecks), and prototypical in its appeal. Strictly a nice and lovely piece for some fortunate connoisseur of proof gold. *From The RNB Collection.* (#7957)

Lovely PR66 1910
'Roman Gold' Quarter Eagle

3454   1910 PR66 NGC. The delicate surfaces are a consistently lovely greenish-gold throughout both sides of this satiny "Roman gold" Premium Gem proof. Garrett and Guth comment that this issue is far rarer than the anomalous mintage, recorded as 682 pieces, would suggest, and that the figure is either just plain wrong or that about two-thirds of the proof mintage was subsequently melted. Regardless of the truth in the story, in PR66 condition this coin is a definite rarity, with three dozen pieces so fine at NGC and PCGS combined (12/06). Scrutiny with a lens shows the Indian's cheek and the exposed, open fields on either side are distraction-free. A lovely piece, suited for a fine date or type set. Census: 30 in 66, 11 finer (11/06). (#7959)

Scarce 1854-D Three Dollar Gold
AU50 PCGS

3455   1854-D AU50 PCGS. Variety 1-A. Only 1,120 pieces were struck of this near-legendary coin. This is the only three dollar gold issue produced at the historic Dahlonega Mint. As always, the striking details are soft with especially weak definition on the U in UNITED and doubling on TED (both of which are diagnostic). The surfaces are remarkably free from handling marks, scratches, or any other type of post-striking impairments, except for a pair of small puncture marks very close to the 4 in the date. Minor die clash marks are noted in the reverse fields, and beneath Liberty's chin. Light green-gold color overall, with attractive peach accents. Faint remnants of mint luster can still be discerned in the more protected areas of the design. (#7970)

Low Mintage 1854-D
Three Dollar Gold AU50

3456 1854-D AU50 NGC. Variety 1-A. Ex: Richmond Collection. As usual for this poorly-produced issue, the striking details are noticeably weak in some areas, especially on the denticles and on the denominational 3 on the upper reverse field. Light straw-gold toning is noted across both sides of this AU survivor. A bit of high-point wear seems evident on Liberty's hair and crown. A small mark is located on Liberty's jaw, and a couple more are situated on the reverse, above DOLLAR. Faint die clash marks are nestled adjacent to Liberty's throat. Because of its extremely low mintage of 1,760 pieces, this date is very popular with collectors. It is also the only three dollar gold issue from the Dahlonega Mint. (#7970)

Famous 1854-D Three Dollar AU50

3457 1854-D AU50 NGC. Variety 1-A. Perhaps no other D-mint issue captures the imagination of Southern gold enthusiasts like the 1854-D three dollar. Both a first year and one-year type, the issue's tiny original production and low survival rate long secured its place among the numismatically elite Dahlonega gold coins. A perusal of Heritage auction records also shows that survivors are often damaged or harshly cleaned. This lightly circulated example has escaped such distractions. It is well defined for an 1854-D and retains glimpses of luster in the areas surrounding the devices. A few shallow blemishes are clustered in the lower left obverse field and faint die clashing is noticed on the reverse. Census: 12 in 50, 58 finer (11/06).
From The Twin Hollows Collection. (#7970)

Popular 1854-O Three Dollar Gold AU55

3458   1854-O AU55 PCGS. The three dollar gold denomination began with a certain amount of fanfare, being struck at three different mints in its initial year - Philadelphia, Dahlonega, and New Orleans - along with the fledgling San Francisco facility which began production the following year. Today, gold collectors covet both of the branch mint issues from 1854 as the acceptance of the three dollar gold piece was so dismal that they were never again minted in the South. Like many O-mint survivors, this still-lustrous example exhibits distinct yellow-gold color and a bit of striking weakness over the central devices. (#7971)

Elusive Near-Mint 1857-S
Three Dollar Gold

3459   1857-S AU58 NGC. Ex: Princess Collection. Well struck and still somewhat lustrous, with distinct semi-prooflikeness and appealing khaki-gold toning that yields to rose accents in the fields. Faint highpoint wear is noted on the obverse, and scattered small abrasions and wispy hairlines appear on both sides. Nearly the entire mintage of 14,000 pieces was either lightly or heavily circulated, and Uncirculated examples are virtually unobtainable. To date, just four coins are recorded in the population data of NGC and PCGS as having achieved any Mint State grade; and a total of only 14 survivors are certified at AU58 at both services. A pleasing example of this historic San Francisco Mint pre-Civil War issue, almost assuredly coined from newly mined California gold. Census: 8 in 58, 3 finer (11/06). (#7977)

Elusive Gem Uncirculated 1859 Three Dollar

3460   1859 MS65 NGC. Breen-6361. Both the 1 and the 9 in the date are repunched. This reverse is from the more difficult of two die marriages utilized in the production of 15,558 business strikes, but is actually more frequently seen on higher grade examples. Perhaps 100-125 Mint State pieces survive of the 1859 three dollar, a quantity that actually places it among the more obtainable issues in the series. Gems, however, are of the utmost scarcity and it has been more than eight years since we have been fortunate enough to offer one. This shimmering yellow-gold Gem is remarkable for its smoothness and displays a soft, frosted sheen over devices that leave only a touch of softness on the often incomplete bow at the base of the wreath. There is little evidence of die clashing on either side. Census: 2 in 65, 3 finer (12/06). (#7979)

Choice 1871 Three Dollar Gold Piece

3461   1871 MS64 PCGS. The never-popular three dollar denomination suffered a drawn-out demise, with the last 29 years of coinage at the Philadelphia Mint only and just two issues with more than 10,000 pieces coined. At 1,300 business strikes produced, the 1871 is one of the many issues that embody the concept of a nominal mintage. This Choice wheat-gold example is one of the best-preserved survivors. The luster is strong and partially prooflike, unsurprising given the low mintage, and the strike is adequate. The overall appearance is clean, and only some small, scattered marks keep this example from a Gem grade. NGC has graded no pieces finer, and the only example awarded a higher grade by PCGS is a solitary Superb Gem (11/06). (#7993)

Flashy 1873 Closed 3 Three Dollar MS61

3462 1873 Closed 3 MS61 PCGS. Among three dollar gold issues, a series replete with rarities and enigmatic issues, the 1873 Closed 3 is unique as the only business strike three dollar gold piece without a recorded mintage. The number of pieces originally produced is generally conceded to be between 600 and 1,000 coins, but these are only estimates. The few known Mint State survivors are known to possesses distinctive prooflike qualities, as does this flashy example. Abrasions are fairly numerous, but evenly distributed with none being worthy of individual mention. Look for considerable bidder interest on this dazzling, unquestionably elusive 1873 Closed 3. Population: 5 in 61, 4 finer (11/06). (#7995)

Gem Mint State 1878
Three Dollar Gold Piece

3463 1878 MS65 NGC. This is a flashy Gem with brilliant yellow-gold color and frosty luster. Both sides have subtle pink toning and a few small copper toning spots. A tiny planchet flake is visible in the field right of the E in UNITED, and a few insignificant blemishes are evident on each side. Although this piece does not have a full strike, it is well-detailed in most areas. The 1878 three dollar has the second highest mintage of any date in the series, and it is clearly the most common date of the Large DOLLARS reverse type, coined from 1855 to 1889. Only the 1854 issue has a Small DOLLARS reverse. (#8000)

Beautiful Gem 1878 Three Dollar Gold

3464   1878 MS65 PCGS. In anticipation of gold being exchangeable at par with paper money on January 1, 1879, as mandated by the Specie Redemption Act of 1875, the Mint produced considerable numbers of gold coins, including 82,304 business strikes of the 1878 three dollar gold. The market achieved parity on its own in late December—but when the public realized they could exchange paper money for gold whenever they wanted, a giant collective yawn was the result. Most of the freshly minted three dollar gold pieces went into long-term bag storage. Contact marks are generally a problem for this issue. Not so with this delightful example, however. Brilliant cartwheel luster radiates from the yellow-gold surfaces, accented by glints of orange-gold at the rims. There are no singular abrasions, and the eye appeal is quite high. This beautiful candidate for a Gem gold type set is certified in a green-label PCGS holder. *From The James Paul Collection.* (#8000)

Lovely Gem 1878 Three Dollar Gold

3465   1878 MS65 NGC. This sparkling Gem displays an effulgent, frosty sheen that radiates palpably over both sides. The tantalizing, light yellow-gold and faintly reddish toning is likewise lovely to behold. All of the design elements are well formed from an obviously sharp striking impression. According to Garrett and Guth (2006): "The 1878 $3 gold piece is the most common date of the series, by far. More than 8,000 examples have been certified by ANACS, PCGS, and NGC combined, more than double that of 1854 and 1874. Uncirculated specimens are very common, even through MS-65. In MS-66, the population begins to drop off and the finest examples stop at MS-67. The 1878 issue usually features a rich, coruscating luster and good to great eye appeal."(#8000)

Choice Mint State 1879 Three Dollar Gold Piece

3466   1879 MS64 NGC. David Bowers and Douglas Winter, in their book *United States Three Dollar Gold Pieces,* wrote: "As coins of this date did not circulate in commerce, the relatively few AU pieces probably represent souvenirs that were not carefully kept. They are rarer than Mint State pieces but are less desirable numismatically." The more ready obtainability of the MS64 specimen in this lot is offset by its vibrant luster and gorgeous greenish-gold patina. Sharply executed design elements complement these attributes, as does the cameo-like effect that arises when the coin is rotated under a light source. Scattered handling marks, especially on Liberty's cheek and in the left obverse field, preclude an even higher grade. Overall, an appealing Mint State three dollar specimen. Census: 83 in 64, 18 finer (3/06). (#8001)

MS64 1879 Three Dollar Gold

3467   1879 MS64 PCGS. Unlike its 1878 predecessor, the 1879 is a low mintage date. Only 3,000 pieces were struck, and although a few hundred Mint State examples are known, only a small portion of these can compete with the quality of the present lustrous near-Gem. The orange and ice-blue toning is original, and the strike is precise throughout. Intense evaluation beneath a strong lens reveals only unimportant field grazes. The 1879 trades for a bit more than a "common" three dollar gold piece, but since it is many times scarcer than the 1878, one can argue that the 1879 remains underappreciated. Encapsulated in a green label holder. (#8001)

Near-Gem 1879 Three Dollar Gold Piece

3468   1879 MS64 NGC. With a mintage of just 3,000 business strikes, the immediate temptation is to call this piece a major rarity, yet a large number of higher grade coins still exist. Garrett and Guth noted: "Collectors and dealers were responsible for preserving a high percentage of the mintage, and mini-hoards were dispersed slowly throughout the first half of the 20th century. The typical Mint State specimen is prooflike and falls in the MS-63 and MS-64 range, with Gems becoming very scarce." This lovely honey-gold piece is at the high end of the range of typical pieces, with reflective surfaces that are not deeply mirrored. The strike is quite sharp and the overall appearance is excellent. (#8001)

Radiant Gem 1879 Three Dollar Gold

3469   1879 MS65 PCGS. Although the skimpy mintage was only 3,000 pieces, quite a few Gems are known of this generally well-produced issue. Most surviving Uncirculated examples, however, average MS63 to MS64, and Gems are nonetheless quite elusive. The present example offers radiant cartwheel luster with semi-prooflike surfaces, brilliant orange-yellow color, and enormous eye appeal. PCGS has graded 32 pieces in Gem condition, with only three examples finer (11/06). This coin would be an excellent acquisition for a high grade type set. Three dollar gold pieces also have enduring popularity among today's collectors. (#8001)

Finest NGC 1882 Three Dollar MS66 ★ Prooflike

3470   1882 MS66 ★ Prooflike NGC. Ex: Freedom Collection. An obviously repunched 2 in the date confirms this coin's status as a business strike. Well struck, essentially untoned, and impeccably preserved, this beautiful Premium Gem exhibits intense reflectivity in the fields and considerable frost on the devices, producing a noteworthy cameo effect on both sides. Some tiny chatter marks in the field area directly beneath UNI are mint-made, non-distracting, and irrelevant to the technical grade of the piece. Three coins have achieved the MS66 grade level at NGC, but two of those are non-Prooflikes without the "Star" designation (for outstanding eye appeal), making this piece the finest-graded NGC example overall. Census: 1 in 66 ★ Prooflike, 0 finer (11/06).
From The Freedom Collection. (#78004)

Gem 1884 Three Dollar, Mintage: 1,000

3471   1884 MS65 NGC. The 1884 has always been a favorite coin of collectors as it has a mintage of only 1,000 pieces. Probably 55 to 75 pieces exist today in the various grades of Uncirculated, but just a handful of those are in Gem condition. In fact, NGC has only graded three others in MS65 and PCGS has certified five, with five in higher grades. This is a splendid MS65 example that has semi-reflective fields mixed in with mint frost. Well, but not fully struck, the surfaces are predictably clean with the only ripple in the surface being a tiny planchet flake out of the field below the O in DOLLARS. (#8006)

Pretty Gem 1888 Three Dollar Gold

3472   1888 MS65 NGC. The few active collectors of gold coins in the late 1880s must have had quite a heyday, as the writing had been on the wall for several years that the three dollar gold pieces would go the way of the woolly mammoth. After 1879 the yearly mintages never again exceeded 7,000 pieces, yet many of the later pieces were saved for posterity. According to Bowers' *The United States $3 Gold Pieces 1854-1889* (2005), New York City-based coin dealer J.W. Scott apparently bought several hundred examples of the 1888 issue directly from the Mint.

The present example, like most of its brethren, shows an "aura" of reflectivity around the central portrait. Excellent luster and pretty apricot-gold surfaces complete the attractive package. The reverse die is rotated about 30 degrees counterclockwise. Census: 36 in 65, 13 finer (11/06). (#8010)

Splendid Gem 1888 Three Dollar

3473   1888 MS65 NGC. The 1888 has long been a popular target for hoarders, because of the tiny mintage of 5,000 pieces. The 1888 is indeed a better date, but a portion of the mintage was set aside, presumably by a few Philadelphia-area dealers. MS62 to MS64 examples are always available for a price, but the issue is undeniably rare as a Gem. This lustrous representative has an exemplary reverse, while the obverse has only faint marks. The strike is intricate except for minor softness on the wreath knot, as it is opposite the high relief plumes. Light die doubling on Liberty's eye and mouth, and more apparent die doubling on UNITED, are diagnostic for the business strike issue. Census: 36 in 65, 13 finer (11/06). (#8010)

Popular Gem 1888 Three Dollar

3474   1888 MS65 PCGS. This sharply struck Gem features refreshingly clean surfaces. Shimmering luster bathes the pumpkin-gold fields and devices. A few trivial light golden-brown freckles are noted upon magnification. UNITED is nicely die doubled, a feature that distinguishes the mere 5,000 business strikes from the even rarer proofs.

The three dollar and one dollar gold pieces had similar designs, and both series ended in 1889. The dollar gold denomination was more popular with contemporary collectors, perhaps because of the lower face value. Mintages of the three dollar denomination actually declined between 1887 and 1889, while gold dollar production climbed during the same period. Population: 70 in 65, 28 finer (11/06). (#8010)

Low Mintage Gem 1888 Three Dollar

3475   1888 MS65 NGC. A beautiful Gem example with satiny surfaces, rich orange-gold luster, and a sharp strike. It is one of a mere 5,000 business strikes minted in the next-to-last year of production for this series. Most examples of this date were not put into circulation, and many were saved in Mint State grades, however, at the MS65 level this issue is anything but common. Several small abrasions are present in the obverse fields, and are mentioned, not because they are overly distracting, but because of the fact that without them, this piece would certainly warrant a grade higher. A beautiful example for the type collector or specialist in the series, and certain to attract many bidders. Census: 36 in 65, 13 finer (11/06). (#8010)

Lovely Gem 1888 Three Dollar Gold

3476   1888 MS65 PCGS. This is a coin of superlative quality, which quickly becomes apparent when it is examined closely. Few gold coins from the 1880s can boast such vibrant luster, which generates a shimmering halo effect on both sides. The lovely, light honey-gold toning yields to even lighter shades of creamy-pink and mint-green near the peripheries. Despite a low mintage of 5,000 pieces, the 1888 is one of the most common dates in the three dollar gold series. Being the penultimate issue probably helped this date to be saved in sufficient quantities to avoid becoming a rarity. Also, by the late 1880s the number of coin collectors in America had increased substantially, compared to the early years of the series. Population: 70 in 65, 28 finer (11/06). (#8010)

Finest Certified 1869
Three Dollar Gold Proof
PR66 ★ Cameo

3477   1869 PR66 ★ Cameo NGC. The Philadelphia Mint only struck 25 proof three dollar gold pieces in 1869 and not more than half of those pieces survive today. This example is the finest of those that appear in our notes, with only three or four other Gem quality pieces known to us, including the Elias-berg-Trompeter coin, and an example that appeared in our January 1998 FUN auction. The Bass Foundation coin probably also qualifies as a Gem proof, and the Garrett coin may likewise be a Gem specimen. We believe that this piece is the finest known proof of the date. NGC and PCGS have graded a total of 14 proofs, and this example is the only one of those coins to be deemed a PR66 grade.

Both sides of this lovely piece have brilliant light yellow-gold color with excellent contrast between the frosty devices and the deeply mirrored fields. It is a sharply struck piece with full design details on both sides. The fields display the usual watery or wavy appearance that is expected on 19th century gold proof coins. The surfaces are essentially perfect, with no useful pedigree markers. A tiny flake above the F in OF may appear on photographic plates, and a wispy v-shaped hairline in the reverse margin at 4 o'clock may or may not be of any use in plate matching. As auction appearances for proof examples of this date are few and far between, it does not seem that pedigree research should be a difficult task. However, many of the earlier auction catalogs had plates of poor quality, showing few of the features needed to make a positive match. When coins of nearly perfect quality are examined, coins such as this piece, it is difficult to be certain about provenance. (#88032)

Important Choice Proof 1872
Three Dollar Gold

3478   1872 PR64 PCGS. The proof 1872 three dollar gold piece has an original mintage of only 30 pieces. It is unlikely, however, that even half of these coins are extant today, a few of which are unfortunately impaired. In addition to being wholly original, this near-Gem is free of unduly bothersome post-production distractions. Both sides display a tantalizing cameo finish with deep, rich orange-gold patina. There is a single, well concealed toning spot on Liberty's headdress, and a series of minute planchet flaws in the reverse field around the 3 in the denomination should help establish the pedigree of this piece. An important coin with both rarity and aesthetic desirability on its side. PCGS has certified three pieces as PR64, one piece as PR64 Cameo, and one specimen as PR65 (10/06).
Ex: Santa Clara Signature (Heritage, 11/00), lot 7097.
From The Jones Beach Collection. (#8035)

1875 $3.00 PR64 Ultra Cameo NGC

1875 $3.00 PR64 Ultra Cameo NGC

Proof-Only 1875 Three Dollar Gold
PR64 Ultra Cameo NGC

3479   1875 PR64 Ultra Cameo NGC. Breen-6386. In most gold series, the 1875 is a major rarity. For the gold dollar, only 400 business strikes and 20 proofs were struck. The 1875 quarter eagle has an identical pair of mintages. The 1875 three dollar is a proof-only issue. The half eagle and eagle have proof mintages of 20 pieces each, and business strike mintages of just 200 and 100 pieces, respectively. Only the 1875 double eagle was struck in reasonable quantities, and despite containing nearly an ounce of gold, it is the most affordable Philadelphia Mint gold product from the year. Why were so few gold coins struck at Philadelphia in 1875? The reason was Gresham's Law. Federal paper money could not be redeemed for specie. Paper money circulated, and gold was hoarded. Gold coin was needed to make export payments, but this demand was met by the double eagle, the largest gold denomination and the most convenient for trade purposes.

The 1875 is a key to all gold series from the dollar to the ten dollar, but it is particularly difficult for three dollar gold collectors. That is because no business strikes were produced, and collectors who need the date must compete for one of the survivors from the original proof mintage. Breen believed there were two proof productions for the 1875, originals and restrikes, both of which he lists as "Very Rare." Breen identified the restrikes by "prominent rust marks" on the OL in DOLLAR. There is no indication of die rust on the present piece, which must be an original, particularly since it meets Breen's diagnostic of a die line near the denticles above the two right maple leaves. This beautiful specimen is well struck aside from the usual minor roughness on the wreath knot. The frosty devices provide pleasing contrast with the prominently reflective fields. Thorough inspection locates a couple of unimportant marks on the fieldnear the profile, but the appearance is splendid for the PR64 level. The importance of this opportunity for the three dollar specialist cannot be overemphasized.

From The Blowing Rock Collection, Part Two. (#98039)

Prized 1876 Three Dollar PR61

3480   1876 PR61 PCGS. Although not quite as rare as the 1875, the proof-only 1876 is an immensely popular issue that is well known among both dedicated gold specialists and more casual numismatists. Actually, the 1876 is not as rare as some other proofs in this series (such as the 1861, 1874, and 1878), but the lack of a similarly dated business strike delivery explains the greater demand that this issue enjoys. Only 45 proofs were originally produced, and (unfortunately) a decent number of the 33 or 34 survivors are impaired. Although the present example exhibits some grade-limiting hairlines, the overall eye appeal is above average for the PR61 grade level. The color is a deep, rich, green-gold shade over which orange-gold highlights have gathered. There are no sizeable or unsightly handling marks, and the only noteworthy pedigree marker is a lintmark in the reverse field above the S in DOLLARS. (#8040)

Esteemed 1876 Three Dollar
PR64 Deep Cameo

3481   1876 PR64 Deep Cameo PCGS. The proof-only status of the 1876 three dollar and close association with the even more elusive 1875 (one of the legendary 19th century gold dates from gold dollar through eagle denominations) have given it considerable notoriety among generations of gold collectors. Its well documented rarity is easily recognized by a quick glance at the mintage figure. While 45 proofs may sound like a minuscule output, it is actually the highest production for the denomination between 1868 and 1880. It is the issue's proof-only status that secures its esteemed standing.

Although produced from a single set of dies, there were two separate deliveries of 1876 proof threes. Improper storage after the first 20 specimens were struck was followed by a second production of 25 coins in June of that year. Evidence of die rust can be detected on these later pieces, found here and on the Gem specimen in the next lot. Other minor disturbances are sometimes found on these so-called restrikes, here a small, but deep planchet void is located just to the right of the wreath at 3 o'clock on the reverse. The contrast on this Choice specimen is quite dramatic, with characteristic halo effect found to the left of the portrait. One must allow for duplication in arriving at the number of surviving 1876 threes, but even so it seems that no more than 25-30 pieces are extant today. Population: 1 in 64, 4 finer (12/06).

From The Blowing Rock Collection, Part Two. (#98040)

Beautiful 1881 Three Dollar
PR66 Cameo NGC

3482   1881 PR66 Cameo NGC. The 1881 three dollar gold issue boasts a limited mintage of 500 business strikes and 54 proofs.
This beautiful Premium Gem offers needle-sharp design details and
mildly reflective fields. A lovely cameo effect is evident on both obverse and reverse. The surfaces exhibit dominant orange-gold coloration intermingled with small amounts of ice-blue toning, mainly on
the portrait. There are no bothersome contact marks, but some minor haziness is noted. Certainly one of the more important survivors
of this low mintage issue. Census: 4 in 66 Cameo, 0 finer (11/06).
(#88045)

Lovely PR66 1883 Three Dollar Gold

3483   1883 PR66 PCGS. 1883 at the nation's mints was a year chiefly dedicated to the spewing out of millions of unwanted and unneeded Morgan dollars, as mandated by the Bland-Allison Act of 1878. Three types of five cent nickels were produced in considerable quantities, but three cent nickel coinage was negligible. Quarters, half dollars, and gold coins below the half eagle were produced in strictly token amounts, while the double eagle was produced only in proof format, to the extent of 92 pieces. The mintage of three dollar gold pieces, as it did in 1881, again dipped below four digits, this time to the extent of 900 business strikes and 89 proofs. Although some earlier researchers, such as Harry W. Bass, Jr., believed that business strikes were struck from the proof obverse die, Breen's proof *Encyclopedia* says that a different die was used. However, both proofs and some business strikes are seen with a speck of die rust in the plume above the T in LIBERTY, as on the present coin. According to Q. David Bowers' *The United States $3 Gold Pieces* the reverse die, however, is definitely different on the proof coins. The wreath tops are unconnected and show an area of proof surface between them, while on business strikes the wreath tips touch. The proofs show the peak of the 1 in the date centered beneath the left tip of the serif of the first L in DOLLARS, while on the business strikes this digit is minutely to the left of that position. The present lovely specimen offers rich yellow-gold centers that meld into amber, copper, and sunset-gold hues at the rims on each side. This is one of four specimens graded PR66 at PCGS, while a single specimen at NGC is graded finer, at PR67 Cameo (11/06). (#8047)

PROOF FOUR DOLLAR GOLD PIECES

1879 Flowing Hair Four Dollar
Gold Stella PR55

3484   1879 Flowing Hair, Judd-1635, Pollock-1832, R.3, PR55 PCGS. Although a contemporary failure in its concept, the four dollar gold piece, or stella, has proven to be a hint with generations of gold collectors, being incorporated into the standard issues of United States gold coins decades ago. The 1879 Flowing Hair stella is a curious piece that was proposed by John Kasson as an international coin whose value would be roughly equivalent to that of an Austrian 8 florin.

The flowing hair stellas were originally engraved by Charles Barber in 1879 after a design his father, William, had executed in the previous year. 415 pieces were struck as patterns (Judd-1635) and another 400 or so backdated restrikes were produced in 1880. These were widely distributed around Washington circles to popularize the proposed new denomination, but were soon forgotten when the international gold coin was rejected by Congress.

The specimen offered here appears to have been carried as a pocket piece for a year or two (one has to wonder if perhaps by a Cabinet member or influential Senator), but displays pleasing reddish and steel-blue highlights over partially glassy surfaces. With the recent upsurge in prices for higher grade specimens (two PR64 examples each realized over $160,000 in our November 2006 Sale) so-called mishandled pieces such as this take on an even greater importance for the budget-minded collector.

From The Twin Hollows Collection. (#8057)

Lightly Circulated 1879
Flowing Hair Stella, PR58

3485   1879 Flowing Hair, Judd-1635, Pollock-1832, R.3, PR58 PCGS. The Flowing Hair stella struck in gold is one of the most famous and desirable pattern issues, perhaps because it has been listed in the *Guide Book* for many years. Most surviving pieces fall into two different categories: Choice to Gem proof or damaged. Many examples show evidence of use in jewelry, yet they still actively trade in numismatic circles due to their desirability and value. Of course, a large number of high quality proof examples also exist today. It is hard to estimate the exact number of survivors, however, a reasonable guess is about 300 coins covering all different grades.

The example that we are offering here is extremely important and should receive a great deal of attention at the auction. It is a lightly circulated proof, significantly lacking any damage. A trace of wear can be seen on the high points of the design, but the fields retain nearly full mirrors and the designs are quite sharp. Light abrasions on the obverse and reverse surfaces are consistent with a coin that may have circulated briefly, although this example probably served as a pocket piece for some time. As always, this stella shows the parallel roller marks across the highest design elements, and they are nearly vertical, oriented from 6:30 to 12:30 on the obverse. Collectors who have always desired a stella, but lack the budget for a Choice or Gem proof, would do well to consider this opportunity. (#8057)

Choice Cameo Proof 1879 Four Dollar Gold Piece, Flowing Hair Design

3486 **1879 Flowing Hair, Judd-1635, Pollock-1833, R.3 PR64 Cameo NGC.** The planchet striations on this piece are nearly vertical, and faintly visible on the highest design points. They also extend into the fields above and below, although this is barely detectable without a magnifier. We always try to mention the planchet striations as they represent an important aspect of production for these pieces. They are also highly useful for pedigree research. A substantial number of stellas still exist today, in a wide range of grades. As the direction or orientation of the planchet striations is a random matter, pedigree researchers realize that two offerings cannot be the same specimen if the striations are running in different directions.

Technically, the gold stellas are pattern issues with limited mintages, although it is now believed that there may have been as many as 800 or even 1,000 of these "patterns," including a number of restrikes made a few years later. For many years, the mintage figure was quoted at just 400 pieces, however, it is known that restrikes were produced, thus the higher figures. It may be the case that nearly 400 of these still survive today in various grades, many impaired.

This lovely proof has rich greenish yellow-gold color with deeply mirrored fields and fully lustrous devices. A thin hairline crosses Liberty's cheek vertically, nearly parallel to the planchet striations, and this undoubtedly accounts for the limited grade of this piece. A hint of rose iridescence is visible above the date with a small patch of hazy blue color behind the hair curls. The upper reverse also has some hazy patina. This is a pleasing example that any collector should be happy to own. (#88057)

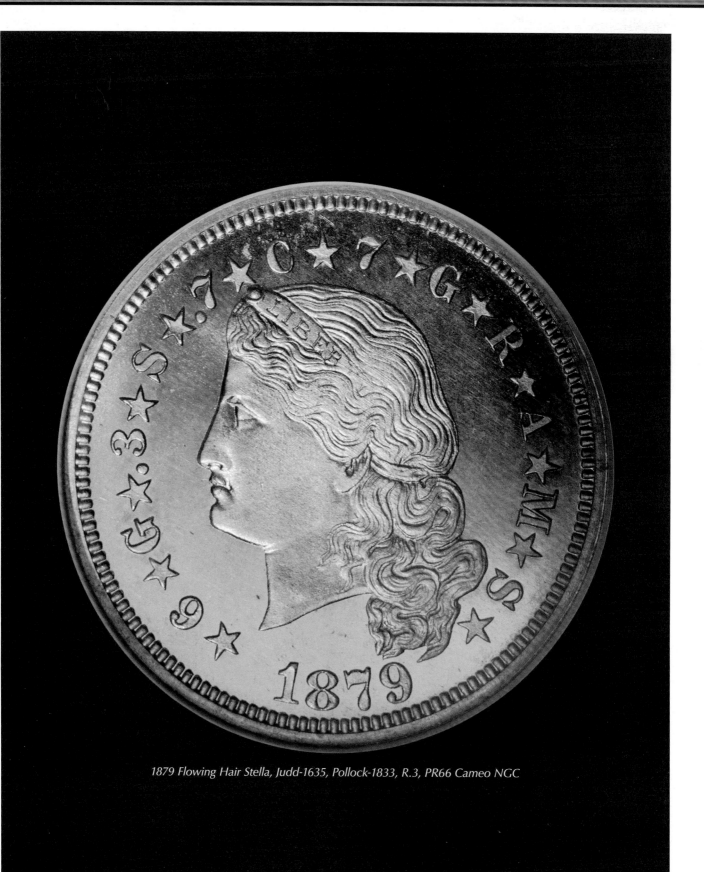

1879 Flowing Hair Stella, Judd-1635, Pollock-1833, R.3, PR66 Cameo NGC

1879 Flowing Hair Stella, Judd-1635, Pollock-1833, R.3, PR66 Cameo NGC

Spectacular PR66 Cameo 1879 Flowing Hair Stella

3487   1879 Flowing Hair, Judd-1635, Pollock-1833, R.3, PR66 Cameo NGC. The successful introduction of a more unlikely coin is difficult to conceive. The 1879- and 1880-dated four dollar gold coins, or stellas, were a pet project of the Hon. John Adam Kasson (1822-1910) of Des Moines, Iowa, "envoy extraordinary and minister plenipotentiary" to Austria-Hungary from 1877 to 1881. Kasson's international background in the multicultural Hapsburg empire undoubtedly played a large role in his proposal for an international coin. (Kasson would later, in 1884 and 1885, serve as foreign minister to Germany. His record also includes various terms as U.S. Representative from Iowa between 1867 and 1884, as well as his 1878 attempt to enlist U.S. support for equal rights for various underprivileged classes of society in Romania and Serbia).

It helped that Kasson was the former chairman of the House Committee on Coinage, Weights, and Measures. At the beginning of 1879 Kasson, through his ally Alexander H. Stephens, then-chairman of the same committee, contacted Treasury Secretary John Sherman, asking that the Mint supply pattern pieces:

Will you please have a specimen or specimens, say five, of this coin struck? The obverse design similar to that of a double eagle = 6G. .3S. .7C., 7 grams — 1879.

The reverse — "United States of America. Four Dollars. E pluribus unum. Deo est gloria," and a large star emblazoned, in the words, 'One stella, 400 cents' ... .

All over the world this will show the intrinsic measure and value of the coin, and exhibit its remarkable adaptation to use as an international coin. (Pollock, United States Patterns and Related Issues).

A chief aim of Kasson was to recommend international coinage that would assist Americans in foreign trade and travel, by alleviating inconveniences in making transactions in various currencies. The proposed four dollar coin would approximate the value of eight Austrian (and Dutch) florins, of 20 French francs, of 20 Italian lire, and of 20 Spanish pesetas.

But facilitating international travel was not Kasson's sole purpose. Kasson was closely connected with Western silver mining interests in the United States and their congressional allies, including Reps. Richard P. "Silver Dick" Bland and William Darrah Kelley, all of whom were highly desirous to see expanded domestic and international uses of silver. Kasson's proposal included a "quintuple stella" or twenty dollar gold piece, along with the stella, both of which were to be in "metric gold," and a silver dollar made of Dr. Wheeler Hubbell's "goloid" alloy—silver with about 4% gold content. Mint personnel also abetted Kasson's cause, remembering his help in overcoming objections in 1864 to introduction of the bronze cent.

And so was born the most unlikely of numismatic curiosities: a four dollar coin with a five-pointed star, with six nominal grams of gold and a seventh of alloy, not exactly worth eight florins. A fa-tal flaw was that the *value of the stella was not precisely that of any of those international measures,* so that transactions made in stellas would require change to be made. Another flaw is that the above-mentioned foreign currencies, just as today's, fluctuate against one another. With no fixed reference point (other than the nameplate value of four U.S. dollars and its content, purportedly six grams of alloyed gold), the stella offered no particular advantage in international commerce over the half eagle or any other U.S. gold coin.

Breen's *Complete Encyclopedia* lists "originals" without planchet striations, but comments that none have been offered in many years. Pollock lists two different metallic compositions—one of standard 90% gold/10% alloy, and another so-called "metric alloy" consisting of 6/7ths gold, 1/7 alloy. Some researchers have professed their belief that the "original" 1879 Flowing Hair patterns were struck in the metric alloy, with the larger number of restrikes of standard composition. The Pollock pattern reference under the "1879 metric dollar" says, "Tom DeLorey notes that 'the term 'metric alloy' refers to the awkward alloy necessary to make a coin of 25 grams, the weight of a French 5 francs, rather than an alloy that was 'metric' or base 10 in nature." Presumably the stella, purportedly an even 7 grams in weight, also was considered "metric," as were the quintuple stella and the "metric goloid" dollars, all supposedly struck in even gram weights.

Despite all the hullabaloo about metric coinage, it is highly doubtful that these proposed stellas were ever struck on anything other than the standard 90/10 gold coinage planchets. The planchet striations seen on all known gold stellas serve as virtual confirmation that the stella planchets, almost the same diameter as a half eagle, were produced by rolling out planchet stock 80% of the thickness of a half eagle planchet. The striations or "roller marks" in the center highpoints remained unstruck, due to the planchet thinness.

The four dollar stella is one of the most desirable of U.S. coins, and is featured in Garrett and Guth's *The 100 Greatest U.S. Coins.* The "original" mintage of the 1879 Flowing Hair stellas was supplemented, likely in 1880, by "restrikes." As far as is known, the so-called originals and restrikes are indistinguishable one from another—although the originals are reputed to lack die striations, and/or to feature the "metric" alloy—and the total mintage is estimated variously from 425 to as high as 800 pieces. The present PR66 Cameo piece is one of 20 pieces so graded at NGC, with eight Cameo pieces finer. Adding the PCGS Cameo pieces brings the total to 27 coins at both services, with 10 pieces finer (10/06). This is a spectacular, deeply mirrored coin that shows a significant amount of mint frost over the devices, which yields strong cameo contrast. The surfaces are a rich orange-gold, and there are no noticeable contact marks on either side of this remarkable specimen. One of the most attractive and eye appealing stellas extant of this curious and widely sought-after issue.

From The Freedom Collection. (#88057)

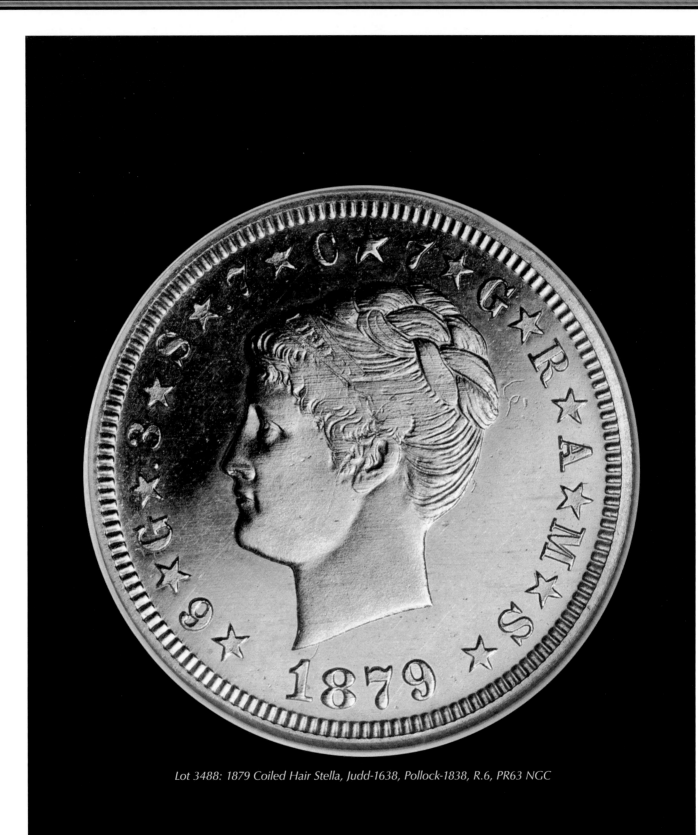

Lot 3488: 1879 Coiled Hair Stella, Judd-1638, Pollock-1838, R.6, PR63 NGC

1879 Coiled Hair Stella, Judd-1638, Pollock-1838, R.6, PR63 NGC

Extremely Rare and Important 1879 Coiled Hair Stella, PR63

3488   1879 Coiled Hair, Judd-1638, Pollock-1838, R.6, PR63 NGC. Of all the many numismatic delicacies created inside (and occasionally outside) the U.S. Mint in Philadelphia during the period of from roughly 1857 to the late 1870s, the 1879 and 1880 Coiled Hair stellas have a special mystique that few other U.S. coins share, a delectable combination of rarity, high demand, beauty, and mystery. The period is renowned for the hijinks, shenanigans, and general free-wheeling of various Mint personnel, often for their own aggrandizement or for those of various VIPs and the numismatically well connected. The four dollar stella, from its outset, was an ill-fated and poorly conceived coin issue, one destined to join the company of odd-denomination numismatic curiosities, those coins that are the object of intense desire on the part of dedicated numismatists, and that are the object of puzzled interest on the part of the uninitiated. A short list of those odd-denomination coins would also include the half cent, two cent and three cent pieces, half dimes (perhaps), the three and four dollar gold pieces, and such oddities as the Pan-Pac commemorative and territorial fifty dollar pieces (and perhaps the quintuple stella and the half union).

The accompanying 1879 Flowing Hair stella lot tells the story of the Honorable John A. Kasson's quest to produce a four dollar coin of international renown, and how it was doomed to failure from the outset. Kasson's proposal included a "goloid" silver dollar, as well as a "quintuple stella" twenty dollar gold piece, composed of 35 grams of gold, 30 pure gold and 5 alloy. Members of Congress had sufficient interest that a number of "original" 1879 Flowing Hair coins were made, likely 15 or 20 pieces. When demand swelled, several hundred more examples were made, probably in the following year. The 1879 Flowing Hair stellas were distributed to Congress in three-coin pattern sets that also included the 1879 "metric goloid dollars," Judd-1618 and -1626. A popular numismatic legend offers that many Congressmen gave their stellas to their wives and mistresses as gifts, accounting for the many pieces seen with jewelry mountings removed.

While Mint Chief Engraver Charles Barber prepared the Flowing Hair obverse, it fell to Assistant Engraver George T. Morgan, of Morgan dollar fame, to prepare the Coiled Hair obverse that was also used on the stellas. The Coiled Hair stellas were produced in numbers that were strictly limited, and their distribution was apparently a highly clandestine "affair" of a different sort. The 1879 Coiled Hair stellas likely were made to the extent of only 15 or so pieces, and their existence was unknown to the numismatic fraternity for many years. Today they are extremely rare, with probably a dozen or so surviving pieces.

The Judd pattern reference, ninth edition, writes tellingly of the circumstances surrounding the issuance of the 1879 stellas:

"It was announced by someone, perhaps a Mint official, that 15 of the 1879 Flowing Hair $4 Stellas were struck,

these as patterns, but there was a sufficient demand for them that a few hundred more were struck for congressmen, who [were] allowed to acquire them for $6.50 each. This was an era of great secrecy at the Mint, and virtually the entire pattern coinage of 1879, including the 'Washlady' and Schoolgirl silver coins, were produced for the private profit of Mint officials. These were not given to congressmen or openly sold to collectors at the time, and, indeed, for many issues, their very existence was not disclosed. ... With regard to Morgan's Coiled Hair Stella, this was strictly a delicacy for Mint officials. None were shown to congressmen, and none were made available to the numismatic fraternity—the wholematter was hush-hush. How many were struck is not known, and estimates have ranged from about a dozen up to perhaps two or three dozen. Whatever the figure, it is but a tiny fraction of the 1879 Flowing Hair style."

All of the stellas enjoy a special status and popularity shared by a small handful of U.S. coin issue, those that are strictly patterns or specimen strikings, but which are collected as part of the regular series of U.S. coinage. The stellas share this favored niche with such legendary coins as the 1856 Flying Eagle cent, most of the Gobrecht dollar issues, the 1859-60 transitional half dimes and dimes, the 1907 Wire Rim eagles, and the 1866 No Motto Seated dollars. Collector fervor for these rarities is also fueled by their listing in popular collector guides such as the *Guide Book,* alongside regular issue coinage. (The *Guide Book* is extremely influential, as legions of collectors make their collecting decisions based on what coins that reference chooses to list or not).

The present PR63 example, certified by NGC, is one of three pieces so graded at that service, with four pieces finer. PCGS has graded no PR63 specimens, but seven finer. Include a handful of Cameo coins, and both NGC and PCGS combined have seen a total of 25 *grading events* for this coin (10/06). Given the high likelihood of multiple resubmissions, the estimate of a dozen or so survivors appears reasonable. This is a well-preserved example of the Coiled Hair stella. There are very few contact marks present on either side. The most notable surface "flaw" is actually a strike-through, a curlicue depression in the right obverse field behind Liberty's hair bun. This strike-through is likely the most reliable pedigree identifier on this important coin. The central details are weakly struck, a fact that explains the presence of roller marks that were not struck out of the coin (as a rule, fully struck coins do not show roller marks). The fields are nicely reflective, and the surfaces display rich orange-gold coloration.

From The Freedom Collection. (#8058)

Sought-After 1795 Small Eagle
Five Dollar AU55

3489   1795 Small Eagle AU55 PCGS. B. 1-B, Breen-6412, Bass-3033, BD-3, High R.3. The obverse die employed on BD-3 is distinguished by the presence of stars 11 and 12 overlapping, with star 11 joined to the upper right arm of the Y. This die was paired with three different reverses, the one here attributed by short vertical die lines above TE in UNITED and by the placement of the wreath opening almost directly between the final S in STATES and the O in OF. We have been fortunate on several occasions in the past to offer several examples of the 1795 Small Eagle five dollar, an immensely popular early gold type. However, in tonight's Platinum session we are thrilled to be able to present no less than five AU and finer representatives culminating with a trio of amazing MS64s.

On this important first year half eagle, appealing reddish-tinged surfaces retain a modest degree of reflectivity after a relatively brief stint in commerce. The obverse displays excellent sharpness on the portrait and only occasional bluntness on the surrounding stars. The central portion of the reverse, more specifically the eagle's neck, head, and right leg (facing) feathers are noticeably deficient beyond the effects of minimal wear. There are no noticeable adjustment marks and the only abrasion worthy of mention is a shallow dig along the reverse border just to the right of six o'clock. An ideal type candidate. (#8066)

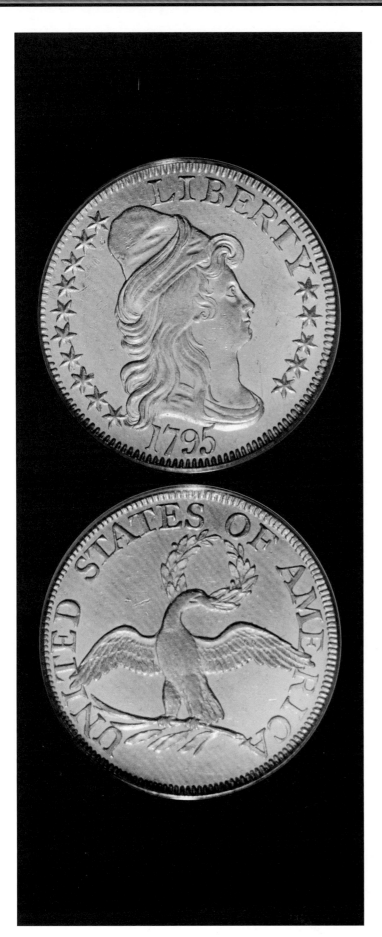

Significant Mint State 1795 Small Eagle Five Dollar

3490   1795 Small Eagle MS61 PCGS. Breen-6416, BD-8, High R.5. The 1795 half eagle was the first gold issue struck by the U.S. Mint. Although copper cents and half cents were issued in 1793, and silver dollars and half dollars were coined in 1794, the production of gold coins had to wait until 1795. This was because of excessive surety bonds required of the Chief Coiner and Assayer. Once these bonds were reduced, 8,705 half eagles were struck, in addition to 5,583 eagles. The final authorized gold denomination, the quarter eagle, was first produced in 1796. The mintage given for the 1795 half eagle excludes the curious Heraldic Eagle reverse varieties, which were coined two or three years later using functional older obverse dies.

Early gold specialists know that the most often encountered 1795 half eagle variety is BD-3, identified by its monogram-like attachment of the ME in AMERICA. BD-8 is considerably more difficult to locate, and in the recent Bass-Dannreuther reference is listed as more rare than BD-1, BD-4, BD-6, or BD-10. For BD-8, the right upright of the N in UNITED is recut, and the top of the 5 in the date overlaps the bust truncation. The wreath terminates beneath the left curve of the O in OF. These diagnostics can be used to identify the die marriage.

This attractive example is crisply struck overall. The eagle's breast and the hair left of the ear exhibit moderate merging of detail, but most design elements are exquisitely brought up. Adjustment marks are virtually absent, seen only on the obverse margin near 10 o'clock. The obverse field has the small mark here and there, as expected of the MS61 grade, but none among these distract. Light honey-gold toning is consistent, except for the infrequent gunmetal-blue highpoint on the major devices. Uncirculated 1795 half eagles are rare, and under tremendous demand from type collectors and early gold specialists. Years may pass before a comparable example of BD-8 appears at auction.

From The Essex Palm Collection. (#8066)

Choice Prooflike 1795 BD-2 Half Eagle, Small Eagle Reverse

3491   1795 Small Eagle MS64 NGC. Breen 1-C, Breen-6412, Bass-3034, BD-2, R.6. The 1795 half eagles were the first gold coins struck at the Philadelphia Mint, from dies prepared by Robert Scot. This design complied exactly with the law established by the Coinage Act of April 2, 1792 regarding obverse and reverse devices. Section 10 of that legislation stated: "Upon one side of each of the said coins there shall be an impression emblematic of liberty, with an inscription of the word Liberty, and the year of the coinage; and upon the reverse of each of the gold and silver coins there shall be the figure or representation of an eagle, with this inscription, UNITED STATES OF AMERICA" The only additional embellishments were the stars on the obverse and the wreath and olive branch on the reverse.

In *Numismatic Art in America,* Cornelius Vermeule discussed this design at some length: "The industrious Robert Scot seems also to have created the bust of Liberty that dominated the gold coinage from 1795 until John Reich introduced his turbaned ladies in 1807 and 1808. His [Scot's] source could well have been an ideal, somewhat backward portrait of Martha Washington arrayed for an evening reception, a considerably more suave, tranquil presentation than that identified with the half-disme of 1792. The Liberty cap is a great tumultuous affair of soft felt, that somehow manages to tower amid a large, curled forelock and long, wavy tresses. It is hard to say what is cap and what is hair entwined about it. The face is flat, blunt, and thoroughly bourgeois. The draped bust is a truncated curiosity. Greco-Roman classicism has been misunderstood here, for this is the type of draped neck ordinarily found in ancient art when a marble bust has been created for insertion into the body of a draped statue. The entire presentation makes little sense as an immediate visual experience.Scot surely did not originate this form of classicism in the Federalist period; no doubt he adapted the design from some case after the antique or some contemporary marble by a sculptor of modest talents." After breaking down the Scot design, Vermeule continued by defending it: "Criticism comes easy, however, and it must not be overlooked that Robert Scot's first gold coinage has a positive character of its own, a healthy individuality and almost-rustic charm that conveys the message of a young nation seeking its identity as well as any monumental manifestation of the early arts in America."

An extensive coinage of gold took place during the earliest years at the Mint, with 12 die varieties for the 1795 Small Eagle half eagles and five more for the 1795 eagles. This variety, currently identified by the variety notation BD-2, is considered the second die marriage produced, probably in early August 1795. John Dannreuther suggested that this variety may have been among coins from Warrant 26, consisting of 520 pieces delivered on August 11. It is also a rare variety among 1795 half eagles. Harry Bass, who collected two dozen half eagles dated 1795, only found one example of this variety during his three decades of collecting gold coins. Only about 20 to 30 pieces are known from this die combination, and this example has the highest numerical grade of any. The surfaces have bright lemon-yellow color with splashes of rich honey-gold toning. Some unusual striations are visible in the lower obverse fields. Both sides are fully prooflike with several visible lint marks, suggesting that the planchet may have received special treatment before this piece was struck.

From The Freedom Collection. (#8066)

Prooflike Near-Gem BD-10 1795 Small Eagle Five

3492   1795 Small Eagle MS64 NGC. Breen-6415, BD-10, R.5. The half eagle denomination was the first gold coin struck for the United States. The 1795 coins are divided into two major types, the Small Eagle and Large Eagle (or Heraldic Eagle) reverses. The mintage of the Small Eagle variety is recorded as 8,707 pieces. The Large Eagle Reverse half eagles dated 1795 are regardless believed to have been struck in 1798, and the *Guide Book* includes their mintage in the figure of 24,867 coins for 1798.

The 1795 Small Eagle coins are divided into 12 varieties, BD-1 through BD-12, according to the new Bass-Dannreuther *Early U.S. Gold Coin Varieties,* with the Large Eagle variants comprising the three BD-13 through BD-15 entries in that reference. All of the Small Eagle variants, with the sole exception of the R.3 BD-3, are listed as at least R.5 or "rare," with some called R.7+, extremely rare, or three-five examples known. The three Large Eagle varieties are R.5, R.6, and R.9 (unique). The Small Eagle varieties are identified through various diagnostics such as the position of star points, the width and positioning of the date, the number and position of the berries on the reverse, and other die markers.

It is worth remembering, in this era of "Buy your U.S. Mint products before December 31 or you can't get the 2006-dated coins," that in the early days of the U.S. Mint, die steel was a scarce commodity, and dies were mostly used *with complete disregard for the year stamped on them.* If coinage of a particular denomination was needed, functional dies, even if dated from previous years or with outdated styles, would again be pressed into service to fill the need. Additionally, the early Mint reported deliveries of coins *according to the year in which they were delivered, not according to the dates on the coins.* This is the reason why Mint Director Samuel Moore in 1834 created an instant rarity when he ordered silver dollars to be struck dated 1804, for diplomatic purposes, from a leftover unused die of that year—but the 19,570 silver dollars reported from 1804 were likely dated 1803!

Even though the BD-10 variant is listed in Bass-Dannreuther as an R.5 or "very rare" coin, it must be remembered that that figure is *within the context of the series,* long considered one of the most difficult in U.S. numismatics. The BD reference estimates a mintage for this variety of 750-1,250 pieces, with the total mintage for the date estimated at 8,707 to 12,106 coins. Star 1 is left of the curl, but touching it, rather than beneath. Star 10 points to and nearly touches the cap. The 1 in the date is barely free of the hair, and the flag of the 5 lies over the drapery. On the reverse, the rightmost (facing) leaf pair shows a stubby, short second leaf. There are four berries in the wreath, two inside and two outside, with the inner right berry small and low. The D in UNITED and the second T in STATES show obvious recutting.

Light adjustment marks show in the center obverse, visible with a loupe. The stars and obverse center are fully struck, but some softness shows on the central reverse. A light reverse die crack is noted from the rim to the last A, through the stem, and into the field. The coin is decidedly prooflike, with brilliantly mirrored fields and thickly frosted devices, and beautiful orange-gold coloration. Light field chatter limits a Gem grade.

The current NGC *Census Report* lists 196 nonprooflike examples of the 1795 Small Eagle coinage, without regard to variety, in all grades, and another seven pieces with Prooflike surfaces. Of those 203 coins, only three pieces are certified MS64, with seven finer. Of the specimens certified Prooflike, this is the only MS64 piece, with a single MS65 finer, again irrespective of rarity. Among the finest, and nearly unimprovable. (#8066)

Choice Mint State 1795 Small Eagle Half Eagle, BD-3

3493 **1795 Small Eagle MS64 PCGS.** B. 1-B, Breen-6412, Bass-3033, BD-3, High R.3. This is easily the most plentiful of all 1795 Small Eagle varieties, and it is the most commonly seen die combination in Mint State grades. The collector or numismatist must always remember that the terms common or plentiful are relevant only to the series under discussion, and have no relationship to similar terms in other series. For example, less than 1,000 1795 Small Eagle half eagles remain in existence, with possibly one-third of the total struck from this single die pair. By comparison, a Morgan dollar or a Lincoln cent, or a coin from one of many other series, would be considered a major rarity if the total population was less than 1,000 coins. It is a basic economic matter of supply and demand. The 1795 Small Eagle half eagle has a rather limited supply, but an equally limited demand.

This piece has a short die crack from the obverse border to star 12. The reverse is nearly perfect with only a short engraving line to the top of E and a tiny crack to the right top of T. Both sides have prominent center dots that are seldom visible as they are each positioned on high points of the design and are usually susceptible to slight wear. This is the second of three die uses for this obverse. The first use (B. 1-C, BD-2) has no trace of the obverse crack at star 12 and the third use (B. 1-A, BD-4) has the crack extending through star 12, into the field. Careful study of all die states for the 1795 Small Eagle coinage led John Dannreuther to the conclusion that Walter Breen's emission sequence was incorrect. The order of production for the first four 1795 half eagle varieties was B. 2-C, 1-C, 1-B, and 1-A, using Breen's numbering scheme.

Both sides of this Choice Mint State example have remarkable surfaces for the grade, with satiny greenish yellow-gold luster and a sharp strike. All design elements on each side are fully defined without any apparent weakness. While the grade is limited by a few faint hairlines, the overall appearance is spectacular. A small blemish, apparently present when this example was struck, appears at eye level in the right obverse field. An even smaller abrasion is present in the left obverse field. Hopefully, these will be useful to the pedigree collector. Among all 1795 Small Eagle half eagles certified by PCGS, this coin lags behind just two others for finest certified, including the entire population of all 12 varieties. (#8066)

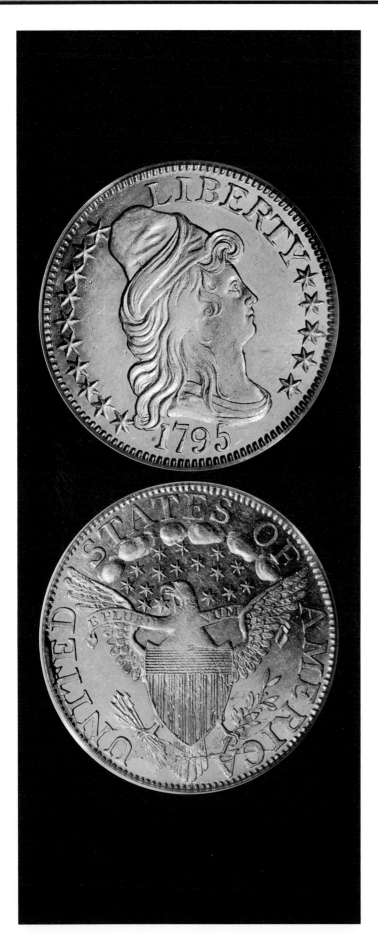

Rare 1795 Heraldic Eagle Five Dollar
BD-15, MS62 PCGS

3494   1795 Large Eagle MS62 PCGS. Breen-6423, BD-15, High R.5. Obverse State C. This is not the terminal die state, which is reserved for the few pieces that are known with a die cud over the TE in STATES. This state, however, shows plentiful die cracks on each side, including the diagnostic crack from star 13 to the lower lip of Liberty. There is some dispute about the exact die emission sequence of this and other 1795 fives. However, it is beyond dispute that this variety was produced in 1797 or 1798. The Heraldic Eagle reverse was first used in 1797. The Bass-Dannreuther reference states that this variety was minted after the 1797 BD-5, as "the common reverse die is in a much earlier state for the BD-5 pairing."

These "1795" half eagles possess a charm and desirability seen on few other early gold coins. Much of their desirability lies in the anachronistic nature of the coins themselves. That is, the 1795-dated obverse is paired with a Heraldic Eagle reverse—an impossibility for coins issued in 1795 or even 1796. Breen postulates that this was an emergency issue in his 1988 *Encyclopedia:*

> "From Aug. 20 through Nov. 1, the Mint was again closed for the [yellow fever] epidemic. On Dec. 5 followed [3,226], emergency issues, possibly comprising some or all of these: 1795 Heraldic, 1797/5, 1798 Rusted Dies. Other issues attributed to Dec. 1798, made in haste in various denominations to fill back orders, also severe die rust and breakage: Evidently any dies that would stand up even briefly were used, no matter how haphazard or anachronistic their combinations."

Of course, another reason for the popularity of this issue is its absolute rarity. Only 30 to 35 individual pieces are known. The average grade is quite high with a number of Mint State coins extant. However, the MS62 level is the breaking point for this issue with a mere six pieces certified (probably even fewer actually accounted for) in MS63 and 64 grades.

This particular piece has bright yellow-gold surfaces. There are numerous small abrasions scattered about, but none are worthy of individual mention.

From The Essex Palm Collection. (#8075)

Brilliant 1800 BD-4 Half Eagle, MS62

3495   1800 MS62 PCGS. Breen-6439, BD-4, R.4. This variety is immediately recognized by the widely recut M in AMERICA, and this example represents Die State a with no evidence of clash marks, lapping, or die cracks on the reverse. Among five 1800 half eagle varieties, this die marriage is the third most common. In fact, BD-2, BD-4, and BD-5 are each considered R.3 or R.4, while BD-1 and BD-3 are both quite rare, R.7 and R.6, respectively. A lovely Mint State example, this piece exhibits satiny luster with reflective fields. Both sides have brilliant green-gold color with hints of orange toning. The PCGS population recorded here includes all varieties of 1800 half eagles, not just this single die combination. Population: 32 in 62, 18 finer (11/06). (#8082)

Lustrous, Appealing BD-5 Near-Gem 1800 Five

3496   1800 MS64 PCGS. Breen-6438, BD-5, High R.3. BD Die State d/b (early). The 1800 issue appears to be among the more available of the early Draped Bust half eagles, and accordingly makes an excellent choice for a type or year set (for the more daring among us). The issue is plentiful in grades up through AU, and even the lower Mint State ranks see numerous occupants. Looking at the data, NGC and PCGS combined have certified a total of 76 pieces in AU50 or AU53. In AU55 and AU58, the total increases to 173 coins, and there are now 168 pieces at both services from MS60 through MS63. In the near-Gem MS64 grade, however, the total thins out substantially, to only 13 examples at both services. In MS65 and higher grades, there are two coins, one each at NGC and PCGS (both MS66 pieces) (11/06). Those figures, of course, will be artificially inflated by the inevitable resubmissions, crossovers, and the sometimes-significant attainment of "one more point."

This variety marks the fourth and final use of this obverse, shared with the BD-2 through BD-5. The 1 in the date lacks a "flag" or top serif. The 1 in the date is separated from the curl. The distance between 1 and 800 is greater than between the other digits. The stars are arranged eight and five, with star 9 very nearly touching the Y of LIBERTY. On the reverse is the key diagnostic that signals this pairing: Both feet of the last A in AMERICA touch the claw of the eagle. The right side of the last S in STATES is about over a space between two clouds. A star point touches the back of the eagle's neck.

In this die state on the obverse, a light die crack crosses IBER, and the early beginning of a crack runs from the rim through L. Several reverse die cracks are noted, including one from the edge through R into the field, another from the lower left (facing) leaves through the left foot, the shield, and the right foot, and another from the edge through the I in UNITED into the field. However, no trace of a crack from ED to the wing is visible.

This example, one of the finest dozen or so certified excluding duplicates (possibly one of the finest eight or so coins certified), offers lovely, lustrous orange-gold coloration. A few light contact marks on Liberty's cheek and in the right field remove this coin from Gem consideration, but its appeal is considerable. (#8082)

Beautiful 1800 Capped Bust Right Half Eagle MS64

3497 **1800 MS64 PCGS.** Breen-6438, BD-5, High R.3. A total of five die pairings were used to coin 1800 half eagles, four of which share a common obverse die as on the BD-5. Here, the 1 in the date is lacking the upper left serif, often referred to as a Blunt 1. The reverse die is unique to this variety, however, and is recognized by a star touching the back of the eagle's neck. The Philadelphia Mint stepped up production of Capped Bust Right Heraldic Eagle half eagles in 1800 to a new high of 37,628 pieces. After a one-year hiatus, comparatively high mintage figures were also recorded from 1802 through 1807 when the new Capped Bust Left design was phased in. This issue and the 1802/1 are generally considered to be the two most obtainable dates from this challenging series.

This lovely, wholly original example is boldly struck in all areas, with especially sharp highpoint definition noted on the reverse. Struck from an intermediate die state, a wispy die crack angles down between the IB in LIBERTY and continues to touch the bases of ER. The reverse exhibits a few more prominent die cracks, the most obvious of which advances from the lower left olive leaves through the right leg (facing), the base of the shield, and onto a claw on the eagle's left leg. Location of this particular die crack is often used for attribution of the BD-5 since it is visible on nearly all examples. An important opportunity for the advanced gold specialist. Population: 6 in 64, 1 finer (12/06). (#8082)

Lustrous Near-Mint 1802/1 BD-1 Half Eagle

3498   1802/1 AU58 PCGS. Breen-6440, BD-1, High R.4. The half eagles of this date have provided a challenge to numismatists attempting to sort out the known varieties from those that are listed but don't exist. The efforts of John Dannreuther, with the notes of Harry Bass, have done much to set the record straight. Two overdate obverse dies are known, with a centered or high 2 in the date. This first obverse has the overdated digit 2 centered between the bust and the border. Five reverse dies were combined with this obverse, and three reverse dies were combined with the high overdate obverse for a total of eight die marriages that are currently known. This near-Mint example has attractive greenish yellow-gold surfaces with reflective fields on both sides. A few scattered abrasions are evident, and they are strictly consistent with the grade. (#8083)

Mint State 1803/2 BD-1 Half Eagle

3499   1803/2 MS62 PCGS. B. 1-C, Breen-6441, Bass-3080, BD-1, R.4. Three of the four known 1803 half eagles varieties are considered scarce, and one is rare. All four varieties are 1803/2 overdates, from two different obverse dies. The obverse die used for the present example, and also used for varieties BD-2 and BD-3, has the former 2 right of center beneath the 3. The other obverse die, that of BD-4, has the 2 just left of center beneath the 3. This example, a pleasing Mint State piece, has brilliant and frosty yellow-gold luster with excellent eye appeal. Although finer examples of this date and variety certainly exist, this piece should satisfy most collectors who have an interest. (#8084)

Lustrous 1803/2 BD-4 Half Eagle MS62

3500   **1803/2 MS62 PCGS.** Breen-6441, BD-4, R.4. The presence of the intact right foot on the Y of LIBERTY aids in prompt attribution of the variety. The overdate is bold, and the prominent die crack through the bottom of the date continues upward faintly on either side, ending beneath stars 1 and 13. On the reverse, an arrowhead ends under the right foot of the N in UNITED. The reverse shows a die crack from the eagle's right (facing) wing, through the top olive leaf, through the E in AMERICA, and to the rim. A second crack proceeds from the left shield point through the left wing and to the rim left of the first S. This lustrous piece shows light adjustment marks through the central obverse—scarcely visible without a loupe—and a few scattered, undistracting abrasions. Certified in an early PCGS green-label holder. (#8084)

Mint State 1803/2 BD-4 Half Eagle

3501   **1803/2 MS62 PCGS.** Breen-6441, BD-4, R.4. Struck from the second overdate die, immediately recognized by the die crack through the base of the date, apparently a constant feature of all known examples. To date, none have been found with a perfect obverse die. This variety was once thought to be a major rarity, although today it is recognized as one of the more common die marriages for the year. Three of the four 1803/2 half eagle varieties are considered R.4 and one other is listed as R.5. This example is fully lustrous with rich orange-gold color with a hint of green. A few tiny surface marks prevent a higher grade, but this is a delightful example for the grade. (#8084)

Important Gem 1803/2 Half Eagle
Late Dies BD-1 With Cud Die Break

3502   1803/2 MS65 PCGS. Breen-6441, BD-1, R.4. A fully lustrous Gem that ranks among the finest 1803/2 half eagles. The strike is exacting save for the eagle's left (facing) claw, which is opposite the comparatively high relief cap. The light canary-gold surfaces lack identifying abrasions, and a slender diagonal roller mark (as made) on the left half of the shield provides the only suitable pedigree marker. It is unlikely that *any* 1803/2 half eagle of similar quality will appear at auction for some time, let alone an example of BD-1 with a cud die break.

All 1803 half eagles are overdates. Two obverse dies were used, and both show prominent remnants of an underdigit 2. BD-1 shares its obverse die with two other varieties, so it is identified by its reverse. An arrowhead is centered beneath the N in UNITED, rather than beneath the right upright of the N, as is the case for BD-2 to BD-4. Most if not all examples of BD-1 exhibit a die crack through TED. Later, slender die cracks emerge along the left shield border and the left curve of the O in OF. The present piece is from the final die state, noted for a cud over the UN in UNITED. A brief survey of Heritage's Permanent Auction Archives failed to locate another example of BD-1 with this cud, and the variety is probably very rare as such. Harry W. Bass, Jr. was likely the first to note this die state; a polished example appears as lot 307 in the Bass IV auction. Bass was blessed with the resources to collect early gold not only by die marriage, but by die state, and his fastidious notes are an invaluable resource for researchers. Encapsulated in a green label PCGS holder. Population: 2 in 65, 2 finer (10/06). *From The Essex Palm Collection.* (#8084)

Bold 1804 Small 8 Half Eagle MS62

3503   1804 Small 8 MS62 PCGS. Breen-6443, BD-1, High R.4. The Small 4 obverse, which comes with two different reverses. BD-1 is identified by a long, straight die line from the left shield tip to the eagle's beak. BD-1 was struck earlier than BD-2, since the vertical die crack through the 0 in the date is light on BD-1 and heavy on BD-2. Unlike the earlier die state Bass specimen, the present piece exhibits a relatively large cud over the T in UNITED. The strike is crisp, since only the left (facing) claw is soft. Minor adjustment marks cross the highpoints of the lower shield, as made. A smooth and slightly subdued canary-gold example without identifiable pedigree markers aside from a short, hair-thin scratch between the cap and obverse star 5. (#8085)

Glowing 1804 'Small 8' Half Eagle MS62

3504   1804 Small 8 MS62 PCGS. Breen-6443, BD-1, High R.4. Dannreuther-Bass (2006) describes this variety as follows: "Key Identifiers: Normal 8 (former Small 8, but it is the correct 8 punch) with blunt top to 1 (missing flag like 1800; Normal/Large 8 coins have perfect 1) and small 4; reverse with a graver line from the left (viewer's) shield point through B in ribbon, through S12 to upper beak, TE apart (keys, as obverse used for next)." This is a fine example with glowing luster, lovely green-gold coloration, and minimally disturbed surfaces for the grade. Most of the grade-limiting elements are wispy pinscratches and hairlines in the fields, but a shallow curving mark is noted on the upper obverse that extends from near 12 o'clock on the rim to the top edge of Liberty's hair tresses. A few faint adjustment marks are located on the reverse. (#8085)

Scarce Near-Mint 1805 Half Eagle, BD-2

3506   1805 AU58 NGC. Close Date, Breen-6445, BD-2, R.4. Substantial bright luster bathes this pleasing near-Mint Heraldic Eagle five dollar piece. The strike is intricate save for the junction of the shield and left (facing) wing. Surprisingly smooth, since no marks are evident to the unaided eye, and the use of a loupe only reveals an inconspicuous pinscratch above Liberty's forehead curl. The eye appeal is equal to many examples certified as Mint State, although a hint of friction on the cap and drapery prevents an Uncirculated assessment. Slender radial die cracks through the 0 in the date and obverse star 13 converge southwest of Liberty's ear. Denticles are clashed above LIBERTY, and letters from LIBERTY are clashed over the CA in AMERICA.

From The Jones Beach Collection. (#8088)

1804 Small 8 Over Large 8 Five MS62

3505   1804 Small 8 Over Large 8 MS62 PCGS. Breen-6442, BD-6, R.5. The Small 8 Over Large 8 feature is dramatic enough to merit a separate *Guide Book* listing. BD-5 and BD-6 share the same obverse, but are readily distinguished by their reverses. BD-6 has lengthy die lines from two olive leaves, and two vertical die cracks through the shield borders bisect the reverse. This well struck representative has rich honey-gold toning, and the fields are mildly proof-like. Two thin vertical marks on the upper reverse and left obverse field combine to limit the grade. Population: 8 in 62, 6 finer (11/06). (#8086)

Attractive 1805 Half Eagle, MS63

3507   1805 MS63 PCGS. Close Date, Breen-6445, BD-2, R.4. The variety is attributed by the top serif of the 1 in the date that touches the curl, the tip of the 5 that overlies the bust, the crack through the 0 in the date to the cap, the lowest arrowhead nearly aligned under the right upright of the N in UNITED, the leaf point free of the I in AMERICA, and a spine from the top of the left (facing) shield point.

This lovely example displays bright yellow-gold lustrous surfaces that show a slight greenish tint. Sharp definition is apparent on the well centered design features, including virtually full detail on the eagle's neck and breast feathers. The grade is defined by a few inconsequential handling marks, and some light adjustment marks are located on the upper obverse. (#8088)

1806 Round 6, 7x6 Stars Half Eagle AU58

3508   1806 Round Top 6, 7x6 Stars AU58 NGC. Breen-6448, BD-6, R.2. Six die marriages of 1806 half eagles are known to exist, but BD-6 is distinctly different in two ways. The 6 in the date culminates with a knob instead of a point, and the obverse stars are arranged seven left and six right instead of the usual eight by five arrangement. Consequently, the right side stars appear crowded when compared with their left side counterparts, since the right periphery is also shared with the legend LIBERTY. This minimally circulated representative, one of several examples included in the Platinum Night sessions, retains considerable luster and bits of reddish patina about the devices. The major devices exhibit average or better sharpness for the issue. (#8089)

Round Top 6 1806 7x6 Stars
Half Eagle MS61

3509   1806 Round Top 6, 7x6 Stars MS61 NGC. Ex: Childs. Breen-6448, BD-6, R.2. The only Round Top or Knobbed 6 variety for the date, and also the sole variety with the obverse stars arranged 7x6. A relatively unabraded piece whose sole defect (a minor rim mark at 8 o'clock) is virtually obscured by the NGC holder. The strike is slightly soft on the left shield border and left obverse stars, but the devices are generally bold. A lovely piece with a desirable pedigree, suitable for a high quality type collection of early gold. The Childs collection is best known for its Sultan of Muscat 1804 dollar, certified MS68 by PCGS.

Ex: Walter H. Childs Collection (Bowers and Merena, 8/99), lot 695.

From The Jones Beach Collection. (#8089)

Pleasing 1806 Round Top
7x6 Stars Half Eagle, MS62

3510   1806 Round Top 6, 7x6 Stars MS62 PCGS. Breen-6448, BD-6, R.2. Half eagles of 1806 have either pointed or knobbed 6's. The former coins have 8 x 5 obverse stars (estimated mintage of 9,676 pieces), and the latter display a 7 x 6 star arrangement (estimated 44,741 pieces). This MS62 Round Top five dollar exhibits rich peach-gold color, and the most potent luster in the areas around the design elements. Generally well struck, though there is a touch of softness in the upper left shield area and adjacent feathers. The reverse is rotated a few degrees. This variety is usually seen with heavy adjustment marks; these are lacking on this specimen, however. (#8089)

1806 Round Top 6
7x6 Stars Half Eagle MS62

3511　**1806 Round Top 6, 7x6 Stars MS62 PCGS.** Breen-6448, BD-6, R.2. This distinctive die pairing is also one of the more plentiful varieties of these popular and desirable Capped Bust Right half eagles. As such, the 1806 knobbed 6 (as it is also known) makes a logical choice for type collectors and the fact that several Mint State representatives are being offered creates a prime buying opportunity. A subtle reddish patina blankets both sides of this satiny, well struck example. There are no appreciable abrasions and adjustment marks are similarly absent. A small area of discoloration between ME in AMERICA is likely from an impurity in the planchet. (#8089)

Choice Mint State 1806 BD-6 Half Eagle

3512　**1806 Round Top 6, 7x6 Stars MS64 NGC.** B. 5-E, Breen-6448, BD-6, R.2. There is no doubt that the 1806 Round Top 6 or Knobbed 6 variety is the single most common Draped Bust half eagle. Perhaps as many as 1,000 examples still exist today, although John Dannreuther estimated the total population between 600 and 900 coins. Although it is commonly named for the distinctive shape of the final digit in the date, seen nowhere else in the series, this obverse is also unusual for its star layout, with seven stars to the left and six to the right. Only this 1806 variety along with the 1807 half eagles have this particular pattern.

This example is a remarkable near-Gem with fully brilliant yellow-gold surfaces tending toward green. Both sides of this piece have frosty luster and the surfaces are nearly mark-free. Slight design weakness is evident in the eagle's wing just left of the shield and among the vertical stripes, but all other details are boldly defined. The reverse has a fine crack through the N and arrowheads, with another visible through stars 10 and 13 to the right edge of the eagle's neck.

From The Freedom Collection. (#8089)

Lustrous 1807 Capped Bust Left Half Eagle MS61

3513 **1807 Bust Left MS61 PCGS.** Breen-6453, BD-8, R.2. This die pairing is easily distinguished by the lone 1807 Capped Bust Left obverse being combined with a reverse where the arrow feathers are directly over the left and right sides of the top of the 5. The other marriage has the 5 positioned lower and further to the right. Despite the fact that production was shared with the Capped Bust Right type in this transitional year, 51,605 pieces were struck of John Reich's new design and survivors of the BD-8 are among the most plentiful in the series. Although bright, frosty, and very well struck, this yellow-gold example is kept within the lower reaches of Mint State by a number of scuffy abrasions in the fields. Those located in the field to the left of the portrait are most noticeable. (#8101)

Pleasing Mint State 1807 Capped Bust Left Five Dollar

3514 **1807 Bust Left MS62 PCGS.** Breen-6453, BD-8, R.2. The new obverse with the head facing left and a floppy cap; on the reverse, the tip of the feather points to the tip of the flag of 5, and the O of OF is centered over the N of UNUM. Bright lustrous surfaces display yellow-gold patina that is imbued with subtle traces of light green. The design features are well impressed, with sharp definition visible in Liberty's hair and the eagle's plumage. A few minor scuffs help to define the grade. Overall, a very nice looking coin for the grade designation. (#8101)

Outstanding Gem 1807
Bust Left Half Eagle

3515   1807 Bust Left MS65 PCGS. Breen-6453, BD-8, R.2. There is something about early gold, and early half eagles in particular, that whets the collector's appetite. Many pieces are excessively rare in absolute terms, and those that are not are blessed with tremendous demand from type collectors as a result. This is an outstanding example of a coin destined for a high quality type collection. It is of interest as the first date of the new Capped Bust to Left type, designed by John Reich, and complete with his trademark notch on star 13. But more importantly, although not rare in absolute terms, the 1807 Bust Left half eagle is tremendously rare as nice as the present piece. The major grading services have combined to grade only eight such coins in MS65, with a scant four known finer. Of these, this is only the third that Heritage has had the opportunity to offer in such a lofty grade, the last of which was in our 2004 June Long Beach Signature Auction.

This apricot to olive-gold Gem is sharply struck, as is common for coins of this date. The abundant luster is of the satin variety, and the few surface abrasions are in line with the high grade. Interestingly, there are faint adjustment marks (as struck) visible on the reverse at 11:30 and 1:30. These are unusual in a coin minted this late and serve mostly as a numismatically intriguing pedigree marker, as they have only a minimal effect on this piece's obvious eye appeal. Population: 5 in 65, 2 finer (11/06). (#8101)

Attractive 1808 Half Eagle MS61

3516   1808 MS61 NGC. Wide 5D, Breen-6457, BD-4, High R.3. The 1 in the date is slightly higher than the adjacent 8. On the reverse the D in the denomination is far from the 5, almost equidistant between it and the last A in AMERICA. While not especially difficult within the context of the Capped Bust Left series, the 1808 is legitimately scarce in better Mint State grades. This more affordable alternative is very well defined on all of the design elements and is void of adjustment marks. The yellow-gold surfaces, while moderately abraded in the fields, are notable for their outstanding luster. (#8102)

1808 Close 5D Half Eagle MS62

3517   1808 MS62 PCGS. Close 5D, Breen-6456, BD-3, R.4. The Normal Date varieties from this year were produced from a single obverse die while the reverse is not only distinguished by the distance between 5 and D in the denomination, but also by the alignment of I of PLURIBUS on the scroll in relation to E of STATES above. The BD-3 variety (offered here) has the I centered below the upright of E, while BD-4 (or Wide 5D) has the I centered below the space between T and E. This reddish-tinged example is sharply struck with minimally abraded surfaces. Only the presence of a faint hairline scratch in the left reverse field seems to preclude a Select or finer rating. (#8102)

Rare Near-Gem 1808/7 Half Eagle, Close Date

3518   1808/7 MS64 PCGS. Close Date, Breen-6455, BD-2, High R.4. Two 1808/7 die marriages are known, both of which share a common reverse die with a closely spaced denomination. Although the obverses for BD-1 and BD-2 are very similar, they can be distinguished by the alignment of denticles below the date. BD-2 also has an open curl above the 0 in the date. According to *Early U.S. Gold Coin Varieties, A Study of Die States, 1795-1834*, (2006), quoting from the Bass Notebook: "OBV: 8 over 7. Wide date. Numerals evenly spaced. Numerals widely spaced. 1 is centered over two denticles. Top of 1 higher than that of 8. Cross bar of 7 within top opening of 8. Serif of 7 atop 8 at left. No foot of 7 visible beneath bottom loop of 8. Large round die center punch lump within a depressed circle on jaw in front of hair curl. Die has been lapped, resulting in bottommost curl being weak and broken at right side. This interior is hollow. REV: That of 1807 (Y). Clash visible within shield. Clashed and lapped."

This scarce near-Gem example has a crisp strike, and the field areas on each side are virtually untouched. One of the lower points of obverse star 13 is malformed (as made—the so-called "secret signature" of designer John Reich). Lovely satin luster illuminates the clean fields and well formed devices. The essentially yellow-gold coloration is imbued with lime-green undertones. Although this piece is remarkably well preserved, thin horizontal marks are noted across Liberty's neck and cheek. The reverse seems virtually blemish-free.

From an estimated mintage of 7,500 to 12,500 (for the BD-2 variety, from a total for the date of 55,578+ pieces), this specimen is one of just four coins certified at the MS64 grade tier, by NGC and PCGS combined, and only a single Gem has been encapsulated, by PCGS (11/06). (#8103)

Choice Mint State 1809/8 BD-1 Half Eagle

3519   1809/8 MS64 PCGS. Breen-6458, BD-1, R.3. Historical numismatic literature describes this obverse as an 1809/8 overdate. While there is obviously "something" under the digit 9, current students of the series have begun to question the status of this as an overdate, a recut date, or simply a defective die. Whatever is eventually decided really doesn't matter as this is the only known die variety for the date. It is considered a relatively common variety, and pieces are routinely available in the lowest Mint State grades. However, Choice or Gem Mint State pieces remain important rarities. This is a fully lustrous and sharply struck representative with satiny yellow-gold luster and sharp design features. Population: 21 in 64, 3 finer (12/06). (#8104)

MS62 1810 Large Date, Large 5 Half Eagle

3520   1810 Large Date, Large 5 MS62 NGC. Breen-6459, BD-4, R.2. Four different die marriages were struck dated 1810. These include all combinations of Large and Small Date, and Large and Small 5. The two Small 5 varieties are formidable rarities. Fortunately for date collectors, the two Large 5 varieties are comparatively available, although all pre-1834 gold coins are rare. The reported mintage of 100,000 pieces is nearly meaningless, since nearly all of this mintage was exported overseas as bullion, then melted. The present sharply struck example escaped this fate, and displays ample satin luster. There are no noticeable marks, and a small spot on the inner points of star 10 provides a pedigree reference.
From The Jones Beach Collection. (#8108)

Uncirculated 1811 Small 5 Half Eagle

3521   1811 Small 5 MS62 NGC. Breen-6464, B. 1-B, Miller-116, High R.3. One of just two die marriages used in striking 1811 half eagles despite a comparatively sizeable mintage of over 99,000 pieces. The Small 5 variety, which can also be distinguished by a re-punched C in AMERICA, is seen with only slightly greater frequency than its Tall 5 counterpart. This sharply struck representative inter-mixes a touch of reddish patina with the yellow-gold alloy. Scuffy abrasions on the obverse seen in both the fields and the portrait are the primary grade-limiting factor. Census: 40 in 62, 47 finer (11/06). (#8109)

Impressive Near-Gem 1811 Half Eagle, Small 5

3522   1811 Small 5 MS64 PCGS. Breen-6464, BD-2, R.3. The 1811 has a mintage of 98,851 pieces. This number was apparently almost equally divided between two *Guide Book* varieties (if surviving population figures are an accurate gauge): the Small 5 and the Large 5. These refer to the size of the punch used to enter the denomination. The Small 5 can also be identified by the C in AMERICA, which is clearly repunched at the base. Regardless of variety, the 1811 is very scarce today, although collectible in Mint State for those with sufficient resources, and the patience to wait for a piece of suitable quality to arrive at auction. All gold coins from this era are elusive. The United States used a ratio of gold to silver that undervalued gold, relative to European trade. As a result, Capped Bust gold coins did not circulate, and were instead exported to Europe, where they were melted and recoined. Although most unimpaired survivors are in XF or better grades, pieces with full mint luster throughout the fields are rarely encountered. The present near-Gem has full luster, and the fields show only occasional faint grazes from long-ago contact with other coins. The striking details are impressive, although slightly imperfect centering has left a few of the upper left obverse denticles off of the planchet. The overall eye appeal of the piece is exceptional, and this example would serve as a highlight of any advanced early gold collection. Population: 16 in 64, 0 finer (11/06). (#8109)

Handsome 1812 Half Eagle MS61

3523   1812 MS61 PCGS. Wide 5D, Breen-6466, BD-1, R.3. 1812 was the final year for Reich's Draped Bust motif on gold coinage, although the portrait style continued on silver coins as late as 1838. The recorded mintage for 1812 was 58,087 pieces, but most of these pieces were exported as bullion, and promptly melted following their overseas arrival. This fortunate survivor has blushes of peach toning, and displays ample glimmering luster. The obverse is well struck, and the reverse shows only moderate incompleteness on the shield, and on the scroll near 10:30. All Wide 5D half eagles exhibit a curious broad, curved die scratch across the horizontal shield lines, probably because of a slip of a tool that no doubt caused considerable exasperation and embarrassment on the part of the engraver. (#8112)

1812 Wide 5D Half Eagle MS63

3524   1812 MS63 NGC. Wide 5D, Breen-6466, BD-1, R.3. As might be suspected by the presence of several Mint State pieces in the sale, the 1812 is one of the more plentiful dates within the Capped Bust Left series of half eagles. As such, it is a logical candidate to represent this popular early type. The example offered here is notable for outstanding satiny brilliance and largely undisturbed fields. There is a hint of striking softness on the highpoints of the eagle and a series of faint adjustment marks can be detected on Liberty's cheek. Census: 32 in 63, 36 finer (11/06). (#8112)

Gem Mint State 1812 BD-1
Wide 5D Half Eagle

3525   1812 MS65 NGC. Wide 5D, B. 1-B, Breen-6466, BD-1, R.3. John Reich's Capped Bust design made its appearance on the half eagles in 1807 and continued through 1812. This design type is also known as the Bust Left design, for the direction that Liberty faces. John Dannreuther discusses the problem of nomenclature in his reference on the early gold varieties: "This type was the result of hiring John Reich as an assistant engraver. His new design with a floppy cap has traditionally been called Capped Bust, but the previous type by Robert Scot also has a capped bust. This design also has drapery, so the nomenclature has bee confusing, to say the least. The definitive difference is the direction Miss Liberty is facing. The previous type has her facing right, while this type has her facing left. So, some have referred to the first series (1795-1807) as Capped Bust Right and this series (1807-1834) as Capped Bust Left. To avoid confusion, we have labeled the two designs as Draped Bust and Capped Bust—no matter what they are called, they are the pinnacles of early American gold coinage."

This example is from the Harry W. Bass, Jr. Collection, and before that from the Nathan M. Kaufman Collection. Dallas businessman Harry Bass spent over three decades collecting coins, primarily gold coins, beginning with the purchase of an 1876 gold dollar that he acquired in 1966. Over the next 32 years, he acquired over 7,000 U.S. gold pieces, along with patterns, remarkable currency, and other desiderata. Kaufman was from Marquette, Michigan, and collected in the earliest part of the 20th century with his last acquisition taking place in 1927. After that time, the collection was displayed in the board room of a Marquette bank.

The Wide Denomination variety is one of two different die marriages coined with the 1812 obverse, and it is somewhat more plentiful than the Close 5D variety. This example is sharply struck with frosty luster and fully brilliant yellow-gold color. A thin scratch in the upper right reverse field, between the eagle's head and the scroll, provides an instant pedigree identifier.
Ex: N.M. Kaufman Collection (RARCOA, 8/1978), lot 802; Harry W. Bass, Jr. (Bowers and Merena, 5/2000), lot 312; Bowers and Merena (7/2002), lot 780.
From The Freedom Collection. (#8112)

Sharply Struck 1813 Half Eagle
MS62 PCGS

3526   1813 MS62 PCGS. Breen-6467, BD-1, R.2. This is the new design, with no drapery on Liberty's bust. The variety is attributed by the reverse, where the first S in STATES is over the right side of the E in the ribbon, the D of the denomination leans left in relation to the 5, the middle arrow points to the left side of the foot of the upright of R in AMERICA, and the lowest arrow points to the center of I in AMERICA.

Apricot-gold surfaces display hints of light green, and the most potent luster is in the areas around, and the recesses of, the design elements. A powerful strike is visible throughout, manifested in sharp definition in Liberty's hair, in the star centers, and on the eagle's feathers. Close examination reveals a few grade-defining marks, none of which are worthy of individual mention. (#8116)

Impressive 1813 Half Eagle MS62

3527   1813 MS62 PCGS. BD-1, R.2. The Capped Head Left Half Eagle is one of the most challenging gold types. Although struck for a generation, between 1813 and 1834, survivors are rare for most dates. This is because the American gold-silver ratio undervalued gold. Thus, mintages were limited, and mostly intended for export overseas, where the pieces were valued solely for their bullion content. This was reclaimed when the pieces were melted. Unlike many dates of the type, the 1813 is available in Mint State, but type demand is formidable, especially for examples as pleasing as the present coin. Lustrous and boldly struck with clean fields and only a couple of unimportant obverse marks. Certified in an older generation green label holder. (#8116)

Pretty 1813 Half Eagle, BD-1

3528   1813 MS62 PCGS. Breen-6467, BD-1, R.2. Widespread melting had a dramatic impact on the survival rate of this series, and among Capped Bust, Small Bust half eagles, the BD-1 variety of the 1813 is the only one Dannreuther and Bass term "readily available." This early gold issue is hardly the average type coin, though, and any available example, no matter how worn or impaired, is sought-after. The present Mint State example is sure to find a home in a worthy collection. The amber-gold surfaces have frosty luster and a blush of peach-rose. Areas of deeper orange-bronze are noted at the lower reverse periphery. The strike is above-average, and only a small number of light to moderate abrasions preclude a Select or better grade. Appealing and important.
From The Hill Country Collection. (#8116)

Impressive Select Mint State 1813 Half Eagle

3529   1813 MS63 PCGS. Breen-6467, BD-2, R.4. The scarcer of the two 1813 die marriages. This was the first year of the new Capped Head To Left, Large Diameter half eagle type, which would continue through 1828. For the type, only the 1813 is considered common in Mint State, with approximately 350 pieces certified in Uncirculated grades through the combined efforts of NGC and PCGS. This example is well struck on most of the design elements, except for the eagle's leg feathers, arrow feathers, and talons, and displays substantial luster for the issue. Minor imperfections in the alloy mixture have left faint red-orange patches near the left obverse periphery; but careful preservation has left the piece with a minimal number of trivial surface blemishes for the assigned grade level. Population: 52 in 63, 56 finer (11/06). (#8116)

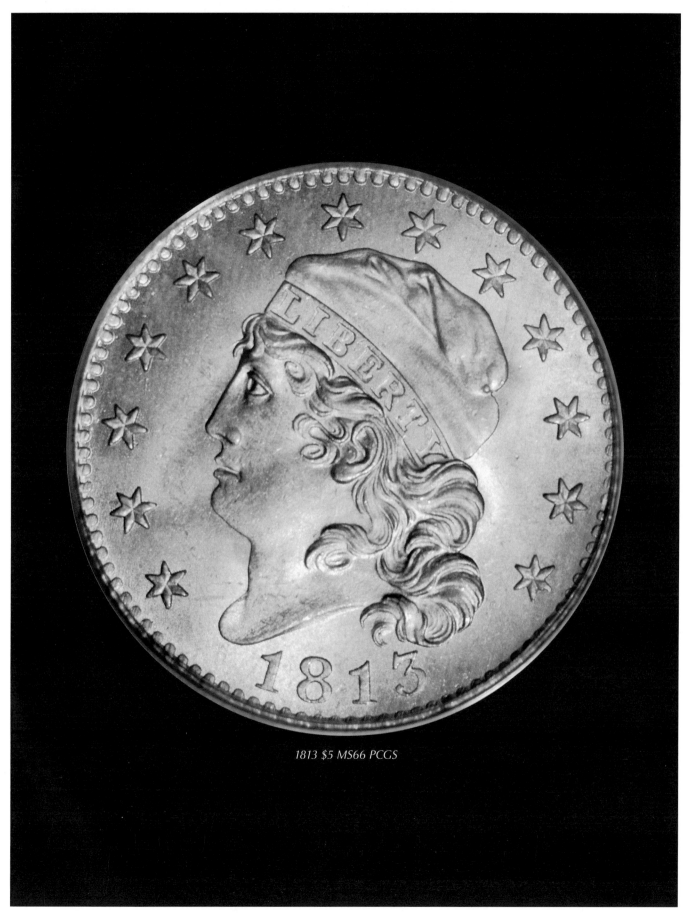

1813 $5 MS66 PCGS

1813 $5 MS66 PCGS

Finest Known 1813 Half Eagle From The Garrett Collection, MS66 PCGS

3530   1813 MS66 PCGS. BD-2, R.4. In 1813 the half eagle was the only U.S. gold denomination being produced. Gold eagles had not been made since 1804 (they were resumed in 1838), and quarter eagle production was interrupted from 1808 until 1821. The Capped Head half eagles, produced from 1813 to 1834, were made during a period when widespread melting took place. Most of the coins never circulated, and they frequently went straight from the Mint into the hands of bullion dealers. Some forty thousand pieces of "recent mintage" were destroyed in a single Paris melt in 1831, according to Walter Breen.

The reason for this mass melting of U.S. gold coinage was simple: the Coinage Act of 1792 had established a 15:1 ratio between silver and gold, but by 1813 the ratio in Europe was 16:1 or more. All circulating U.S. gold coins were now worth more than their face value in silver, as bullion dealers swiftly realized. Fifteen ounces of silver would buy one ounce of gold in the United States, but that same ounce of gold would bring sixteen ounces of silver in Paris or London.

The 1813 half eagle is important to collectors for several reasons: First, it is the initial year in the Capped Head series. Second, it is by far the most affordable and obtainable date in the series, a series which few would dispute is the most difficult in all of U.S. numismatics. Of the seventeen major issues (excluding varieties) in this series, only the 1813, 1814/3, 1818, 1820, 1823, and 1826 are offered for sale with any degree of regularity. This means that the "average" Capped Head half eagle issue is a rarity. According to Jeff Garrett and Ron Guth, writing in *The Encyclopedia of U.S. Gold Coins 1795-1933* (2006): "The Capped Head to Left, Large Diameter type, issued from 1813 to 1829, contains some of the greatest rarities in American numismatics—coins such as the 1815 half eagle, the 1822 (three known), the 1825/4 (two known), and the 1829 Large Date. Most of the dates in this series have low mintages, usually below 50,000 coins. The 1820 half eagle has the highest mintage (263,806 coins), and the 1815 has the lowest (635 coins). Some dates, such as the 1819, have a reasonably high mintage (51,723 coins) but remain extremely rare today."

Approximately 600 examples of the 1813 half eagle have been encapsulated through the combined efforts of NGC and PCGS; but that figure probably reflects numerous resubmissions over the past twenty years. It is possible, however, that as many as 500 pieces still exist, and perhaps a few more. Many of the known examples have survived in Mint State, including quite a few near-Gems. However, the population drops off dramatically at the Gem level, and any 1813 half eagle in MS65 or better condition is an extreme rarity.

Two varieties of the 1813 half eagle are known, and these are identified as Bass Dannreuther-1 (BD-1) and Bass Dannreuther-2 (BD-2). BD-1 is also sometimes known as Miller-119, based on the reference by Robert W. Miller, Sr.; and has the D in the denomination leaning sharply to the left. A second variety, BD-2, has both the 5 and the D in the denomination upright, with the left serifs of D showing evidence of recutting. The BD-1 variety is about twice as common as the BD-2. As both varieties are from the same obverse die, determination of the emission sequence is as simple as comparing die states of the obverse on each of the two varieties. No die cracks have been observed on the BD-1 variety. A thin die crack from the border left of the date to the bust is seen on this example of BD-2, as on a couple of the other known specimens. The appearance of this die crack clearly tells us that the BD-2 variety was struck second.

This Premium Gem is possibly the finest-known example of the date, and almost certainly of the variety. It is sharply struck with all details on both sides exceptionally well detailed. Although the centering is not perfect, the borders on both sides are complete. All of the hair curls on the obverse are well defined, and each of the stars has complete center lines. The reverse detail is similarly sharp, with the sole exception of the eagle's claws which are a bit bluntly defined. The surfaces are frosty and fully lustrous with lovely yellow-gold color. Light orange toning is visible on the reverse, and near the obverse periphery, and adds to the overall aesthetic appeal of the piece.

This was the first year of issue for the Capped Head design type, modified from the Draped Bust type introduced by John Reich in 1807. According to Walter Breen, writing in 1966: "Obverse shows head of Liberty, without drapery, on a much larger scale than previous profiles. The cap is much more close-fitting. Curls somewhat resemble those on the 1807-12 design but are not identical. Rounded truncation of the bust shows. This head continued to be used until 1829, in which year modifications of design appeared in the new hub introduced by William Kneass. Stars are no longer divided 7+6 but rather form a continuous line around and above head. Dates are larger than on previous years except for 1810 and 1812. The eagle is also different in minor details, most noticeably at wing feathers nearest his body; shield is smaller, arrows much wider and more spread apart, motto letters taller, claws much larger and the individual ones more spread apart, leaves longer and wider, etc. Border denticulation on both sides is much more coarse than formerly."

From the famous Garrett Collection that was originally formed by T. Harrison Garrett in the latter 19th century and bequeathed to his son, Robert. As Robert Garrett was more of an art aficionado, and his brother John Work Garrett was more the numismatist, the two traded collections. After John Work Garrett passed away, his widow willed the collection to the Johns Hopkins University in Baltimore. Eventually the collection was sold in a series of auctions, the first in 1976 and the others from 1979 to 1981. Population: 1 in 66, 0 finer (11/06).

Ex: Garrett Collection; Johns Hopkins University (Bowers and Ruddy, 11/79), lot 458; Gold Rush Collection (Heritage, 1/05), lot 30045. (#8116)

1814/3 Capped Head Half Eagle MS62

3531   **1814/3 MS62 PCGS.** B. 1-A, Miller-121, R.4. While not one of the elite rarities in the ultra-challenging Capped Head Left series of half eagles, this issue of just 15,454 pieces is nevertheless a very difficult coin in Uncirculated grades and enjoys popularity as the most obtainable of four overdates (one a great rarity) within the brief series. This satiny greenish-gold representative is well defined save for a few of Liberty's highest curls and the eagle's claws. Die clashing, a hallmark of the issue, is visible on both sides. Census: 12 in 62, 14 finer (11/06). (#8117)

Lovely Select 1814/3 BD-1 Half Eagle

3532   **1814/3 MS63 NGC.** B. 1-A, Breen-6468, Bass-3127, BD-1, High R.4. All known examples of the 1814 half eagle are from this single die pair that features an overdated obverse die. The reverse die was used for three different varieties spanning three years. Its first use was in 1813 and its final use was for the extremely rare 1815 half eagle. This 1814/3 half eagle is an important and scarce issue, although it is not the rarity once believed. Current estimates suggest between 80 and 100 pieces exist, including several Mint State examples. This example has a clear overdate feature with all of the other design features sharp. The surfaces have frosty luster and brilliant yellow-gold color. A few tiny abrasions on each side are consistent with the grade. The obverse has a faint crack at the base of the date and the reverse has a light crack through MER and another at the base of the denomination.
From The Freedom Collection. (#8117)

Select Prooflike Mint State 1820 BD-3 Half Eagle

3533   1820 Square Base 2 MS63 PCGS. Large Letters. Breen-6476, BD-3, R.5. The Capped Head design half eagle was coined from 1813 to 1834, and the highest annual mintage occurred in 1820 with a total production of 263,806 coins. Not surprisingly, the largest number of individual die varieties have been identified from this year. In his new reference on the varieties of early gold coinage, John Dannreuther recorded nine different varieties representing three major types. All Square Base 2 coins have Large Letters on the reverse, while Curved Base 2 pieces have either Large Letters or Small Letters on the reverse.

The reverse die of this example was not used with any other varieties, thus the tiny rust lumps left of the digit 5 are a diagnostic identifier. The BD-3 variety is the most readily available of the year, as pointed out by Dannreuther: "This is the only scarce variety of 1820 half eagle with a few more than 50 examples as the surviving population. The other eight varieties existing for this year are either rare, very rare, or exceedingly rare."

This lovely Mint State piece has brilliant greenish-gold color with prooflike fields and a hint of cameo contrast. The surfaces have the usual light abrasions and tiny hairlines that are expected at the grade level. This piece is similar quality to the Bass-ANA example, and is one of the finest known of this die marriage. (#8125)

Lovely 1820 BD-3 Half Eagle, MS63

3534   1820 Square Base 2 MS63 PCGS. Large Letters. Breen-6476, BD-3, R.5. This is a stunning Mint State example with satiny honey-gold surfaces and nice cameo contrast. The surfaces are not prooflike, but they do display excellent reflectivity in the fields. This example is sharply struck with nearly full design details. Aside from the small die chips left of the digit 5, there is no evidence of any die imperfections such as clash marks or cracks. This is the only appearance of the reverse die, thus it is logical to assume that a later, terminal die state exists, but so far none have been discovered. Population: 17 in 63, 14 finer (12/06). (#8125)

Bass 1820 Curl Base 2, Small Letters Half Eagle MS61

3535   1820 Curl 2, Small Letters MS61 PCGS. Breen-6478, BD-8, High R.7. Ex: Harry W. Bass, Jr. The half eagles of 1820 are divided into nine varieties depending on the style of the 2's base and the size of the reverse lettering. This piece is among the Curl Base 2, Small Letters variants, which include the BD-6 and BD-8. While the BD-6 has the lowest tight hair curl mostly over the 2 in the date, the BD-8 has that curl mostly over the 0. The bottom of the 2 points to the right side of a dentil. The reverse letters are small, and the lowest arrow points to the bottom of the C in AMERICA. The tip of an arrow feather is over the right side of 5 in the denomination.

This coin is different from that pictured in the *Bass Museum Sylloge* (and duplicated in the Dannreuther-Bass *Early U.S. Gold Coin Varieties*), because *it is the second example of this R.7+ (four to six pieces known) variety that Harry Bass owned.* Nonetheless, most of his comments in those volumes are pertinent. Especially notable are the following, which we summarize: Star 7 points in front of a cap angle; star 8 points at a cap angle. A minute die center punch is in front of the ear. Vertical rust lumps show in the field at the tip of the front lock, and in front of L. On the reverse there are distinctive raised horizontal line fragments within openings of the shield's lower section.

Although not noted in those references, the eagle's left (facing) wing shows a small spine of metal at the tip, and there is a dotlike die rust spot nearby at the border. This delightful piece shows good luster and attractive green-gold color with a bit of light field chatter on each side. Light die rust shows microscopically on the portrait, visible under a glass. A pleasing and historic Mint State coin of the utmost rarity, from one of the most difficult U.S. coin series, and pedigreed to the fabled Bass Collection. It doesn't get any better than this. (#8126)

Mint State 1823 Half Eagle, High R.5

3536   1823 MS61 NGC. B. 1-A, Breen-6481, Bass-3145, High R.5. Only a single die marriage is known for this date. The Capped Bust Left half eagle series likely has suffered higher attrition rates than any other U.S. coin series, due to the widespread and extensive meltings that occurred in the 1830s when these pieces' intrinsic value exceeded their face value. A note in the Bass *Museum Sylloge* under Bass-3143 (1821 half eagle) reads, "This issue begins the trend of very rare half eagles, which continues throughout the decade. Interestingly, several die varieties exist for extremely low populations, suggesting that the recorded mintages are realistic, despite very low survival rates." The same reverse die was used for half eagle issues from 1820 through 1824, and again in 1826, featuring a letter punch that had a triangular notch at the base of the upright of the T's in UNITED STATES OF AMERICA. The 1823, while still quite rare, is one of the most available issues from the 1820s. This piece shows a few light, undistracting adjustment marks through the central obverse, and a bit of the usually seen strike weakness on the eagle's claws and the leftmost olive leaves; otherwise, the striking details are complete. The surfaces overall are bright yellow-gold with a semi-reflective finish evident in the fields. A few small marks are scattered over each side, but the only one that bears mention is located in the reverse field between the eagle's right (facing) wing and the ME of AMERICA. Population: 5 in 61, 16 finer (11/06). (#8131)

Desirable Mint State 1823 Half Eagle

3537   1823 MS61 PCGS. Breen-6481, BD-1, High R.4. Only one variety was produced for the year, with 80 to 100 coins surviving today, according to the estimate of John Dannreuther. Other students of the series feel that a smaller number of coins may actually exist. This design type was produced from 1813 to 1834, and the most easily obtainable dates are 1813, 1818, 1820, and 1823. This piece is a sharply struck Mint State example with brilliant green-gold surfaces and satiny luster. A few minor abrasions, especially on Liberty's face, prevent a higher grade. Population: 5 in 61, 16 finer (12/06). (#8131)

Sharp 1825/1 Five Dollar, MS61

3538   1825/1 MS61 NGC. Ex: Reed. Breen-6483, BD-1, High R.5. David Akers, in his *United States Gold Coins: An Analysis of Auction Records,* places the number of extant 1825/1 half eagles at between 35 and 40 pieces, and are mostly in XF or AU grades. A total of 20 coins have, to date, been graded by NGC and PCGS.

This MS61 specimen displays a blend of yellow-gold and apricot-gold color with decent luster. A powerful strike manifests itself in sharp definition on the design elements, that are well centered on the planchet. The surfaces exhibit prooflike tendencies, especially when the piece is rotated under a light source. Some wispy hairlines in the reverse fields are mentioned for accuracy. Census: 4 in 61, 3 finer (11/06). (#8133)

Condition Census 1830 Large 5D Half Eagle MS64

3539   1830 MS64 PCGS. Large 5D, Breen-6491, BD-1, R.6. The Large 5D variant, at R.6 (13-30 pieces extant) is a bit rarer than the Small 5D (Breen-6492, BD-2), ranked as a high R.5 (31-45 pieces known). Suffice it to say that both varieties are incredibly elusive. The Mint produced the PR67 1828 Smithsonian Institution half eagle specimen using a "close collar"—essentially a die for the edge of the coin. Partway through 1829, the Mint expanded the use of the close collar to all coins and reduced the diameter of the half eagle to 22.5 mm.

The new invention, a heavy steel block with a hole the same diameter as the finished coin, had grooves that provided the edge reeding. The close collar provided coins with a "mathematical equality to their diameters," according to Mint Director Samuel Moore. According to the Breen *Complete Encyclopedia:*

> *"Earlier coins had been struck in an open collar, which is a flat metal plate with a hole somewhat larger than the diameter of a finished coin, serving to position a planchet atop the lower die for striking, but not to restrain its expansion. Edge lettering, reeding, or other ornamentation were imparted in a separate operation by the Castaing machine (parallel bars) before the blanks went to press; the open collar did not affect them. Because centering was not always exact, dies were normally of much greater diameter than the finished coins, and included long radial-line dentilated borders so that any unstamped areas might not tempt the ungodly to clip or shave off precious metal before spending the coins."*

By 1834 the gold content of old-tenor coins exceeded their intrinsic value; most were melted. Like gold coins from earlier decades, the 1829-34 half eagles are exceedingly rare. The present example has a small date, with the 1 taller than the remaining digits. Recutting is most evident at the top of the 0, and stars 8-9 and 12 show re-engraving. The 5 in the denomination is small but the D is large, with a small period. The U's in E PLURIBUS UNUM are visibly taller than the other letters of the motto. A small die crack joins the tops of NITE.

Many past auction catalogs and catalogers have failed to distinguish between the Small and Large 5D variants. Curiously, PCGS lists 18 examples of the Large 5D variety but none of the Small 5D in its online *Population Report.* There are two pieces graded MS64, with two finer (10/06). The NGC *Census Report* shows 18 examples of the Small 5D, versus only five examples of the Large 5D, the finest graded MS65 ★.

This lovely coin has especially strong mint luster and notably well-defined devices and appears to have been well cared for since Andrew Jackson was president. The rich orange-gold surfaces deepen considerably around the margins, with especially deep red patina around the reverse. There are a few tiny field marks on the obverse that account for the less-than-Gem grade, but none are worthy of mention or consideration. (#8152)

Choice Mint State 1834 Capped Head Half Eagle

3540   **1834 Capped Head, Crosslet 4 MS64 NGC.** B. I-3, Breen-6500, Bass-3166, BD-2, R.5. The final "old tenor" design type was coined from 1829 through early 1834, with few surviving examples. Although Mint records suggest that over 700,000 of these coins were produced from 14 different die combinations, the total estimated population today is less than 400 coins with a cumulative total of 284 to 370 pieces according to John Dannreuther, including 80 to 100 examples of this date alone. Some numismatists will be surprised to learn that the 1834 With Motto half eagle is the most plentiful date of this design type.

The actual mintage figures have no relationship to the rarity of these pieces today. Newly minted half eagles during the 1820s and early 1830s were immediately worth a premium, and were hoarded and melted in this country, or exported. In the *Harry W. Bass, Jr. Sylloge,* Dave Bowers relates: "Beginning by the autumn of 1821, virtually all half eagles were exported, a situation that remained in effect through the summer of 1834. Even the Philadelphia Mint would pay a premium over face value for contemporary half eagles! Thus, striking was specifically to the order of bullion depositors who realized that a freshly-minted $5 would be worth more than face value, and that on the international market it could be exchanged for its bullion value. At foreign destinations such as London and Paris, American half eagles would be melted and converted into national coinage—to facilitate exchange, accounting, and trade. Although hundreds of thousands of Type IV [1813-1829, Type V was issued from 1829-1834] half eagles were struck, only a few survived exportation and subsequent melting. Thus, the general mintage figures in no way relate to the availability of such pieces today."

The Coinage Act dated June 28, 1834 reduced the authorized weight of half eagles to 129 grains of standard 899.2 fine gold. The previous standard had been 135 grains of 916.7 fine gold. These standards yielded a gold value of $5.33 for the old standard pieces. The new standard, accompanied by the new Classic Head design, took effect on August 1, 1834. It is fascinating to learn that the most prolific private gold manufacturer in the country at that time, Christian Bechtler, adapted the new standard to his coinage as well. In fact, one of the Bechtler five dollar gold pieces actually includes the August 1, 1834 date as part of the design. The Bechtler piece actually contains 116.67 grains of pure gold instead of 116 grains, about three cents worth of extra gold at the time.

Although the 1979 photograph makes plate matching difficult, we are quite certain that this example piece is from the famous Garrett Collection, sold on behalf of Johns Hopkins University by Bowers and Ruddy in a series of four sales from 1979 to 1981. A tiny rim bruise directly above star 7 appears to match the photo of the Garrett coin. Despite a few insignificant abrasions, this is a lovely example with bright greenish yellow-gold color and full prooflike surfaces. The obverse has a die crack joining stars 9 through 13. John Dannreuther described to different die cracks for his die state b, but the other crack from the rim to cap at the right side of star 6 is not visible on this piece. The reverse has a crack through MERICA and the denomination.

Apparently Ex: John W. Haseltine (69th Sale, 6/1883); Garrett Collection; Johns Hopkins University (Bowers and Ruddy, 11/1979), lot 477.

From The Freedom Collection. (#8161)

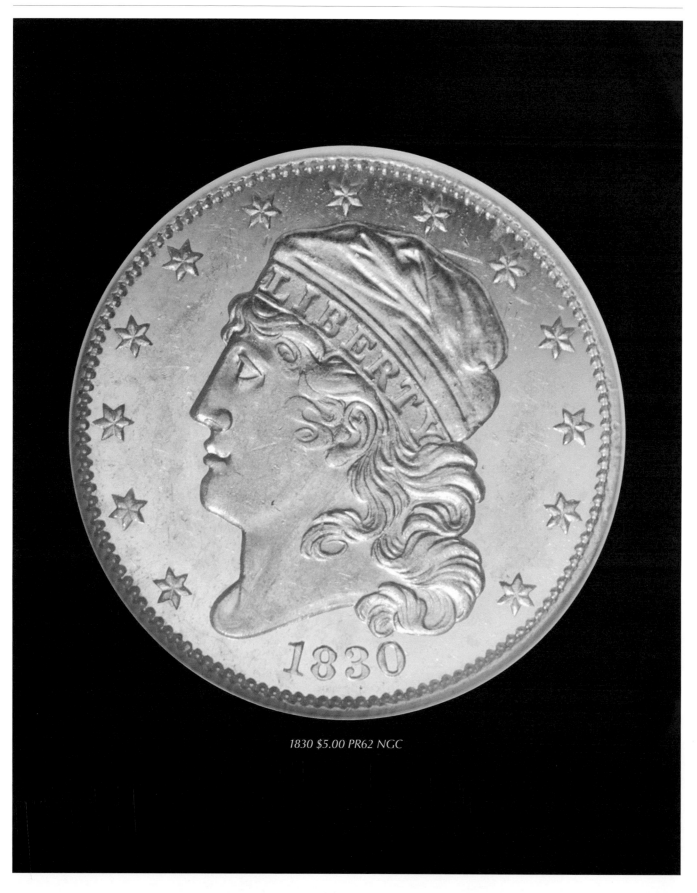

1830 $5.00 PR62 NGC

PROOF LIBERTY HALF EAGLES

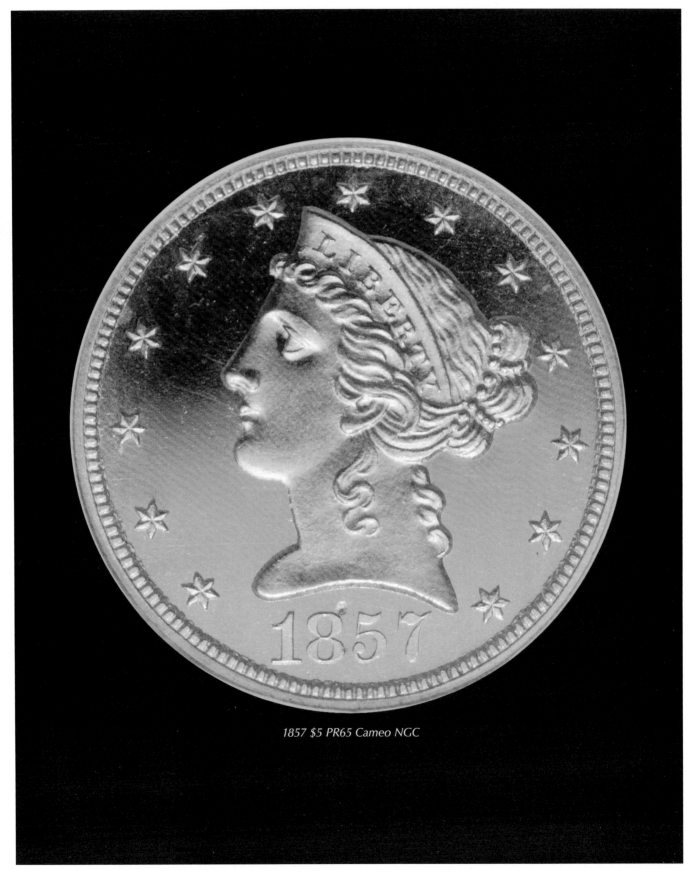

1857 $5 PR65 Cameo NGC

1857 $5 PR65 Cameo NGC

Extraordinarily Rare 1857 Gem Cameo Proof
Half Eagle Unique in Collectors' Hands

3565   1857 PR65 Cameo NGC. Just two proof half eagles of 1857 are known to exist, and Harry Bass once owned both pieces! One of these was sold in November 2000 in Part IV of the Harry Bass auctions by Bowers and Merena, and the other example was retained by the Bass Foundation for display at the American Numismatic Association in Colorado Springs, CO. It is illustrated in *The Harry W. Bass, Jr. Museum Sylloge* by Q. David Bowers. The Smithsonian Institution does not have a proof example of this date.

While we certainly don't know which example is finer, this remarkable Gem Cameo Proof should be considered the landmark specimen that it is. There is no rumor of a third example.

When Jeff Garrett and Ron Guth prepared their 2006 *Encyclopedia of U.S. Gold Coins,* it appears that they did not consult the Bass Museum Sylloge, for they wrote: "Only two examples are currently known for the date. The most recent appearance of a specimen was in the 2000 sale of the Harry W. Bass, Jr. Collection. The coin was graded by PCGS as PF-64, and realized $78,200. Bass had purchased the coin in a 1978 Stack's sale. The other surviving example was in the collection of Louis Eliasberg. His collection crossed the auction block in 1982. Just one example is now on the population rolls of NGC, ANACS, and PCGS. The current NGC PF-65 is probably the Harry W. Bass, Jr. coin." As wonderful as the Garrett-Guth reference is (and we use their information constantly), the commentary regarding this date would suggest that both pieces are available to collectors, and this is clearly not the case. This coin is unique in collectors hands, and the present opportunity to acquire this issue in proof format must be carefully considered. As Dave Bowers wrote in the Bass catalog: "The opportunity is incredible, and whether or not you ever own a proof 1857 may well be dependent upon whether you purchase [this] Bass Collection coin. Here is a numismatic beacon, an American landmark, a coin for the generations."

This example has frosty yellow-gold design motifs with deeply mirrored olive-gold fields on both sides. A shallow planchet depression above the right side of the digit 8 is the only imperfection that we see, and this planchet flaw was present when the coin was struck. This tiny characteristic provides positive identification of the pedigree of this specimen.

The following roster provides the currently known pedigree of both specimens of this amazing rarity.

Proof. Ten Eyck Collection (B. Max Mehl, 5/1922), lot 223; John H. Clapp Collection (1942); Louis E. Eliasberg, Sr. Collection (Bowers and Ruddy, 10/1982), lot 482; Superior (Auction '85, 7/1985), lot 948; Harry W. Bass, Jr. Core Collection.
PR65 Cameo NGC. The piece offered here. Stack's (4/1978), lot 866; Stanley Kesselman; Harry W. Bass, Jr. Collection (Bowers and Merena, 11/2000), lot 462. (#88447)

Exceptional PR64 Deep Cameo
1864 Five Dollar

3566   1864 PR64 Deep Cameo PCGS. The 1864 proof five has a mintage of 50 pieces. While this is a tiny output, the survivorship is higher than other dates from the era and as such it is considered the most "common" date as a proof in the No Motto series. In spite of the multiple resubmissions that have artificially inflated the population data, with more than 30 pieces certified today, probably only 12-15 individual proofs are actually still extant. This number includes three pieces that are held in institutional collections—two in the Smithsonian and one in the ANS. Because of the artificially high numbers seen at the services, it is also difficult to discern just how many coins are known in this and better grades. That being said, at least several (whatever number that is) are known finer than this piece.

Proofs of this date all show a common diagnostic: a die scratch (or is it a short die break?) below Liberty's ear. According to Breen (1988) this diagnostic was observed on the Auction '80 and the Clapp/Eliasberg coins.

This is a lovely example and one that also is numismatically interesting. A streak of slight granularity is seen in the lower obverse field that extends to the rim and then runs between the denticles and stars 10-13. Otherwise, the surfaces display the deeply reflective fields one would expect from a proof gold coin. Also, given the limited mintage of this date, the devices are heavily frosted and present a strong gold-on-black contrast on both obverse and reverse. A few small, stray marks keep the coin from a full Gem classification, but this is a singularly impressive No Motto proof five that will undoubtedly be included in a high grade proof type set. (#98454)

Extremely Scarce 1865
Half Eagle PR64 Deep Cameo

3567   1865 PR64 Deep Cameo PCGS. Production of 1865 proof half eagles dropped from an average of more than 50 pieces over the preceding six years to a miniscule 25 pieces in 1865. Of that already tiny number, only 12-14 specimens are believed to survive. Over the past decade, the most noteworthy example to appear on the market was the PCGS PR66 from the Harry W. Bass Collection which was sold in November, 2000 for $66,700. The demand for proofs from this year is further enhanced by the difficulty of 1865 business strikes, of which a mere 1,270 pieces were produced.

The desirable proof 1865 five dollar offered here is a dramatically-contrasted specimen whose fields offer illimitable depth of mirrored reflectivity that provide stark contrast against the needle sharp devices. Both sides are coated in a beautiful orange-gold patina that in no way undermines the strong reflective qualities. Close inspection of the obverse reveals a long, paper-thin facial blemish that curves down from Liberty's nose to her jawline. A couple of glancing disturbances are found on the reverse. One is noted in the field above the eagle's head and the second is an almost imperceptible pinscratch that begins beneath the first T in STATES and continues to the juncture of the eagle's left (facing) wing. A significant find for the specialist in early proof gold. Population: 3 in 64 Deep Cameo, 0 finer (12/06). (#98455)

PR65 Cameo 1879 Half Eagle
Only One Finer

3568   1879 PR65 Cameo PCGS. Only 30 examples were coined of the 1879 proof half eagle in two deliveries, the first in January of 20 pieces, the second in November of 10 pieces. The two deliveries are apparently indistinguishable. While this mintage is slightly higher than for the 1878 and 1877 issues, each of which saw 20 pieces minted, the Garrett-Guth gold *Encyclopedia* says regarding the 1879 half eagle, "There have actually been fewer examples (of the 1879) offered at public auction than either of those two issues. The Smithsonian collection contains an example, but the coin is lightly hairlined, and is one of the lesser-grade coins in their collection of Proof Liberty half eagles. There are probably fewer than 10 survivors in all grades, and the 1879 half eagle is a great rarity in Proof." One cannot help but wonder if the issuance of the four dollar stella proof gold coins in 1879 could have influenced the number of survivors of the similarly dated half eagle. Could collectors owning specimens of both the four and five dollar coins have chosen to keep the unusual stellas and part with the more "common" half eagles by putting proofs into circulation when hard times came a-knocking?

The Breen proof *Encyclopedia* notes die polishing is present at ERT, the eye and ear, and on the scroll at WE ST, while his *Complete Encyclopedia* also notes a small "dent on top point of seventh star, rather than the notch seen there 1864-78."

The surfaces of this piece are unfathomably deep in their reflectivity. By way of contrast, the devices on each side are heavily frosted and show a cameo effect that most would perceive as borderline Deep Cameo. Bright yellow-gold color and nearly flawless.

Only once before within the past dozen-plus years have we handled a proof example of this issue. Its rarity is borne out by the current population data. While NGC shows five proof 1879s certified, PCGS adds only three more. The present PR65 Cameo specimen is the finest certified at PCGS, and exceeded only by a single PR66 Cameo piece at NGC (10/06). (#88474)

Vivid 1884 Gem Proof Half Eagle
Ultra Cameo

3569   1884 PR65 Ultra Cameo NGC. The 1884 half eagle is considered one of the underrated issues in proof format due to its sheer rarity. Breen, in both his *Encyclopedia of United States Proof Coins* and *Complete Encyclopedia of U.S. and Colonial Coins* considered the number of pieces extant to be fewer than a dozen, calling it "extremely rare" and "one of the great sleepers" in the former tome. Garrett and Guth, in their *Encyclopedia of U.S. Gold Coins 1795-1933* state that fewer than 20 are known in all grades. The major grading services have combined to certify a total of sixteen pieces, likely including resubmissions, and at least three are in museums and permanently off the market.

Perhaps more importantly to the collector interested in acquiring such a piece, proof 1884 half eagles are rarely offered at auction at all in any grade. The last record of one having sold in public auction belongs to the Bass specimen, a Proof 65 piece, in November 2000. A Proof 64 Deep Cameo piece appeared in our 2003 Spring ANA auction, but did not sell.

Breen's diagnostics of proof 1884 half eagles include a die scratch slanting up from the right base of the T in LIBERTY and a rust pit on the lower end of the upright of 1, between and above the serifs. Both are clearly present on this coin. Of course, if there were any doubt about this coin's proof status, they would be allayed by the sheer visual effect this coin possesses. It is a vivid black on bright gold in appearance, with deeply mirrored orange peel surfaces giving way to smoothly frosted devices. The strike is complete, and only a few slight marks in the fields appear to determine the Proof 65 grade. For pedigree purposes, this piece appears to have a tiny planchet flake below Liberty's hair bun. No coins of this date have yet received a higher grade with deep contrast, and only a single Proof 66 piece exceeds this Gem's numerical grade. For the serious gold collector, this is an opportunity that may not soon be repeated. (#98479)

Magnificent 1888 Half Eagle
Proof 66 Ultra Cameo NGC

3570   1888 PR66 Ultra Cameo NGC. The Philadelphia Mint produced 18,296 business strike and 95 proof half eagles dated 1888. Proof survivors are understandably rare. Walter Breen's *Complete Encyclopedia of U.S. and Colonial Coins* estimates that 30 to 35 proof examples survive, but they are more easily obtainable than Mint State representatives. Breen's proof coin *Encyclopedia* comments: "Date very low and to left, slanting up slightly to r.; polish around eye, mouth, and ear; left base of 1 over left edge. Rev. Polish within stripes, unlike the last few years. Rarer than lower denominations, much rarer than its mintage figure suggests ..." All of these diagnostics are observable on the present specimen, which also displays snappy, gold-on-black contrast between the deep, glassy fields and the devices, with heavy, wintry frost. The fields are remarkably smooth and problem-free. Accuracy compels mention of a tiny obverse scrape between star two and Liberty's neck, visible only under a glass. The highpoint details of the coronet and the eagle are sharp and well defined. This is an opportunity to acquire a Premium Gem example of this difficult and virtually unimprovable issue. NGC's *Census Report* shows this to be the sole specimen graded in Proof 66 Ultra Cameo, with just one coin, a Proof 67 Ultra Cameo, graded higher (11/06).
Ex: Byron Reed Collection (Spink/Christie's, 10/96), lot 147, which realized $18,700. (#98483)

PR64 Cameo 1889 Half Eagle

3571   1889 PR64 Cameo PCGS. Half eagle production at the Philadelphia Mint fell to just 7,565 pieces in 1889, 45 of those being proofs, and neither the San Francisco nor Carson City mints delivered any coins. Survivors are rarer than most of the other proof Liberty half eagles from the 1880s, as well as all of those from the 1890s. This well-contrasted specimen shows a touch of haziness over both sides that minimizes the effect of wispy hairlines. A tiny area of planchet roughness below star 12 should easily pedigree this piece in the future. While NGC has certified six coins similarly and three higher, this is tied with one other PCGS example graded PR64 Cameo, with none finer (11/06).
From The RNB Collection. (#88484)

PR66 1898 Ultra Cameo Half Eagle

3572   1898 PR66 Ultra Cameo NGC. This PR66 Ultra Cameo half eagle is a charming and delectable counterpart to several other 1898 proof gold coins from a single consignor in the present sale, also including the quarter eagle, eagle, and double eagle, graded from PR66 Ultra Cameo to PR68 Ultra Cameo by NGC. The proof mintage of this issue, numbering 75 pieces, is a considerable decrease from other years of this era. For example, the 1896 proof emission numbers 103 coins, and 1899 saw 99 proof specimens produced. However, high grade pieces appear at auction with some regularity. The Garrett-Guth *Gold Encyclopedia* notes that the survival rate is quite high compared to most proof gold coins, but that perhaps 30 to 40 coins exist, still a tiny number when compared to the masses of collectors who desire proof gold.

A search through Heritage's own auction records, stretching back more than a dozen years, shows the present PR66 Ultra Cameo example to be the second finest of this issue that we have ever had the privilege to offer, second only to a PR68 Ultra Cameo piece from our August 2006 Signature Auction. The present specimen is one of seven pieces graded PR66 Ultra or Deep Cameo at NGC and PCGS combined, with five coins finer (11/06). The black-on-gold contrast so desired in proof gold of the late 19th century is quite prominent on this lovely coin. There are no notable blemishes on this high grade example, and the fields have the distinctive orange-peel texture seen on proof gold in the latter part of the 19th century. In fact, the reverse of this piece is at the far end of the orange-peel spectrum and almost has a crinkly texture. (#98493)

Superb Gem Proof 1898 Half Eagle
PR67 Deep Cameo

3573   1898 PR67 Deep Cameo PCGS. Both sides of this amazing piece have rich orange-gold color. This piece is fully struck with every individual design detail boldly rendered. The deeply mirrored fields and highly lustrous devices combine to present incredible "black and gold" contrast. A tiny break in the frost is evident on Liberty's chin, and a miniscule v-shaped lint mark just inside star 3 are the only readily apparent pedigree markers on the obverse of this piece. The reverse has an extremely small black dot on the upper edge of the left facing wing, vertically below the G in GOD. This will also serve the pedigree researcher.

Unlike other denominations, the proof half eagles are generally found in lower grades. This piece is the finest 1898 proof half eagle certified by PCGS, and the only example to receive this grade (11/06). NGC claims a PR67 ★ Ultra Cameo and a single PR68 Ultra Cameo example, the only two coins to be given a better grade assessment.

The half eagles boasted a much smaller mintage than the similarly dated proof quarter eagle. Just 75 of these pieces were coined as proofs, and about 25 or 30 still exist today. The mintage difference obviously represents an increased demand for quarter eagles with their smaller face value. In his *Proof Encyclopedia,* Walter Breen pointed to the lower mintage and the small number of auction appearances, and called this date "a sleeping golden elephant."(#98493)

Beautiful, Bold PR66 1903 Half Eagle

3574   1903 PR66 NGC. In 1902 the Mint switched from the former proof format that featured brilliantly mirrored fields and deeply frosted cameo devices to an all-brilliant format. The 1903 half eagle accordingly is not found with the deep cameo contrast of the issues from 1901 and before. The 1903 is one of the most common Liberty Head proof half eagles, but any proof issue as a type is still quite rare. The surfaces on each side are a gorgeous canary-yellow, brilliantly mirrored, as expected, and uncommonly free of distractions, even for a well-preserved proof. Bold and beautiful! Census: 2 in 66, 1 finer (11/06). (#8498)

Gem Cameo Proof 1903 Liberty Half Eagle

3575   1903 PR65 Cameo NGC. Early 20th century proof gold coins (and also silver coins) are seldom found with any degree of cameo contrast. For example, NGC and PCGS have combined to certify only 26 Cameo pieces out of a total population of 116 coins for the date. The mintage for the year was 154 proof half eagles, and it is universally believed that about 75 or 80 of these coins still exist today. This Gem Cameo proof is an exquisite representative of the date, with light yellow-gold color, deeply mirrored fields, and fully detailed devices that retain light mint frost. Census: 8 in 65 Cameo, 9 finer (12/06). (#88498)

Stunning Gem Proof 1905 Half Eagle

3576   1905 PR65 NGC. In the world of proof Liberty gold, where 108 pieces is a comparatively large mintage, the 1905 half eagle does not manage to distinguish itself that way. A Gem example, on the other hand, is a completely different kettle of fish, since the tiny mintages of the issues and the effects of time have combined for a tiny available supply of high-grade examples. On this deeply reflective lemon-gold specimen, even the most intricate details are bold. The reverse has a degree of cameo contrast, though the comparative brilliance of the obverse precludes such a designation. Only trivial flaws, none of them distracting, affect the mirrors and the devices. A stunning piece that would be a wonderful addition to a 20th century proof type set. Census: 3 in 65, 0 finer (11/06). (#8500)

Near-Gem Cameo Proof 1905 Liberty Half Eagle

3577   1905 PR64 Cameo PCGS. This brilliant yellow-gold proof has a hint of green color on both sides. The fields are deeply mirrored and the devices are slightly reflective with just enough luster remaining to be assigned the Cameo descriptor. A few tiny abrasions prevent calling this coin a Gem.

Just seven pieces have been designated as Cameo proofs out of 38 total examples certified by PCGS. None have been given the Deep Cameo designation. Among the Cameo proofs graded by PCGS, only one higher grade coin has been certified (11/06). This piece appears to be typical of most proof 1905 half eagles, with Garrett and Guth reported an average grade of 64.4 among coins they have tracked in various auctions. (#88500)

INDIAN HALF EAGLES

Delightful Gem 1908 Indian Head Half Eagle

3578   1908 MS65 NGC. The Yale-educated Bela Lyon Pratt, a student of Augustus Saint-Gaudens, among others, was responsible for the novel incused-design Indian Head quarter eagles and half eagles that debuted in 1908 as part of President Theodore Roosevelt's push to implement coinage redesign. A generous mintage of 578,000 pieces, plus a collecting public that saved numerous examples as first-year issues, is responsible for most of the high grade survivors. A couple of hundred Gem pieces exist at both NGC and PCGS combined, and those examples are generally lovely and well produced. The present specimen is no exception, with lustrous orange-gold, abrasion-free surfaces. A well-struck and delightful representative of its type. (#8510)

Handsome Gem 1908 Indian Five

3579   1908 MS65 PCGS. Rich peach-gold patina confirms the originality of this luminous first-year Gem. The strike is intricate, since the eagle's shoulder and the headdress feathers exhibit essentially full definition. Luster sweeps across the fields and devices when the piece is rotated beneath a light. Only trivial marks are encountered, and the eye appeal is excellent. While the eagle and double eagle denominations have both Motto and No Motto varieties for 1908, all quarter eagles and half eagles with this date bear the Motto, since it was part of the initial design. Encapsulated in a green label holder. (#8510)

Scintillating Gem 1908 Half Eagle

3580   1908 MS65 NGC. One of several Gem or better examples of this first year Indian Head half eagle issue offered in tonight's Platinum session. In terms of availability in high grades, the 1908 is actually one of the more common issues in this series. Better grade Mint State representatives, however, are scarce and always in demand among both date and type collectors. This boldly struck Gem displays yellow-gold surfaces that are not only sparingly abraded, but also possess a uniform radiance that adds immensely to its considerable eye appeal. (#8510)

Superb Gem 1908-S Indian Half Eagle

3581   1908-S MS67 PCGS. This frosty Superb Gem is a gorgeous piece, an aesthetically desirable example with few peers, although NGC and PCGS each report a finer grade coin in their population data, examples that can be difficult to envision. This example has brilliant and frosty yellow-gold luster with sharp design details. The surfaces are pristine and nearly perfect. Although only 82,000 of these coins were minted, this date is considered a common date among the Indian half eagles. Jeff Garrett and Ron Guth had this to say: "The 1908-S is one of the most common dates in all grades despite the low mintage, and in Gem grades these are generally frosty and highly attractive. Many of the surviving Gem coins are likely from a hoard attributed to Virgil Brand."

This is the date often chosen by type collectors who only need a single example of the Bela Lyon Pratt incuse design. PCGS has only certified 13 Indian half eagles in MS67 or finer grades, and eight of those 13 coins are examples of this date. Three others are from the 1910-D issue, and one each are dated 1908 and 1909-S. Garrett and Guth further wrote: "If a single coin is desired from this series, this date and mint should be considered for the overall quality and availability." And if a single example of this date is desired, the present piece should be considered for its exceptional luster and superior strike. Population: 7 in 67, 1 finer (11/06). (#8512)

Gem Mint State 1909 Half Eagle

3582   1909 MS65 PCGS. Just 80 examples of this date have been certified in MS65 or MS66 grades, a seemingly small number but this is the second largest Gem population for the entire Indian Head half eagle series, tied with 1909-D and lagging behind the 1908 for honors as the most common issue. This highly lustrous honey-gold example has excellent eye appeal with frosty surfaces. It is sharply struck on every obverse and reverse design element. The surfaces are pristine without any significant marks on either side. Population: 74 in 65, 6 finer (11/06). (#8513)

Lovely Gem 1909-D
Indian Head Half Eagle

3583   1909-D MS65 NGC. The 1909-D Indian Head half eagle is the most common issue of the series, and more than 35,000 pieces have received Mint State grades from NGC and PCGS. Most of those coins fall between MS61 and MS64, however. At the Gem level, this issue suddenly becomes relatively scarce, with approximately 130 pieces so graded, although that number is also rather high compared to the average Indian half eagle issue.

The current offering is a lovely example with great luster and attractive, light peach-gold coloration. A heavy peripheral die break encircles each side, possibly an indication of die buckling, but all of the design elements are sharply delineated, including the mintmark. Surface marks are few in number and all of them are very trivial. *From The Freedom Collection.* (#8514)

Gem Mint State 1909-D Half Eagle

3584   1909-D MS65 PCGS. Although this date is clearly the most common of the Indian half eagle series, it is a condition rarity in Gem quality, as are all dates of this type. The mintage of nearly 3.5 million coins is well more than double the next closest issue, the 1911-S with 1.4 million coins minted. These two dates are the sole entries in the list of 1 million plus mintages for the entire series. This piece is sharply struck with rich honey-gold luster and frosty obverse and reverse surfaces. It is an exceptional example for the date and type, a coin for the connoisseur who appreciates the finest. Population: 74 in 65, 5 finer (12/06). (#8514)

Well Struck 1909-D Gem Five Dollar

3585   1909-D MS65 NGC. The 1909-D half eagle, with a mintage of 3,423,560 pieces, is the most common date of the Indian Head five dollar series. Several thousand examples have been certified by NGC and PCGS through the near-Gem grade level. After that, the population falls precipitously. Only 130 or so pieces have been given the MS65 designation, and fewer than 10 finer.

Apricot-gold patination is imbued with subtle traces of light green and red, and rests upon lustrous surfaces. A powerful strike makes itself known on the design elements, including crispness in the eagle's plumage. A few minor handling marks do not disturb. Census: 58 in 65, 2 finer (11/06). (#8514)

Key Date 1909-O Indian Head Half Eagle AU58 NGC

3586   1909-O AU58 NGC. The 1909-O is the most conditionally challenging Indian half eagle. Only 34,200 pieces were struck, easily the lowest mintage of them all, and this mintmarked date is therefore also the premier absolute rarity of its type, and the key date to the series. This issue is usually seen in VF to XF condition, and weakly struck. The AU58 coin presented here displays better-than-average definition, though the eagle's left shoulder is a tad soft; the mintmark, though not fully impressed, is quite clear. The honey-gold surfaces exhibit luster in the recessed areas, and the expected light abrasions are scattered over each side. There is little perceptible wear, except over the highest points of the design. (#8515)

Important Near-Mint 1909-O Half Eagle

3587   1909-O AU58 PCGS. The 1909-O has the lowest mintage of the Indian half eagle series, and would have been the unquestioned key date were it not for Franklin Roosevelt's 1933 gold recall, which transformed the 1929 from a common date into a coveted rarity. However, nearly all surviving 1929 half eagles remain in Mint State, while most 1909-O half eagles are circulated. In fact, the 1909-O is the rarest issue in Uncirculated grades. Because of the cost and rarity of the 1909-O in Mint State, most advanced collectors choose a near-Mint example. This sharp and generally lustrous piece has a bold strike and only faint friction on the cheekbone. Wispy reverse field marks are of little consequence for the AU58 grade. (#8515)

Coveted 1909-O Half Eagle AU58

3588   1909-O AU58 NGC. The 1909-O enjoys a trifecta of advantages over its Indian half eagle rivals. It not only is the only O-mint of any Indian head denomination, but it also boasts the lowest mintage of the type, and is perhaps its greatest condition rarity as well. The opportunity to choose from several AU or better examples of this coveted New Orleans is extremely unusual, even for a Heritage Platinum Night sale. This lightly circulated representative boasts a strong mintmark and appealing, rich golden color. A few minor marks are well situated in the field above the eagle's wing. (#8515)

1909-O Indian Half Eagle Rarity, MS62

3589   1909-O MS62 PCGS. The opportunity to bid on a Mint State 1909-O half eagle is a rarity, indeed, but the opportunity to bid on multiple Mint State '09-O's is virtually unheard of. Even AU grade pieces are only offered from time to time. This date, from an extremely limited mintage of just 34,200 coins, is clearly the rarest Indian half eagle, and it is also among the elite issues of 20th century U.S. gold coinage. Jeff Garrett and Ron Guth remarked: "This is one of the most sought-after issues in the series because of the low mintage and general rarity in any Mint State grade. It has long been considered a key date and is always in feverish demand." This piece is sharply detailed with a bold mintmark and excellent luster. The obverse is frosty orange-gold while the reverse is lighter yellow-gold with faint hairlines that limit the grade. (#8515)

Exceptionally Pleasing and Rare
MS63 1909-O Half Eagle

3590   1909-O MS63 PCGS. Variety One, the mintmark is sharply doubled. This variety usually is weakly impressed on the mintmark, but this coin shows stronger-than-normal definition, although in truth it is a bit weaker than other mintmarks in the series.

The 1909-O is one of the key absolute and condition rarities among U.S. gold. A client of Heritage once summed it up this way: "Go to a small coin show and you will never see an '09-O. Go to an ANA and you *might* see three or four, and most of those will only grade XF or maybe AU." Which explains why an Uncirculated coin such as this is being offered in a major auction with other important rarities.

When coinage production resumed in New Orleans in 1909, the half eagle was the only gold coin struck. Very few were minted (34,200 pieces) and only a tiny percentage survive today in all grades. It is estimated that no more than 300 to 350 coins are known today in all grades. Of those survivors, it is believed that a mere 10 to 15 Uncirculated examples have survived.

The Winter book on New Orleans gold (2006) gives a good summary of the striking characteristics of this issue: " ... typically found with a good quality of strike. Usually, the center of the obverse will not be fully defined, but the intricate feather details on the obverse and on the reverse are often full." With that being the standard expected for an '09-O, this piece is definitely above average. There is almost no striking weakness seen on either side of this magnificent coin. Additionally, the below average luster that is usually seen on this issue is pleasing on this coin and more akin to the softly frosted luster seen on Philadelphia coins. Attractive, although somewhat unusual tan-gold color covers each side and there are no obvious or detracting marks present, which is quite a surprise given the MS63 grade and the reduced relief design that seems to be a magnet for abrasions on most five dollar Indians.

The specialist will certainly recognize the offering of this coin for the rare opportunity that it truly is. Population: 7 in 63, 13 finer (11/06). (#8515)

Pretty 1909-S Five Dollar Gold Piece, MS64

3591   1909-S MS64 PCGS. Compared to the key-date 1909-O, this San Francisco issue has comparatively little glamour, and in circulated grades, pieces command little, if any, premium over the price of a type coin. Yet in Mint State grades, particularly Choice and better, specialists respect how elusive it is and actively seek appealing examples. The slightly coppery wheat-gold surfaces of this shining near-Gem have splashes of orange in the centers and vibrant luster. Strong detail is the rule, and though the lowest parts of the Indian's necklace are incomplete, the strike is solid elsewhere. A few light, scattered marks on each side define the technical grade, which the eye appeal surpasses. Population: 16 in 64, 4 finer (12/06). (#8516)

Scarce MS64 1910-S Five Dollar

3592   1910-S MS64 NGC. The 1910-S compares favorably to the 1909-S in terms of striking characteristics. This is a sharply impressed coin with lovely copper-gold patina. The texture is softly frosted, the mintmark is well defined, and the only mentionable abrasions are several tiny reeding marks in the reverse field behind the eagle's head.

The San Francisco Mint delivered 770,200 half eagles in 1910, a respectable total for the Indian series. Nonetheless, this issue is rare in all Mint State grades, and nearly all Uncirculated survivors are confined to the MS60-63 grade levels. No more than 8-10 coins are believed extant at or above the MS65 level. Census: 12 in 64, 2 finer (12/06). (#8519)

Choice Mint State 1911-D Half Eagle

3593   1911-D MS64 PCGS. An interesting comparison can be made between issues of the Indian half eagle series. The 1908-S date has a mintage of 82,000 coins, and it is considered one of the most common dates in the series. This 1911-D issue has a mintage of 72,500 coins, only 9,500 less than the '08-S, yet it is considered one of the great rarities of the series. Indeed, this rare date is difficult to find in any Mint State grade, being rarely offered. Unlike the key-date 1911-D quarter eagle with about 20 examples offered in this 2007 FUN auction, this is the only 1911-D half eagle presented for sale. PCGS has only certified 98 Mint State examples of this date in all grades from MS60 to MS65.

This piece is an impressive near-Gem, exhibiting lustrous honey-gold color and remarkable surfaces that are virtually mark-free. While the present piece just misses the Gem grade level, it should still be considered seriously by Set Registry collectors. Only two half eagle collectors can possibly own a finer example certified by PCGS, and just 12 more can own a piece of this quality, based on the current PCGS population data (11/06). Jeff Garrett and Ron Guth provided a handy summation: "The 1911-D Indian Head half Eagle is one of the great rarities of the series, and a very difficult coin to find in any Uncirculated grade, ... as such, this date currently ranks as the fifth most difficult coin in the series to obtain in Gem MS-65 or higher." Population: 12 in 64, 2 finer (11/06). (#8521)

Remarkable Gem 1912
Indian Head Half Eagle

3594   1912 MS65 NGC. This Gem Indian Head half eagle is unusual in several respects. It features shimmering mint frost, in contrast to the typical satiny surface texture of its type, and it also has beautiful reddish honey-golden color, unlike the more commonly seen greenish yellow-gold toning scheme of a 1912. The striking details are crisp throughout, and the bright surfaces are remarkably clean. If not for two or three scattered ticks, and a couple of insignificant marks beneath the E in LIBERTY, the piece would be essentially immaculate. Census: 34 in 65, 3 finer (11/06). (#8523)

Radiant Near-Gem 1913-S Half Eagle

3595   1913-S MS64 PCGS. The 1913-S follows the pattern of several S-mint Indian half eagles, being relatively available in the circulated and lower Mint State grades, but legitimately scarce once the Choice level is reached. Offered here is splendid near-Gem representative that displays excellent sharpness except for a shallow, shapeless mintmark that is nearly diagnostic for a 1913-S. The luster, however, is especially vibrant and the satin surfaces exude vivid orange-gold patina. Outstanding, virtually unsurpassable quality for this conditionally scarce half eagle. Population: 14 in 64, 2 finer (11/06). (#8526)

Sharply Struck 1915 Gem Five Dollar

3596   1915 MS65 PCGS. The 1915 half eagle boasts a mintage of 588,000 pieces, and is readily available in grades VF through Mint State 63. Near-Gems become more difficult to locate, and MS65 pieces are quite scarce. Fewer than 60 examples have been assigned the MS65 grade by PCGS and NGC, and none finer. The specimen in this lot exhibits vibrant luster and attractive yellow-gold and orange-gold color. The design features are powerfully struck, as is characteristic of the issue; the hair at the Indian's temple is strongly defined, as is the eagle's plumage. A few light handling marks prevent an even higher grade. Population: 29 in 65, 0 finer (11/06). (#8530)

Near-Gem 1915-S Indian Half Eagle

3597   1915-S MS64 NGC. This is an impressive near-Gem, and it is virtually the finest known for the date. PCGS has never graded a finer piece, and NGC has only graded one example at a higher level. Both sides have frosty light yellow luster with full mint brilliance. It is sharply struck; even the mintmark is unusually bold. This is one of the rarest Indian half eagle issues, and it ranks among the most important 20th century gold coins. Even at this near-Gem grade level, the '15-S is a rarity with only 18 similar quality pieces certified, nine by PCGS and nine by NGC (11/06). (#8531)

Near-Mint State 1929 Half Eagle

3598   1929 AU58 PCGS. The 1929 half eagle is the last issue of the long-running denomination that began in 1795. It is also a reminder of the historic (and economically catastrophic) Wall Street Crash of 1929 that ushered in the Great Depression of the 1930s. The peach-gold surfaces show the slight color change—hazel on the highpoint of the Indian's cheek and the highest wing feathers—that signal slight rub. The strike is generous and well executed. The few light contact marks are consistent with the grade. Certified in a green-label holder.

From The Twin Hollows Collection. (#8533)

Gorgeous 1908 Five Dollar, PR66

3599   1908 PR66 PCGS. Proofs of this first-year Indian Head half eagle display a dark, matte finish. Concerning this distinctive finish, gold specialists Jeff Garrett and Ron Guth (2006) write: "It is believed that a special grain powder was used on the planchets to give them this curious finish, which was not reflective, unlike the finish seen on prior Proof coins. The matte finish proved generally unpopular with collectors and the Philadelphia Mint changed the Proof finish in 1909."

Virtually pristine surfaces display a rich straw-gold color with subtle hints of light green, and a wisp or two of light orange on the reverse. A sharp, even strike emboldens the design elements, with no areas that reveal hints of softness. Impeccably preserved surfaces exhibit no marks that are worthy of note. We mention a hard-to-see linear mark immediately to the right of the eagle's head strictly for pedigree purposes. Nicer examples of this gorgeous matte proof are difficult to imagine. Population: 12 in 66, 1 finer (10/06). (#8539)

EARLY EAGLES

Gem Matte Proof 1911 Indian Half Eagle

3600   1911 PR65 PCGS. Today, matte proof gold coins are among the numismatic elite, delicacies that maintain a high level of desirability and demand. At the time they were issued, this was not the case. Only those collectors who desired to maintain their run of proof gold coinage sought out examples like this. A mustard-yellow Gem, this proof has traces of olive and hints of deep orange color, with faint gray toning lines on the obverse. Each side has a single tiny spot that may aid the pedigree researcher. The obverse has a tiny spot between stars 7 and 8, near the corner of the top feather in the headdress. The reverse has a similar spot immediately below the first A in AMERICA. Matching photos of matte proof gold coins for identical pedigree markers is one of the most challenging aspects of numismatic research. Population: 8 in 65, 7 finer (11/06). (#8542)

1795 BD-1 Gold Eagle, AU Sharpness

3601   1795 13 Leaves—Plugged—NCS. AU Details. Breen-6830, BD-1, R.3. This piece will fit the bill for an affordable 1795 Small Eagle ten dollar gold piece, for the collector who would like a piece representative of our Nation's early gold coinage. The young Philadelphia Mint coined half eagles in July 1795, and the first eagles just two months later. Looking past the rather obvious plug between I and B, and also visible at the bottom of the reverse, the balance of this piece has attractive medium yellow color with only slight evidence of cleaning. *From The Lanterman's Mill Collection.* (#8551)

AU55 Details 1795 13 Leaves Eagle

3602 **1795 13 Leaves—Polished, Tooled—ANACS. AU55 Details.** Breen-6830, Taraszka-1, BD-1, High R.3. The 13-leaf reverse has a leaf nearly touching the U of UNITED, and a leaf pierces the bottom of the last S in STATES. On the obverse the 5 in the date touches the bust. Star 11 is quite near to the Y. The fields on both sides are quite bright, overmuch, from the zesty polishing, and the obverse hair curls appear to have been lightly strengthened, although this detail is much less obvious. Little actual wear is clear, although a few light scrapes are seen under a lens. (#8551)

Important Near-Mint 1795
13 Leaves Eagle

3603   1795 13 Leaves AU58 PCGS. Breen-6830, BD-1, Taraszka-1, R.3. The largest denomination authorized by the Mint Act, the eagle was not only the flagship gold coin of the United States, but also a confirmation of the young nation's commitment to the decimal system, according to Breen in his *Encyclopedia.* Unfortunately for the eagle, that very commitment caused it to run into several problems. While the half eagle was close enough to other major currencies of the day to pass in international channels (a fact that ultimately doomed many later coinage proposals, including the Stellas of 1879 and 1880), the eagle was neither close enough to major currencies to pass well, nor was it large enough to be useful for bulk transactions, and so the denomination languished, with sporadic production in the early years of the Mint and a hiatus of more than 30 years after 1803.

This is a pleasing example of the most common die marriage of the 1795 eagle. Widely saved by the public at the time of issue, the 1795 is an immensely popular coin among type collectors, especially those who prefer first-year issues. This coin obviously circulated for a very limited amount of time, and the amount of wear is neither excessive nor distracting. Rather, the surfaces have acquired a pleasing blanket of original olive-gold patina with iridescent lemon-gold shadings around many of the devices. There is a lot of definition on both sides, as well as some traces of mint luster in the protected areas. A shallow planchet indention in the right obverse field is noted as a pedigree marker. For all 13 Leaves varieties, Population: 20 in 58, 45 finer (11/06). (#8551)

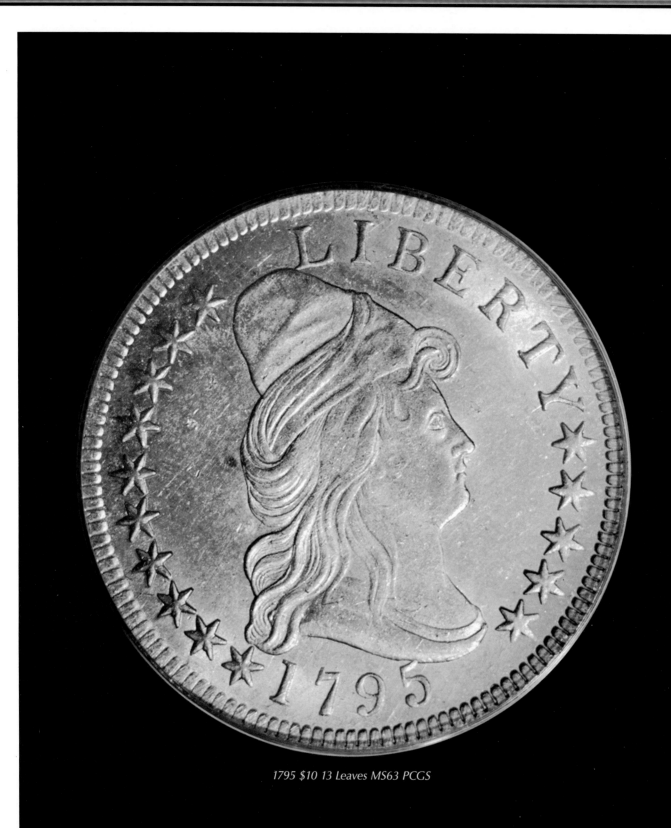

1795 $10 13 Leaves MS63 PCGS

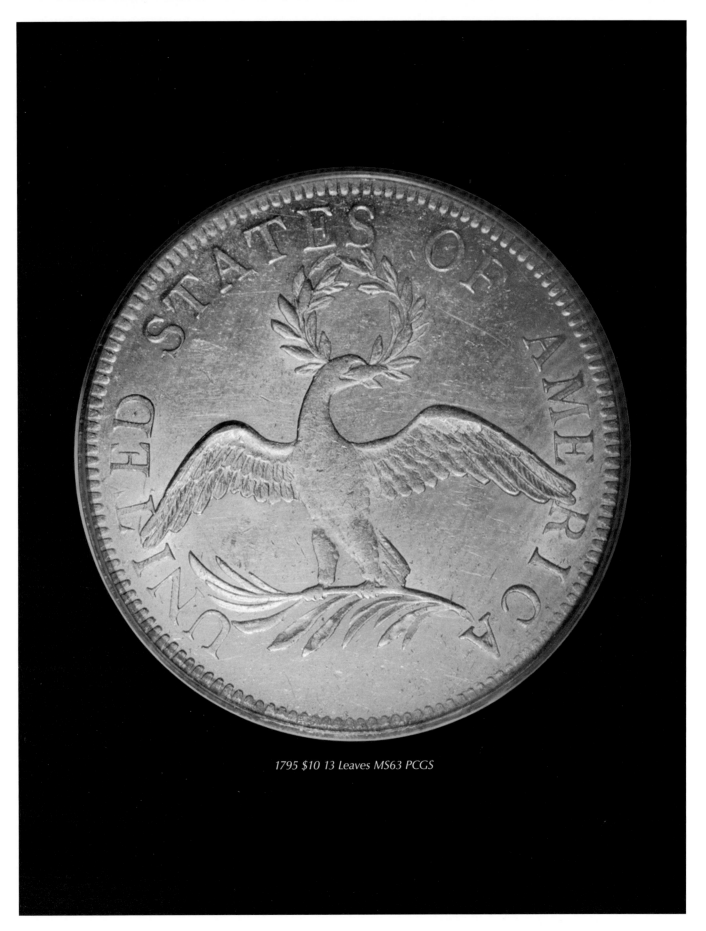

1795 $10 13 Leaves MS63 PCGS

Select Mint State 1795 BD-2 Eagle

3604   1795 13 Leaves MS63 PCGS. Breen 2-A, Breen-6830, Taraszka-2, Bass-3170, BD-2, High R.4. Most authors worry that new information will be discovered shortly after a book is published. This coin seems to present new information regarding the BD-2 variety of 1795 half eagle. This following the publication of Early U.S. Gold Coin Varieties by John Dannreuther and the late Harry Bass just last summer. The die state of this example is not consistent with known states previously reported. There is no visible evidence of any obverse cracks described by John Dannreuther or Anthony Taraszka, but a clearly visible die crack joins the northeast point of star 13 and the border. The reverse die appears perfect with no evidence of any die cracks. This means that this coin was struck prior to the latest die states of BD-1 except conventional wisdom dictates otherwise. It is currently believed that BD-1 was struck first, followed by BD-2. The obverse also shows no evidence of die lapping although the reverse is lapped.

This is either an early die state, struck before a second group of BD-1 coins, or it is a late die state with die cracks lapped away. We believe the former is more accurate. This coin was struck immediately after the earliest die states of 1795 BD-1, before the reverse die cracked. There is no doubt that the obverse die crack from star 13 to the border was merely overlooked by earlier observers.

This specimen is a lovely 1795 eagle with frosty mint luster and brilliant greenish yellow-gold color. The surfaces have a few minor abrasions that are consistent with the grade. It is highly attractive and free of all but the slightest peripheral adjustment marks. The central obverse and reverse design details are characteristically weak. Although the reported PCGS population shows several finer examples, most all of those are the BD-1 variety. This 1795 BD-2 variety is much scarcer with fewer than 100 pieces known in all grades. We believe that this example is approaching the finest known status. Population: 10 in 63, 8 finer (10/06). *From The Essex Palm Collection.* (#8551)

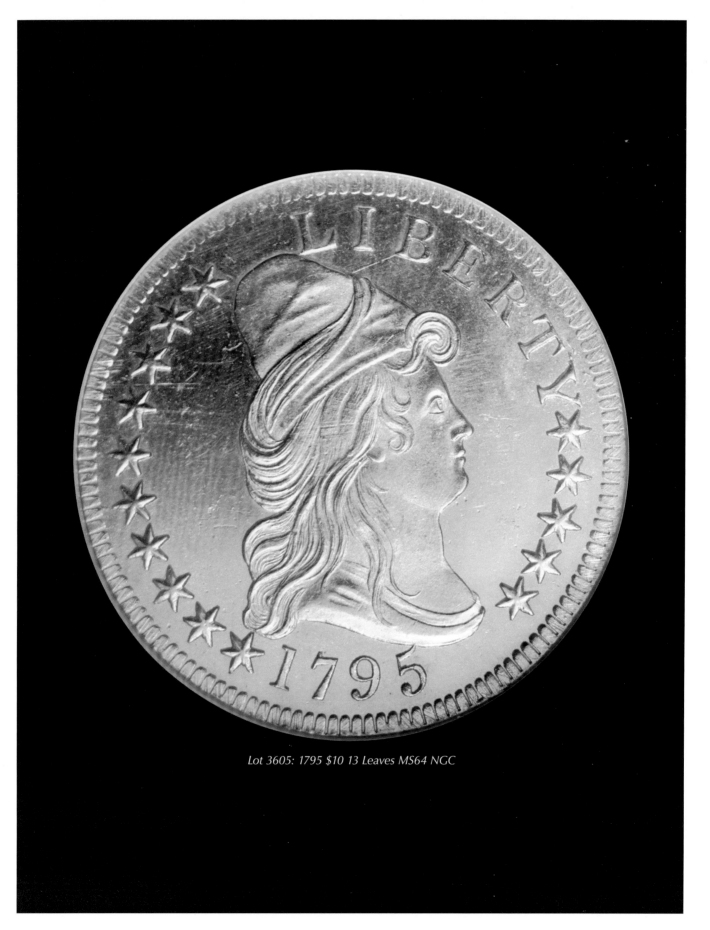

Lot 3605: 1795 $10 13 Leaves MS64 NGC

Lot 3605: 1795 $10 13 Leaves MS64 NGC

Near-Gem 1795 BD-1 Eagle, Prooflike Surfaces

3605   1795 13 Leaves MS64 NGC. Breen 1-A, Breen-6830, Taraszka-1, Bass-3169, BD-1, High R.3. The ten dollar gold pieces, given the name "eagle," were the largest gold coins produced by the first U.S. Mint from 1795 through 1804. Like all early gold coins, these pieces did not carry an actual denomination as part of the design. John Dannreuther explains: "The eagle was the second gold denomination struck by the United States Mint. Calling it a *denomination* is actually a misnomer. Even though a gold eagle was denominated as a ten-dollar coin, our forefathers traded gold by the tale. [Tale, in this instance, means count or tally, a number of things taken together (i.e., the weight and purity of an individual coin).] The weight and purity were the only things important to merchants and individuals—money was gold, and gold was money. In most cases, transactions of even a nominal sum had to be settled in gold, especially whenever governments were involved. There really was no need at first for a stated denomination on either gold or silver coins, because it was known that our coins would be under extreme scrutiny and would likely be assayed by foreign mints and others as to their weight and purity."

A similar problem exists for both the half eagles and the eagles. For both denominations there were multiple varieties dated 1795 and only a single variety dated 1796, despite mintages that suggest this is illogical. During the course of 1795, just 2,795 eagles were minted from September 22 through November 27. In 1796, the Mint produced 6,934 eagles from January 9 through December 22. If we take these annual production totals at face value, an average of 560 coins per die marriage were struck in 1795 while a single die marriage produced all 6,934 coins in 1796. Clearly there is something wrong, unless many of the coins produced in 1796 were from dies dated 1795, and we can be certain that this was the case. According to the *Guide Book*, the 1795 mintage totaled 5,583 coins and the 1796 mintage totaled 4,146 coins, but even these figures are suspect, suggesting a survival rate of 10% for 1795 eagles and only 4% for 1796 eagles. This discussion illustrates the challenge that numismatists have today when attempting to reconstruct the events of the earliest years at the Philadelphia Mint. There were no records of mintages for individual die varieties, and any attempt to make such estimates today is plagued with problems.

In his new reference, *Early U.S. Gold Coin Varieties,* Dannreuther provides estimated mintages for every variety, as well as estimates of the number of survivors for each variety. The only thing we know for sure is the number of die marriages known from 1795 through 1804 (32) and the total mintage for that period (132,714 coins including 122 pieces reserved for assay). By using the midpoint of Dannreuther's survival estimates, we can also establish an approximate survival rate for the series of 2.5%. Is this enough information to establish original "mintage figures" for each variety or even for each coinage date? This cataloger has spent considerable effort over several years attempting to correlate mintage figures with individual varieties, and now feels that it is not possible. There are at least two variables that cannot accurately be determined. First, the exact emission sequence needs to be determined (including both die marriages and remarriages). In a series like the early eagles, the emission sequence alone is enough to give a numismatist nightmares. Once the emission order is known, an accurate estimate of the survivors must be established for each variety and remarriage, and this is nearly an impossibility. Finally, differing survival rates from one coinage date to the next must be pinpointed, a seemingly impossible task.

The 1795 BD-1 is considered the first variety coined for the year, therefore it is the first eagle minted by the United States! There are more of these surviving today than all other 1795 varieties combined, and it is actually one of the five most common die varieties of the entire series from 1795 to 1804, a fact that would probably surprise most collectors. Quite a few examples survive in Mint State grades, giving collectors a reasonable chance of obtaining a high-quality example of the Small Eagle reverse design. Many of the Mint State pieces have prooflike fields, much like this coin does. Although the fields are not deeply mirrored, they are clearly reflective. The surfaces are exceptional and almost totally mark-free with only a few scattered abrasions. Faint adjustment marks are evident at the center of the obverse, and also on some of the obverse dentils. All of the design elements on both sides are sharply struck, suggesting to some the possibility that this may have been some type of presentation piece. This example is a relatively early die state of the variety, with faint obverse die cracks but no evidence of any reverse cracks. Despite the existence of several Mint State pieces, this example is one of the best we have handled. In fact, in our previous sales we have only handled two 1795 eagles in grades better than MS61! Census: 4 in 64, 4 finer (10/06).

From The Freedom Collection. (#8551)

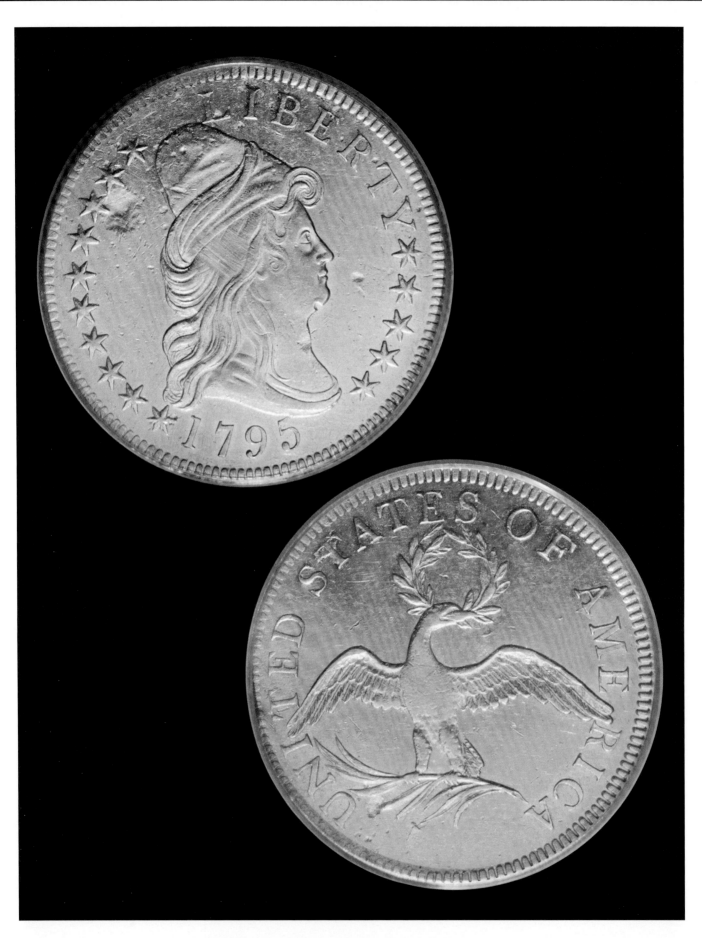

Choice AU 1795 Nine Leaves Eagle
A Legendary Early Gold Rarity

3606   1795 9 Leaves AU55 PCGS. Breen-6831, BD-3, Taraszka-3, R.6. Although all early eagles are rare, the Heraldic Eagle type (1797 to 1804) is more obtainable than the introductory Small Eagle type (1795 to 1797). The latter type has a total recorded mintage of 13,344 pieces, unevenly divided between seven known die marriages. For the first year 1795, five die varieties are known. Four of these have 13 leaves on the reverse. BD-3 has only nine leaves, and has to be regarded as an engraving error. Presumably, the die engraver used 9 leaves to prevent a crowded appearance, and was unaware that four states (presumably Southern states) were symbolically removed as a result. The Nine Leaves is the rarest among the seven Small Eagle varieties, and is the key to a *Guide Book* collection of early eagles, if the virtually non-collectible mid-1830s novodel proof 1804 is excepted.

This is an evenly struck example that has consistent yellow-gold toning. A strike-through is noted over the inner point of star 8. This strike-through, like most others, was caused by a small amount of packed debris on the die at the moment of striking. This debris acts as part of the die, but since it is raised, and the die is in opposite relief to the coins it produces, the debris causes a depression on struck pieces. Often, this debris remains on the die for many strikes, and reflects a lack of attention on the part of the coiner, who should clean the dies once strike-throughs begin to appear on struck pieces. Breen-6831 notes, "Usually with flan chips (foreign matter adhering to dies?)." A smaller strike-through of similar origin affects the tip of the middle palm leaf, and other mentionable strike-throughs are present on the right edge of Liberty's neck and on the obverse field midway between Liberty's mouth and star 12. Sometimes, strike-throughs are referred to as planchet flaws, but this term is inaccurate, since the cause of the depression is the die and not the planchet.

The obverse features parallel striations, most apparent on the hair beneath the cap, but also noticeable near the date. These striations are mint-made, and were present on the planchet prior to strike. They are adjustment marks, believed caused by a mint worker filing the planchet to bring it within weight standards. These are usually found on only one side of the coin, and are generally located near the edges and on the devices. They are rarely visible on the open fields, since this represents the highpoint of the die. A third mint-caused feature of note is the die breaks through the first T in STATES and the tip of palm leaf 8. These are present on every coin struck from this die state, and should not be confused with laminations, which they somewhat resemble. The Harry W. Bass, Jr. specimen, currently on loan to the ANA museum, has these identical die breaks.

Since the grade is AU55, slight wear is appropriate, and is present on the eagle's neck, and on portions of Liberty's cheek, forehead, cap, and drapery. Satin luster percolates across the devices and legends, and is diminished across the exposed fields. Relevant marks are few, although we mention a minor rim nick on the reverse before 9 o'clock, and a small cluster of faint pinscratches between the IB in LIBERTY. The dies are lightly rotated counterclockwise. Certified in a green label PCGS holder. Examples of the Nine Leaves variety appear in Heritage auctions only about once per year, and the last three offerings were in NCS holders, with problems such as a harsh cleaning or a removed mount. The appearance of an unimpaired Choice AU example presents an uncommon opportunity for the advanced early gold collector.
From The Essex Palm Collection. (#8552)

Rare AU53 1797 Heraldic Eagle Ten

3607   1797 Large Eagle AU53 NGC. Breen-6835, Taraszka-11, BD-3, R.5. According to the new Bass-Dannreuther reference, BD-3 is the scarcest of the three Heraldic Eagle die marriages for this date. There is no star beneath the eagle's beak, and this promptly separates the variety from BD-2 and BD-4. Type demand is drawn to the 1799 and 1801 dates, since the 1797 is clearly more scarce. A richly detailed apricot-gold half eagle from the first year of the Heraldic Eagle type. This subdued piece is notable for its lack of mentionable marks, although for pedigree purposes we note a curly, brief lintmark at 7 o'clock on the reverse. As usual for BD-3, a spindly die crack journeys through the second 7 in the date, and connects it to both the bust and the rim. (#8559)

First Year 1797 Heraldic Eagle
Ten Dollar Gold Piece

3608   1797 Large Eagle—Scratched, Cleaned—ANACS. AU55 Details. Breen-6834, BD-2, High R.4. Bright greenish-gold surfaces exhibit numerous fine scratches in the fields, the result of this piece being improperly cleaned. The Mint produced three different varieties of 1797 Heraldic Eagle tens, all from a common obverse die. Approximately 250 examples are thought to survive from all three die combinations, with 80 to 100 being this BD-2 variety. This is an excellent candidate for the date collector, or for the first year of issue type collector. (#8559)

Lovely MS62 1797 BD-3
Large Eagle Ten, R.5

3609   1797 Large Eagle MS62 PCGS. Breen-6835, Taraszka-11, BD-3, R.5. The eagle on the reverse has a short, thin neck, and stars 7 through 10 on the reverse are in a straight line, with stars 7 and 10 lower than the others. The arrowheads run to the center of the N in UNITED. A wispy die crack runs through the tops of UNITED. The eagle has a short, thin neck, and no tongue. A small die center punch shows on the center of the eagle's breast. On the obverse, the 10 stars on the left side, because of lapping, have shortened inner points, with the inner point of star 10 considerably shorter. Two small die cracks appear through the last 7; the leftmost joins the diagonal of that number with its lower serif, while the rightmost runs from the rim through the upper serif and thence to the bust. The dentilation is quite weak or nonexistent from 3 o'clock on the obverse to 5:30.

According to the Dannreuther-Bass *Early U.S. Gold Coin Varieties* (and Anthony Taraszka as well), this very scarce variety was struck after both varieties of the 1798/7 eagles. This is the rarest of the three varieties of Large Eagle (or Heraldic Eagle) coins dated 1797. The Dannreuther-Bass reference continues, "This singular reverse die seems to be prepared by John Smith Gardner, though it employs a Short Thin Neck eagle for the reverse die. If it is a Gardner product, it is the only short neck Large Eagle die he created, as all his other reverse dies have either a long neck (thick or thin).

"The star pattern on the reverse has elements of both a cross pattern and an arc pattern. Perhaps this reverse die was the product of John Smith Gardner *and* Robert Scot, as Scot used only thick, short necks on his Large Eagle dies and no tongue for the eagle. In favor of Gardner is the use of seven solid vertical stripes with six clear stripes and the two rows of tail feathers. The debate will continue." This lovely and rare coin offers greenish-gold, lustrous and frosty surfaces. A few light adjustment marks are limited to cloud 5 on the reverse. PCGS has graded only 11 pieces of the 1798 Large Eagle (all varieties) in MS62, with three finer (11/06). (#8559)

Beautiful BD-4 1797 Large Eagle Ten MS63

3610   1797 Large Eagle MS63 NGC. Breen-6834, Taraszka-12, BD-4, High R.4. Breen-6834, Taraszka-12, BD-4, High R.4. Take a one dollar bill out of your pocket or purse and look at the reverse. If you are not a specialist in early gold and yet the Large Eagle design on this early eagle looks familiar, it is because both are renditions of the Great Seal of United States. Even today the one-dollar-bill version shows a straight-sided shield attached to the eagle's breast, with outstretched wings and E PLURIBUS UNUM on a scroll. On the early eagle design, however, a heraldic miscue exists: The eagle clutches the olive branch of peace in his sinister, or less-honorable, claw, while the arrows of war are in his dexter, or more-honorable claw, in effect signaling "war is more honorable than peace." That heraldic snafu is rectified on the one dollar bill.

The twenty dollar double eagles were latecomers to American numismatics, making their debut in 1850 only after the discovery of vast reserves of gold in California. The Bass-Dannreuther *Early U.S. Gold Coin Varieties* (2006) makes some interesting comments regarding the majesty and impressive beauty of this largest of early U.S. gold coin denominations:

> *The early eagles are some of the most prized acquisitions in all of numismatics. The Large Eagle type is full of rarities and there really are only two dates that can be considered available. Calling the 1799 and 1801* common *is only relative, as the number of survivors of each date is probably in the high hundreds or certainly not many more than a thousand of each date. Every early eagle date is rarer than, say, an 1856 Flying Eagle cent and many times rarer than a 1909-S V.D.B. Lincoln cent. These too are great collector coins, but when one gazes upon an early eagle, there is a certain thrill in just viewing such an impressive coin.*

The Small Eagle ten dollar pieces were struck with dates 1795, 1796, and 1797, but the mintage was probably produced only from September 1795 until June 1797. A single variety of 1797 Small Eagle is known, while there are three variants of the 1797 Large Eagle coins, from a single obverse die and three reverse dies. The common obverse shows a die crack running from the rim through the last 7 in the date and onward to the bust on all known specimens. The stars are arranged 10 and six. The inner point of star 10 grows successively shorter, through lapping, when paired with each subsequent reverse.

The reverses are distinguished chiefly by the style of the eagle's neck and the arrangement of stars. On the BD-4 Large Eagle reverse, the eagle's neck is long and thick, but tapered, and the stars have an unusual cross pattern. On the BD-3 the neck is short and thick, and the stars are arranged in equidistant arcs. The BD-2 shows the long thin neck, but the stars have an even, symmetrical cross pattern. (Although not noted in Bass-Dannreuther, perhaps an easier way to distinguish BD-2 from BD-4 is to look at the position of the S in the motto compared to the eagle's breast. On BD-4 the breast intersects the scroll bearing the motto to the *left* of the S, while on BD-2 it intersects to the *right* of the S.) On BD-4 stars 1, 7, and 12 are in a straight line, as are stars 9, 10, and 11.

The present example boasts beautiful yellow-gold color and rich luster. From the last die state recorded in Bass-Dannreuther, with obverse star point 10 shortest; reverse die cracks from rim to tail; another from rim to left side of R to top leaf; and another from rim through C to leaf. Both sides are free of adjustment marks, but a couple of scrapes are noted left of the date. Beautiful and rare. Population: 2 in 63, 1 finer (12/06). (#8559)

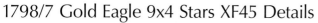

1798/7 Gold Eagle 9x4 Stars XF45 Details

3611   1798/7 9x4 Stars—Repaired, Cleaned—ANACS. XF45 Details. Breen-6836, Taraszka-9, BD-1, High R.4. Somewhat bright from an old cleaning, this example displays rich golden coloration and numerous faint die polish lines in the fields. A round area of lavender discoloration appears on the cheek, and several instances of apparent repair may indicate that the piece is ex-jewelry. A few small marks are noted on each side, along with some wispy hairlines. According to Bass-Dannreuther (2006): "Only 80 to 100 examples of this variety are thought to exist, making it merely scarce among early eagles, although the strong overdate and 18th-century date make it immensely popular with collectors."(#8560)

AU Details 1798/7 9x4 Stars Eagle

3612   1798/7 9x4 Stars—Obverse Repaired—NCS. AU Details. Breen-6836, Taraszka-9, BD-1, High R.4. The variety is instantly distinguished by the distinctive obverse star arrangement, one of the 13-star designs after Mint personnel wised up, subsequent to Tennessee's admission in 1796, to the fact that stars could not be added for every new state in the Union. The die crack from the L in LIBERTY down through the cap also aids attribution. Telltale swirls in the left obverse field and on the rear of the lower hair curls attest to the repair, which is well done and undistracting. Otherwise the surfaces are a pleasing, beautiful orange-gold, with considerable luster remaining. An appealing piece of early gold, deserving strong bids regardless of the NCS disclaimer. (#8560)

Sharp 1799 Ten Dollar, Unc Details

3613   1799 Large Stars Obverse—Tooled, Cleaned—ANACS. Unc Details, Net AU50. Breen-6841, BD-10, Taraszka-22, R.3. Key identifiers for this variety are: large obverse stars (this is key, as one of only two varieties of 1799 with large stars); leaf touches I in AMERICA at its lower right; the lowest berry is under the right foot of the last A in AMERICA; and the lower beak of the eagle touches the star point and the upper beak nearly gets another one, as it "extends" to the lower arm of the star touching the lower beak.

The specimen offered in this lot displays bright yellow-gold surfaces that show ample luster residing in the recessed areas. Sharp definition is noted on the design features that are well centered on the planchet, and the dentilation is strong on both sides. Light hairlines are noted on both faces, but are not terribly offensive. Likewise, the few light tooling marks in the right obverse field are not that distracting. Overall, this is a nice 1799 eagle; prospective bidders should not be intimidated by the ANACS disclaimer. (#8562)

1799 Large Stars Ten Dollar AU58

3614   1799 Large Stars Obverse AU58 NGC. Breen-6841, BD-10, Taraszka-22, R.3. By far the more obtainable of two die pairings sharing the large stars obverse, identified by a leaf tip that points to the right base of the I in AMERICA. Much semi-reflective luster navigates between a number of small to medium-sized abrasions on each side, being broken by modest wear on the highpoints and exposed fields. A small grease stain beneath the 1 of the date is enough of a distraction that it quickly distinguishes this piece from other examples of this popular 18th century gold coin. (#8562)

Desirable Near-Gem 1799 Eagle

3615   1799 Large Stars Obverse MS64 PCGS. Breen-6841, BD-10, Taraszka-22, R.3. Only one 1799 die (Breen's obverse 5) has Large Obverse Stars. This obverse was paired with two different reverses, BD-9 and BD-10. These are promptly distinguished by the location of a leaf tip, which points between IC for the very rare BD-9, and points to the I on the collectible BD-10. The *Guide Book* distinguishes between the Large and Small Obverse Stars varieties, but prices them equally in all grades, since the Small Obverse Stars BD-7 is comparable in rarity with BD-10. Breen, in his 1988 *Encyclopedia,* breaks the Small Obverse Stars into further subtypes: the Wide Date (BD-1 to BD-3), the Close Date (BD-4 to BD-6), and the Irregular Date (BD-7 and BD-8). It is possible that the *Guide Book* will someday recognize these different Small Date subtypes, and those collecting by *Guide Book* variety would then diminish the supply of 1799 eagles available for date collectors.

This is a splendid example of the Large Obverse Stars subtype. The strike is enticingly close to full. The eagle's left (facing) leg shows slight softness, but the eagle's breast and neck feathers are intricate, and Liberty's hair also has complete definition. Some of the obverse denticles, near 3 and 9 o'clock, are lower in relief and display roller marks. However, the fields and the major devices show no evidence of either adjustment marks or roller marks. Further, no abrasions are visible to the unaided eye. Once studied at length beneath a glass, a few wispy field marks become apparent, but although these determine the grade, they do not limit the eye appeal. The khaki-gold toning is even, and billowy luster dominates the legends and devices. *From The Essex Palm Collection.* (#8562)

Crisply Struck BD-7 1799 Eagle AU53

3616   1799 Irregular Date, Small Stars Obverse AU53 PCGS.
Breen-6840, Taraszka-19, BD-7, R.3. The 7 in the date is high and
leans right, while a mint-made die line is found below the right serif of the T in UNITED. This attractive specimen is from an early die
state, lacking the vertical die crack through the E in LIBERTY. This
coin is also without the crack through IBERTY and the right-side
stars, documented for the late-state example in the *Harry W. Bass,
Jr., Museum Sylloge.* This canary-gold example has abundant bright
luster and a crisp strike. A few moderate abrasions along the upper
left obverse border appear also to be of mint origin and do not reduce the eye appeal. (#98562)

Desirable 1799 Small Stars Obverse Eagle MS62

3617   1799 Small Stars Obverse MS62 PCGS. Irregular Date,
Breen-6840, BD-7, Taraszka-19, R.3. Incorrectly designated by
PCGS as a Large Stars Obverse variety. BD-7 is most interesting for
its diminished clouds, which were inadvertently reduced in scale
by a mint worker, either to remove clash marks or simply to prepare
the die for coinage. This luminous example has mildly prooflike luster, and a hint of orange toning on the fields. No adjustment marks
are present, and the strike is unusually sharp for this large denomination. Careful evaluation beneath a loupe fails to locate any consequential marks. Early eagles are under formidable demand from
gold type set collectors. (#98562)

1799 Small Stars Obverse
Ten Dollar MS62

3618   1799 Small Stars Obverse MS62 PCGS. Irregular Date, Breen-6840, BD-7, Taraszka-19, R.3. One of the two "Irregular Date" varieties of this year, being distinguished on most examples by rim crumbling over star 7 and a vertical die crack through the E in LIBERTY to her forecurl. Here a on this intermediate to late die state another peripheral crack on the obverse advances from the T through stars 9-11, and culminates on the border adjacent to star 12. The strike on this attractive yellow-gold example is well executed in virtually all areas and a semi-prooflike sheen emanates from both sides. (#98562)

BD-2 1799 Small Stars Obverse
Eagle MS63, R.5

3619   1799 Small Stars Obverse MS63 NGC. Breen-6839, Taraszka-14, BD-2, High R.5. The BD-2 is the only Small Stars Obverse variety that shows star 9 away from the Y in LIBERTY and star 13 away from the bust. Star 1 points toward the bottom of a curl. Two points of star 8 are close to the cap. Stars 1 and 13 are about equally distant from the bust, and the second 9 is a bit further than the other digits are from each other. There is a center dot in the hair behind Liberty's ear. Numismatic researchers believe that the 1799 Large Stars varieties were created after the Small Stars punch broke during the creation of a die, since the Large Stars device is seen on several 1799 variants and carries over to the single 1800 obverse (and variety for the year) and one of the 1801 obverse dies. The reverse of this variety was married successively with four different obverses to create the BD-1 through BD-4 varieties.

On the reverse a berry is centered under A, and a leaf tip touches the I in AMERICA at the center of the base. The first A in AMERICA does *not* touch the wing feathers, a diagnostic for this die. A die rust lump shows between the U and N. The present example shows clashing of the dentils from the obverse inside the reverse rim from above F through AME. Otherwise both dies appear to be from early die states, with no other visible clashing or cracks. Considerable luster shows on the obverse, a bit less so on the reverse, and both sides are a pretty antique-gold color. No adjustment marks are present save for a few visible under a loupe below OF, and there is some light buildup in the protected areas of each side. The Bass-Dannreuther reference estimates that 35 to 45 pieces are known of this rare variety. While NGC has not attributed this piece, that service has graded 60 coins of the 1799 (all varieties) in MS63, with 49 finer. Both NGC and PCGS have graded several examples of the 1799 Small Stars in MS64, although not necessarily this BD-2 variety. (#98562)

Low Mintage 1800 Eagle AU55

3620   1800 AU55 NGC. Breen-6842, BD-1, Taraszka-23, High R.3. A single pair of dies was used in striking the drastically reduced mintage of 5,999 pieces. As with most seen, a familiar die crack connects the letters of LIBERTY and extends to the denticle above the right side of the B. This mildly prooflike example is accented in rich reddish-orange patina and is well defined except for a bit of curious, localized weakness over the first five letters of STATES. There are no mentionable abrasions or adjustment marks on this comparatively underrated early eagle. Census: 16 in 55, 55 finer (11/06). (#8563)

Appealing 1800 Mint State Eagle

3621   1800 MS60 NGC. Breen-6842, BD-1, Taraszka-23, High R.3. This is the only known variety of the year. In *Early U.S. Gold Coin Varieties,* authors John Dannreuther and Harry Bass state that: "...some of the mintage for 1801 undoubtedly was dated 1800. This corresponds with the availability of this 1800 variety...as it is more available than the calendar-year mintage of 5,999 would indicate. In fact, this is one of the more available varieties of early eagles, with more than 200 examples extant with some estimates as high as 300 known.

This particular specimen exhibits bright yellow-gold surfaces that show the most potent luster in the areas around, and in the recesses of, the design features. Excellent definition is noted on Liberty's portrait, the stars and dentils on both sides, and on most of the eagle's plumage. Several minute contact marks are evenly scattered over each side, but none are worthy of individual mention. This piece exudes considerable eye appeal for the grade designation.
From The Hill Country Collection. (#8563)

1801 BD-2 Eagle AU50

3622   1801 AU50 PCGS. Breen-6843, Taraszka-25, BD-2, R.2. The 1801 BD-2 is the most common of early eagles produced from 1797 to 1804. Star 8 has two points oriented toward Liberty's cap, and the eagle's beak nearly touches star 13 at its top. The two lowest left stars on the obverse are softly struck on this piece. This example show still-lustrous canary-gold centers that deepen to amber-gold near the peripheries. A bit of highpoint rub is visible as a color change on the cheek and highpoints of the hair, and a bit of light field chatter is consistent with the grade. A small dig is noted through the I in LIBERTY. An excellent choice for a type coin. (#8564)

Handsome 1801 AU Ten Dollar

3623   1801 AU50 NGC. Breen-6843, Taraszka-25, BD-2, R.2. On this variety, the large obverse stars are thinner with longer spines than is the case for the BD-1 variety with thick spines, star 8 displays two points to the cap, and is close to it, and star 13 almost touches the bust. On the reverse, the upper beak just about touches the star right below its point.

This lightly circulated example displays bright yellow-gold surfaces that are accented with whispers of reddish-gold around the borders. Both sides retain considerable luster in the recesses, and exhibit nicely detailed motifs. There is an even distribution of light marks, none of which are individually bothersome. A handsome AU50 early ten dollar.

From The Hill Country Collection. (#8564)

Pleasing 1801 Early Eagle, AU53

3624   **1801 AU53 NGC.** Breen-6843, B. 2-B, Taraszka-25, BD-2, R.3. The variety is confirmed by the distance between star 1 and Liberty's Bust; on Taraszka 24, the only other variety of the date, star 1 is much closer. The 1801 is one of the more plentiful dates of the Capped Bust Eagle series, and this is perhaps the most common die variety in the series, making it perfect for type collecting purposes. This is a bright green-gold coin with a minimum of wear, indicative of the grade. The strike is a bit soft through the shield and motto, and a number of surface abrasions are evident. Hints of luster remain in the recessed areas of the coin. (#8564)

Exceptional 1801 Eagle, AU53

3625   **1801 AU53 PCGS.** Breen-6843, Taraszka-25, BD-2, R.2. One of two varieties for the year. One of the keys that distinguishes this variety from BD-1 is that star 13 almost touches the bust on the BD-2; another is that the upper beak does not quite touch the star beneath on the BD-2, whereas the previous reverse has both upper and lower beak touching a star.

Beautiful canary-gold color adorns bright, relatively clean surfaces that display ample luster, along with exceptionally well delineated design elements. Liberty's hair is bold, as are the eagle's wing and tail feathers. Even the neck and breast feathers are nearly full. A few small marks on Liberty's cheek are not bothersome, and may help to pedigree the coin. This lovely specimen reposes in a first generation PCGS holder.
From The Hill Country Collection. (#8564)

AU55 Sharpness 1801 Eagle

3626   1801—Cleaned—ANACS. AU55 Details. Breen-6843, Taraszka-25, BD-2, R.2. A sharp yellow-gold example of the desirable Heraldic Eagle type. The eagle's breast feathers are distinct, and only slight wear is noted on Liberty's cap, forehead, and drapery. The rims are problem-free except for a brief obverse mark past 7 o'clock. Slightly bright from a mild cleaning. The fields are abraded from long-ago indifferent storage, but most collectors would be delighted to own such an impressive large denomination gold piece that dates from the Thomas Jefferson administration. (#8564)

Pleasing AU55 1801 Ten Dollar

3627   1801 AU55 PCGS. Breen-6843, Taraszka-25, BD-2, R.2. According to Harry Bass, this variety can be distinguished by: "OBV: New large star punch, type III 1, first usage. Star 1 away from curl, star 8 close to cap. Star 9 away from Y, star 13 very close to bust. Star 9 has spine pointed at Y. Nine vertical spines in cap. Rust lump at denticle between stars 2 & 3. REV: That of 1803/A. Lumps at bottoms of left serifs of T(A) and (T)A. A(M) rests on feather tip. Lapped."

This is an especially well struck example that shows even, strong definition on Liberty's hair curls as well as the eagle's plumage. The surfaces are bright yellow-gold with an accent of reddish patina around the margins. There are no mentionable abrasions on either side of this lovely, high grade, early gold type coin. (#8564)

Choice AU 1801 BD-2 Eagle

3628   1801 AU55 PCGS. Breen-6843, Taraszka-25, BD-2, R.2. Although myriad abrasions are evident on both sides, this lovely green-gold piece has subdued satin luster on the obverse with fully reflective fields on the reverse. Faint hairlines on each side were not of concern to the grading service. A few of the stars on the obverse and the wing tips on the reverse are weakly defined, but all remaining details are fully visible. As it is the most common variety of all early eagles struck from 1797 to 1804, this issue is an excellent choice for type and date collectors. (#8564)

Borderline Uncirculated
1801 Ten Dollar Gold

3629   1801 AU58 PCGS. Breen-6843, BD-2, Taraszka-25, R.2. Prolonged examination finds slight friction on the drapery and on the highpoints of the cap and scroll, but this sharply impressed example would have been considered Uncirculated throughout most of the pre-certification era. Indeed, substantial luster is present, particularly on the reverse, and the absence of detectable abrasions and adjustment marks further confirms its quality. An outstanding slider of the highest gold denomination from the first Philadelphia Mint.

BD-2 is noteworthy for its glimpses of prooflike surface within selected areas of the portrait: below her ear, beneath the base of the cap, and within the neck curls. Presumably, the dies clashed, evidence of which remains. The dies were then lapped by a mint worker to efface the clashmarks, but certain low relief elements of the design were also removed. (#8564)

1801 Heraldic Eagle Ten Dollar MS60

3630 **1801 MS60 NGC.** Breen-6843, B. 2-B, Taraszka-25, R.3. Among early tens, the 1801 has the highest mintage in the series and is surpassed in availability only by the 1799. This fully lustrous yellow-gold example is well detailed throughout and displays the often-seen "spines" in Liberty's cap. A number of scuffy abrasions across the obverse dilute the effectiveness of the luster. As is typical of these early eagles, the reverse is far less prone to surface marks. Ideal quality to represent the extremely popular Capped Bust, Heraldic Eagle type. (#8564)

Appealing Uncirculated 1801 BD-2 Eagle

3631 **1801 MS61 NGC.** Breen-6843, Taraszka-25, BD-2, R.2. Star 1 is further from the lowest hair curl than on the Taraszka-24, BD-1 variety, where it is quite close. On the BD-2, however, star 13 is very nearly touching the tip of the bust. On the reverse the upper beak nearly touches the star point below. This is the most available early eagle variety, and the BD-2 is much more common than the R.5 BD-1. The present piece shows the characteristic die spines in the Liberty cap, with considerable luster and no mentionable abrasions. A bit of strike weakness shows on the eagle's left (facing) claw and the fletchings, but the overall eye appeal is much nicer than one might infer from the conservative grade. (#8564)

Mint State 1801 BD-2 Eagle

3632 **1801 MS61 NGC.** Breen-6843, BD-2, R.2. This is a lustrous example with mottled green-gold and orange coloration on both sides. The obverse field is slightly reflective while the reverse is highly reflective, nearly prooflike in quality. The 1801 BD-2 variety is the single most common variety in the entire series of early U.S. gold eagles from 1795 to 1804. More Mint State examples of this date are available than for any other issue, although the 1799 Large Obverse Stars variety gives this issue a run for its money. An ideal piece for the type collector. (#8564)

Select Mint State 1801 Heraldic Eagle Ten

3633 **1801 MS63 NGC.** Breen-6843, Taraszka-25, BD-2, R.2. The *Guide Book* reports a mintage of 44,344 pieces for the 1801. What the *Guide Book* omits is that most of this production was exported overseas, where gold was valued more highly relative to silver. Soon after their arrival at a foreign port, the pieces were melted down to recoin in local currency. This trend of small domestic mintages and heavy melting was a direct consequence of an incorrect gold to silver ratio in the United States, and continued until 1834, when the dollar was finally devalued relative to gold. By that time, it was too late to save most early eagles, and among those that had escaped export, many had been put to use in jewelry, or otherwise mishandled. Thus, the present piece is rare in three different ways: it is from a low mintage, it has a low survival rate, and it is a condition rarity. The 1799 and 1801 are the two most available dates of the Heraldic Eagle type, but Select Mint State examples are under enormous demand from early gold type collectors. In addition, the pieces are scarcer in Uncirculated grades than the third party population data suggests, since over the past twenty years, many coins have been repeatedly submitted in the hopes of receiving a higher grade. The current lot is an intricately impressed and thoroughly lustrous representative of this desirable early gold type. The radiant sun-gold surfaces are pleasing for the MS63 level. Adjustment marks are limited to stars 9 through 11 on the obverse margin. Refreshingly void of abrasions, other than a minor reverse rim mark at 8:30. Census: 37 in 63, 32 finer (10/06). (#8564)

Possibly Finest 1801 BD-1 Eagle, Choice Mint State

3634   1801 MS64 NGC. Breen 1-A, Breen-6843, Taraszka-24, Bass-3193, BD-1, R.5. Specialists in the series of early eagles will immediately recognize the importance of this offering. Nearly every known 1801 eagle, regardless of grade, is an example of the *other* variety, and only about 5% of the existing population of the date is this die combination.

We have records of just five Mint State examples of this die marriage, and the present piece is the finest of those. Even the Harry W. Bass, Jr. Core Collection coin, retained by the Bass Foundation and currently on display at the ANA, is no finer than this piece. That coin was graded MS63 by Superior in their session of Auction '89. Bass had two duplicate examples of this variety, an MS61 example and an AU58 coin.

The rarity of this variety is directly related to obverse die cracks, especially the crack between the 0 and 1 of the date. Further die cracks appeared and the die was soon unserviceable. The reverse faired much better, seeing use with obverse dies dated 1799, 1800, and 1801. John Dannreuther discusses the emission sequence: "This variety was struck between the first 1800 coins and the later states of that same issue. Because this 1801 obverse and its 1799 reverse were both in advanced stages of failure, the production of this variety was limited. The obverse quickly was rendered totally useless because of severe cracking, thus the 1800 obverse was remarried with this reverse die for more strikes. The reverse, as noted, was also failing and soon would also be replaced; it appears that the 1800 obverse and this reverse simultaneously fail, as the next variety employs a new obverse and reverse."

This specimen is an impressive near-Gem example and, as we noted earlier, is probably the finest existing specimen of this die combination. It is sharply struck with excellent design definition, especially on the reverse. A few wispy hairlines and faint abrasions on each side keep it from a Gem grade level. Both sides are fully brilliant with soft, frosty luster. The obverse has a die crack between the 0 and 1 of the date, and the reverse has a die crack through the eagle's tail and the olive branch. Faint clash marks from dentils are visible above STAT. Anthony Taraszka notes that the final states of the *1800* eagle have a vertical die crack right of the eagle's tail, but that crack does not appear on this example, thus confirming the emission sequence.

Ex: Heritage Internet (1/2000), lot 2256; Heritage Bullet (2/2000), lot 399; Heritage (1/2001), lot 8263; Bowers and Merena (1/2003), Lot 711.

From The Freedom Collection. (#8564)

Attractive 1803 Large Stars Reverse
Eagle AU53

3635   1803 Reverse AU53 PCGS. Breen-6845, Taraszka-30, BD-5, R.4. Misattributed as a Small Stars reverse on the PCGS holder, and distinguishable from other Large Stars variety, BD-6, by the faint extra star visable within the rightmost cloud. This briefly circulated example rates high in eye appeal, being wholly original with ample signs of prooflike luster still in evidence. Although mentionable post-minting disturbances are not to be found, a series of mostly vertical adjustment marks affect the central portion of the reverse. *From The Collection of Louis E. Eliasberg, Sr.* (#8565)

Desirable 1803 Small Stars Reverse
Ten Dollar, AU53 Details

3636   1803 Small Stars Reverse—Cleaned—ANACS. AU53 Details. Breen-6844, Taraszka-29, BD-4, R.6. The 1803 mintage is reported as 8,979 pieces, in two deliveries: warrant 281, August 19, 4,816; warrant 286, November 19, 4,163 pieces. To this must be added an unknown quantity made in 1804 from 1803 dies. This example displays bright yellow-gold surfaces that reveal some wispy hairlines. The design elements are sharply defined and well centered, and the dentilation is strong on both sides. Some diagonal adjustment marks are noted on the obverse. (#8565)

AU58 1803 Large Reverse Stars 'Extra Star' BD-5 Eagle

3637   1803 Extra Star AU58 PCGS. Breen-6845, Tarasz-ka-30, BD-5, High R.4. To the present cataloger the cessation of eagle coinage, ordered in 1804 by President Thomas Jefferson, is one of the greatest tragedies in U.S. numismatics, from an aesthetic point of view. These were the nation's largest and most impressive gold coins for more than half a century, from 1795 until the double eagle was introduced in 1850. But the large gap in their production has led many numismatists to favor the early quarter eagles and half eagles. In 1795 an ounce of gold, worth 15 ounces of silver in America, was worth 15.5 ounces of silver in Paris—enough differential for bullion brokers and speculators to buy U.S. gold coins and ship them to Paris for sale. By 1813 the ratio had reached 16.25 to 1, and the vast majority of all early U.S. gold coinage was melted. At the end of 1804 President Thomas Jefferson ordered eagle production stopped. Even though the half eagle and quarter eagle contained gold proportional to their face values with the eagle, those series continued, intermittently and with unreduced gold content, until the 1830s. Eagle production would resume 34 years after it was halted, in 1838.

Only a single obverse die was married polygamously to six different reverse dies to create the varieties known for 1803. A die line on the obverse runs from the drapery fold at left of the neck curl, upward and right to the juncture of the neck with the bust. The large, pointed stars are of a style also used on the B. 2-B, Taraszka-25 1801-dated eagle variety. Some light clash marks in the hair, from the second of three known sets of die clashes from the Taraszka-29 Reverse D (B.1-B), remain visible throughout the life of this obverse. Stars 11 through 13 are a bit weak, along with the top row of reverse stars, both as on the Bass specimen, but this example lacks the die crack through BERTY of the piece plated in the Bass *Museum Sylloge.* On the reverse of this R.4 variety a small extra star, about half the area of a "regular" star, is lightly punched within the peripheries of the rightmost cloud. A leaf points to the left edge of the I in AMERICA, and the last A has a partial foot.

Numismatist *par excellence* and gold specialist Harry W. Bass, Jr., discovered the extra star (and thus the variety) at the 1966 ANA Convention. The extremely useful new Bass-Dannreuther *Early U.S. Gold Coin Varieties* comments, "There have been several theories to explain the extra star. The punch that made the extra star is smaller than any used on eagles, so it may be an intentional addition to this reverse die by a Mint employee. It is hard to imagine an accident causing this feature, as a punch would have had to drop into this working die at some point. This is another early gold mystery that defies explanation." Mellow green-gold surfaces contribute to this piece's superb eye appeal. Light field chatter and just a trace of rub confirm a small spate in circulation, but this piece remains a charming and distraction-free example of this historic early gold series. (#88565)

Important 1838 Ten Dollar, MS63 NGC
Tied For Finest Known

3638   1838 MS63 NGC. While other denominations of gold coins were struck with minimal breaks in production, the ten dollar gold piece was deemed not necessary or convenient for 34 years between 1804 and 1838. Its relevancy to the channels of commerce was revived by two mint provisions of the mint act that was passed in January 1837. The first changed the legal fineness of all gold coins from the awkward standard of .9167 gold and .0833 copper to .900 gold and .100 copper. The second section of the mint act (actually Section 10) provided a reduction in the weight of these coins: " ... the weight of the eagle shall be two hundred and fifty eight grains ..." The previous weight for ten dollar gold pieces had been 270 grains. This 12-grain reduction was enough to make it unprofitable to melt U.S. gold coins, thus ensuring these pieces would actually circulate.

Christian Gobrecht was Assistant Engraver at the mint at that time. It fell to him to redesign the new gold coins, and his designs from 1838 were minimally altered until major changes occurred in 1907 and 1908. Gobrecht apparently copied the head of Venus in Benjamin West's painting *Omnia Vincit Amor.* According to Breen, he slightly changed the headdress "but with the same triple-beaded cord on her bun, and the same coronet (here inscribed LIBERTY)." Only 7,200 business strikes were produced in 1838 (plus four proofs), and high grade survivors are rarely encountered. In fact, at the MS63 level this is the only NGC coin certified and there is one PCGS coin graded also, and most significantly there are none finer.

What immediately grabs the attention of the viewer is the incredible mint luster that swirls around each side of this coin. The fields are semi-reflective and soft mint frost races around each side as the coin is tilted beneath a light. A few tiny field marks are seen on both obverse andreverse, but none are worthy of individual mention. The striking details are equally strong on each side. This is a significant opportunity to acquire a rare date, a coin that is tied for finest known, and the first of only two years this important subtype was produced. *From The Freedom Collection.* (#8575)

Choice AU 1839 Eagle, Type of 1838

3639   1839 Type of 1838, Large Letters AU55 PCGS. This variety has been called many different things over the years, quite often by the Large Letters name from the reverse. Every example is described by PCGS as an 1839/8 Overdate, although others label these pieces as Normal Dates. It appears that the Normal Date coins are merely late die states of the overdate, and not a separate variety. This piece has subdued greenish yellow-gold surfaces with traces of reflectivity in the fields, especially where protected by the devices. A few tiny nicks and abrasions are consistent with the grade. (#8576)

Brilliant AU58 1839 Type of 1838 Large Letters Ten

3640   1839 Type of 1838, Large Letters AU58 NGC. Easily distinguished from the Type of 1840, also known as the Small Letters, not only by the Large Letters reverse, but more prominently by the pointed bust truncation that hovers over star 13. On the Type of 1840 the bust truncation is rounded and to the left of that star. The surfaces are brilliant canary-yellow, with light rub on the eyebrow and wingtips separating the piece from Mint State. The unobtrusive abrasions are grade-consistent, with high overall eye appeal. NGC has certified only 10 coins finer (12/06). *From The Temecula Collection.* (#8576)

Elusive, Lustrous MS62
1839 Type of '38 Eagle

3641   1839 Type of 1838, Large Letters MS62 NGC. There are numerous differences between the 1839 Type of 1838, also known as the Large Letters variety, and the 1839 Type of 1840, also known as the Small Letters variety, but the easiest and quickest confirmation is to look at the bust truncation. On the Type of 1838 it is quite pointed and lies over star 13, while on the Type of 1840 it is much more rounded and lies considerably to the left of that star. Most examples of this issue are believed to be overdates, although Breen lists a normal-date variety that may be an example of a late die state. This piece has great luster and attractive green-gold surfaces. A few light, miscellaneous field ticks and small digs account for the grade, but the eye appeal is right. An elusive coin in Mint State: NGC has graded only one piece in MS62, with one coin finer (11/06). (#8576)

Pleasing AU58 1839 Eagle
Type of 1840

3642   1839 Type of 1840, Small Letters AU58 PCGS. The Type of 1840 eagle boasts a completely new obverse from that used on 1838 and prior 1839 issues. The most noticeable difference between the two types is the tilt of Liberty's head; on the Type of 1838 star 6 is located directly above Liberty's coronet, while on the Type of 1840 the coronet points directly at star 6. Liberty's bust is rounded on the Type of 1838; and more pointed on the Type of 1840. Of the two types of eagles minted in 1839, this is easily the rarer. It has roughly half the mintage of its predecessor, and about as many have been certified by the major grading services in total as the Type of 1838 has examples graded in Mint State alone. Indeed, the current near-Mint piece has to be considered among the finest available to collectors. Breen called the 1839 Type of 1840 "prohibitively rare AU," while Akers states that it is "very rare in any condition and most known specimens are VF or EF." Only two pieces have been certified in Mint State: one graded MS64 by NGC and another graded MS62 by PCGS. This leaves collectors searching for the finest available quality to consider attractive high-end AU specimens such as the current coin. The surfaces boast a pleasing medium gold color and a good deal of remaining luster, most notably in the recessed areas near the edges. A bit of highpoint wear is evident, most noticeably on the hair above Liberty's ear, yet the overall level of detail is outstanding. The lightly abraded surfaces are appropriate for a coin that has spent a short time in circulation. A series of spindly die cracks, as struck, encircles much of the obverse. This lot represents an opportunity for the specialist to acquire a rare coin in an uncommonly high grade without having to wait the years or even decades it might take to encounter a finer specimen. Population: 2 in 58, 1 finer (11/06).
From The Temecula Collection. (#8580)

Impressive MS64 1849 Eagle

3643   1849 MS64 NGC. Although No Motto Liberty eagles are relatively plentiful in XF grades, pieces with full mint luster are seldom seen. On those extraordinary occasions when a completely lustrous No Motto eagle appears at auction, it is often abraded or an indifferent strike. Here is an impressive piece that has both booming luster and unmarked surfaces. In addition, the strike is above average, since only star 2 is soft. Rich orange-gold toning contributes further to the eye appeal. A minor L-shaped lintmark above the jaw serves to identify this exceptional gold type coin. Census: 6 in 64, 0 finer (10/06).
From The Freedom Collection. (#8601)

Near-Gem 1853 Eagle
Tied for Finest Certified

3644   1853 MS64 PCGS. Among gold type coins, the No Motto half eagles and eagles rank high in desirability, regardless of date, and this is especially true in Choice or Gem Mint State condition. The 1853 is considered one of the more common dates in this series of rarities, yet only 26 Mint State examples have been certified by PCGS, and none finer than this coin. We have only sold an MS64 example of this date on one previous occasion, more than a decade ago in October 1995, and the next best piece offered by us grades just MS62. This piece is a different example than the 1995 offering, exhibiting sharp central details with exceptional surfaces for the grade. The stars on the obverse and the wing tips just inside the reverse border are a bit weakly defined, but all other details are fully brought up. Both sides have frosty luster with brilliant yellow-gold color, accented by hints of pink and orange toning. A small nick between the top arrow and the base of the right (facing) wing it the only mark large enough to help track the pedigree of this near-Gem. A faint hairline in the upper reverse field is barely visible. Die characteristics are few, but the upper left border of the shield is clearly doubled, with the horizontal shield lines extending past the inner border and a couple of these extending past the outer border as well. Population: 3 in 64, 0 finer (11/06). (#8610)

Finest NGC-Graded 1857-S Eagle, MS63
Ex: *S.S. Central America*

3645   1857-S MS63 NGC. Ex: *S.S. Central America.* Writing in 1980, David Akers commented regarding this issue, "Low grade specimens are the norm for this date yet the 1857-S is sufficiently rare that even VF and EF examples are seldom seen. I have seen two or three AU's but have neither seen nor heard of a strictly uncirculated piece. The 1857-S is just as rare as the lower mintage 1857-O and is very nearly as rare as the 1855-S. It is considerably more rare than the 1854-S or 1856-S." Of course, Akers wrote those words before the Columbus-America Discovery Group began hauling up 1857-S double eagles by the bucketload up from the ocean's depths during the salvage of the *S.S. Central America* bounty. However, the 1857-S *eagle* remains today quite rare: **This is the finest Mint State piece at NGC by two full points, and the only specimen that NGC has encapsulated with the *S.S. Central America* pedigree.** The other Mint State piece at NGC is an MS61, ex: *S.S. Republic.* PCGS has graded six Mint State coins, two each in MS62, MS63, and MS64, none with the SSCA pedigree.

While the ill-fated steamship carried large crates full of freshly minted double eagles, this eagle might have been a piece carried by a passenger who boarded the *S.S. Sonora* in San Francisco for the trip to Panama. (The *S.S. Central America* made the second, Atlantic Ocean leg, bound for New York from the eastern side of Panama.) This piece offers brilliant yellow-gold surfaces with only a touch of light haze around the obverse periphery. A couple of light reeding marks and other signs of contact account for the grade. The mintmark is large and close to the fletchings. (#8624)

Among the Finest Known
1858-S Eagles, AU58 NGC

3646   1858-S AU58 NGC. According to Jeff Garrett and Ron Guth in their *Encyclopedia of U.S. Gold Coins, 1795-1933,* "The 1858-S is a low-mintage, low-population coin that has proven to be a resilient rarity over the past two decades. While the populations of other dates have swelled, that of the 1858-S issue has remained small, creating a new appreciation for this date. It is nearly as rare as the much more highly regarded 1858 eagle, but unlike the 1858, no Mint State examples of the 1858-S are known." The NGC/PCGS population data bear this out, as the AU58 specimen we offer here is one of only ten such coins certified, all by NGC; no finer coins have been seen by either service.

Yellow-gold surfaces are tinted with light tan-red, and exhibit ample residual luster, and nice definition is noted on the design elements. Some minor marks are evenly scattered over each side, but none are worthy of individual mention. The gold specialist does not want to miss out on the chance to acquire one of the finest known 1858-S eagles. (#8627)

Elusive 1860-S Ten Dollar AU55

3647   1860-S AU55 NGC. In the early years of San Francisco Mint gold production, far more attention was given to the minting of double eagles. After similar quantities of S-mint eagles and double eagles were struck in 1854, only token mintages were recorded for most ten dollar issues well into the 1870s. Among the lowest of these is the 1860-S, an issue with an original production of just 5,000 pieces. The few pieces that survived the rough and tumble commerce of the Pacific West tend to be well circulated and heavily abraded. This absolute as well as condition rarity not only escaped heavy circulation, but also came away with no overtly distracting marks. The strike is a trifle soft, as always, and tinges of reddish-orange patina cling to the devices. Census: 2 in 55, 4 finer (11/06). (#8632)

Rare Near-Mint 1865-S Perfect Date Ten

3648   1865-S AU58 NGC. Perfect Date. The Blundered Die or Inverted Date variety of this year received a higher premium for many years because of its dramatic, clearly visible mint error. Only recently has it become clear that the Perfect Date variant is even rarer. This is among the finest known examples of this rare issue. Garrett and Guth comment, "The quality of survivors is lower than average for a No Motto eagle with most examples falling into the VF category. Extremely Fine and About Uncirculated examples are extraordinarily rare ..." This important near-Mint example has most of its original satiny luster, displaying occasional softness on the obverse stars and the eagle's neck feathers. There is a slight reddish tint overall. Unobtrusive abrasions are generally limited to the exposed fields. Census: 4 in 58, 1 finer (12/06). (#8642)

Significant Choice AU 1871-CC Ten

3649   1871-CC AU55 PCGS. The 1871-CC is less famous than its 1870-CC predecessor, but is also a major rarity within the Motto Liberty eagle series. Only 8,085 pieces were struck, and these pieces were strictly regarded as bullion for at least another twenty years, when J. M. Clapp became the first numismatist to seriously collect contemporary gold series by date and mintmark. The 1871-CC spent years in circulation, and most were eventually melted. PCGS has graded examples as low as VG8, and has certified only one piece in Mint State. This nicely struck and lightly abraded piece possesses lovely orange-gold toning, and displays considerable remaining luster. A small strike-through at star 4 is mentioned for pedigree purposes. Population: 3 in 55, 2 finer (10/06). (#8661)

Lower Condition Census 1875-CC Ten, AU53

3650   1875-CC AU53 NGC. The 1875-CC is a rare Carson City ten with a mintage of only 7,715 pieces. Only 65-75 coins are believed known in all grades. The finest known is an NGC MS63, and this AU53 piece is tied with several others at the lower end of the Condition Census. Every researcher who has written about the 1875-CC has agreed on one feature: its poor strike. Apparently it only a matter of degree with all coins showing some variant of softness. Doug Winter went so far as to say: "The 1875-CC is the most poorly struck eagle from the Carson City mint. I have seen examples on which the obverse appeared to be twenty to twenty-five numerical points lower than the reverse (i.e., the obverse had the sharpness of Very Fine-20 to Very Fine-25 while the reverse had the sharpness of Extremely Fine-40 to Extremely Fine-45)." However, this coin does not show that particular feature like most 1875-CC tens. The obverse and reverse are well balanced in respect to each other. There is weakness present on the devices, but significant portions of mint luster remain around the devices. The fields show a few small marks, as one would expect, with an overall pleasing appearance for this notoriously difficult Carson City issue. (#8673)

Scarce 1876-CC Ten Dollar, AU50

3651   1876-CC AU50 NGC. Winter 1-A, the only known dies. The 1876-CC eagle is scarce in all grades, and most known examples are in the Very Fine to Extra Fine grade range. AU specimens are considerably more challenging, and Uncirculated examples are virtually unknown. Unfortunately, the typical 1876-CC survivor also has obtrusive and deep abrasions on the surfaces, and is generally poor in luster.

The AU example presented in this lot does have a scattering of light abrasions, but none of worthy of individual mention. The honey-gold surfaces display traces of orange and light red, and exhibit traces of luster in some of the recessed areas. All in all, a better-than-average Carson city representative. Census: 10 in 50, 22 finer (11/06). (#8675)

Impressive AU 1879-CC Liberty Eagle

3652   1879-CC AU50 PCGS. With only 1,762 coins minted, this date has the lowest mintage of any Carson City Mint eagle, indeed, it is actually the lowest mintage gold coin produced at Carson City, regardless of denomination. This piece is a pleasing AU example with deep honey-gold color and considerable remaining luster on each side. The surfaces have the usual quota of tiny handling marks that are always seen on these pieces. Typical of most survivors, the strike is acceptable but not sharp. The present example misses the Condition Census for the issue, but it is still far finer than average. For example, the single piece in the Smithsonian Institution grades just VF25. Population: 8 in 50, 4 finer (11/06). (#8684)

Lustrous Near-Mint 1882-CC Eagle

3653   1882-CC AU58 PCGS. Winter 2-A. This interesting variety is actually a mispunched date. Two lunules of the top of the two 8s in the date were mispunched in the dentils below the date. It is estimated that some 30-33 examples of this issue are extant today in AU condition. This is a very attractive piece that is fully struck and has bright surfaces with strong remnants of mint luster and a glimmer of semi-prooflikeness in the fields. A couple of tiny marks on Liberty's cheek are the only abrasions that bear mentioning on this near-Mint example. (#8696)

Condition Census 1892-CC Eagle, MS64

3654   1892-CC MS64 NGC. In terms of overall rarity, the 1892-CC is not a particularly noteworthy issue among Carson City tens. 40,000 pieces were originally struck, a comparatively high figure for eagles from the historic Western Mint, but only a tiny percentage of survivors qualify at the Mint State level. The Choice representative offered here is by a full two points the nicest 1892-CC we have ever offered and easily merits Condition Census status. Not only are both sides boldly defined with luxuriant frosty luster, the surfaces reveal only a minimum of wispy field marks. A few small alloy stains are scattered across the obverse, the most noticeable being located to the right of star 3. Simply outstanding quality for the issue. Census: 2 in 64, 0 finer (11/06). (#8722)

Astounding Premium Gem
1893-S Ten Dollar

3655   1893-S MS66 PCGS. Looking over Heritage auction records one is immediately taken back by the fact that no other 1893-S eagle has been sold above the MS63 grade level, an astounding three points less than the Premium Gem offered here. Further investigation into gold references and census data proves this inexplicable void to be no accident, only a handful of Choice or better examples are known to exist despite a total Mint State population in the hundreds. One glimpse at this meticulously preserved, satiny example is all it takes to recognize the coin's special qualities. The strike is razor sharp, surface marks are virtually non-existent, and both sides are accented in lovely blue and orange pastel shades. Population: 1 in 66, 1 finer (11/06). (#8728)

Rare, Unsurpassed 1907-S
Liberty Eagle MS66

3656   1907-S MS66 NGC. Few Liberty Head ten dollar coins can rival this one in terms of eye appeal. Radiant luster emanates from the flashy rose-gold surfaces, and surface marks of any kind are nearly nonexistent, save for two or three trivial nicks on the obverse. These comments by Jeff Garrett and Ron Guth are instructive: "The 1907-S eagle is easily the scarcest of any Liberty Head eagle of the 20th century, even though the mintage is not among the lowest. Akers called this date one of his favorites and considered it one of the most underrated of all U.S. coins (of any denomination)." This beautiful Premium Gem is the single highest-graded example at NGC, with none finer. PCGS has certified two pieces at MS66; likewise with none graded any higher (11/06). (#8765)

PROOF LIBERTY EAGLES

1839/8 Type of 1838 Eagle PR67 Ultra Cameo NGC

1839/8 Type of 1838 Eagle PR67 Ultra Cameo NGC

The Eliasberg 1839/8 Large Letters Proof Eagle
An American Numismatic Classic

3657   1839/8 Type of 1838 PR67 Ultra Cameo NGC. This is an amazing opportunity for the advanced collector, the connoisseur of early American gold coinage, or the numismatist who appreciates the combination of quality and rarity. This masterpiece is the finest of just three proofs known, and one of just two examples available to collectors. Three additional proofs are known for the 1838 eagle, bringing the total population to six coins for this first design type. One of each date is held by the Smithsonian Institution, and the other four are available to collectors. This specimen is the finest of all six known proofs of this first Liberty Head eagle design.

In the Eliasberg catalog, Dave Bowers wrote: "The 1839 Large Letters or Type of 1838 eagle has traditionally been one of the most desired issues in the series. Specimens are very elusive in high grades, and in proof grade this piece ranks as one of the most important rarities in the field of American numismatics. A marvelous opportunity for the specialist."

Previous Discussions

Walter Breen wrote in his *Encyclopedia of United States and Colonial Proof Coins:* "Large Letters, type of 1838. Date low, to left, many die file marks near rev. border. (1) Smithsonian, from Mint collection. (2) Parmelee: 1097 to Chapman, Jenks: 5735, John H. Clapp, now in Eliasberg collection. No rumor of a third specimen."

A decade later, the same author mentioned the third specimen in his *Complete Encyclopedia:* "East European pvt. coll., 1981, Mark Emory for NERCG, in a proof set including $2 1/2 and $5."

In *United States Gold Coins, An Analysis of Auction Records,* David Akers commented briefly: "There are only two known proofs, one in the Smithsonian Institution and the other in the Eliasberg Collection." His 1980 reference was published just a year before the third example was discovered.

Recently, Jeff Garrett and Ron Guth wrote *Encyclopedia of U.S. Gold Coins, 1795-1933,* published in 2006. Every U.S. gold issue, business strikes and proofs, was given a third page of space. For this proof issue they wrote: "The Proof 1839, Type of 1838 eagle is an exceedingly rare coin of which only three examples are known. The first is the PF-66 deep cameo in the Smithsonian Institution, obtained in the year of issue as were virtually all of the Proof gold coins in that collection (the only exception being additions from the Lilly Collection.) The second example (and the finest of the three) is the Eliasberg Proof coin that later sold as an NGC PF-67 ultra cameo in a 1999 auction for $690,000. The third examples is a PF-61 listed in the PCGS Population Report, a coin that reportedly came out of Eastern Europe in 1981, along with a Proof quarter eagle and half eagle."

Historical Commentary

According to the Mint Act of 1792, the ten dollar gold piece was declared the unit of all gold coinage and was named the eagle. Smaller gold denomination coins were called the half eagle and the quarter eagle.

Once gold coinage actually began in 1795, the eagle remained in use only for a decade, being discontinued in 1804 in favor of the half eagle. Much of this had to do with the increasing price of gold and the extremely limited production of gold coins by the Philadelphia Mint. Gold value eventually exceeded face value for all of the gold coins.

For many years, the half eagle was the denomination of choice among those who deposited gold with the mint. Few depositors requested eagles and even fewer asked for quarter eagles. In 1804, President Thomas Jefferson halted production of both the eagle and the silver dollar. It was another 30 years before the Philadelphia Mint coined another 10 dollar piece, in 1834. The "1834" eagles were actually dated 1804, and were produced for inclusion in special presentation sets to be given to foreign monarchs such as the King of Siam.

Finally, full scale production of gold eagles resumed in 1838 by order of the Secretary of the Treasury, a few years after the standard weight for gold coinage was reduced to levels that brought gold value and face value back in line. With an internal supply of gold discovered in Georgia and the Carolinas a few years earlier, the necessity of a larger gold coin became evident.

Christian Gobrecht created the Liberty Head design, the first style used only in 1838 and 1839, before slight modification. The second head style remained in use from 1839 through 1907. In the earliest years of this design, few proofs were coined, usually only upon request by an occasional collector, or by government authority for presentation purposes. Today, less than 40 proof eagles are known for the entire two decades from 1838 to 1857, and this total includes a dozen such pieces in the Smithsonian Institution.

The Design

The Liberty Head design was created by Christian Gobrecht who is best known for his silver dollar design of 1836. During his brief tenure at the Mint's engraving shop, Gobrecht also created the Braided Hair design for half cents and large cents, as well as similar designs for several pattern issues.

The obverse has a bust of Liberty facing to the left, with her hair bound into a triple bun at the back, and held in place by a beaded cord. A coronet or crown in her hair is inscribed with the word LIBERTY. The bust truncation is smoothly curved, forming a sharp point at the back. Thirteen stars are placed just inside the obverse border, beginning at 7 o'clock, clockwise to 5 o'clock. The 1839 date is placed below the bust.

For the reverse design, Gobrecht chose an eagle with its wings reaching skyward, gazing to the West. The eagle holds an olive branch in its dexter claw and three arrows in its sinister claw. A shield covers the eagle's breast, composed of six vertical two-line stripes and nine horizontal crossbars. The statutory legend UNITED STATES OF AMERICA follows the border clockwise from 7:30 to 4:30 with the denomination abbreviated TEN D. below.

Nomenclature

Over the years, this issue has become known as the "1839 Large Letters" eagle. While there is a slight difference in the size of the reverse lettering, obvious when coins of each type are side-by-side, this difference is not obvious when examining one coin or the other. The difference in the appearance of the obverse is much easier to discern when looking at an individual coin. The date is farther left on the Type of '38, the bust truncation is much more noticeably curved, and the hair over the ear has an entirely different treatment. For these reasons, we refer to this piece as the 1839 Type of '38 eagle.

Individual Die Characteristics

The digits 1 and 9 show evidence of recutting, visible at the serif and top of the upright of the 1, and along the outer right side of the 9. A short diagonal die line joins the ball of the digit 3 to the border below the right side of the 8. Short raised die lines extend up from the hair below the right serif of T and the left serif of Y.

The reverse has myriad fine die lines, along with a series of heavy die file marks between the border and lettering, especially visible over STATES OF, ERICA, and below N D.

This Coin

A numismatic masterpiece, this coin is easily the finest known 1839 proof eagle, and far beyond the quality of the only other example available to collectors. All of the individual die characteristics on both sides are intricately detailed, with the sole exception of stars 7 through 10, each lacking most or all of their radial lines. Struckin brilliant yellow gold, the fields on both sides are exceptionally deep with fully mirrors. The devices are highly lustrous with complete mint frost. This is an amazing cameo proof with extraordinary aesthetic appeal. A few insignificant flakes and lint marks are visible on each side, along with light clash marks.

Roster and Provenance

1. **PR61 PCGS.** Recorded in the PCGS Population Report. This is the piece from the European private collection mentioned by Breen in his *Complete Encyclopedia*. It was purchased by Marc Emory in 1981 for New England Rare Coin Galleries as part of a three piece gold proof set. No further details regarding this coin are known.

2. **PR66 Deep Cameo.** U.S. Mint; National Numismatic Cabinet; Smithsonian Institution. Illustrated by Jeff Garrett and Ron Guth in *Encyclopedia of U.S. Gold Coins.*

3. **PR67 Ultra Cameo NGC. The coin offered here.** Lorin G. Parmelee (New York Coin and Stamp Co., 6/1890), lot 1097; John Story Jenks (Henry Chapman, 12/1921), lot 5735; John H. Clapp; Clapp Estate; Louis E. Eliasberg, Sr.; Eliasberg Estate (Bowers and Ruddy, 10/1982), lot 662; Mike Brownlee; later, Goldberg Coins & Collectibles (9/1999), lot 1817; Bowers and Merena (8/2003), lot 4042. An anonymous document from the late 1980s or early 1990s, discussing the proof 1838 eagle issue, records this piece as part of the Harry Bass Collection. It is doubtful that Bass actually owned this coin, as it was not retained for his collection. (#8771)

The Single Finest PCGS Certified
1863 Eagle, PR65 Deep Cameo

3658   1863 PR65 Deep Cameo PCGS. A regal coin which
is graced by strong contrast between the mirror fields and devices. The color is bright canary-gold throughout. As expected for the grade, the surfaces are very attractive with minimal
hairlines and virtually no signs of handling. The only identifying lintmark we could find is a tiny one right of the Y in LIB-
ERTY near the edge of the coronet, and we also note a trivial
speck tucked between the upper inside points of the third star.
NGC has graded five coins as such of this date, with none finer in the Cameo category, and another eight pieces equal or
higher in their Ultra Cameo designation. This lovely Proof eagle would make a welcome addition to any collection, and
such magnificent beauty will never go out of style. There are
minute but interesting die diagnostics on this issue, we note a
few small raised lumps from die rust on Liberty's truncation,
another one near her earlobe on her jaw. In addition, a small
lintmark somehow adhered to the hub when the die was engraved, right on Liberty's cheek below her eye, the coiner noted this raised line on the die atop Liberty's cheek on the die,
and carefully wire brushed most of it off her cheek, but telltale
faint swirling lines are seen on her cheek and portions of the
hubbed lintmark are still present on the Proofs coined from this
die. On the reverse we note the last vertical shield line extends
up to the third horizontal stripe. These tiny diagnostics are
unique to the obverse and reverse die, and would appear on
each coin struck from these dies unless the dies were further
lapped or altered by the Mint employees. This is the single finest PCGS-certified 1863 eagle, and would be the centerpiece
of any proof gold collection. (#98799)

Impressive 1879 Gold Eagle
PR65 Cameo NGC

3659   1879 PR65 Cameo NGC. Researching auction records for the 1879 proof Liberty eagle is quite instructive. Only nine auction appearances are recorded for the issue, within the past thirteen years, and *five of these are apparently for the same coin, a PCGS example graded at PR64 (non-cameo).* While not as well known as the 1877 and 1878, the 1879 proof Liberty eagle is just as elusive. Only 30 specimens were struck, and today no more than 10 to 12 individual coins are known. This lovely Gem is tied for the finest certified with one other Cameo and one non-Cameo coin (assuming the other Cameo is not a resubmission of this piece). Altogether, only 10 Cameo and non-Cameo coins have been certified by the two major services. As with all proofs of this date, the hair curls behind Liberty's head are detached by excessive die polishing and seem to "float" in back of the neck. Further evidence of this heavy die polishing can also be seen on the detached left end of the scroll, and below the second T in TRUST. The surfaces display lovely honey-gold coloration and the fields are deeply mirrored with a significant amount of mint frost over the devices; this produces impressive cameo contrast on each side. Close examination with a magnifier shows a few very light hairlines, but these do not impair the overall appearance or Gem quality of this important 19th century gold coin. Census: 2 in 65 Cameo, 0 finer (11/06). (#88819)

PR65 Deep Cameo 1888 Eagle
Finest Certified

3660   1888 PR65 Deep Cameo PCGS. Despite its recorded mintage of 72 pieces (the *Guide Book figure of 75 appears to be in error,* the 1888 eagle is an elusive gold coin as a proof. The current combined population data at NGC and PCGS show 13 proofs in all grades at NGC, with eight proof pieces at PCGS. The present PR65 Deep Cameo coin is the *single finest example certified at either service.* NGC has graded no coins finer than PR64 (11/06). As an added indication of the rarity of this coin, since the mintage of the first With Motto proofs in 1866, only four other issues through the 1880s—1871, 1874, 1877, and 1878—show a total NGC/PCGS population of one coin in PR65, PR65 Cameo, and PR65 Deep/Ultra Cameo with none finer, making this is the *only 1880s issue with a combined NGC/PCGS population of one coin in PR65 between both services, with none finer.*

Proofs from 1888 have a date that is low in the field and slants minutely up to the right. The left bottom serif of the 1 is over the left half of a dentil. The proof reverse, which was shared with the 1887 eagles, shows "four stripes thin, feathers attenuated below second," according to Walter Breen's proof *Encyclopedia.* Breen comments that the 1888 eagle is the "rarest denomination of the year, seldom offered, probably between 20 and 30 survivors at most, possibly fewer."

The present example offers bold contrast between the deeply frosted devices and the well-mirrored fields as its chief hallmark. The fields show the orange-peel texture frequently seen on gold proofs from this era. The sharp strike succeeds in fully delineating all of the star centrils, and the individual beads in Liberty's hair cord are fully articulated. On the reverse, there is no apparent weakness on any of the eagle's feathers, which are distinct and fully struck, and full detail appears present as well in the eagle's claws and the horizontal stripes in the shield. This coin represents a considerable opportunity to obtain what is clearly the *finest certified example* of this elusive proof issue. (#98828)

Amazing Gem Ultra Cameo
Proof 1891 Eagle

3661   1891 PR65 Ultra Cameo NGC. Present controversies about the numerous Mint products scheduled for 2007 (and the five-figure sums required to acquire one of everything) bring to mind the difficulties collectors faced in earlier years. While the minor proofs of the 19th century usually had mintages at least in the hundreds, if not the thousands, far fewer numismatists had the financial wherewithal to put away examples of the gold proofs of the era. Often forgotten is the substantial financial cost, which could easily reach the thousands of dollars as reckoned in modern currency. The 48 proofs of this issue almost all display cameo contrast, according to Garrett and Guth, but anything stronger is difficult to come by. In the NGC *Census,* 17 Cameo pieces are listed, along with five Ultra Cameo coins, and only one specimen received neither designation. In addition, the vast majority of examples grade Choice, with Gem examples far more elusive.

Interestingly, this is the first Ultra Cameo example of this issue ever offered by Heritage, and as far as starts go, it is difficult to do better. The deeply reflective mirrors are essentially free of haze, and the richly frosted devices engender stunning black-and-gold contrast. A tiny contact mark below the eagle's beak is a minimal distraction at worst. The minor hairlines so often found on 19th century proof gold are absent on this piece, and a quick look is sufficient to assure any viewer of the quality of this specimen, though anyone with any interest in this lot will want to take more than a glance. Census: 2 in 65 Ultra Cameo, 1 finer (11/06). (#98831)

Beautiful PR64 Cameo 1892 Eagle

3662 **1892 PR64 Cameo NGC.** Despite the fairly high proof production of 72 pieces, there are few high grade examples that appear in the numismatic marketplace. Only nine times in the last dozen-plus years have we offered examples in PR64 or finer grades. Furthermore, only a handful of the proofs of this year show deep cameo contrast, making the Cameo designation of the present example a bonus. Beautiful deep sunset-gold coloration, arm's-length eye appeal, a bold strike, and an absence of visible distractions complete the package. Census: 3 in 64 Cameo, 2 finer (11/06).

From The RNB Collection. (#88832)

Magnificent 1897 Eagle
PR65 Ultra Cameo

3663   1897 PR65 Ultra Cameo NGC. From a limited mintage for the 1897 proof eagle of a mere 69 pieces, attrition appears to have taken its toll on up to half of the original production. Even an estimate by Breen (whose survival figures were calculated years ago and are often found to be low) of only 35-40 survivors seems to hold up on this issue. Not that there could ever be any doubt about this spectacular coin's proof status, it does meet the criteria set out in Breen's *Comprehensive Encyclopedia* for proofs of this date: "low date slanting up to right, light repunching on base of 1."

The standards for proof gold coinage appear to have reached their zenith during the closing years of the 20th century. This tendency is also borne out in the offerings of two spectacular 1898 four-piece gold proof sets appearing in this year's FUN Sale. The fields of this solid Gem representative exhibit glittering, glassy mirrors of unfathomable blackness that provide stark contrast with the heavily frosted design elements. One has to closely examine the fields under magnification to locate even the slightest post-minting disturbance. Two pinpoint planchet voids on the obverse are useful for attribution, one between stars 11 and 12 along with a more obvious one between Liberty's forecurl and star 5. Magnificent quality for this extremely challenging proof Liberty eagle. Census: 2 in 65, 2 finer (12/06). (#98837)

Impressive Proof 1898 Liberty Eagle
PR67 Deep Cameo

3664   1898 PR67 Deep Cameo PCGS. Like the other pieces in this impressive 1898 gold proof set, this Superb Gem has rich orange-gold color with deeply mirrored fields, frosty and highly lustrous devices, and exceptional Deep Cameo contrast. A few faint splashes of coppery toning are barely visible on each side, and these should not be confused with "copper spots" as they are entirely different. Not only is this piece the finest certified 1898 proof eagle graded by PCGS, it is the only PR67 example that PCGS has seen, regardless of designation (11/06).

With a mintage of only 67 coins, this date is a rarity in proof format, despite the comments of Jeff Garrett and Ron Guth who claimed: "The 1898 eagle is one of the more common proofs of this era." These authors suggested that between 30 and 40 proofs are known, representing approximately half the original mintage. Our own research in the field of proof gold coins indicates that the actual population may prove to be in the range of 20 to 30 pieces. Over the past three decades, a large number of old collections have come on the market, as well as a few newer collections. These include names such as Garrett, Norweb, Eliasberg, Pittman, Carter, Bass, Trompeter, Bareford, Starr, and others. All of these collections were responsible for many proof gold coins across various denominations. As a result, a small number of pieces have been actively making the auction rounds in the last several years, giving the appearance of a much higher population than actually exists. (#98838)

The Norweb PR68 Ultra Cameo 1898 Eagle
Single Finest Graded of the Entire Liberty Head Type

3665   1898 PR68 Ultra Cameo NGC. Ex: Norweb. With great pride we present the **highest graded proof Liberty Head eagle,** another entry in our consignment of high grade 1898 gold coins from the quarter eagle through double eagle, all grading PR66 to PR68 by NGC, and all with Ultra Cameo surfaces. The recorded mintage for proof 1898 eagles is 67 pieces. The Garrett-Guth *Gold Encyclopedia* comments concerning this issue and this specific piece, "The 1898 eagle is one of the more common Proofs of this era, found in a wide range of grades from lightly circulated PF-58 to PF-68. In case the PF-68 number failed to impress, note that this is the *only* date in the entire series that has ever earned that lofty grade. The certified population ballooned in this year, doubtless because of resubmissions, but the variety of grades is so well dispersed that it is impossible to determine where the numbers have been inflated. There are probably 30 to 40 coins known today, which is still a very tiny number. The Smithsonian has two PF-64 examples, both of which are deep cameos."

Ambassador and Mrs. R. Henry (Emery May Holden) Norweb were another famous "collector couple" fortunate enough to be present at the 1954 Palace Collection sale of the numismatic treasures of the deposed King Farouk of Egypt. As a young girl, Emery May Holden learned the love and lore of coins from her father, Albert Fairchild Holden, publisher of the *Cleveland Plain Dealer* newspaper and an active collector from 1910 to 1913, as well as her grandfather Liberty Holden, who had interests in mining and newspapers, and specialized in medals of George Washington. A gift of a 1795 pendant-mounted gold eagle to young Emery May from her grandfather, made when she was 11 or 12 years old in 1915, launched her lifetime of coin collecting. Many years later she and her diplomat husband resumed collecting with a vengeance, through purchases from illustrious auction sales such as the memorable King Farouk offerings. Among the more memorable coins in the massive Norweb collection, dispersed in 1987 and 1988 after the Norwebs' death through three auction sales, were: a 1913 Liberty Head nickel; an 1894-S Barber dime; an 1876-CC twenty cent piece; an 1838-O half dollar; an 1870-S Seated Liberty dollar; an 1885 Trade dollar; an 1861 P-mint Paquet Reverse double eagle; and a 1907 Ultra High Relief double eagle.

The present coin, while not as legendary as those ultra-rarities, in another way is every bit as memorable as those phenomenal specimens. This PR68 Ultra Cameo 1898 eagle is the highest graded example of the issue at either NGC or PCGS. **This piece is also the single finest graded of the entire Liberty Head type at either service (11/06).** A close perusal of the NGC and PCGS population data, indeed, will confirm that precious few coins of the type—numbering less than three dozen pieces—are graded PR67, a fact that makes this spectacular PR68 Ultra Cameo coin even more rare and memorable. Most of the pieces grading PR67 understandably date from 1890s and 1900s, although NGC has graded one PR67 Ultra Cameo eagle dating back to 1839! It is also noteworthy—as our spectacular run of high grade proof gold coins from 1898 bears out—that the year was an especially good one for proof gold. NGC has also graded a total of five 1898 eagles in PR67, as Cameo or Ultra Cameo.

As might be expected, the present example approaches perfection in every conceivable aspect. The fields go "black" when tilted at the proper angle with thick, frosted golden luster. Each side is nearly perfectly preserved. Like the quarter eagle from this set, this coin shows extreme orange-peel texture—only on this piece it is on the obverse rather than the reverse. (#98838)

Glittering 1904 Eagle PR64 Cameo

3666   1904 PR64 Cameo NGC. Although the official proof mintage for this year is recorded to be 108 pieces, survivors are at least as scarce as other dates with noticeably lower mintage figures. Perhaps attrition just took a greater toll during the eventful decades that followed. This specimen is notable for deep, watery reflectivity and appreciable contrast for a proof from this era. The yellow-gold surfaces are not without a few modest blemishes, one easily found between Liberty's chin and star 2. A few more pinpoint marks are located beneath ME in AMERICA. If the coin's glittering appearance isn't convincing enough, a die line within the curl below the ear, located near the top of the neck, serves as a diagnostic for this rare proof issue. Census: 6 in 64, 8 finer (11/06). (#88844)

INDIAN EAGLES

Beautiful Choice Proof 1907 Liberty Eagle

3667   1907 PR64 NGC. This is the final year of mintage for the proof Liberty eagle and the lowest mintage of the 20th century. The piece's status as a proof is confirmed by the exquisitely and deeply mirrored fields, orange peel surfaces, and sharply struck devices. A significant amount of contrast exists between the devices and the fields, giving a nice black-and-white (or black-and-gold) effect when examining the coin from straight on, but apparently not quite enough to justify a Cameo designation. The Choice grade appears to be determined by a few pinpricks in the fields, and belies the more than ample eye appeal this coin possesses. (#8847)

Lovely Mint State 1907 Wire Rim Eagle

3668   1907 Wire Rim MS62 NGC. Light yellow-gold surfaces with faint greenish tendencies. This piece is satiny and fully lustrous with thin wire rims around the entire coin on both sides, much like the wire rim High Relief double eagles. For the specialist in Indian gold coinage, this piece represents the art of Augustus Saint-Gaudens as he intended it to be, before Charles Barber got his hands on the design to make his "improvements." The generally accepted mintage figure is 500 coins, but many were saved and pieces are usually available for a price.
From The Twin Hollows Collection. (#8850)

Historic 1907 Wire Rim Ten
MS65 PCGS

3669   1907 Wire Rim MS65 PCGS. This is a Gem quality representative of the famous Indian Head design created for the ten dollar gold piece by Augustus Saint-Gaudens. The model for the head of Liberty on this piece is not known to the present generation, but it probably derived from several sources. Homer Saint-Gaudens, the designer's son, commented that "the profile head was modeled from a woman supposed to have negro blood in her veins. Who, other than an Indian, may be a 'pure American' is undetermined. In reality here, as in all examples of my father's ideals sculpture, little or no resemblance can be traced to any model; since he was always quick to reject the least taint of what he called 'personality' in such instances."

Cornelius Vermeule discussed this topic in *Numismatic Art in America:* "The tale about a woman of negro blood serving as the ultimate source for the head of Liberty on the ten-dollar coin may be correct in that artists had constant recourse to living models, but there is a clear line of classical progression from the so-called 'Beautiful Head' made at Pergamon about 165 B.C. to the Nike of the Sherman Monument and thence to the coins. The sculptures at Pergamon had been excavated in the previous generation, and they were artistic sensations of the decades when Saint-Gaudens was at the height of his fame and creativity."

Only 16 finer examples of this issue have been certified by PCGS (12/06). It is a sharply struck Gem with finely granular surfaces that were imparted at the time it was minted. The reverse has considerable die polish in the fields that impart a satiny appearance. Both sides are fully brilliant with a hint of green over bright yellow surfaces. (#8850)

Elite 1907 Wire Rim Indian Eagle MS65

3670   1907 Wire Rim MS65 PCGS. Approximately 500 Wire Edge tens were struck by the Philadelphia Mint to provide a test run for Augustus Saint-Gaudens' original Indian Head eagle design. As none of these coins were intended for circulation, this issue is technically a pattern and at least half of the original mintage of this issue survives for the benefit of today's collectors. Like the 1856 Flying Eagle cent and 1836 Gobrecht dollar, issues struck under similar circumstances, the Judd reference number (here Judd-1774) has been dropped in most popular references. Never actually released into circulation, lower grade or damaged survivors of this elusive variety are more the result of collector mishandling or abuse.

This is a satiny greenish-gold Gem with a delicate reddish tinge about the devices. Normal die polish or finishing lines are especially prominent on the reverse. We notice a shallow luster grazes on the neck and a few others of less severity are found in the headdress. Trivial marks also affect the lower half of the reverse. It sounds odd to make such a statement, but this high quality representative is one of several Gem or better Wire Rim eagles in tonight's Platinum session. Population: 39 in 65, 16 finer (11/06). (#8850)

Bright, Frosted 1907 Wire Rim Ten
MS65 PCGS

3671   1907 Wire Rim MS65 PCGS. The Wire Rim tens are the equivalent to the Ultra High Reliefs, in that each represents Augustus Saint-Gaudens' concept of how circulating coinage should appear in the United States. Much has been written about the antagonism between Saint-Gaudens and Chief Engraver Charles Barber. Much of what has been written about the animosity between these two is true, but the fact is Charles Barber was correct in certain regards. Nevertheless, that does not keep writers from demonizing him in the story of the development of the ten and twenty dollar coins—after all, every good story needs an antagonist. What Barber knew from decades of experience was that coins like the Ultra High Relief, the regular High Relief, and the Wire Rim tens could not be struck for use in the channels of commerce. In the case of the twenties, they required too many blows from a medal (hydraulic) press. In the case of the tens, Charles Barber's lack of skill with the new Janvier Reducing Lathe gave the coins soft, mushy design elements. The next attempt at commercial production was even less successful when Barber reduced the ten dollar design and the result was the Rolled Rim coins.

The Wire Rim tens were never really circulated as Saint-Gaudens intended. They were largely sold to collectors, museums, and administration officials as mementoes. As a result, most examples survive today in high grade. This is a particularly attractive coin that shows the usual bright yellow-gold surfaces with a hint of reddish patina around the margins. The slightly granular surfaces are essentially free of contact marks, the only interruption in the flow of the mint luster coming from the die polishing marks in the field that are seen on all Wire Rim tens. (#8850)

Rare 1907 Wire Rim Eagle, MS66 ★

3672 **1907 Wire Rim MS66 ★ NGC.** Breen-7094. The Wire Rim pieces are technically patterns (Judd-1774), as they were never intended for circulation. The Breen *Complete Encyclopedia* (1988) says that "Almost all survivors are UNCs. distributed to officials and VIPs." Designed with triangular dots for periods and a "knife" or wire rim, these rare pieces show another distinction: Breen adds that "[Saint] Gaudens's standing-eagle device is splendid in its original form, reminiscent of late Egyptian and early Roman work at its best, though it is seen in untampered form only in the rare experimental pieces [Breen-7094 to -7096]." The eagle treads upon an olive branch and strikes a truculent, powerful pose, with an aggressive expression that says it is competent to deal with any threat.

The obverse design is more compromised. Were it not for President Theodore Roosevelt's insistence that Augustus Saint-Gaudens place an unlikely Indian war bonnet on the female head, this design would likely be called the Nike Head or Victory Head: It is based on "General Sherman Led by Victory," a bronze statue at the entrance to New York's Central Park that took Saint-Gaudens 11 years to complete.

Doubt lingers as to whether these pieces, with a mintage of about 500 examples, were struck in proof format or not. A February 1907 letter from Mint Superintendent Frank Landis, cited in Taxay's *U.S. Mint and Coinage,* mentions 50 proof pieces, but Breen's proof *Encyclopedia* calls any purported examples "so rare in proof as to be controversial." The more recent Garrett-Guth gold *Encyclopedia* makes no mention of confirmed proof examples, citing the Smithsonian's finest piece as an "MS-66." Our own experience with this issue also leads us to doubt that true proof examples exist, and neither NGC nor PCGS has certified any proofs. The present specimen is one of 30 MS66 coins currently certified at NGC and PCGS combined, which have graded 11 pieces finer (10/06).

This is an absolutely amazing coin. The surfaces have a thick, frosted finish, quite unlike the bright satiny luster usually seen. Also, Wire Rim tens usually have a bright yellow-gold finish, but this piece has rich reddish-orange coloration. Each side is also remarkably well preserved—one could literally count the number of contact marks on one hand that are present on this piece. While finer examples have been certified, it is difficult to imagine a coin with stronger eye appeal, thicker mint luster, and fewer obvious marks.

From The Freedom Collection. (#8850)

Historic Gem 1907 Rolled Rim Indian Head Eagle

3673   **1907 Rolled Rim MS65 NGC.** Judd-1903. As part of Augustus Saint-Gaudens' commission to rede-sign the four circulating gold coins plus the cent at the behest of President Theodore Roosevelt, at one point the sculptor proposed to Roosevelt that the head of Liberty wearing the feather headdress for the obverse, combined with the flying eagle on the reverse, should be used on the twenty dollar piece (and on the cent), rather than the striding full figure of Liberty on the obverse that was ultimately adopted. So that Saint-Gaud-ens could see the concept embodied on a coin, Roosevelt ordered a piece to be made, creating one of the rarest and most celebrated of all pattern coins, the Judd-1905 gold Indian Head double eagle. Only a single piece was produced. Roosevelt reviewed the concept coin with Mint Director George E. Roberts, who re-plied to Saint-Gaudens that the walking figure of Liberty would apply to the double eagle, with the "feath-er head of Liberty with the standing eagle" on the ten dollar coin (Roger Burdette, *Renaissance of American Coinage 1905-1908)*. Roberts made no further mention of the cent.

The first models for the ten dollar coin had deeply cut edges, soft detailing, and the date in Roman nu-merals, which Roberts deemed impractical. The first production coins had a wire or knife rim, and triangular dots for periods before and after TEN DOLLARS. Coins of the new design would not stack. During this time Mint personnel were still experimenting with the 46-star edge collar, and early specimens had irregularly spaced, different-sized stars along the edge. Mint Engraver Charles Barber, curtailing his summer vacation (and deeply resenting Saint-Gaudens, apparently to the end), redesigned the eagles with a rounded rim. Al-though in the meantime a third version of the eagle had been received (from Homer Saint-Gaudens, Augus-tus's son). Saint-Gaudens died from intestinal cancer in August 1907 and general confusion resulted in the production of 31,500 coins with the rounded rim and soft central details. The Judd pattern reference, eighth and ninth editions, list these as Judd-1903, renumbered from Judd-1775 in the seventh and earlier editions. Burdette says, "These are not patterns and are best described as abandoned production trials." The rounded rim allowed the coins to stack, and protected them from wear. All except 50 pieces (according to Burdette; most other experts say 42) were ordered melted, apparently at Barber's insistence. These coins retained the triangular, raised dots as periods of the initial Wire Rim coins. The surfaces are bright yellow-gold with thick, satiny mint frost. The strike through the centers is soft, a diagnostic for the issue. The combined NGC/PCGS population data show a total of 69 pieces graded at both services, although that total is still a far cry from the 189 pieces that the Garrett-Guth gold *Encyclopedia* puzzlingly claims those two services have certified.

The present MS65 specimen is one of 12 pieces so graded at NGC, with five coins finer (10/06). This is another dazzlingly elusive and historic coin of the seminal early days of Saint-Gaudens' coinage designs, one destined to be a centerpiece of any fine numismatic collection.
From The Freedom Collection. (#8851)

Delightfully Toned 1907 No Periods Ten MS66 PCGS

3674   1907 No Periods MS66 PCGS. A spectacular beauty, with a cameo effect given not by the field-device contrast but by contrasting color schemes between the fields and highpoints on each side. While the pristine fields sport greenish-gold hues, the device highpoints are beautifully colored in yellow-gold and orange-gold shades. While this issue of one of the most available of the series in high grades, with numerous pieces grading MS67 and one piece each at NGC and PCGS in MS68, is doubtful that many examples, regardless of their numeric grade, could be more aesthetically appealing. Population: 59 in 66, 6 finer (12/06). (#8852)

Superb Gem 1907 No Periods Indian Ten

3675   1907 No Periods MS67 NGC. A magnificent Superb Gem of this introductory business strike issue. Cartwheel luster dominates both fields and devices, and both sides are virtually immaculate. The strike is bold, since only the eagle's right (facing) claw lacks absolute detail. A partial wire rim is present along the right borders. By the standards of the Indian type, the 1907 is plentiful in bagmarked Mint State grades, since pieces were careless stored as bullion holdings or bank reserves. At the MS67 level, however, the 1907 emerges as a significant conditional rarity. Census: 19 in 67, 1 finer (11/06). (#8852)

Outstanding Gem 1908 No Motto Eagle

3676   1908 No Motto MS65 PCGS. Of the 184 No Motto Gem eagles certified by PCGS, fully 164 of them are dated 1907. While not so elusive in MS65 as the 1908-D (of which PCGS has graded just two examples in that grade), this issue, with its picayune mintage of 33,500 pieces, still presents a significant challenge for those who would collect the series. Anyone who acquires this lot would lift a significant roadblock to a complete set of Saint-Gaudens eagles. The devices are well struck, and the softly lustrous apricot-gold surfaces have only a handful of small marks. A few minor ticks on Liberty's cheek and on the eagle's leg prevent an even higher grade. Population: 18 in 65, 9 finer (12/06). (#8853)

Gorgeous 1908-D No Motto Ten Dollar MS64 PCGS

3677   1908-D No Motto MS64 PCGS. The 1908-D No Motto ten dollar is considered to be one of the least attractive in the Indian Head series. This is because it is generally flatly struck on the obverse and is somewhat lackluster. These characteristics account, at least in part, for the paucity of high-end Mint State coins in the certified population. The near-Gem specimen offered here is a notable exception. Peach-gold surfaces are tinted with yellow-gold and light green, and exhibit pleasing luster. The design elements are well brought up, including good definition in the Indian's hair, and on the feathers of the bonnet and the eagle. A couple of minute marks are noted on the Indian's neck, but we hasten to mention that this gorgeous coin reveals fewer marks than what might be expected for the grade designation. (#8854)

Fantastic 1908-S Gem Ten Dollar

3678   1908-S MS65 PCGS. Jeff Garrett and Ron Guth assert in their *Encyclopedia of U.S. Gold Coins, 1795-1933* that: "This date is available in Gem and even Superb Gem grades in spite of the very low mintage (59,850 pieces). Most examples were very sharply struck and quite lustrous, some with a fine granular appearance, and others frostier. One of the requirements for a Gem grade from the grading services is eye appeal, and this date was blessed with splendid eye appeal."

This MS65 example exudes dazzling luster and a medley of peach-gold, yellow-gold, and mint-green patina. The surfaces are somewhat fine-grained, and exhibit well struck design features. A few light reverse marks in no way detract from this coin's fantastic eye appeal. (#8861)

Beautiful Near-Gem 1909-D Eagle

3679   1909-D MS64 PCGS. An appealing example of this luster-challenged issue, here with blazing luster on both sides complementing alternating areas of peach-gold and greenish-gold. A simply beautiful near-Gem, the present piece under a loupe reveals a couple of tiny ticks on the cheek and chin that limit a Gem grade, but they also disclose enormous eye appeal and appealing depth of character. Since so few Gem examples have been graded (currently only a half-dozen at NGC and PCGS combined), the present specimen appears to offer both aesthetic quality and monetary value. Population: 28 in 64, 10 finer (11/06). (#8863)

Dynamic Superb Gem 1909-D
Saint-Gaudens Eagle

3680   1909-D MS67 NGC. When the Denver Mint started production in 1906, it, like the New Orleans Mint before it, began by striking silver and gold coinage. The fledgling Colorado establishment quickly proved its usefulness, and in conjunction with the resurgent "Granite Lady" in San Francisco, it demonstrated by comparison how outmoded the facility at New Orleans had become. In the year Denver minted this attractive ten dollar gold piece, one of 121,540 such examples, America's southernmost branch mint produced dimes through half dollars and half eagles only, and the New Orleans Mint never struck another coin before it was decommissioned in 1911.

Although the spotlight is rarely on the 1909-D eagle when numismatists think of gold coins from that year, it is impossible to deny the remarkable condition rarity of this representative. It is the *only* Superb Gem of this issue graded by NGC, and PCGS has certified just two examples in this lofty grade (12/06). Interestingly, now Heritage can claim to have offered all three of them, the first at the FUN 1999 sale, and the second (which was pedigreed to the Price collection) at the Morse sale of November 2005. The present piece has vivid orange-gold surfaces and strong, slightly satiny luster. A trace of emerald graces the reverse fields. The strike is generally solid and trumps the norm for this issue, though, as always, a trace of softness affects the hair below the headband and the eagle's talons. The obverse is incredibly clean, and only a handful of tiny marks and grazes on the reverse preclude an even higher grade. Overall, the eye appeal is highly favorable, and this piece holds its own when compared side-by-side with photographs of the Price-Morse specimen. This lot offers a remarkable second chance for those who vied for that piece and a fleeting opportunity for all other interested collectors. (#8863)

Elusive 1910-S Ten Dollar MS64

3681   1910-S MS64 NGC. The 1910-S eagle is one of the true condition rarities of the series: Gem and finer pieces of this issue number only eight specimens at both services, so this high-end near-Gem poses an especially attractive alternative. Luscious, deep orange-gold surfaces with coruscating luster are the hallmark of this elusive and important coin. The few light abrasions, mostly visible only under a loupe, are completely consistent with the near-Gem grade. Only a single tick is noted on the Indian's cheek, along with a small luster break on the reverse just above the motto. Extremely appealing! Census: 8 in 64, 4 finer (12/06). (#8867)

High-End Near-Gem 1910-S Eagle

3682   1910-S MS64 PCGS. In near-Gem and Gem grades the 1910-S is one of the most difficult and hard-to-obtain issues in the entire Indian Head eagle series. As of this writing (12/06), NGC and PCGS combined have certified an even dozen pieces in MS65, with only 28 coins in MS64. This lustrous coin must certainly rank among the top of the certified MS64 survivors. Deep orange-gold predominates over the reverse and portions of the obverse, which adds greenish-gold and canary-yellow into the mix. Even for an MS64 grade the abrasions are minimal, and the eye appeal is enormous. Population: 20 in 64, 4 finer (11/06). (#8867)

Beautiful Satin 1912 Eagle, MS66 NGC

3683   1912 MS66 NGC. Thick satin luster, almost matte in appearance, is immediately evident over the surfaces of this eagle, which boasts a considerable amount of attractive light rose color over its gold sheen. The strike is strong, with the exception of a bit of weakness on the highest point of the eagle's wing, as sometimes seen on this date. Surface marks are at a minimum, and the eye appeal is uncommonly high even for a coin in such a lofty grade as the present piece. Not a rare date in absolute terms by any means, yet quite rare as a Gem and obviously even more so in MS66. Only two pieces have been certified finer, one of which is the MS67 piece we offered in April 2006. This is a beautiful coin, likely destined to highlight an outstanding date or type set. Census: 18 in 66, 1 finer (11/06). (#8871)

Eye-Appealing MS66 1913 Eagle

3684   1913 MS66 NGC. The generous mintage of nearly a half-million pieces is hardly indicative of this issue's rarity in Premium Gem grade, where both services combined have certified less than two-dozen pieces, even before resubmissions are excluded. Brilliant luster exudes from the satiny, yellow-gold surfaces that virtually *drip* with that most desirable of numismatic characteristics, *eye appeal*. We mention a tiny luster graze beneath E PLURIBUS UNUM for accuracy. Collectors seeking a pleasing alternative to the pedestrian 1926 and 1932 eagle issues for their type sets would do well to ponder—and bid—on the present example. Census: 9 in 66, 0 finer (11/06). (#8873)

Scarce 1913-S Ten Dollar MS63

3685   1913-S MS63 PCGS. Fully lustrous surfaces with deep or-ange-gold color and excellent eye appeal. This example is housed in an older green-label holder. Each side has the typical quota of light surface marks expected at this grade level. The mintage of this date was pegged at 66,000 coins, the sixth lowest of the series, and yet David Akers ranked this date as first out of 32 issues for rarity in Mint State grades. He commented: "The 1913-S is the premier rarity of the series and is extremely difficult, if not virtually impossible, to obtain in MS-64 or better condition." Population: 19 in 63, 15 finer (11/06). (#8874)

Lofty 1914 Indian Eagle MS66

3686   1914 MS66 PCGS. A well struck Premium Gem with booming luster and lovely apricot and yellow-gold toning. Deter-mined evaluation locates only trivial contact. Philadelphia Mint ea-gle production annually exceeded 400,000 pieces between 1911 and 1913, but in 1914, the mintage was limited to 151,000 business strikes and 50 proofs. Presumably, the reason for the reduced mint-age was the outbreak of the World War in Europe. Shipping bullion was dangerous during wartime due to enemy submarines. Mintages at Philadelphia did recover to 351,000 pieces in 1915, but the facil-ity omitted the denomination thereafter until 1926. Population: 7 in 66, 2 finer (11/06). (#8875)

Superb 1915 Indian Head Eagle MS67

3687   1915 MS67 NGC. This is one of the plentiful dates in the series, from a mintage of 351,000 coins, and yet it is virtually impossible to locate in Gem quality. Noted gold coinage authority David Akers commented about this issue: "True gems are rare but are seen more often than all but a handful of the series' 32 issues. In addition to the MS65 quality coins, there are also a small number of superb MS67 quality specimens known, including several nearly perfect ones." While we are not certain that Mr. Akers actually saw this particular coin, it certainly qualifies as a nearly perfect example. Both sides have fully brilliant yellow-gold luster with frosty surfaces. Hints of pinkish toning complement the color of this Superb Gem. The reverse has a few tiny copper toning spots, but these are hidden in the design work, and not readily apparent. No finer examples of this date have been certified, and, in fact, this is only the fourth Superb Gem example that has appeared in any of our auctions since 1993. Census: 4 in 67, 0 finer (12/06). (#8878)

Scarce 1920-S Indian Head Ten Dollar MS60

3688   1920-S MS60 NGC. According to Jeff Garrett and Ron Guth, writing in the new *Encyclopedia of U.S. Gold Coins, 1795-1933*: "This is the third-rarest date overall in the entire series, behind the coveted 1933 and 1907, Rolled Edge variety. Obviously, the three-year hiatus did little to drum up excitement for this series, and most of these entered circulation unnoticed soon after the time of issue." The current example exhibits admirable striking detail and pleasing, if slightly muted satiny luster. An interesting planchet lamination (as struck) occurs over the U in UNITED. Scattered small abrasions and a few moderate marks, on the lower left obverse, determine the numerical grade designation. Census: 3 in 60, 15 finer (11/06). (#8881)

Prized 1930-S Indian Head
Ten Dollar MS64

3689   1930-S MS64 PCGS. A quick perusal of tonight's Platinum session offerings of 1930-S eagles will certainly prompt the gold specialist to do a double take. The immediate response might be something like "that must be some kind of misprint" or for the less well informed "maybe I am confusing the 1930-S ten dollar with the 1932 ten dollar." We can think of a few others that best stay off the record. To be sure, it almost boggles the numismatic mind to consider that no less than five MS64 and MS65 examples of the highly prized 1930-S Indian eagle will cross the auction block on one night. Since most of what could possibly be said about this low mintage S-mint Indian will be presented in the other four Choice or better examples, we will concentrate here on the coin itself.

This splendid, wholly original example derives much of its beauty from the bountiful frosty luster that shimmers over each side. Light blushes of orange patina can be seen over the major design elements, attractively accenting characteristic yellow-gold surfaces. The strike is more than adequate for the issue, with only a nominal degree of softness noted on the eagle's leg feathers. A few mostly paper-thin luster grazes affect the lower left obverse field and neck area of the portrait. These relatively minor disturbances are all that separates this attractive 1930-S from a Gem rating. Housed in an old second generation PCGS holder.

From The Twin Hollows Collection. (#8883)

Elegant Choice 1930-S
Ten Dollar Gold Piece

3690   1930-S MS64 PCGS. Production of eagles could best be described as fitful in the years leading up to the gold recall of 1933. After 1915, the Philadelphia Mint would coin examples in just three other years, though two of them were the million-plus mintages for 1926 and 1932. (The third, of course, is the famed rarity of 1933.) San Francisco was the only mint to produce the ten dollar pieces in 1916, and it would coin just two more issues, those of 1920 and 1930. Both of these later issues faced heavy melting, though the 1930-S was less affected than the coins of a decade earlier. This may seem counterintuitive, particularly with the trend of increasing difficulty for later-date issues, Garrett and Guth cleverly note that few European banks, one of the best sources of American gold coinage, were ill-equipped to acquire such coinage in 1920, as that continent was still recovering from the Great War. While the 1930-S is significantly more available than its 1920 counterpart, such availability is relative, particularly as one moves up the Mint State grades.

The present example is a highly lustrous and suitably struck survivor from the original mintage of 96,000 pieces. The surfaces are predominantly apricot-gold, and jewel-toned swirls of pale citrine and emerald grace the frosty fields. Overall, the appearance of the piece is clean, and only a pair of light abrasions on the obverse, one on the cheekbone, the other on the jaw, keeps this near-Gem from an even higher grade. A remarkable representative of this late-date issue, best appreciated in person. Population: 35 in 64, 18 finer (11/06). (#8883)

Impressive Gem 1930-S Indian Eagle

3691   1930-S MS65 NGC. In September 2002 we offered three examples of this rare date Indian eagle in a single sale, and the finest of those was just MS64. Today, we are pleased to offer three MS65 grade pieces, nearly the finest available examples of the date. In 1926, the Philadelphia Mint coined over 1 million eagles, an ample supply for commerce of the remainder of the 1920s. The mintage of this 1930-S issue was halted after 96,000 coins were produced, and even these pieces were not needed in commerce, thus most remained in Mint or Treasury vaults until they were melted in 1933. Although this date is not impossible to locate in Gem quality, examples are certainly elusive, with just 27 MS65 examples certified by NGC and PCGS, and only eight finer pieces.

This gorgeous Gem is just a few marks shy of being the finest graded, with just three coins certified as high as MS67. Both sides have highly lustrous and brilliant orange-gold surfaces with no breaks in the luster on either side. A minor blemish is evident in the left obverse field with a tiny tick on Liberty's cheek. Otherwise, both sides are pristine and exceptionally attractive. This piece has a sharp strike. Only a couple hair strands below LIBERTY show any inconsistency of detail. Every detail of the eagle on the reverse is remarkably full and complete. Even the claws show nearly full detail. For the connoisseur who seeks exceptional aesthetic appeal, this coin and the present sale offer an exceptional opportunity. (#8883)

Gem Mint State 1930-S Indian Eagle

3692 1930-S MS65 NGC. A highly lustrous Gem with intermingled orange-gold and lemon-yellow frost. A small scrape in the left obverse field is the only blemish of note. The strike is sharp, as usual for this issue, with bold details on both sides, save for a few hair strands behind Liberty's eye. The eagle is bold with crisp wing feathers and sharp claws. A few tiny splashes of orange toning are evident on the reverse.

Among Mint State Indian eagles, the 1930-S ranks in the middle, rarity wise. This issue is not known in grades below MS60. Every survivor has been preserved in the best possible condition. In his 1988 *Handbook of 20th Century United States Gold Coins,* David Akers wrote: "In my opinion, this issue ranks pretty much in the middle of the series with respect to both population rarity (in Mint State only) and condition rarity. The fact that it is priced so much higher than other issues that are less rare is due solely to the fact that the 1930-S is not generally available in circulated grades while the others are." Akers went on to discuss the existence of small hoard: "A small hoard of original Mint State pieces (reportedly 40 to 50 pieces) is still intact in the San Francisco area; I have taken this hoard into account in my rarity ratings and I estimate the total population of this issue to be around 95 to 100 pieces." Now, nearly 20 years later, we are not aware that this, or any other hoards, remain intact.

The most recent entry into literature for U.S. gold coinage is the *Gold Encyclopedia* penned by Jeff Garrett and Ron Guth. These authors speculated a much higher survival for this issue: "In overall terms of rarity, this date ranks a little behind the 1920-S, with just a few hundred known in all, and those are scattered over the grading spectrum." In our opinion, the true population is in the 125 to 140 coin range. (#8883)

1933 and the Recall of American Gold

"Therefore, pursuant to the above authority, I hereby proclaim that such gold and silver holdings are prohibited, and that all such coin, bullion or other possessions of gold and silver be tendered within fourteen days to agents of the Government of the United States for compensation at the official price, in the legal tender of the Government. All safe deposit boxes in banks or financial institutions have been sealed, pending action in the due course of the law. All sales or purchases or movements of such gold and silver within the borders of the United States and its territories, and all foreign exchange transactions or movements of such metals across the border are hereby prohibited.

"Your possession of these proscribed metals and/or your maintenance of a safe-deposit box to store them is known to the Government from bank and insurance records. Therefore, be advised that your vault box must remain sealed, and may only be opened in the presence of an agent of The Internal Revenue Service.

"By lawful Order given this day, the President of the United States."

In 1933, as the saying goes, the times were "hard." This land of ours had known almost unprecedented growth as a nation. America had started as one of numerous colonies of Great Britain, with a people of great ethnic diversity but not so much as today, for most Americans in 1933 were of European descent—solid stock from England, Ireland, Germany, Sweden and other pockets of the Continent. Few countries were not represented by the bloodlines of other nations, and the "work ethic" was common among all these peoples. They came from oppressed situations to make a new life, in a new land full of opportunity. In a little more than a century, America had broken away from its former master, had expanded, had nearly been split in two but had mended, had grown first by agriculture and then by the discovery of gold in California, and then by industry and invention. Yet we remained an isolated nation to a great extent, not part of the company of major countries—until our military might proved itself in World War One. But then came the great crash on Wall Street in 1929, which devolved into the Great Depression—a downturn in both the economy and the spirit of the land. By 1933, America was struggling. Many people were afraid of the future.

Then came a new presence to the White House. In 1933 Franklin Delano Roosevelt took office. He had been born at a golden moment, in 1882. He had a checkered career in government before being elected President, but many Americans felt he could rescue them from the dire economic times of the early 1930s. One of the first things he did was to change the course of American history—he signed into law the executive order quoted above.

There had been a fairly recent precedent for the Presidential action of 1933. In 1917, during World War One, Congress had passed a bill which became known as the Trading with the Enemy Act. It stated in article 5(b) that the "President may investigate, regulate or prohibit, under such rules and regulations as he may prescribe, by means of licenses or otherwise, any transactions in foreign exchange for the export, hoarding, melting, or earmarking of gold or silver coins or bullion or currency." So, in 1933, FDR was simply re-enacting the law of 1917, hoping to stabilize the difficult economy and to outlaw the hoarding of gold.

Most citizens complied with the law and dutifully turned over their gold coins. Ironically, another act of Congress would have made all of them richer by almost double only months after the recall law of 1933. The Gold Reserve Act was passed on January 30, 1934, revaluing gold from the former $20.67 (which prevailed when gold coins were recalled) to a new official rate of $35 per ounce.

Many Americans, of course, hid their gold and did not turn it over to their federal government. Many coins were also exported, to remain hidden in Europe and in Caribbean countries for half a century. These actions explain the existence of earlier gold coins today, as well as the fact that many "new coin collectors" were born in 1933, not so much in fact as in name, as the only legal means of hanging on to their U.S. gold coins struck in earlier years.

But almost all the gold coins struck early in 1933 did not escape. Most remained in the vaults of the Treasury and went into the melting pots, creating today's rarities. That is because, while many pieces were minted prior to the change in the law in 1933, few had been released to banks or to the public. In fact, none had been officially released (save one, or perhaps others—as future litigation with the federal government will some day prove) of the twenty dollar denomination. A mere handful of tens had been released, however, accounting for their legal status today. But it was a mere handful! It is not known exactly how many escaped the melting pots in 1933, but today 1933 Indian ten dollar coins are among the rarest of all our coins, of any period in our history. All were minted at Philadelphia. A best guess is that only about three dozen survived—just 1/10,000th of the mintage. They were the last of a breed that began in 1795, named for one of the great native symbols of the land—the American bald eagle. From the controversial gold-recall law of 1933 was born a numismatic classic.

1933 Eagle, Numismatic Highlight in Near-Gem Condition

3693   1933 MS64 NGC. Ex: Freedom Collection.

The Presidential order of March 9, 1933 exempted items of "recognized special value to collectors of rare and unusual coins." Late in 1933 a revised order removed the statement allowing individuals to hold up to $100 worth of gold coins or gold certificates (in addition to pieces with recognized numismatic value), so that afterward, only numismatically valuable pieces could be legally held. Although the government during 1933 issued several pronouncements that it would remain on the gold standard, in early 1934 legislation terminated the production of current gold coinage, removed the remaining gold coins from circulation, removed the gold metal backing from paper money, and took the United States off of the gold standard. A true fiat money was created in the United States, one backed by nothing other than the citizens' trust in their government. Needless to say, many other world governments and owners of gold coinage had a much more cynical view, and they chose to maintain their possessions of U.S. gold coins. (This was a short decade after the German hyperinflation of the Weimar Republic, and only four years after America's great Stock Market Crash of 1929.) Later, when import restrictions were loosened, Europe, Latin America, and some Asian countries became fertile ground for the repatriation of many gold pieces, some of them quite rare and elusive.

As with all three pieces in this auction, this coin has thick mint frost. This example differs from the other two by the rich golden color that is interspersed by light lilac in the recesses of the design. The striking details are strong on each side, and the only marks worthy of note are a couple behind the mouth of the Indian, one along the jawline, and another at the front of the neck. The reverse is remarkably clean with only one, barely noticeable mark which is located in the field above the P in PLURIBUS. One of a remarkable offering of three of these rarities, this piece is certainly worthy of consideration by the specialist.
From The Freedom Collection. (#8885)

Outstanding 1933 Ten Dollar, MS64 PCGS

3694   1933 MS64 PCGS. The 1933 eagle and double eagle issues are inextricably linked, owing to the great Gold Recall of 1933 and the subsequent Bank Holiday, beginning on March 6. The order of President Franklin D. Roosevelt barred private U.S. citizens for many years from owning gold coins (and related paper certificates) *except for items of numismatic significance.* Both the 1933 eagle and the 1933 double eagle are fabled rarities. On the surface, the coins bear many similarities, but, fortunately for bidders on the current lot, there are key differences.

The United States continued minting gold coins intermittently for several months after Roosevelt took the country off the gold standard. Two executive orders banned the release of additional gold coins for circulation, but by longstanding practice, collectors could obtain copies of the current year's coinage from the Mint cashier, a practice that apparently continued through at least the first several months of 1933. On April 5, 1933, a Presidential order decreed that owners of gold coins (and gold certificates) were to return them to the Federal Reserve System by May 1, except for amounts of less than $100 per person.

The 1933 double eagle issue has no record of release through official channels before the President's declaration, and as of this writing only a single specimen is clearly legal to own, having been "remonetized" by the U.S. government. That coin, the former possession of King Farouk of Egypt, set a price of $7.59 million in a Sotheby's/Stack's auction in July 2002, a record that still stands today as the highest price ever paid for a single coin, U.S. or otherwise. The legal status of several other 1933 double eagles remains unclear (at least to many persons), and those pieces are the subject of ongoing litigation. However, the legal status of the 1933 ten dollar issue has never been in question.

This upper-end MS64 coin shows the same frosted mint luster as the other two examples in this sale, but this piece differs slightly with a brighter sheen and a silkier texture. As always, the striking details are strong throughout. The abrasions that account for the less-than-Gem grade are almost all located on the reverse. This is a fortunate occurrence, especially if the coin is displayed obverse-up, in which case the coin appears to be a full blown Gem. Each side shows even reddish patina with just the slightest hint of lilac around the eagle on the reverse. An outstanding example of this 20th century rarity. (#8885)

Delectable Matte PR66
1908 With Motto Eagle

3695   1908 Motto PR66 PCGS. The 1907 No Motto eagles released into circulation reflected President Theodore Roosevelt's personal conviction that the name of the Deity should not appear on coinage. Those first eagles entering the channels of commerce were Mint Engraver Charles Barber's reworking of sculptor-designer Augustus Saint-Gaudens' original design concept. However, the Mint Act of 1865 mandated that the motto IN GOD WE TRUST should appear on all larger coins, and Congress insisted upon it. Acceding to the majority rule (and knowing where his bread was buttered), Roosevelt accordingly had the motto added to the 1908 eagles and double eagles. Other minor design tweaks were made, including making the first U in UNUM more prominent. Proofs of this year are apparently found in three different finishes: a dark-olive matte proof finish; a "Roman gold" finish with a light yellow satiny semibrilliant surface; and a satin finish. The Garrett-Guth *Encyclopedia of U.S. Gold Coins 1795-1933* notes that "The finish most commonly seen is a dark matte Proof finish, and of the 116 coins struck, this represents virtually all known examples. As a date, this is the most commonly available of the Proof issues."

This piece is definitely one of the dark-olive proofs. The surfaces are virtually flawless on the obverse. The only "defects" on the reverse are a series of light, diagonal specks of green (the origin of which we really cannot determine or even speculate about), and two tiny marks on the upper part of the eagle's wing.

The current online NGC *Census Report* enumerates two satin finish proofs, both graded PR64, alongside 64 survivors with the matte finish, ranging from PR62 to PR68. PCGS's online *Population Report* also lists two satin finish proofs, both graded PR64, along with 34 matte proofs. The present specimen, graded PR66 by PCGS, is one of seven so graded, with none finer (11/06). Both of those population totals for matte proofs include the inevitable resubmissions. As the most available proof issue in the finest obtainable grade, this wonderful coin would make an ideal acquisition for a high grade type set. (#8890)

Enchanting Superb Gem
Proof 1909 Indian Eagle

3696   1909 PR67 NGC. This is an exceptionally rare proof gold coin, with only 74 specimens struck in this year of issue. It has been variously reported that between 7-9 and 20 proofs still exist. Akers uncovered only 13 appearances in auction over the decades he surveyed for his work on the series. We believe the number of pieces extant to be somewhat higher and estimate that perhaps 30-45 pieces may still exist. The proof process for this year and the next is the enchanting Roman Gold finish. This gives the coins a bright, satiny appearance with light color, obviously quite different from the traditional, darker matte finish. (Breen noted in his *Encyclopedia of U.S. and Colonial Proof Coins* that two 1909 coins are known that exhibit the matte finish that was also used on most 1908 proof eagles.) Roman Gold Indian eagles are very rarely seen today, and infrequently appear at major auctions.

The surfaces of this piece are bright and satiny and, as the grade would indicate, there are no mentionable marks or flaws that might be mentioned as identifiers for future research. The reddish-golden coloration is enchanting, and is one of the most noteworthy attributes of this particular piece. A rare opportunity for the gold specialist to purchase a Superb Gem example of one of the most elusive proof Indian eagle issues at this lofty grade level. Census: 4 in 67, 1 finer (11/06). (#8891)

Unique 1910 Matte Proof $10, PR66 NGC

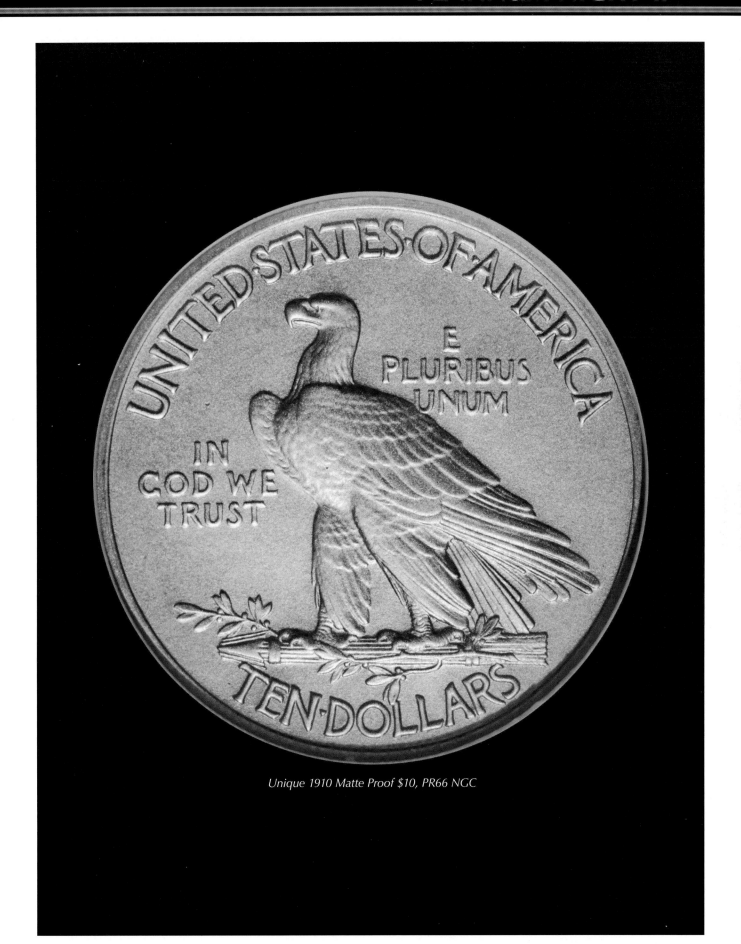

Unique 1910 Matte Proof $10, PR66 NGC

Unique 1910 Matte Proof Ten Dollar, PR66 NGC

3697   **1910 PR66 NGC.** This auction contains the last two coins from a unique four-piece set of matte proof gold coins from 1910. The existence of this set was not generally known until Jeff Garrett purchased it several years ago at a North Carolina coin show and then sold it soon thereafter.

The difference between the matte finish and so-called Roman Finish is profound. The matte finish was first used in the mint on regular production coins in 1908, and had been used on several medals previously. Like the previously produced brilliant finish proofs, planchets were carefully selected; however, the dies were not polished. Instead, the planchets were inserted in the high pressure medal press and struck once. After striking, the coins were taken to a small, enclosed cabinet and carefully sandblasted on each side with a stream of fine, industrial sand that imparted a dull, granular effect. The new, European-inspired proofs were not popular with collectors. But the fix in 1909-1910 proved even more unpopular. In those two years, the mint produced proofs that were struck with special dies on special planchets, but the coins received no post-striking treatment (that is, sandblasting). These coins were variously called bright proofs, Satin proofs, new style proofs, and yellow proofs. These coins proved even more unpopular with collectors than the previous matte proofs from 1908. William Woodin commented to Assistant Treasury Secretary A. Piatt Andrew in August, 1910: " ... The present [satin] proofs of the Saint-Gaudens designs and the Pratt designs are simply rotten. I know of no other word to express it ..." Collectors today would surely agree that Woodin overreacted to the new finish, but the mint in 1910 was sensitive to the comments by collectors and especially one as influential as William Woodin.

As a result, mint personnel prepared to revert to the matte finish in 1911. But trial strikes had to be prepared, and that is what this coin, and the others from this set that we have offered, represent. There is no trace of the semi-brilliant finish seen on the Roman Finish proofs from 1909 and 1910. Rather, this piece shows fine granularity with darker reddish-tan color. Perfectly preserved since the year of issue, there are only two tiny pedigree identifiers that we see. One is a minute planchet flake above the star at 1 o'clock on the obverse; the other is another tiny flake in the reverse field between the N in UNITED and the foremost curve of the eagle's wing.

Only one set of matte proofs were struck in 1910. This piece represents a unique opportunity for the collector of ten dollar proofs or the collector of varieties of special strikings from the period of the American Renaissance of Coinage. (#8892)

LIBERTY DOUBLE EAGLES

Extraordinary Gem 1850 Double Eagle

3698   1850 MS65 NGC. According to *The Encyclopedia of U.S. Gold Coins, 1795-1933,* (2006): "In 1848 the discovery of gold in California turned the American economy on its ear. Suddenly, vast quantities of gold were available to be quickly converted into money. Although the $10 gold piece was perfectly suited for the job, the Treasury took the opportunity to create a new denomination called a double eagle, worth twice the face value of the $10 eagle." The design for the series was executed by James B. Longacre. Approximately 1.1 million pieces were produced bearing the 1850 date.

A semi-reflective Gem and one of the two finest-known examples of this first-year regular issue double eagle. The devices of this extraordinary specimen are firmly struck on the peripheral areas and show nary a hint of softness in the centers. There is the possibility that this piece was saved for presentation to an important official or dignitary, as both sides are mildly prooflike in the fields, being struck from freshly polished and striated dies. Only minimal coin-to-coin contact is indicated on either side. The lovely lime-gold toning reveals hints of underlying pastel color, mainly near the obverse stars and the date. Any Mint State 1850 double eagle is an important offering, but here is an example that is certainly among the finest, if not *the* finest available to collectors. Census: 2 in 65, 0 finer (12/06). (#8902)

Attractive Near-Mint
1850-O Double Eagle

3699   1850-O AU58 NGC. Both Philadelphia and New Orleans coined double eagles in 1850, and New Orleans was the only branch mint to produce them until 1854, when the San Francisco Mint struck its own from California gold. This is an appealing near-Mint example of the first branch mint double eagle issue, partially prooflike with pale greenish-gold surfaces that retain practically all of their original luster. The stars have unusually strong definition, with none of the mushiness often seen at the centers, and Liberty's hair displays above-average detail. Light highpoint friction denies this piece a Mint State grade, but the relative lack of distracting marks is a refreshing change from the typical representative. Census: 11 in 58, 4 finer (12/06). (#8903)

Elusive Near-Mint State 1850-O Twenty

3700   1850-O AU58 PCGS. Even the Smithsonian Institution lacks an example as fine as the present specimen, having only an XF40 piece. Gold experts Jeff Garrett and Ron Guth note that the numerous yearly offerings of this issue as mostly well circulated, in the range of Very Fine to Extremely Fine at best. Fully Uncirculated examples are very rare, making this near-Mint State specimen an excellent choice, and likely one of the finest readily obtainable. A search through our permanent auction archives shows that only five times previously have we offered as fine an example. The 1850-O is quite popular, both as the first year of issue and as the first branch mint emission. The present specimen offers reflective orange-gold surfaces with the light field chatter characteristic of a short spate in circulation. There are no singularly mentionable abrasions, save for a couple of small ticks on Liberty's cheek. Population: 5 in 58, 0 finer (11/06).
From The Temecula Collection. (#8903)

Sharp 1852-O Double Eagle AU58

3701   1852-O AU58 NGC. Despite an original mintage of 190,000 pieces that is quite modest when compared to Type One issues from the Philadelphia and San Francisco Mints, the 1852-O is one of the more obtainable issues in the entire run of New Orleans double eagles. The typical survivor, however, rarely surpasses low-end AU grades and those approaching Mint State enjoy strong demand from Southern gold specialists. This is a satin finished example whose lightly rubbed surfaces reveal flashes of original luster at most angles. The devices are sharply impressed, the number of abrasions is consistent with the assigned grade. A bright, yellow-gold representative. Census: 69 in 58, 16 finer (11/06). (#8907)

Enticing Near-Mint 1853/2 Double Eagle

3702   1853/2 AU58 NGC. FS-301, formerly FS-008. The remnants of a 2 are visible beneath the 3 in the date and plain under magnification, and a diagnostic raised area (a rusted spot on the die) appears below the R in LIBERTY. Though this variety commands a comparatively modest premium in Very Fine and lower grades, the relative scarcity of overdated examples becomes plain in higher grades, with only eight Mint State pieces graded by NGC and PCGS combined (12/06).

Light highpoint friction keeps this piece from a higher grade, but that makes it an opportunity to acquire a representative with a similar appearance for a considerably lower price. The apricot-gold surfaces have nearly full luster and few marks overall, and the strike is pleasing. Listed on page 254 of the 2007 *Guide Book*. (#8909)

Exceptionally Pleasing MS63 1856-S Double Eagle

3703   1856-S No Serif, Left S MS63 PCGS. When a ship begins to slip beneath the waves, it has a tendency to focus the attention of passengers on what is important and what is not so important. That was brought out in this passage as related by Q. David Bowers:

> "Ladies left behind unnecessary baggage. Some, 'as if to illustrate how little value was the gold, brought out bags (not entrusted to the purser) and scattered it on the floor, asking all who wanted money to help themselves.' A few ladies picked up pieces, but none took more than two $20 coins."

This is an amazingly well-preserved example that has superior luster for the grade and attractive, light rose and lilac coloration. Fully struck throughout. All the Blanchard packaging is included with this piece. (#70024)

Lustrous MS63 1856-S Twenty Dollar

3704   1856-S No Serif, Left S MS63 PCGS. Prior to the establishment of the mint in 1854, private minters struck coins of questionable fineness. This was followed by the quasi-official Assay Office tens and twenties. Augustus Humbert also struck the fifty dollar "slugs," coins that Tommy Thompson called "wildly unpopular" in *America's Lost Treasure*. Prior to the discovery of the *S.S. Central America*, Type One twenties were among the rarest 19th century gold coins in mint condition. This is a truly remarkable coin, regardless of whether it is a Type One, Type Two, or Type Three. The mint luster is phenomenal, as seen on all the recovered coins. Fully struck, the only marks that account for the grade are located on the highpoint of Liberty's cheek and across the bridge of the nose. A wonderful type coin. Accompanied by all the packaging from Blanchard. (#70024)

Clean MS63 1856-S Twenty Dollar

3705   1856-S No Serif, Hi Right S MS63 PCGS. The loss of so much gold bullion and coined gold in 1857 affected the country's monetary markets to such an extent that it was one of the contributing factors in the Panic of 1857. There were 1,085 1856-S twenties recovered from the *S.S. Central America*. So many, in fact, that a study of die varieties was done of this and the 1857-S. This is an attractive coin that differs slightly from other SSCA twenties. The luster is not quite as pronounced, but the surfaces are exceptionally clean and show a slight accent of reddish patina. Fully struck, as usually seen. Accompanied by the Blanchard boxes of issue. (#70023)

Desirable 1857-O Double Eagle AU55

3706   1857-O AU55 PCGS. The 1857-O double eagle has long resided in the shadows of the three O-mint issues that preceded it, most notably the 1854-O and 1856-O rarities. Of the 30,000 double eagles coined at the New Orleans facility in 1857, only a small percentage survives. Indeed, it is doubtful that more than 150 examples are currently known, just half of one percent of the original mintage. Uncirculated coins are essentially non-existent, so any example that approaches Mint State status takes on even greater importance. This example is an attractive green-gold representative, with traces of wear only on the highest design points. Prooflike surfaces exhibit a moderate quota of the small abrasions that these large gold coins are known for. Although the date and mintmark are both weakly impressed, all remaining design details are boldly rendered. A bit of extra metal along the left reverse border may assist in pedigree tracking. Population: 13 in 55, 11 finer (12/06). (#8921)

Highly Lustrous MS65
1857-S Double Eagle

3707   1857-S MS65 NGC. Ex: *Central America.* Few realize the horrors involved of a ship sinking at sea, but we have the written memories of some of the survivors. On the night of September 12, 1857, the *S.S. Central America* plunged at a 45-degree angle, disappearing beneath the waves of the North Atlantic, and the suction of the sudden sinking of the ship pulled many passengers far below the surface. Some managed to swim back to the surface. One survivor, John C. Taylor, described the scene that night: "Men, some holding planks, and others without anything, were tossed about through the sea for a great space, and appeared to me like so many corks. The cries of despair which were uttered by all faintly reached me. I could not describe my feelings at this awful moment."

Along with the hundreds of men, women, and children who lost their lives that night, a fabulous treasure in California gold also slipped beneath the waves. The gold coins and bars sank to such a depth that the mint luster remained undisturbed on the coins. Since they were salvaged in 1988 and sold into the market several years later, these pieces have provided collectors with numerous high quality examples of Type One double eagles—coins that were generally unavailable in mint condition. This piece shows bright, swirling mint frost and full definition on all the devices. An exceptional Gem 1857-S and rarely seen any finer.
From The Freedom Collection. (#8922)

Pleasing 1859-S Double Eagle, MS62

3708   1859-S MS62 PCGS. Like most of the early San Francisco gold issues, the 1859-S double eagle saw heavy circulation, and few survived unworn. Yet the total mintage of more than 636,000 pieces dwarfs the figures for both the Philadelphia and New Orleans issues for that year, and of the three, only the San Francisco double eagle is available in anything above minimal Mint State.

The key is available, not readily available, as such pieces are still condition rarities, especially in MS62. One such example, well struck and softly lustrous, is offered here. The apricot-gold surfaces are lightly abraded overall, and a slightly deeper mark affects the hair behind the coronet, but the overall visual appeal is high. Population: 15 in 62, 1 finer (11/06). (#8928)

Lustrous 1861 Double Eagle MS64

3709   1861 MS64 NGC. Uncommonly sharp with a bright, frosty appearance and satiny, sparingly abraded fields. This issue's mintage of nearly 3 million pieces is the highest among Type One double eagles and the heavy production accurately forecasts its relative availability up to and including lesser Mint State grades. However, the unflagging popularity of this Civil War issue has always quickly absorbed the existing supply. Choice and better 1861 twenties such as this lustrous example represent only a small minority of Uncirculated survivors. Census: 20 in 64, 10 finer (11/06). (#8932)

High-End VF30 1861-S Paquet Reverse Twenty

3710   1861-S Paquet VF30 PCGS. The distinctive Paquet reverse is easy to spot, with its tall letters on the reverse, and for many years the issue, produced to the extent of 19,250 coins, was thought to be a pattern. More recent numismatic scholarship, however, has shown the coins to be a regular issue, but a flawed one whose production was ceased shortly after it began. Sufficient numbers of the S-mint issue were struck that today perhaps 200 coins are known, most of them in circulated grades. The present piece, certified in a PCGS green-label holder, still shows a bit of mint luster in the fields, suggesting a higher grade despite the obvious wear. There are no singular impairments, and as such this piece may represent good value for someone wanting an example for a type or date set without paying the Mint State price.
From The Twin Hollows Collection. (#8936)

Rare 1861-S Paquet Reverse Double Eagle AU50

3711   1861-S Paquet AU50 PCGS. At a casual glance, few observers would notice any difference between the Paquet and the normal reverse of an 1861-S double eagle. A side-by-side comparison reveals subtle differences, however, most notably in the taller, thinner lettering. The width of the eagle is also greater, and the reverse stars are placed lower within the rays.

The 1861-S Paquet reverse double eagle was not discovered until 1937. Walter Breen notes that: "Paul Wittlin turned up 25-30 in French and Swiss banks in the mid-1950s, mostly VF to EF with plenty of bagmarks." Apparently, these coins account for most of the known examples. The four pairs of dies that the Philadelphia Mint shipped to California, in November 1860, each contained an experimental tall letter reverse. Attributed to Assistant Engraver Anthony C. Paquet, these dies produced 19,250 1861-S double eagles that were destined to become the rarest issue of their denomination from the San Francisco Mint. Unknown in Mint State, AU examples are highly desirable. An undeniably attractive specimen, this coin displays reddish-golden surfaces, with a single red alloy spot noted near the eagle's left (facing) talon. A few trivial circulation marks are seen on each side, but these are minimal in terms of the coin's overall eye appeal. With ample remaining definition, this is a problem-free and immensely desirable representative of this prized rarity.

From The Oak Island Collection. (#8936)

Highly Lustrous 1864 Double Eagle, MS61

3712   1864 MS61 PCGS. The symbolic thirteen stars on each side of the double eagle, engraved by Longacre in accordance with numismatic tradition in the United States, remained even during the Civil War, which saw four of the states represented by those stars secede from the Union. On this highly lustrous lemon-gold double eagle, the central devices have a touch of softness, but the peripheral details are strong, and no part of the design displays any wear. Three reeding marks and a moderate abrasion affect the cheek and chin, but the obverse fields have only light, well-distributed abrasions, and the reverse is cleaner than the other side, as is often the case. Appealing for the grade. Population: 14 in 61, 9 finer (12/06). (#8941)

Exceptional Mint State 1864 Double Eagle

3713   1864 MS62 PCGS. Although the 1864 double eagle is not considered a rare date when all grades are considered, it is a condition rarity in Mint State. A few pieces were found among coins recovered from the treasure of the *S.S. Republic,* with 29 coins certified by NGC at an average grade of MS60. The treasure of the *S.S. Brother Jonathan* did not include any examples of this issue. This frosty and lustrous piece has brilliant lemon-yellow color. It is sharply struck with excellent details on both sides. The obverse is lightly abraded and the reverse is nearly mark-free. Population: 8 in 62, 1 finer (11/06). (#8941)

Beautiful Gem 1865-S Double Eagle
Ex: *S.S. Brother Jonathan*

3714 **1865-S MS65 NGC.** Ex: Brother Jonathan. Prior to the *S.S. Brother Jonathan* sale, in 1999, the 1865-S double eagle was rare in high grades. The condition-conscious Harry W. Bass, Jr. was only able to find an XF example for his collection. The *Brother Jonathan* and the *S.S. Republic,* however, each contained hundreds of pieces, many of them in Mint State. According to Garrett and Guth (2006): "Today the 1865-S double eagle is available in grades unheard of several years ago. These coins are tangible links to these fascinating treasures and an important time in American history." The current offering is a lustrous Gem representative with amazingly smooth, matte-like surfaces. Except for a few of the obverse stars, the design elements are boldly impressed, and distracting marks or blemishes are nonexistent. (#8944)

Eliasberg Choice XF 1866-S
No Motto Twenty, Never Before Offered

3715   1866-S No Motto XF45 PCGS. The last of the Type One double eagles from the San Francisco Mint, the 1866-S was struck in both No Motto and With Motto formats during the post-Civil War time when the United States elected to again recognize God on its coinage. Of the two formats, the No Motto is far more elusive; the typical example is well circulated, and there are likely only two hundred or so pieces known. The present Eliasberg example offers still-lustrous yellow-gold surfaces that meld into deep amber-gold near the rims. A few moderate abrasions on each side attest to some circulation, but none are overly distracting. This piece has never before been offered in any of the auctions of Louis E. Eliasberg's coins. *From The Collection of Louis E. Eliasberg, Sr. (#8945)*

Difficult 1866-S No Motto
Double Eagle AU50

3716   1866-S No Motto AU50 NGC. The last of the Type One double eagle issues, the 1866-S No Motto was struck early in the year prior to the arrival from Philadelphia of the new reverse dies featuring IN GOD WE TRUST within the cluster of stars above the eagle. The exact mintage of this formidable scarcity is unknown, with estimates ranging from 12,000 pieces (the current *Guide Book* estimate) to an unrealistically high figure of 120,000 coins. Representatives in AU and finer grades are among the elite survivors. This example, while liberally abraded, retains a generous amount of luster and pleasing reddish accents. Census: 18 in 50, 36 finer (11/06). (#8945)

Borderline Uncirculated 1866-S No Motto Double Eagle
A Famous Low Mintage Conditional Rarity

3717   **1866-S No Motto AU58 PCGS.** The 1866-S No Motto has long been regarded as one of the rarest San Francisco Mint double eagles. In his seminal 1982 volume on double eagles, Akers asserts, "This issue is very rare in any condition, second among S-Mint issues only to the 1861-S Paquet ... In rarity according to average grade, the 1866-S No Motto is tied for first with the 1870-CC and 1871-CC. It is also at the top based on rarity in high grade ... The 1866-S No Motto is typically VF and heavily bagmarked. A strictly graded EF is very rare and, above that level, the 1866-S No Motto is excessively rare and, for all practical purposes, unobtainable."

In recent decades, several important shipwreck hoards of Type One double eagles have come to market. These include the 1854 *S.S. Yankee Blade,* the 1857 *S.S. Central America,* the 1865 *S.S. Republic,* and the 1865 *S.S. Brother Jonathan.* Since all four of these shipwrecks occurred before the 1866-S No Motto was struck, they have had no impact on the limited number of survivors. These much-promoted shipwreck recoveries have, however, increased collector demand for Type One double eagles, to the benefit of the 1866-S No Motto, the final entry of the type.

According to Breen (1988), the No Motto issue was coined in February 1866 using obverse dies shipped from Philadelphia in November 1865. The first Motto reverse dies were shipped March 1866. The mintage of the 1866-S No Motto is uncertain. The 2007 *Guide Book* and the Douglas Winter-Adam Crum reference *An Insider's Guide to Collecting Type I Double Eagles* (2002) both estimate a production of 12,000 pieces. Breen (1988) states 120,000 pieces, as does Q. David Bowers in his 2004 *A Guide Book of Double Eagle Gold Coins.* Bowers adds that "at least two reverse dies still on hand were used." A footnote in the Bowers reference gives Mint records researcher R.W. Julian as the source for the 120,000 mintage. Bowers agrees that the issue is the "Second rarest 'S' mint $20." If 120,000 pieces were struck, then the 1866-S No Motto has an unusually high attrition rare, especially in better grades. Only a single 1866-S No Motto has been certified as Mint State by either NGC or PCGS, compared to a Mint State census of a combined 48 pieces for the 1866-S Motto. In their 2006 *Encyclopedia of U.S. Gold Coins 1795-1933,* Jeff Garrett and Ron Guth assert, "Even by today's more liberal standards, there are no known Mint State examples. Both the Bass and Smithsonian specimens grade just Extremely Fine."

The present Condition Census example has essentially complete mint luster. Luster penetrates the open fields, and covers the cheek and wingtips. As expected of the AU58 grade, a few faint vertical hairlines are present on the left obverse field. Bagmarks are surprisingly minimal, and two tiny overlapping ticks on the cheek are mentioned primarily to identify the present piece for pedigree purposes. Probably, the piece would have been designated as Mint State were it not for a few minute specks of PVC residue north of the ear and above the ER in LIBERTY, which PCGS has factored into the AU58 grade. These specks are completely unobtrusive to the unaided eye, and even once examined with a loupe, take time to locate. The reverse is gorgeously smooth. Given its shimmering cartwheel luster, the reverse, on its own merits, might grade MS64. Although we have not seen the only piece certified finer, an MS61 PCGS example, we suspect that the eye appeal of the present smooth and lustrous piece is competitive, if not superior, to any other 1866-S No Motto twenty. This is the first time this particular coin has ever been offered for sale, as it has been in the family of the consignor since the 19th century. (#8945)

Unheralded 1870 Double Eagle MS63

3718   1870 MS63 PCGS. There are quite a few issues in the Liberty double eagle series that are very scarce in MS63 condition, but drop down a point or two and the flood gates can be opened. This scenario certainly does not apply to the 1870, an unheralded issue of 155,150 business strikes that is challenging in any Mint State grade and an extreme rarity at the Select level. Even the ambitious Eagle Collection was only able to locate an MS61. This Condition Census representative exhibits crisp, frosty devices and unbroken satiny luster in the fields that shimmers from side to side. A T-shaped abrasion in the field before Liberty's mouth and a cut on her hair keep this attractive example from unprecedented quality. Population: 2 in 63, 0 finer (11/06). (#8957)

Significant Select 1871 Double Eagle

3719   1871 MS63 PCGS. Booming luster sweeps this sharply struck better date Type Two twenty. Well struck, and lightly abraded despite a few faint marks at 1 o'clock on the reverse. Only 80,150 pieces were struck, and most of these were eventually melted. The 1871 is actually difficult regardless of grade, although the few XF and lower grade pieces carry only a moderate premium over bullion. In Mint State, the 1871 is a rarity. PCGS has certified 11 pieces in MS60 or higher grades, and NGC has certified only nine such pieces. Presumably, at least a portion of these figures represent resubmissions. Encapsulated in an old green label holder. Population: 2 in 63, 1 finer (11/06). (#8960)

Splendid 1871-CC
Double Eagle Rarity, XF45 PCGS

3720   1871-CC XF45 PCGS. Attractive yellow-gold surfaces are accented by pale olive overtones. This is an excellent, lightly circulated example of the second rarest Carson City Mint double eagle. A few light abrasions are consistent with the grade, and are the result of its brief exposure to circulation in Western commerce during the latter part of the 19th century. The substantial population of certified pieces does not tell of the rarity and importance of this double eagle, due to numerous resubmissions of a much smaller number of coins. Nearly all examples are in lower grades than this specimen. Only one similar quality example is held by the Smithsonian Institution. While a couple Mint State examples and a few more AU examples have survived to this day, such coins are clearly the exception and not the rule when it comes to 1871-CC double eagles. In his *Double Eagle Red Book,* Dave Bowers commented: "These pieces circulated extensively, and most show extensive wear and, often, damage." Fortunately for today's collector, the present example shows neither of those characteristics. Population: 36 in 45, 30 finer (10/06). (#8961)

Challenging 1871-CC Twenty Dollar
XF45 NGC

3721   1871-CC XF45 NGC. Jeff Garrett and Ron Guth, in their book *Encyclopedia of U.S. gold Coins, 1795-1933,* write that: "By a large margin, the 1871-CC double eagle is the second rarest Carson City issue. The mintage is small (17,387 pieces), and most of the production was destined for circulation in Nevada and the surrounding areas....most of the coins found of this issue are well worn and heavily bagmarked."

This Choice XF example exhibits semi-bright honey-gold surfaces with scattered whispers of reddish-gold. The design elements retain sharp detail, and traces of luster can be seen clinging to the protected areas. A few expected marks are scattered about, but none are really detractive. (#8961)

Attractive 1872-CC Twenty AU58

3722   1872-CC AU58 PCGS. The 1872-CC is a rarity, like many of its CC-mint siblings of the era, as most of the issue saw extensive circulation in the West. The average piece grades only Very Fine to Extremely Fine; Mint State pieces are quite elusive. PCGS has graded only 27 AU58 pieces, with two finer (11/06). This attractive example offers mellow orange-gold coloration, with good luster and eye appeal, a bold strike, and a few light scuffs and abrasions consistent with the grade and a short stint in circulation in the rough-and-tumble West of the 1870s.
From The Temecula Collection. (#8964)

Conditionally Scarce 1873 Open 3 Twenty MS63

3723   1873 Open 3 MS63 PCGS. The Open 3 is the more common of the two 1873 varieties. The obverse die shows minor doubling, particularly on LIBERTY. Bright and lustrous with clean surfaces and plenty of eye appeal. This is a decently struck coin, despite partial weakness on four or five of the obverse stars. It shows flashy yellow-gold color throughout and excellent surfaces for the assigned grade. According to Garrett and Guth: "In Mint State this issue is scarce, as are all Type 2 double eagles. Most are in grades of MS-60 to MS-61. Choice examples are actually quite rare and seldom available. Just a few examples are known above MS-63. A PCGS MS-63 coin sold in May 2005 for $9,200." Population: 95 in 63, 5 finer (11/06).
From The Freedom Collection. (#8967)

Select 1873 Open 3 Double Eagle

3724   1873 Open 3 MS63 PCGS. A very attractive coin for the grade with strong luster in the fields and exceptional quality for a Type II double eagle. The strike is typically sharp, with no weakness present. Apparently the double eagles of this period were shipped about in loose containers which allowed for the abundance of bagmarks, and obtaining an example from this period in Gem grades is virtually impossible. Furthermore, no vast shipwrecks have been recovered which contain sparkling Mint State coins by the thousands for collectors as seen from the 1850s and early 1860s. Thus, the number of MS63 Type II double eagles remain quite small, and finding a coin in higher grade requires not only patience, but a substantial sum of money. For identification purposes, there is a moderate nick from below Liberty's eye to the curl near above her ear, and a minor scuff near the ribbon below the I of AMERICA. (#8967)

Select Mint State 1873 Open 3 Double Eagle

3725   1873 Open 3 MS63 PCGS. This Type Two double eagle issue is considered a common date in the context of this short-lived design type. However, in MS63 grade it is an important condition rarity as the PCGS population data shows. Both sides have soft, frosty luster with brilliant yellow-gold color and few abrasions.

Of the basic types of double eagles, the Type Two design, with the addition of the IN GOD WE TRUST motto on the reverse and the denomination abbreviated TWENTY D., is considerably rarer in Mint State grades than either the Type One or Type Three designs. The Type Three design is common due to substantial hoards from Europe and elsewhere. The Type One design is available thanks to three important treasure discoveries. But the Type Two double eagles did not figure in many European holdings, and had not been minted when the treasure ships went down. Population: 95 in 63, 5 finer (11/06). (#8967)

Nearly Mint State 1873-CC Double Eagle

3726   1873-CC AU58 NGC. This issue has the Closed 3 date logotype as always for the Carson City Mint double eagles. It is a lovely piece with essentially full luster and brilliant yellow-gold surfaces. A trace of wear on the highest points defines the grade assigned by NGC. This example is a wonderful piece that lacks the usual heavy abrasions that so often plague the early Carson City Mint gold coins. While the 1873-CC double eagle is not a date usually mentioned when rare CC gold is discussed, it is seldom found in such fine condition. Census: 73 in 58, 18 finer (11/06). (#8968)

Mint State 1874-CC Type Two Twenty

3727   1874-CC MS61 PCGS. As a collectible Type Two Carson City issue, the 1874-CC enjoys great popularity in all grades, and CC-mint type collectors can expect to locate an XF or even a low-end AU without too much difficulty. Uncirculated examples, however, are an entirely different matter altogether, since perhaps less than 20 pieces are believed to survive. This well detailed Mint State survivor is tinted of soft reddish-golden hues and has the normal quota of small abrasions in the fields and on the devices. The absence of individually obtrusive marks ensures pleasing eye appeal for the MS61 level. Population: 4 in 61, 1 finer (10/06). (#8971)

Well Struck Select 1875 Double Eagle

3728   1875 MS63 PCGS. The 1875 double eagle, with a mintage of nearly 300,000 pieces, is not rare in grades VF to MS62. It becomes more difficult to locate at the MS63 level of preservation, however, where PCGS and NGC have certified fewer than 70 specimens; a mere seven coins finer have been seen.

This particular specimen displays a delicate blend of yellow-gold and orange-gold coloration that rests upon lustrous surfaces. Nice definition characterizes the design features, that exhibit good detail in the star centers, in most of Liberty's hair, and in the eagle's plumage. A few obverse contact marks and scuffs define the grade. Population: 45 in 63, 3 finer (11/06). (#8973)

Lovely 1876-S Twenty Dollar Gold Piece, MS62

3729   1876-S MS62 PCGS. The 1876-S has the second-highest mintage of the Type Two double eagles, and if one divides the 1873 into Open 3 and Close 3 varieties, the 1876-S might take the crown. Garrett and Guth consider the 1876-S "easily located in grades of Very Fine to MS-61," coincidentally the grade of the finest Smithsonian example, according to them, but anything finer becomes surprisingly elusive. The straw-gold surfaces of this unworn example have vibrant luster. Scattered light to moderate abrasions appear on the devices, well struck for this issue, and in the gleaming fields. The overall look of the coin suggests a finer grade at first glance, though closer inspection reveals that the coin is not so well-preserved. It is, however, an attractive representative. (#8978)

Sharp 1876-S Double Eagle MS63

3730   1876-S MS63 PCGS. Production of 1876-S double eagles almost reached 1.6 million pieces, the second highest mintage among Type Two twenties behind the combined output for the 1873 Open 3 and Closed 3. Availability of the issue is similarly generous, including Mint State survivors that total well into four figures. This Select example is not only better struck than the vast majority of these Uncirculated pieces, but abrasions are also far less severe. Both sides exhibit radiant luster with tinges of lemon-yellow patina. Population: 75 in 63, 9 finer (11/06). (#8978)

Scarce 1878-CC Double Eagle AU58

3731   1878-CC AU58 NGC. Variety 1-A, by far the most obtainable of three pairings believed to have been used during this scarce Carson City issue's limited production. This example is satiny and generally light in color, with tinges of delicate reddish patina on the reverse. A few reeding marks and other small abrasions can be seen on and to the left of the portrait. Modest luster breaks on Liberty's cheek and in the surrounding fields indicate only a brief amount of circulation. An important offering for the condition conscious gold specialist. Census: 31 in 58, 5 finer (11/06). (#8986)

Borderline Unc. 1878-CC Double Eagle

3732   1878-CC AU58 PCGS. Variety 1-A. The 1878-CC twenty is a scarce, low mintage issue that enjoys perpetual demand from advanced gold collectors and Carson City specialists alike. Perhaps fewer than a dozen Uncirculated pieces survive, lending added importance to those that approach Mint State quality. This bright, shimmering representative is modestly abraded for the grade and mintmark, and shows only the slightest interruption of luster on the highpoints of the obverse. Desirable quality for this sought-after CC twenty. Population: 8 in 58, 7 finer (11/06). (#8986)

Brilliant MS63 1878-S Twenty

3733   1878-S MS63 PCGS. The San Francisco Mint did yeoman service in the 1870s through the 1890s, producing the bulk of the vast numbers of double eagles yearly, most of them quite well produced and of good quality. The 1878-S issue is typical, with a generous mintage and many splendid Mint State coins available, for a price, up to MS63 or so. This lovely example offers peach-gold surfaces, brilliant luster, and excellent eye appeal. A boldly struck piece, and minimally abraded for the MS63 grade. PCGS has graded six pieces in 63, with none finer (11/06).
From The RNB Collection. (#8987)

1879 Twenty, MS63 ★
An Important Condition Rarity
Among Type Three Twenties

3734   1879 MS63 ★ NGC. Philadelphia Mint double eagle production amounted to 207,630 pieces in 1879. Winter (2002) suggests that, because few examples grade below the AU53 level, the '79-P did not see widespread circulation. This may be true, but most of those coins that were preserved were carelessly handled, as the issue is also a prime rarity in Mint State grades above MS61. Fully prooflike with glowing, orange-gold features, the present example is a delight to behold. Apparently NGC agreed, as it gave this piece its Star designation. Pinpoint striking definition is noted throughout, and only a few scattered obverse abrasions seem to rule out an even higher Choice designation. We are aware of only three 1879 double eagles certified MS63 that have appeared at auction in recent years, all of which qualify for Condition Census standing:

1. Ex: Harry W. Bass, Jr. Collection (Bowers and Merena, 11/2000), lot 914, where it realized $9,488; Santa Clara Signature Sale (Heritage, 11/2002), lot 7823, where it realized $13,800. PCGS-certified.
2. Ex: FUN Signature Sale—The "Eagle Collection" of Liberty Double Eagles (Heritage, 1/2002), lot 4080, where it realized $9,488. Certified by NGC.
3. The present example, prior pedigree unknown, but traceable by a few arcing abrasions over, and in the field before and after, the point of Liberty's bust.

NGC and PCGS combined report only 10 examples in MS63, and there are none finer (11/06).
From The Temecula Collection. (#8988)

Appealing AU53 1879-CC Double Eagle

3735　**1879-CC AU53 PCGS.** We are fortunate in this auction to be able to feature multiple examples of the 1879-CC double eagle, a better date among Type Three Carson City twenties. Mint State pieces are quite rare, with only 15 coins having been certified in such lofty grades by the combined major grading services (11/06), so most collectors searching for a quality example of this date are forced to look for an AU piece with eye appeal. This coin more than fills the bill in that regard, with a good deal of luster remaining in the recessed areas of the lettering and devices, and only a minimum of wear, most notably on the highpoints of the crown and hair. Peach-gold color predominates over surfaces which hint at having been prooflike at one time. (#8989)

Challenging 1879-CC Double Eagle AU58

3736　**1879-CC AU58 PCGS.** Variety 1-A. An even finer representative of this low mintage scarcity that is, despite multiple offerings, not at all indicative of this coin's difficulty in grades approaching Mint State. The surfaces on this flashy, boldly struck example are far less abraded than the typical survivor and show only a nominal amount of wear on the highpoints of the portrait. If considered separately, the reverse shows little or no loss of luster. Of the 8-10 Uncirculated pieces generally accepted to exist (combined MS60 and higher population is actually 15), only a handful of coins could surpass the eye appeal of this outstanding example. Population: 16 in 58, 9 finer (11/06). (#8989)

Notable 1882-CC Double Eagle MS62

3737   1882-CC MS62 PCGS. The 1882-CC double eagle was the first twenty dollar gold issue made at the Carson City Mint since 1879. The two-year suspension is attributed to two unrelated factors. The local cause was a reduction in Comstock Lode ore, as silver yields were all but expended, in turn causing temporary coinage suspensions at the local Mint. In 1882 floodwaters deluged the rich lower portions of the mine, effectively rendering Virginia City a tourist attraction. On the national scene, the U.S. Treasury began decreasing double eagle output (mostly visible in the P-mint emissions from the next few years), in the process of implementing a new policy to expand the distribution of half eagles and eagles. These coordinating influences resulted in a paltry double eagle mintage of only 39,140 pieces of the 1882-CC. This example offers lovely orange-gold surfaces, with the reverse fairly prooflike (and a small alloy spot), while the obverse shows only moderate contrast. The few light abrasions are less than might be expected, and the eye appeal is extremely high. Population: 11 in 62, 1 finer (10/06). (#8997)

Prooflike Mint State 1885 Double Eagle

3738   1885 MS61 NGC. In 1885, the Philadelphia Mint coined a meager 828 double eagles, a figure that includes 77 proofs, among the lowest mintage issues in the entire regular issue series of U.S. gold coinage. It is only these proofs that provides a supply of the date to collectors, keeping the price of business strikes somewhat subdued. Like nearly all others, this piece has fully prooflike surfaces with a hint of contrast between the fields and devices. Radial flowlines just inside the border on each side are the only characteristic that distinguishes this business strike specimen from the proofs. It has deep greenish-gold color with hints of orange. An attractive example, and extremely rare at this grade level. Census: 7 in 61, 4 finer (11/06). (#9003)

Attractive 1885-S Double Eagle MS64

3739   1885-S MS64 NGC. The challenge with the 1885-S double eagle is not in locating an Uncirculated representative for it is an issue of relative abundance at that level, but in finding a Choice, minimally abraded example. While not without a few scattered obverse abrasions, this example is one of the nicer 1885-S twenties we have seen. The strike is typically bold and potent luster even incorporates a bit of prooflike flash on the reverse. Importantly, one a single Gem has been certified by both major services combined. Census: 10 in 64, 0 finer (11/06). (#9005)

Lovely 1888-S Double Eagle MS64

3740   1888-S MS64 PCGS. The 1888-S is a typically well produced S-mint double eagle that is seen with greater frequency in Mint State than any other date from the decade. That said, Uncirculated survivors have a propensity for heavy abrasions and are seldom located above the Select grade level. Offered here is one of the flashiest and best preserved 1888-S twenties seen by this cataloguer and, more importantly, no Gems have been certified by either PCGS or NGC. Both sides are draped in lovely reddish-orange patina and show only the most incidental signs of contact. Population: 39 in 64, 0 finer (11/06).
From The Temecula Collection. (#9009)

Scarce 1891 Double Eagle AU58 PCGS

3741   1891 AU58 PCGS. The 1891 was underappreciated by numismatists as a rare issue in the Liberty Head double eagle series, until recently; yet probably fewer than 100 pieces survive from a low mintage of 1,390 business strikes. This near-Mint example is well struck with prooflike fields and rich reddish-gold and green coloration. Little or no highpoint wear exists on either side, but numerous wispy marks are noted in the fields. Similar to the NGC AU58 Prooflike that sold for $69,000 in our 2006 August Denver Signature. In our experience, it is very difficult to locate an 1891 in AU, and a mere four pieces have been certified in Mint State by the two major services: three by NGC and one at PCGS. The highest-graded of these is an MS62, at NGC. Population: 9 in 58, 1 finer (11/06). (#9016)

Near-Mint Low Mintage 1891-CC Twenty

3742   1891-CC AU58 PCGS. The 1891-CC has an unusually low mintage of 5,000 pieces. Among CC-mint double eagles, only the 1870-CC has a lesser production. Bullion was relatively plentiful at Carson City in 1891, since the 1891-CC half eagle and eagle have the highest mintages of their denominations from the legendary Western facility. Since the production of half eagles and eagles required more man-hours to coin than double eagles for a given bullion deposit, perhaps the Mint director simply wished to keep personnel occupied. Another possibility is that the comparatively generous mintage of 1890-CC double eagles was sufficient to satisfy local demand.

This example is well struck aside from the first three obverse stars, which exhibit soft centers. Luster is complete across the reverse, and obverse luster is only slightly muted on the cheek and open field. A few moderate marks are located on the right obverse field near the hair bun, but these are characteristic of briefly circulated double eagles. An opportunity for the determined specialist. Population: 22 in 58, 18 finer (10/06). (#9017)

Low Mintage 1892 Twenty MS62

3743   1892 MS62 PCGS. The 1892 double eagle has long been a prized rarity among P-mints in the series as a result of its impressively low business strike production of 4,430 pieces. From this already brief mintage, demand for large gold in the Eastern part of the country quickly forced almost all 1892 twenties into commercial channels, leaving only a few dozen Mint State survivors. This example, while showing moderate to heavy abrasions over both sides, exhibits pleasing reddish-golden color and semi-prooflike sparkle. Population: 6 in 62, 6 finer (11/06). (#9019)

Radiant 1893-CC Double Eagle MS62

3744   1893-CC MS62 PCGS. The 1893-CC is known as one of the best produced double eagles from the Carson City Mint and fortunately for collectors is also one of the more frequently located CC twenties in Uncirculated grades. Of course the popularity of the issue is intensified by the fact that it is also the final issue from the Nevada facility. This frosty, boldly struck example displays radiant cartwheel luster that is hampered only by a few wispy field marks on the obverse. A long, vertical blemish on the portrait is the coin's sole noticeable distraction. (#9023)

Popular 1893-CC Double Eagle MS62

3745   1893-CC MS62 PCGS. The decision to close the Carson City Mint after the production of 1893 coinage may have been initiated by the dismal outlook for the production of silver dollars over the short term or perhaps greater cost effectiveness and ease in shipping gold ore to the Philadelphia Mint. In any case, Mint State survivors from this popular final year of issue, while not particularly rare, enjoy extraordinary demand from 21st century collectors. This wholly original example is typically bold and well frosted beneath uniform reddish patina. Shallow facial marks are the primary deterrent to a higher grade. (#9023)

Rare Premium Gem 1898-S Double Eagle

3746   1898-S MS66 NGC. This issue is very common in the lower Mint State grades, with thousands certified by NGC and PCGS from MS60 through MS64. At MS65 the '98-S becomes scarce, and it is rare any finer. Remarkable eye appeal is the hallmark of this lustrous, richly toned Premium Gem. The deep rose-gold toning is accented on each side by mint-green traces that occur near the peripheries and into some of the fields. The beautiful coloration is highlighted by intense cartwheel luster that radiates from each side of this wonderfully preserved double eagle. If not for a couple of wispy luster grazes in the left obverse field, and a small alloy spot located between stars 3 and 4, this piece might have been graded as a Superb Gem. Census: 3 in 66, 3 finer (11/06). (#9034)

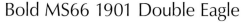

Bold MS66 1901 Double Eagle

3747   1901 MS66 PCGS. According to the Bowers double eagle reference, this issue is the first Type Three issue for which Gem coins are "common" (although, as always, that is a relative term, best used within the context of the series), adding that "even MS66 coins are not rare." Despite that bold assertion, PCGS has certified only three pieces in MS66, with none finer and none at NGC. This coin has bold orange-gold coloration, great luster, and a total paucity of post-strike distractions. A few light roller marks are seen through the central obverse. Certified in a green-label holder. (#9039)

Pristine Gem 1903-S Double Eagle

3748   1903-S MS65 PCGS. Gem examples of this issue are quite rare, according to Garrett and Guth's *Gold Encyclopedia,* much more so than for the 1903 Philadelphia coinage. Like so many Liberty Type Three double eagles, this issue is plentiful in the lower Mint State echelons, but quite elusive in the higher reaches; this is one of only seven pieces at PCGS that have attained the Gem grade, with none finer. Areas of orange-gold and green-gold alternate, with brilliant luster and few singular abrasions. The reverse is especially pristine, although there are few marks on Liberty's cheek. (#9044)

Delightful PR64 Cameo 1864 Twenty

3749   1864 PR64 Cameo NGC. In 1858—only one year after the discontinuation of the large cent and half cent created the first (but certainly not the last) numismatic mania in America—the U.S. Mint began publicly offering wholesale proof sets to collectors. Mint records from those early years of public proof production are spotty at best; while some annual figures may be accurate, oftentimes any specimens that went unsold were reconsigned to the melting pot. The mintages of proof Type One double eagles—those produced from 1858 through 1866, without the motto IN GOD WE TRUST—are recorded in the *Guide Book* as ranging from 80 pieces for the 1859 (the 1858 mintage is unknown) down to 25 pieces for the 1865. Those mintage figures, which are in line with those in the Breen *Proof Encyclopedia,* are largely meaningless in terms of the surviving population, however, and the population data are not particularly helpful, either. Like so many rare coins where a one-point increment in grade can mean potentially huge price increases, the Type One double eagle certified populations are artificially swollen by multiple resubmissions, crossovers, and "crack-outs."

For what they are worth, here are the present population data: NGC has graded a total of 15 proof 1864s, including two Cameo coins in PR63 and nine PR64 Cameos, and four Ultra Cameo pieces, two PR64s, one PR65 ★, and one PR67 piece. This latter PR67 Ultra Cameo is the finest known at either service. PCGS has graded a total of five coins, all PR64s, including three graded PR64 Cameo, with none finer. So the number of *submission events* at both services for this issue totals 20 pieces. In 1977 the Breen *Proof Encyclopedia,* calling this the rarest proof gold denomination of 1864, enumerated nine or 10 different coins. More recently, the authors of the Garrett-Guth *Gold Encyclopedia* noted that, "Despite the fact that only 12 to 15 examples of the Proof 1864 double eagle are known, it is probably the most available year for the type in the Proof format." Given our estimates based on the available data it appears that those numbers might be a bit on the high side, but suffice it to say that the number of *different coins* certified is certainly not over the midteens, and possibly as low as 10 pieces.

The proof 1864 double eagle has the date slanting downward slightly from left to right, with the 4 closer to the dentils than the 1. The largest space is between 86 and then between 18, with the 64 quite close together. The left serif of the 1 is slightly right of the center of a dentil, and the right base of the 4 is nearly to the right edge of a dentil. There are scattered die rust marks near the eye, the brow, and below LIBER. We also see on this piece a short, squiggly die crack at the top of Liberty's forehead, a crack that simulates a bulging vein. The reverse die for this issue was repolished and used again from the 1862-3 proof issues. The present PR64 Cameo specimen shows a bold strike over distraction-free yellow-gold surfaces, with considerable mint frost and good field-device contrast. All star centrils are boldly brought up on this piece, and there are no weak spots apparent in Liberty's highpoint hair. A small copper alloy spot on the reverse, to the right of the shield border, and a second less-noticeable dark area to the left side of the glory of rays, will serve as a future pedigree markers for this delightful Civil War-era piece. Census: 9 in 64 Cameo, 0 finer (11/06). (#89076)

Rare 1868 Proof Double Eagle
PR64 PCGS

3750   1868 PR64 PCGS. Only 25 proof double eagles were struck in 1868, and of that number estimates range from 7 to 8 pieces surviving (Akers), to as many as 12 (Garrett & Guth). An unquestioned rarity among proof twenties, Akers stated that the 1868 was, "among the rarest of the decade. In fact, only the 1861 is unarguably more rare in proof." This piece is probably one of the first proofs to have been struck, as evidenced not only by the thick mint frost on the devices, but also by the lack of die clashing to the left and right of the tail to the scroll, as seen on some proofs (and business strikes).

This specimen displays razor-sharp striking details seemingly on every design element, down to the last denticle. Careful examination with a magnifier fails to reveal any mentionable hairlines or contact marks, per se, but two or three nearly microscopic pinscratches are noted on each side, which may have prevented the Gem grade assessment. The obverse has a light coating of milky patina, while the reverse is entirely untoned. The devices are heavily frosted, yielding a pleasing cameo contrast when set against the endless depths of watery reflectivity in the fields. This is especially true on the brilliant reverse. Truly a breathtaking coin and one of the most visually appealing gold pieces in a sale replete with magnificent, high grade rarities. Population: 3 in 64, 1 finer (12/06). (#9083)

Cameo PR64 1868 Twenty Dollar

3751   1868 PR64 Cameo PCGS. It is remarkable, and perhaps unprecedented, that three 1868 proof twenties are offered in the same auction. The PR66 Cameo, offered elsewhere, is the finest proof known of this date. This coin may not be the finest in technical terms, but it surely represents the best value in this rarity. While one might not believe it from looking at the two coins in this sale, the 1868 proof twenty is actually a great rarity. Of the 25 coins struck, probably no more than a dozen pieces are extant today in all grades. On average, one proof of this date has been offered per year at public auction over the past 13 years—and almost all of them have been non-cameo coins. This piece has distinctive gold-on-black contrast, a finish that makes one think this must have been one of the first coins struck from a fresh pair of dies. With a disproportionate number of non-cameo coins certified, it makes the curious mind wonder just how many impressions were required before the intense cameo contrast wore off a new set of dies. The answer it seems is not very many.

This is a splendid proof striking, regardless of the date, and it is even more remarkable that it is this well preserved from 1868. Close examination with a magnifier shows only the tiniest imperfections. The only surface "flaws" worthy of mention are a cluster of three minute planchet flakes out of the lower obverse field directly below the point of the bust. The coin has even orange-gold color, and as stated above, the cameo contrast is stark on each side. As stated previously, if one wants the ultimate in technical preservation, regardless of price, then the PR66 offered in this sale would be the coin to pursue. However, many collectors will find the value this coin represents to be its main attraction, and we believe (expect ?) that this piece may bring a surprisingly high price when sold. (#89083)

Extremely Rare Proof 1872 Double Eagle, PR63 Ultra Cameo

3752   1872 PR63 Ultra Cameo NGC. Proof double eagles are the creme de la creme of American numismatics, true rarities regardless of date or grade. From the start of record keeping in 1859, through the end of the proof double eagle cycle in 1915, a total of just 3,793 such coins were produced, for an average of just 66 pieces per year! In 1872, for example, just 30 of these proof coins were minted. Just how many survive today is anyone's guess, although the usual survival figures suggest that about 50% to 60% of all proof double eagles are still around. For this date, these figures imply just 15 to 18 surviving examples, although in this instance those figures may be a little high. In his *Complete Encyclopedia,* published nearly two decades ago, Walter Breen reported only 8 to 10 examples. More recently, in the October 1997 catalog of the John Jay Pittman Collection, Part I, David Akers suggested that 10 to 12 examples survive. A dozen known examples seems about right. Of course, some of those, like the Pittman example, are impaired and grade PR60 at best.

This lovely specimen is a remarkable proof. While the obverse has light hairlines that limit the grade, the overall eye appeal is excellent. Both sides have rich orange-gold color with deeply mirrored fields. The devices have full mint frosty, thus creating the impressive cameo appearance that is so highly desired. Aside from the light obverse hairlines, both sides have excellent, unblemished surfaces. Identified by two curved lint marks in the field next to Liberty's neck and a short diagonal mark in the margin below I of LIBERTY. Census: 1 in 63, 2 finer (11/06). (#99087)

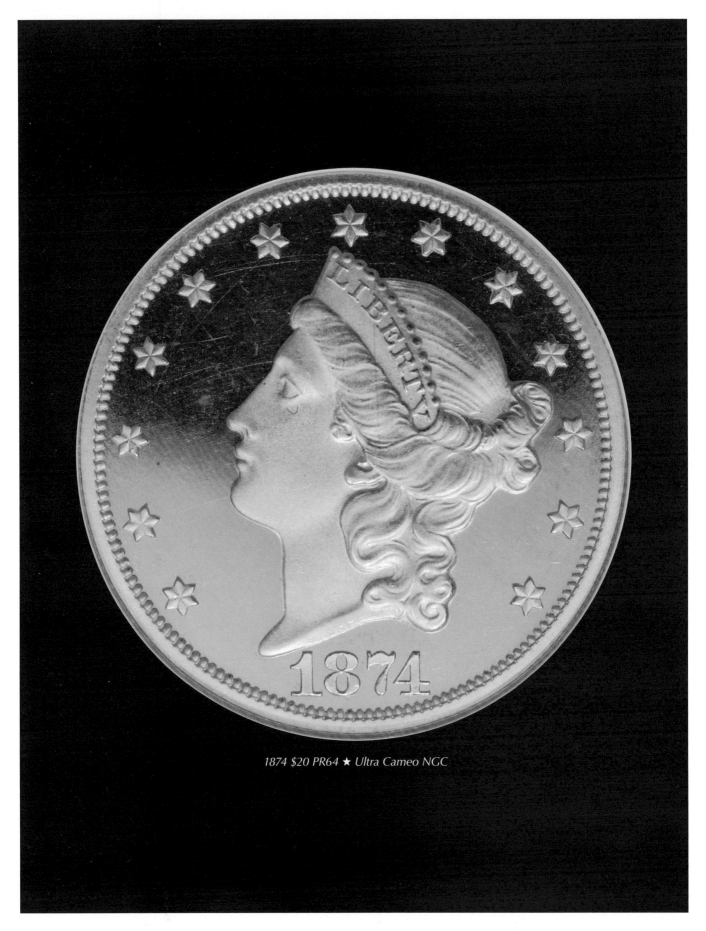

1874 $20 PR64 ★ Ultra Cameo NGC

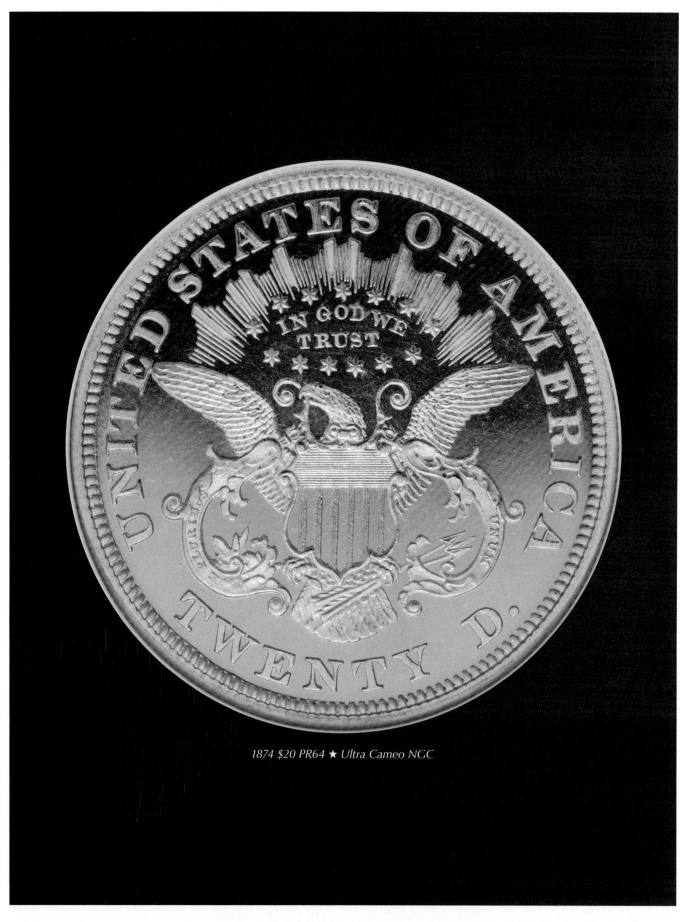

1874 $20 PR64 ★ Ultra Cameo NGC

Finest Known 1874 PR64 ★ Ultra Cameo Double Eagle

3753   1874 PR64 ★ Ultra Cameo NGC. While the circulation-strike examples of the 1874 double eagle are relatively common (366,780 mintage), proofs of this date are extremely rare. Only 20 coins were struck, making this the lowest number of proof double eagles produced after 1858. Writing in their recent book *Encyclopedia of U.S. Gold Coins, 1795-1933,* Jeff Garrett and Ron Guth say that: "Today, fewer than 10 examples can be traced, including the two that are housed in the Smithsonian and the American Numismatic Society. At least one or two examples known are seriously impaired. The date has also been missing from many important collections offered in the last two decades, including the Harry W. Bass Jr. Collection, which was nearly complete. An NGC PR-64 coin sold at auction in mid-2004 for $103,500."

David Akers, writing in *United States Gold Coins, An Analysis of Auction Records, Volume VI, Double Eagles, 1849-1933,* states that: "Proofs of this date (1874) are among the rarest after 1860. Of the 20 minted, less than half can be accounted for today." Douglas Winter and Michael Fuljenz, in their treatise entitled *Type Two Double Eagles, 1866-1876: A Numismatic History and Analysis,* state: "It is estimated that seven to nine of these (1874 proof double eagles) exist today with the finest being a lovely NGC Proof-64 which is part of the Ed Trompeter Collection of United States proof gold coins." And Walter Breen suggests that: "Possibly 7-9 proofs survive."

The population figures indicate that a total of 11 1874 proof twenties have been seen by NGC and PCGS. A PR60, a PR63, and two PR64's have been certified by PCGS. NGC graded one PR63 Cameo, and three PR64 Cameos. NGC certified one PR62 Ultra Cameo, while a PR62 Deep Cameo was seen by PCGS. An NGC-graded PR64 ★ Ultra Cameo, the piece offered in the current sale, is the finest known of all certified 1874 double eagle proofs.

Both sides of this gorgeous 1874 near-Gem ★ Ultra Cameo are embraced with attractive peach-gold color, and outstanding motif-field contrast assumes a gold-on-black appearance when the coin is viewed from directly overhead. A well-executed strike manifests itself in sharp definition on all of the design features, including the star centrils, Liberty's hair, the eagle's plumage, and the horizontal and vertical lines of the shield. An even higher grade is precluded by a few wispy obverse handling marks. A curved lint mark located beneath Liberty's eye may help to pedigree the coin. This outstanding example is sure to draw the interest of aficionados of gold coinage who want nothing but the best. As such, we expected spirited bidding on what is the finest known 1874 proof double eagle. Census: 1 in 64 ★ Ultra Cameo, 0 finer (12/06). (#99089)

Cameo Proof 1878 Double Eagle
PR63 ★ NGC

3754   **1878 PR63 ★ Cameo NGC.** In all grades and all designations, PCGS and NGC have combined to grade just 14 proof 1878 double eagles, from a total mintage of just 20 coins. It is probably reasonable to estimate a true population of less than 10 coins for this issue. We are aware of examples in the Smithsonian Institution and the American Numismatic Society. In addition to these, both the Garrett and Eliasberg Collections included examples, and another was in the F.C.C. Boyd Collection. One additional example appeared in the Bass Collection, acquired from Stack's in 1973. The Bass specimen may or may not be the same as the Boyd example. Most others that have appeared in auctions over the past 25 years are probably duplicates of the privately held coins discussed above.

This is an impressive Cameo proof with extraordinary eye appeal. The central obverse and reverse designs are executed in bright yellow-gold with fully mirrored fields. Darker yellow color is limited to the border on each side, and this serves as a nice frame for the balance of the coin. The surfaces exhibit a few faint hairlines, thus the limited numerical grade, yet few blemishes are of any significance. The most notable pedigree marker is a small field nick just over the rays below D of UNITED. All of the design elements on each side are fully impressed. A visual treat. Census: 1 in 63, 2 finer (11/06). (#89094)

Rare 1879 Double Eagle
PR61 Cameo NGC

3755   1879 PR61 Cameo NGC. As with all proof double eagles of this design type, the 1879 is very rare in the absolute sense. Only 30 pieces were produced, and from that number, the estimated number of survivors is in a narrow range. Akers estimates that only 10 or 11 pieces are extant, while Breen states that only 8-10 pieces have survived. With numbers like those, there are very few coins, and opportunities to buy those coins, that the collector has in the course of a lifetime.

While obviously hairlined, which explains the grade of this coin, there is still a remarkable amount of deep reflectivity in the fields on each side. Likewise, the devices show a noticeable amount of mint frost which gives the coin its cameo contrast. A few irregular patches of golden-brown patina are scattered around the peripheries, but the only contact marks of any importance are one just below the point of the bust and a couple of even smaller ones just above. Census: 1 in 61 Cameo, 4 finer (12/06). (#89095)

Proof-Only Cameo Gem 1887 Double Eagle, A Landmark Rarity Within the Series

3756   1887 PR65 Cameo NGC. If the 1849 pattern is excluded, the 1887 is one of the three proof-only dates within the Liberty double eagle series. The proof mintage of 121 pieces is misleadingly high, since far fewer examples are known today. NGC has certified 12 pieces, and PCGS has encapsulated another 19 pieces. Since the two major grading services have been in business for 20 years, there has been ample time for several of these coins to get resubmitted, and most major collections have by now been certified. Breen's estimate of 20 to 25 pieces is likely accurate. What happened to the rest of the mintage? It is possible that a small quantity was melted by the mint as unsold. In addition, it must have been a temptation for collectors and their heirs to simply spend the coin, since the face value of 20 dollars went a long way during one of the country's economic panics. Large denomination gold coins were seldom collected by date prior to the 1940s, and the enormous premiums given to proof gold coins today did not exist in the 19th century. PCGS has certified two pieces in circulated grades, one each as AU50 and AU53. Other examples likely remained in circulation until Roosevelt's gold recall, which swept in a large percentage of all the double eagles ever struck.

This pleasing specimen has a penetrating strike, with essentially complete detail within Liberty's hair to the right of the ear. The glassy fields are beautifully smooth, and the portrait exhibits impressive frost. Subtle aqua and tan tints on the reverse further confirm the originality. While many collectors over the years have begun a collection of Liberty double eagles, only a handful of collectors, such as Eliasberg and Trompeter, have managed to string together lengthy date runs of proofs. All proof double eagles are both rare and desirable, but the proof-only issues are subject to even greater demand, since they provide the only means of obtaining the date. A Cameo Gem specimen, such as the present coin, may not appear again at auction for many years, and the opportunity is fleeting. (#89103)

Significant 1892 Double Eagle
PR65 Cameo

3757   1892 PR65 Cameo NGC. Although not quite as rare as the Philadelphia issue from the preceding year, the 1892 is a significant date within the Liberty double eagle series. The bulk of production this year was delegated to the half eagle and eagle denominations and only at the San Francisco facility was the production of double eagles pursued in earnest. A mere 93 proofs were originally produced in addition to only 4,430 business strikes, and the number of survivors in each category is far too small to satisfy today's ever-expanding group of gold collectors. Apparently more than half of the proof production went unsold and was melted at year's end or was eventually spent, since proof double eagles did not carry a significant numismatic premium above their already significant face value until well into the twentieth century.

As with all of the proof 1892 twenties we have been privileged to offer, including the PCGS PR65 Deep Cameo that follows, this specimen boasts appreciable contrast between the mirrored fields and the design elements. The color is a pleasing yellow-gold and the strike is executed with pinpoint precision. A thin veil of streaky haziness is seen over much of the reverse, which may explain why this elusive Gem Proof did not receive the Ultra Cameo designation. An important opportunity for the advanced double eagle specialist. Census: 1 in 65, 0 finer (11/06). (#89108)

Gem Deep Cameo Proof 1892 Double Eagle

3758   1892 PR65 Deep Cameo PCGS. Although the mintage of 93 coins is the second highest of any proof double eagle coined in the 1890s, the related business strike mintage of this date was just 4,430 coins, the second lowest mintage of any date in the 1890s. This latter detail is an extremely important consideration as it limits the available supply for date collectors.

This example is an impressive Gem that features rich orange-gold color, deeply mirrored fields, and remarkable contrast. The devices are highly lustrous with frosty texture. Every design detail is sharply impressed with no sign of weakness on either side. A few faint hairlines limit the grade, but do not change the aesthetic appeal of this lovely jewel.

In the Pittman catalog, David Akers discussed the difference between proof mintage and proof distribution, an important concept that is worth repeating: "The 93 piece mintage figure for proof 1892 double eagles is misleading, in the sense that it might give one the impression that proofs of this date are only moderately rare. However, it is important to recognize that a mintage figure for any proof issue represents only the number struck, not the number actually sold. It was common practice for the Mint to strike a number of proofs (how the figure was determined is not known) and then use this existing supply to fill orders throughout the year. At year's end (usually January or February of the following year, to be exact), the unsold pieces were melted. Now, in 1892, it certainly was not very likely that 92 people were willing to pay $20.50 for a proof double eagle (face value plus a $0.50 'proofing' charge), and so it is probable that half, or even fewer, of the original mintage were actually distributed." Today, only about 20 or 25 examples are known, and the only rivals to this example that we recall are the Gem Pittman Collection coin and the similar Gem example in the Dallas Bank Collection.

Proofs and business strikes were apparently produced from different die pairs. Proofs have the date logotype deeply impressed and just a trifle above center, with the digit 1 slightly closer to the bust than the border. The date appears to slant slightly up to the right. The reverse has the leftmost line of the sixth vertical stripe thin at its center. The right claw and right tail feathers are broken. Business strikes have the date centered in the space, with the appearance of slanting slightly down to the right. Population: 3 in 65, 2 finer (11/06). (#99108)

Contrasted Proof 1896 Double Eagle

3759   1896 PR60 PCGS. The 1896 has the highest mintage of any 19th century proof double eagle issue, and is similarly the most available of such coins. This piece has unfortunately seen more than its share of surface contact, explaining its modest grade, yet it also retains the fully mirrored, orange peel fields expected from a proof of the date. The coin is deep orange-gold in color, and there remains a considerable amount of contrast between the fields and the devices, which retain a good deal of frosty luster. For the grade, this coin presents quite well, and it represents an opportunity for the type collector to acquire an unimpaired proof at an affordable price. (#9112)

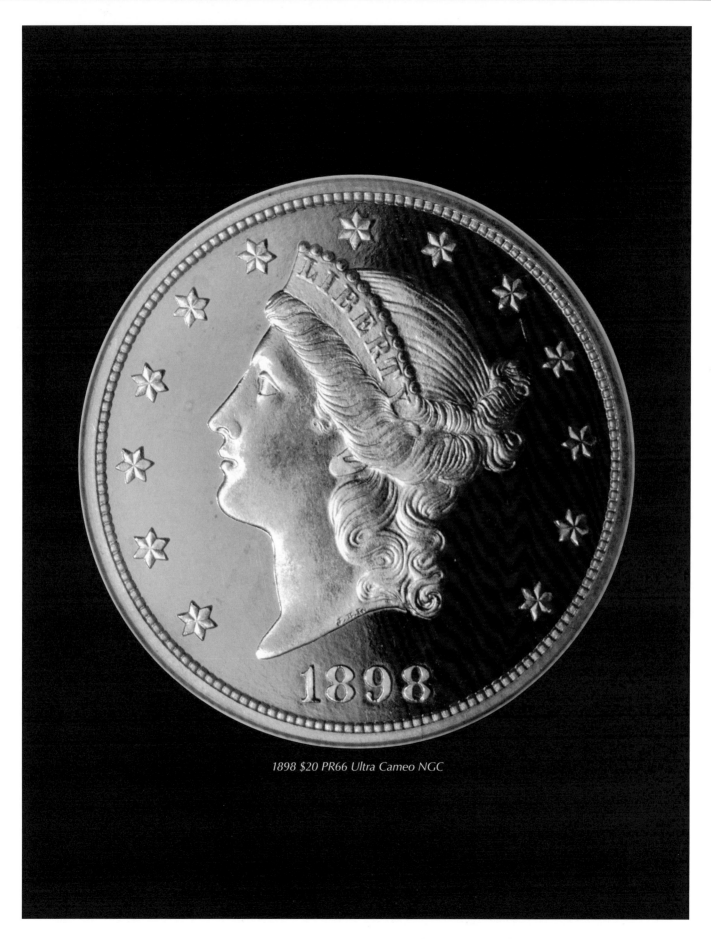

1898 $20 PR66 Ultra Cameo NGC

1898 $20 PR66 Ultra Cameo NGC

The Garrett-Bass 1898 Double Eagle, PR66 Ultra Cameo

3760   1898 PR66 Ultra Cameo NGC. This phenomenal double eagle concludes our offering of a complete run of 1898 proof gold from a single consignor, all ranging from PR66 Ultra Cameo to PR68 Ultra Cameo. When one stops to consider, the larger a coin's surface is, the more unlikely it is to receive an extremely high grade because of the many more opportunities for various surface insults—abrasions, slide marks, hairlines, surface impurities, etc.—to show upon its surfaces. Large proof gold coins in extremely high grades, such as the present coin, make a memorable and lasting impression on all but the most jaded viewer.

Even the business-strike double eagles of 1898 were produced in skimpy numbers at the Philadelphia Mint, to the tune of only 170,395 pieces. Complementing that number was a recorded mintage of 75 proof double eagles. The Garrett-Guth *Gold Encyclopedia* notes, "Although the number of examples offered at auction in the last two decades is on the high side, many of the coins are mishandled pieces. Just six or seven choice coins have been sold. The population numbers are also highly inflated by resubmissions. It can be estimated that only 35 to 40 coins remain in all states of preservation."

Legendary collector Harry W. Bass, Jr., acquired this piece from the collection of the equally legendary Garrett family. T. Harrison Garrett, whose family managed the Baltimore & Ohio Railroad, began collecting coins while a student at Princeton in the mid-1860s. He and his two sons, Robert Garrett and John Work Garrett, formed the Garrett collection, an assemblage that was unrivaled in terms of rarity, quality, and provenance. But the Garretts were far more than mere coin collectors, with far-flung, wide-ranging tastes that also comprised rare books, art, porcelain, music, and theater. The Garrett family purchased Evergreen House, an Italianate home with classical revival additions, in 1878 for T. Harrison Garrett. The 48-room Gilded Age mansion, with its soaring portico, elaborate cornices, and Tiffany-designed glass canopy, offers 26 surrounding acres of gardens and meadows, and elaborate detail throughout its interior. John Work Garrett inherited the house in 1920 and continued augmenting the family's collections—not only coins, but other collectibles as well. Throughout Evergreen House, period rooms feature post-Impressionist paintings, drawings by Degas and Picasso, collections of Chinese blue-and-white porcelain, Japanese lacquerware, and one of the world's largest private collections of Tiffany glass and Japanese minor arts. The rare book library contains more than 8,000 volumes: Shakespeare's four folios, natural history works by Audubon, Catesby, and Gould, and the signatures of every signer of the Declaration of Independence. There is also a fine incunabula collection.

Upon John Work Garrett's death in 1942, Evergreen House and its collections became part of Johns Hopkins University, subject to Garrett's stipulation that the house remain open to "lovers of music, art, and beautiful things." The Johns Hopkins University sold the Garrett Collection of U.S. Coins in a four-part auction (Bowers and Ruddy Galleries, 1979-1981), and it is there that Harry Bass acquired this memorable coin.

The present example is one of three PR66 Ultra Cameo coins so graded at NGC, which has also certified two PR67 Ultra Cameo pieces (11/06). The highest pieces of the issue certified at PCGS are two PR66 Deep Cameo pieces. True connoisseurs of proof gold, the *crème de la crème of American numismatics,* will want to make their maximum bids on this memorable piece, accompanied by its impeccable and unmatched pedigree. (#99114)

Finest PCGS Proof 1898 Double Eagle
PR66 Deep Cameo

3761   1898 PR66 Deep Cameo PCGS. An amazing Premium Gem proof with exceptional contrast between the watery, mirrored fields and frosty, lustrous devices, this piece has rich orange-gold color and is nicely matched with the others in this set. Also like the others in this set, this example is fully and boldly detailed with every individual design element detailed as intricately as it was on the original die. The surfaces are pristine and virtually perfect. There is no evidence of any useful pedigree markers to help establish the provenance of this coin.

Although PCGS has certified 40 proof 1898 double eagles, just four have been assigned the PR66 grade, and only two of those have also been given the coveted Deep Cameo designation. Like the 1898 proof half eagle, just 75 of these large double eagles were coined in proof format, and the current number of survivors is estimated at 35 to 40 coins, although we would not be surprised to learn that the real quantity is much smaller. Not only are population numbers inflated by resubmissions of the same coins on multiple occasions, but auction appearances are similarly inflated by repeated offerings of the same coins. Walter Breen once called this the "musical chairs effect." Breen discussed the population of this issue as he knew it in 1977, when he wrote in his *Proof Encyclopedia:* "This is one of the low mintage Philadelphia dates which has lately begun to stimulate date collector pressure. There are about enough proofs to satisfy the blue chip specialists, though. ... Not too many have lately shown up in the bourses. Possibly 30-odd survive, including the really badly nicked ones and the hairlined pieces."

Here at Heritage, we have offered quite a few examples of this issue over the years, but rarely have we offered pieces as fine as this. Last August, we had the pleasure of presenting a PR67 Ultra Cameo piece, certified by NGC, and in the current sale we are also offering a PR66 Ultra Cameo NGC example. Those two coins, along with this piece, are the finest proofs of this date that we have ever offered. We would not hesitate to declare this piece as one of the five finest known 1898 proof double eagles. (#99114)

PR65 Deep Cameo 1899 Twenty

3762   1899 PR65 Deep Cameo PCGS. According to Jeff Garrett and Ron Guth, fewer than 30 coins are known today of the 1899 proof double eagle, a popular entry in the series as the last issue dated in the 1800s. Of the Smithsonian's multiple examples of most issues in the Liberty Head double eagle series, only a single 1899 is found, grading PR63. The current population reports do show, counting the inevitable resubmissions, a total of 47 pieces in all proof grades, with the median grade about PR64. A perusal through our own auction archives shows that only once before, in the past 13 years, have we offered an example graded finer than the present piece, that by a single point and lacking the Deep Cameo designation from PCGS. We have offered four PR65 pieces in that same length of time, none of them certified Deep Cameo.

The date on proofs of this issue is low in the field, closer to the denticles than to the truncation of the bust, and placed somewhat to the right. Deep sunset-orange coloration is the prime hallmark of this delectable Gem proof. A single straight, undistracting contact mark on Liberty's cheek appears to be the only negative, but there are loads of counteracting positives besides the pretty coloration. The desired black-on-gold contrast is noteworthy, with the pristine fields deeply mirrored and essentially pristine, showing a watery, glasslike clarity. The strike is bold and absolutely flawless. Despite extensive perusal with a loupe, the pristine surfaces yield few pedigree markers. The most promising is a minuscule dot in the planchet, invisible without a lens, between stars 3 and 4 and nearly in front of Liberty's nose. Accompanied by an old first-generation PCGS green-label tag showing the previous grade, PR65. Population: 3 in Deep Cameo, 0 finer (12/06). (#99115)

Dazzling 1904 Double Eagle PR64 Cameo

3763   1904 PR64 Cameo PCGS. Although perhaps unconsciously tainted by their abundant 1904 business strike counterparts, proof double eagles from this year are on equal footing with other 20th century specimen strikings of this largest gold denomination. Nearly two generations after their introduction, proof gold coinage in this country was largely a numismatic cult of the extremely wealthy. Whenever production of proofs was increased, the overage almost invariably had to be later melted as unsold. No doubt, the increased production of 158 proof twenties in 1903 met this fate and the mintage a year later was reduced to a mere 98 pieces.

As America's influence around the world grew ever stronger and the Roosevelt trust busting era was nearing its height, 1904 also marked the centennial of the Louisiana Purchase and the opening of the 1904 World's Fair in St. Louis. The familiar, widely despised Morgan dollar was discontinued after this year and would not be revived until 1921.

This splendid double eagle boasts aesthetic appeal that places it on equal footing with many Gem survivors. Both sides exhibit rich, uniform golden color with an outstanding degree of contrast between the glassy mirrored fields and the design elements. A few small spots of discoloration along the obverse border from 8 o'clock to 1 o'clock are more of a curiosity than a distraction, but a similar spot between RU in TRUST on the reverse stands in the way of a Gem designation. Population: 6 in 64, 7 finer (12/06).
From The RNB Collection. (#89120)

Glittering Gem Cameo Proof
1904 Double Eagle

3764   1904 PR65 Cameo PCGS. Although the 1904 Liberty double eagle is the single most common date in the series in business strike format, proofs of this date are just as rare as any other date in the last decade of this design. Only 98 of these proofs were coined, and a little more than half that number still exist today.

When Walter Breen penned his *Proof Coin Encyclopedia,* he included die characteristics for many of the proof coinage issues. For example, he described the obverse as: "Date to right, slanting down; left base of 1 barely right of left edge, right base of 4 right of center of dentils." The example that we are offering appears to be different, with the left base of 1 about over center of a dentil and the right base of 4 nearly over the right edge of a dentil. It is possible that the different positions may actually be a result of differing perspectives on the part of individual viewers. The date clearly appears to slant down to the right. A tiny area of polish is visible just above Liberty's earlobe, with swirling die polishing lines in that area. The reverse is from the new hub of 1900, with a smooth curve to the back of the eagle's neck. The old hub features feathers that protruded into the field.

This is a nearly flawless Gem with bright yellow-gold color and excellent contrast. The fields are deeply mirrored with satiny luster on the devices. The design motifs are nicely frosted, unlike most proofs from this period that had polished devices. This example is a glittering jewel that completely lacks identifying characteristics. Only a few faint hairlines limit the grade. Population: 7 in 65, 0 finer (11/06). (#89120)

Exciting Gem Proof 1906 Double Eagle

3765   1906 PR65 NGC. Although a prized rarity in Gem condition and seldom offered in any grade, the 1906 is among the more frequently encountered proof Liberty double eagles. Nevertheless, the number of survivors is still limited in an absolute sense, being on the order of only 50-60 coins from an official mintage of 94 proofs. Moderate attrition on these high denomination proof gold coins is understandable since their numismatic value did not substantially exceed their face value for several decades. A certain amount of date pressure also falls on the 1906 double eagle, while perhaps less than in days gone by, because of the issue's low business strike mintage and scarcity in better Mint State grades.

This lovely specimen displays unfathomably deep, glassy mirrors and at least a modest amount of contrast between the fields and devices, especially considering the era in which is was produced. The bright yellow-gold surfaces are faintly striated and show a hint of striking deficiency in the centers, both characteristics found on every proof double eagle seen by this cataloger. A small coppery alloy spot is tucked away on the obverse border adjacent to star 9. While not at all distracting, this feature is particularly useful for future attribution. An exciting, high quality proof twenty for the quality conscious gold collector or investor. Population: 3 in 65, 0 finer (12/06). (#9122)

Lovely 1907 Liberty Double Eagle PR64 Cameo

3766   1907 Liberty PR64 Cameo NGC. Only 78 proof double eagles were struck in 1907, the final year of the Liberty design. Production of business strikes continued well into the year and it wasn't until November that the 1907 Saint-Gaudens twenty made its appearance. The somewhat lower mintage of proof 1907 twenties, the lowest output in fact of the 20th century, can perhaps be explained as being the result of anticipation for the debut of Saint-Gaudens design.

An educated estimate based on auction appearances and population data places the number of survivors to be in the range of 45-55 pieces. Both Breen and Akers in their notations on 1907 proof twenties make a point of mentioning that of the known survivors, many are impaired or somehow damaged, and that 2-3 pieces are impounded in museums, further reducing the number of collectible specimens.

Offered here is a wonderfully preserved specimen with a veil of warm orange-gold patina over each side. Considering the era in which it was struck, the deeply mirrored fields offer exceptional contrast against the rich mint frost on the devices. While essentially free from hairlining, inspection with a glass identifies a solitary luster graze down Liberty's cheek, a disturbance that is virtually undetectable to the naked eye. All in all, one of the more appealing 1907 proof twenties we have offered. Population: 7 in 64, 3 finer (12/06). (#89123)

EARLY PROOF SET

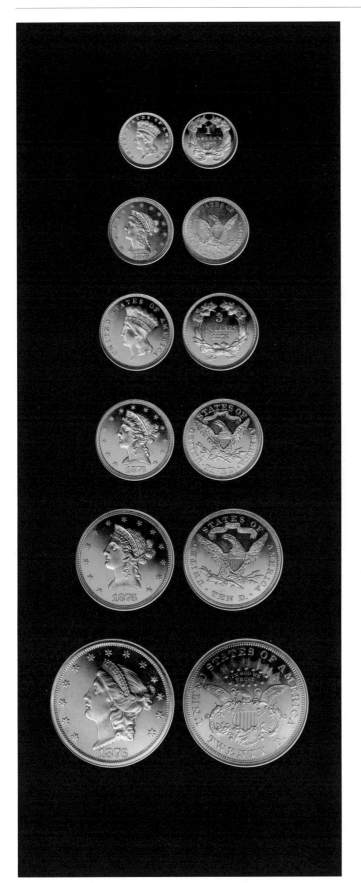

Six-Piece 1876 U.S. Centennial Gold Proof Set

3767   1876 Gold Proof Set PR63 to PR65 NGC. A splendid U.S. Centennial proof set, each piece is certified as a Cameo or Ultra Cameo by NGC. Included is a custom wood case specifically made for this set.

Proof gold coins of 1876 are slightly more populous than those of adjacent years due to increased sales at the Centennial Exposition held that year in Philadelphia. According to Mint records, all six denominations had identical mintages and delivery dates; 20 pieces were coined on February 19, 1876 and 25 more were struck on June 13. These production totals were more than double those of adjacent years. In 1874, 1875, 1877, and 1878 just 20 proof coins of each denomination were coined per year. Estimated survival rates and auction frequency are both consistent with the various mintages for this five year period.

The business strike mintage for most denominations of the 1876 gold coinage was quite low, resulting in a disproportionate number of prooflike Mint State survivors, coins that are often confused with true proofs, especially in older auction catalogs. This fact alone has made pedigree research nearly impossible.

1876 Gold Dollar PR65 Ultra Cameo NGC.

Today, most researchers believe that 20 to 25 of these small gold pieces are known, but few survive in Gem quality. In fact, our own research indicates that just four or five pieces grade PR65 or finer, including this example. Other Gem quality coins include an example in the Smithsonian Institution, one of the two Bass coins, and the Trompeter specimen.

Die characteristics for this issue are documented by Walter Breen and others. Among the clearly visible features are a short die scratch through the right base of A toward the neighboring M and a shallow rust lump on the cheek. Business strikes reportedly have another rust lump on the neck, absent on proof strikes. Breen noted that certain letters of the legend on the obverse have extra outlines, but this does not seem to be consistent from one coin to another, or from proofs to business strikes, thus should not be relied upon. Another characteristic recorded by Breen is the relative position of the date, which he stated slants down to the right. This date placement is not readily visible, thus also should not be relied upon for attribution as a proof. Patterns of the 1876 proof gold dollar were coined in copper and aluminum from these same dies.

It appears that a second obverse die was used for some of the proofs, identified by the leading feather in the headdress retaining few details. The Broken Feather obverse, used to strike most proof gold dollars from 1862 to 1873, is found on the Bass May 2000 specimen, the Trompeter coin, and possibly a few others. Logic dictates that the Broken Feather obverse was used for the delivery of February 19 and the new obverse was used for the June 13 delivery, but there is certainly no documentation to support this concept.

The devices are phenomenally frosty, forming an extreme, deep "gold on black" contrast against the highly mirrored proof fields. Yet another obvious diagnostic attesting to this coin's proof status is the superlative strike, making bold devices that are often sadly lacking on business strikes. These include the obverse highpoint hair curls and headdress plumage and, on the reverse, a full wreath of corn, cotton, maple, and other flora. Finally, the date and ONE DOLLAR are completely and boldly struck up, showing no trace of the central weakness (a function of their presence opposite those aforementioned hair curls above Liberty's ear) that business strikes often demonstrate. Only a few wispy hairlines, noted only with a strong glass, prevent an even higher grade.

Ex: Heritage (1/2006), lot 3400.

EARLY PROOF SET

1876 Quarter Eagle PR65 Cameo NGC. Ex: Pittman.

Like the gold dollar, it is believed that about 20 to 25 of these proof quarter eagles still survive from the 45 coin centennial year mintage. Also like the gold dollar, only four or five Gem quality pieces exist, including the Bass coin, the Childs Collection example, and the Eliasberg specimen.

Business strikes are immediately identified by a raised horizontal bar on Liberty's jaw and this characteristic is entirely absent from proofs. The date is minutely closer to the border than the bust, and it is placed slightly right of center with the final digit close to the right point of the truncation. A tiny die dot is visible directly above the eye lid on this coin.

This piece has excellent cameo contrast, although it is not quite as fully contrasting as the gold dollar. A few trivial hairlines and tiny contact marks have prevented a higher grade for this Gem proof quarter eagle. The strike is sharp as shown by the crisp details on both sides, In fact, we consider this piece to be "fully struck," and that term is not often used.

Ex: B.A. Seaby (8/25/1947); John Jay Pittman Collection (David Akers, 5/1998), lot 1834; Heritage (8/2006), lot 5431 $57,500.00.

1876 Three Dollar PR65 Cameo NGC.

In 1875 and 1876, three dollar gold pieces were only coined in proof format, and both dates are rarities, although a couple dozen of these pieces dated 1876 are believed to exist. A comparison of this coin to the plate in the October 1999 Bass catalog leads us to our belief that this specimen is the Bass Collection coin.

The date appears to slant down slightly to the right with the digit 1 centered below the extreme left corner of the first L in DOLLARS. Just one variety is known in two distinct die states. Examples of this proof issue are known from a perfect obverse and from a rusted obverse, the latter with considerable die rust visible within the headdress.

Opinions regarding the late die state pieces are varied. In his notes, Harry Bass considered this coin and other similar examples to be restrikes, struck at an unknown later date. Walter Breen considered the rusted die pieces to be the delivery of June 13, 1876, and not restrikes in any sense. In the Bass catalog, Dave Bowers made an interesting comment: "Regarding the rusted obverse on the present piece, this would seem to be irrelevant with regard to any issue of restrike versus original, as the obverse is undated and it would seem to have been an easy matter to have taken an unrusted die had restrikes been made. In other words, there is no reason why a particular obverse would have been saved from 1875 and used

years later to make restrikes, when years later another obverse could have been used. This element remains somewhat of a mystery." Alternatively, if it can be shown that the same undated obverse die was used for later date proof threes before the die rust developed, the existence of 1876 restrikes would be proven.

The number of auction records for 1876 proof threes is much greater than for any other denomination, and similarly the total certified population is also considerably greater. These facts suggest that the number of actual pieces known should also be larger, perhaps adding credence to the restrike theory, although this may not be the case. Because this is a proof-only issue, individual pieces tend to appear more frequently, and every example is described as a proof, even when circulated. Proof-only issues also tend to have a higher resubmission rate. We believe that the actual number of survivors is no different than the number of gold dollars and quarter eagles that are known.

This Gem Cameo proof has extraordinary eye appeal with deeply mirrored fields and fully lustrous and frosty devices. A few faint hairlines do little to distract from its aesthetic desirability. Both sides have vibrant yellow-gold color with exceptional surfaces.
Apparently ex: Stack's (12/1970), lot 109; Harry W. Bass, Jr. (Bowers and Merena, 10/1999), lot 695.

EARLY PROOF SET

1876 Half Eagle PR65 Ultra Cameo NGC.

It appears that about 12 to 15 of these pieces are known, including a disproportionately large number of Gems, perhaps half the population. Among others, the Trompeter, Eliasberg, Bass, and Smithsonian coins have been called Gems. This example brings the Gem population to five, and one or two others may also exist.

Two different dies are known for the proof 1876 half eagles. Most proofs are easily identified by the small lump on the cheek, between the lower lip and earlobe. Business strikes have a lump on the neck, vertically above the 1 in the date and just below the jawline. In his *Proof Encyclopedia*, Walter Breen reversed the characteristics of proofs and business strikes. The second variety has tiny die lumps on Liberty's neck in entirely different positions. The Bass Collection specimen, most recently offered as lot 3502 in our January 2006 sale, is an example of the second obverse, thus both varieties were offered by us in consecutive lots just a year ago.

This is a fully brilliant, fully struck example. A few hairlines are detected in the fragile fields with light magnification, but there are no singularly mentionable marks or spots worthy of consideration as pedigree identifiers, other than a tiny flake below the left side of the 8 in the date.
Ex: Heritage (1/2006), lot 3501.

1876 Eagle PR64 Ultra Cameo NGC.

The rarity of this proof gold eagle is approximately equal to the rarity of the half eagle, or about 12 to 15 examples known, but fewer Gem quality pieces exist. It appears that only three or four Gem proofs survive out of this population. In its 1979 appearance, this piece was graded by Paramount as Gem PR65, although now it is considered a near-Gem representative.

Die characteristics to distinguish between proofs and business strikes are limited. A triangular die chip is evident on the neck just below the end of the hair strand beneath the ear. This die chip is clearly visible on plates of proof examples, even in some older catalogs, and appears to provide an immediate attribution diagnostic for the proof pieces. Fine die file lines are visible through much of LIBERTY, although Breen described a similar feature for business strikes.

This piece has superlative rich yellow-gold color with brilliant and highly lustrous devices surrounded by deeply mirrored black-gold fields. All of the design elements are boldly and fully struck and only a few trivial hairlines keep it from the full Gem grade category. A tiny dark spot at the bottom of the bust, and located directly above the space between the 8 and 7, serves to positively identify the pedigree.

Ex: Auction '79 (Paramount, 7/1979), lot 337; Heritage (1/2006), lot 3545.

EARLY PROOF SET

1876 Double Eagle PR63 Cameo NGC. Ex: Eliasberg-Trompeter.

This may be the most spectacular coin in this 1876 Centennial gold proof set, even though it has the lowest grade. It is pedigreed to two famous collections of gold coinage, and it is markedly double struck. The obverse exhibits 16 distinct stars, for example. Approximately five to 10 degrees of rotation appears between the two impressions. Doubling can also be seen above the hairbun. The most evident doubling on the reverse is located at ICA and TY D to the lower right.

Although Walter Breen did not provide any die characteristics for this proof double eagle, certain attribution features are evident. A prominent die chip is located on the eye brow, with other smaller chips in a vertical line down from the corner of the eye. These tiny die chips are not visible on business strikes.

Only about 10 or 12 proof double eagles dated 1876 survive today, and just one of these, a coin in the Smithsonian Institution, can be called a Gem proof. This gorgeous Cameo proof has rich orange and yellow-gold color with lustrous devices and black-gold fields that providing for the contrast. The surfaces have minute hairlines, consistent with the grade.

Ex: Eliasberg Collection (Bowers and Ruddy, 10/1982), lot 942; Ed Trompeter Collection; Heritage (7/2005), lot 10418.

Deep Cameo Gem 1879
Proof Gold Dollar

3768   1879 PR66 Deep Cameo PCGS. Without exception, every regular issue proof gold coin dated 1879 is an important rarity. Only 30 proofs of each denomination were coined, and few of these survive today. Auction records suggest that the proof gold dollars are not as rare as the larger denomination pieces, although many deceptive first strike coins exist, and some of those have been called proofs in the past. Both proofs and business strikes were produced from the same die pair, creating further confusion in proper identification.

However, there is no doubt about the proof status of this beauty. It displays amazing cameo contrast with brilliant yellow-gold luster on the devices and deeply mirrored fields. In fact, we believe that this piece might be the finest known proof example. It is one of just two pieces certified by PCGS as PR66 Deep Cameo, with no finer examples in any designation. This piece is a different example than the other similar grade coin, which we handled in July 2003.

There are about a dozen examples known, possibly as many as 15, including two in the Smithsonian Institution and one in the Western Heritage Museum, ex Byron Reed. Others include the Garrett, Eliasberg, Bass, Carter, and Trompeter specimens, all different coins than this piece.

Choice Proof 1879 Quarter Eagle
PR64 Deep Cameo

3769   1879 PR64 Deep Cameo PCGS. Only 12 to 15 proof quarter eagles exist, including a couple of Gem pieces. It is certainly rarer than the proof-only 1863 quarter eagle, and also seen less frequently than the highly regarded 1875 proof quarter eagle issue. The finest known specimen appears to be the Superb Gem Eliasberg specimen, followed by a couple Gem PR65 coins. At least two examples are held by museums, one in the Smithsonian and another in the Western Heritage Museum.

Myriad planchet flakes on the obverse and wispy hairlines on each side have prevented a Gem grade assignment for this desirable piece. Both sides have intense yellow mint frost on the devices, surrounded by deeply mirrored fields. The contrast on this piece is deeper than usually seen, although most known examples have some degree of a cameo appearance.

This piece is different than the Eliasberg coin, and is not the Bass, Garrett, or Trompeter example. An interesting feature of this coin is the rotated reverse die, turned about 30 degrees counterclockwise in relation to the obverse. We do not know if all proofs have a similar alignment, although it is not frequently mentioned in the literature. The reverse has a tiny point from the wire edge, on the border over the left serif of R in AMERICA.

Splendid Deep Cameo Gem Proof
1879 Three Dollar Gold Piece

3770   1879 PR65 Deep Cameo PCGS. Although Walter Breen estimated a total population of 15 to 18 coins, our research suggests a population that is in the range of 10 to 12 coins, and pieces infrequently appear for sale at auction. Two pieces are part of museum holdings, with one example at the Smithsonian Institution and the other retained by the Harry Bass Foundation and on display at the ANA museum in Colorado.

At least two others were acquired by their owners directly from the Philadelphia Mint in the year of issue, including the Garrett and Childs Collection coins. Among the remaining pieces, a few are impaired and possibly two others are similar to this Gem, representing the finest available quality for this issue.

This impressive Gem proof has exceptional aesthetic appeal created by deeply mirrored fields and brilliant yellow-gold devices that retain their full quota of mint frost. A prominent lint mark diagonally through the A of DOLLARS will serve as an excellent pedigree marker. Traces of light die rust can be seen on the devices, a die characteristic that Breen attributed to the first delivery of proofs on January 25, 1879. The existence of these die rust marks confirms the proof status of this example, not that it was in question.

Very Rare PR64
Deep Cameo 1879 Half Eagle

3771   1879 PR64 Deep Cameo PCGS. We believe that only six or seven proof half eagles of this date are known, including one in the Smithsonian Institution. Walter Breen suggested that: "Survivors probably number less than a dozen, possibly less than nine" in his *Proof Encyclopedia* and Jeff Garrett and Ron Guth wrote in their *Gold Encyclopedia* that: "There are probably fewer than 10 survivors in all grades."

In over 30 years of coin auctions, this is only the second time we have handled an example. Previously, we sold a PR65 Cameo piece in August 2001. In addition to that coin, the Smithsonian piece, and the example offered here, we are aware of the Bass coin, the Garrett coin, and an example once owned by Ed Trompeter. None appeared in the Carter, Eliasberg, or Pittman Collections, among others.

This piece, certified as a near-Gem Deep Cameo proof, is similar in quality to most of the known coins. In fact, each of the six coins that we are aware of grade between PR63 and PR65, always with some degree of contrast. It has lovely yellow-gold devices with full mint frost and deeply mirrored fields as expected. A small scrape in the left obverse field and a tiny field mark on the reverse near the D of UNITED are all that keep it from a Gem grade.

Extremely Rare 1879 Choice Cameo Proof Gold Eagle

3772   1879 PR64 Cameo PCGS. We believe that exactly eight proof 1879 eagles survive today, nearly all Choice or Gem proof quality, although one polished proof example appeared at auction over a decade ago. It is possible, but doubtful, that the population could increase to 10 coins. In addition to the present example, whose previous pedigree has not been established, we are aware of the following pieces:

> **PR64 Cameo.** Smithsonian Institution.
> **Proof.** American Numismatic Society.
> **PR64 PCGS.** Stack's (10/1970), lot 955; Harry Bass Collection (Bowers and Merena, 10/1999), lot 1571
> **PR64 Cameo NGC.** Garrett Collection (acquired directly from the Philadelphia Mint); Trompeter Collection.
> **PR64 Cameo NGC.** Genaitis Collection (Heritage, 8/2001), lot 7946.
> **PR65 Cameo NGC.** Heritage (1/2006), lot 3546.
> **PR60, polished.** Bowers and Merena (5/1992), lot 1541.

Die lapping has caused the "floating curl" situation, with the curl hanging down behind the neck essentially detached at the top. Slight lapping of the reverse die is also evident, particularly at the left ribbon end. There are few other die characteristics to attribute this piece as a proof, although it clearly is an unmistakable proof. It is not as highly lustrous as some of the smaller denominations, yet the devices still retain exceptional mint frost with brilliant yellow-gold devices and impressive mirrored fields. Although a few faint hairlines are visible on each side, a tiny lilac toning spot in the right obverse field may be the only visible pedigree marker. Unlike the smaller denomination gold proofs of this date, eagles and double eagles are extremely rare with deep cameo contrast, and may not exist for this denomination.

Little has been written about this issue over the years, despite its extreme rarity. Walter Breen wrote in his *Proof Encyclopedia:* "Exceedingly rare, seldom offered. Survivors number about 10." David Akers had little more to say in his *Auction Analysis* of the series: "Proofs of this date are more rare than the mintage would suggest and they are just as rare as the proofs of 1877 and 1878." Akers examined 369 auction catalogs for his survey of gold eagles, including nearly every important sale from 1921 to 1980, and found only five auction appearances of proof eagles dated 1879. Our current survey, still a work in progress and numbering more than 500 catalogs already examined, shows just 13 auction appearances of this date in proof format, including several repeat appearances of the same coin.

Choice Cameo Proof
1879 Double Eagle

3773   1879 PR64 Cameo PCGS. Like the eagle in this set, the double eagle is extremely rare in proof format, with about 10 examples known. Although the mintage totaled 30 coins, several were likely melted without ever being sold, and others were almost certainly spent and failed to survive for this reason. We are aware of the following nine different pieces:

> **PR66 Cameo NGC.** Trompeter specimen; Heritage (5/2000), lot 7892.
> **PR64 Cameo.** Smithsonian Institution.
> **PR64 Cameo PCGS.** Heritage (8/2004), lot 7692.
> **PR64 Cameo PCGS.** The specimen offered here with unknown previous pedigree.
> **PR64 Cameo NGC.** Genaitis Collection (Heritage, 8/2001), lot 8200.
> **PR63.** Philadelphia Mint; Garrett Collection (Bowers and Ruddy, 3/1980), lot 796.
> **PR63 PCGS.** Harry Bass Collection (Bowers and Merena, 10/1999), lot 1871.
> **PR61 Cameo NGC.** Heritage (9/2004), lot 7984.
> Proof. American Numismatic Society.

Although a few blemishes and contact marks keep this away from a Gem grade level, it is an aesthetically pleasing piece with excellent cameo contrast and sharp design details. Both sides have brilliant yellow-gold color and a full quota of mint frost with deeply mirrored fields. A small mark on the chin and another just below the chin may assist in tracing the pedigree of this piece.

Like the other proofs of this date, little has been written in the past about these coins. Most recently, Jeff Garrett and Ron Guth wrote: "Although the mintage for the 1879 is slightly higher than for the last few [previous] years, the date is extremely rare in the proof format. There are only 10 to 12 coins known. Many of these are slightly impaired and not of choice quality. Just a few coins of the date have appeared at auction in the last two decades. These have been primarily from major collections such as Bass and Trompeter." Among Heritage sales of the past 30 years, this is only the seventhtime we have offered a proof 1879 double eagle.

Like all of the proofs in this set, there is no question that this piece is a true proof, just by its visual appearance. Each one of the six proofs in this set has the typical wavy or watery appearance that is associated with proof gold coinage from this time period. They all have deeply mirrored fields and lustrous or frosty devices that create a wonderful cameo appearance. Each coin has exceptional aesthetic appeal, extreme desirability, and impressive rarity.

Mint State 1907 High Relief Double Eagle

3775   1907 High Relief, Wire Rim MS62 PCGS. This pleasing High Relief double eagle provides collectors with the optimal combination of grade and price. It is nicely struck with most details fully evident, although a touch of weakness is evident on the highest design points. The grade is limited by a few imperfections in the fields, including a limited area of chatter at the left obverse. This appears to be a product of the same pair of dies used for proof pieces, although it is clearly not as sharp as those certified with the proof designation. (#9135)

Lustrous Mint State 1907 High Relief Double Eagle

3774   1907 High Relief, Wire Rim MS62 NGC. A sharp strike and frosty mint luster characterize this attractive High Relief double eagle, the famous and beautiful design created by Augustus Saint-Gaudens in his Cornish, New Hampshire studio. A few fine hairlines and moderate rim chatter limit the grade of this example. Both sides exhibit pleasing green-gold color with hints of rose toning in the protected areas, and traces of light tan color on the high points of the devices. Collectors are provided with a varied choice of pieces in the present sale. (#9135)

Sharp 1907 High Relief
Wire Rim Twenty Dollar, MS63

3776   1907 High Relief, Wire Rim MS63 NGC. One of the goals of President Theodore Roosevelt was to improve American coinage. With respect to the High Relief double eagle, Jeff Garrett and Ron Guth, in their 2006 treatise entitled *Encyclopedia of U.S. Gold Coins, 1795-1933,* write: "The aging (Augustus) Saint-Gaudens rose to the challenge and rendered this magnificent design. With a full figure of Liberty walking toward the viewer with the blazing sun behind, the reverse design depicts a bald eagle in full flight above the rising sun. Arguably the most beautiful coin ever struck for circulation, these American classics were coveted from the time of issue, and remain so to this day."

Apricot-gold color adheres to highly lustrous surfaces on this MS63 example. The design elements exhibit an impressive strike, that manifests itself in sharp delineation on Liberty's hair, facial features, fingers, and toes, as well as on the eagle's feathers. A few minute marks on each side are all that prevents the attainment of a higher grade. A wire rim is visible on good portions of both obverse and reverse, though it is difficult to discern in places because of the holder. (#9135)

Select MCMVII Wire Rim
High Relief Twenty

3777   1907 High Relief, Wire Rim MS63 PCGS. The green label insert does not specify whether the present High Relief twenty is a Flat Rim or Wire Rim, but a Wire Rim is present where the holder allows visual inspection. Since the extremely rare Ultra High Relief pieces are out of the reach of all but a few collectors, the High Relief pieces are the only affordable souvenirs that approximate the designs as Augustus Saint-Gaudens intended them to be. The High Reliefs were struck in sufficient numbers for the advanced numismatist to secure an example, but worldwide demand for this ambitious and spectacular gold type is ceaseless, especially for attractive Mint State pieces such as the present coin. This satiny and assertively struck representative possesses only minimal marks, and the eye appeal will please even the demanding collector. (#9135)

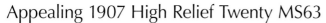

Appealing 1907 High Relief Twenty MS63

3778   1907 High Relief, Wire Rim MS63 PCGS. According to Walter Breen, the Wire Rim variant of the High Relief double eagle was coined in December 1907, with 8,250 pieces struck. This figure seems to confirm today's ratio of Wire Rim versus Flat Rim survivors, as roughly 70-75 percent of High Reliefs offered are Wire Rims and 8,250 pieces represents 73 percent of the total mintage of 11,250 pieces. This appealing yellow-gold representative is strongly and displays generally modest blemishes in the fields. A pair of shallow, parallel marks in the obverse field between 9 and 10 o'clock are well suited for future identification. (#9135)

Impressive 1907 High Relief Twenty MS64

3779   1907 High Relief, Wire Rim MS64 NGC. David Akers, writing in 1982, once said: "The 1907 High Relief Double Eagle is, in my opinion, the most beautiful coin ever issued for normal circulation. Unfortunately, it was not as practical as it was beautiful; the high relief of the standing figure of Liberty and the eagle made the coin impossible to stack properly and thus unpopular and unsuitable for commercial purposes. Minting was also impractical since it reportedly required five blows of the minting press to fully bring up the design making high speed, mass production impossible."

This near-Gem is well struck with pleasing, satiny luster. There are a few shallow marks, mostly located on the lower reverse, that account for the grade of the coin. An attractive example overall with good eye appeal. (#9135)

Desirable Near-Gem
1907 High Relief Double Eagle

3780   1907 High Relief, Wire Rim MS64 NGC. A splendid example of this scarce, historic, and enormously popular gold type. The strike is absolute except for the base of the rays above the sun, which are always indistinct on High Reliefs. The preservation is exemplary for the MS64 level, since the obverse has only a few faint grazes, and the reverse is even closer to pristine. A minor mint-made lamination is noted above the E in LIBERTY, and this serves as an identifier. The possession of the famous Augustus Saint-Gaudens High Relief separates the major gold collections from less ambitious assemblages. (#9135)

Famous 1907 High Relief
Double Eagle MS64

3781   1907 High Relief, Wire Rim MS64 PCGS. A satiny and impressive olive-gold example of this famous rarity. Careful rotation beneath a light locates a couple of wispy grazes on the left obverse field, but the overall preservation is exemplary for the MS64 level. The obverse strike is virtually complete. Only the highpoint of the knee shows a trace of incompleteness. On the reverse, the eagle is completely brought up. A few letters near 12 o'clock are slightly soft near the rim. As always for the High Relief type, the base of the rays above the sun is indistinct. This area of the reverse was enhanced for the Arabic Numerals 1907 issue, perhaps the only part of the design to be raised in relief instead of lowered, relative to its High Relief predecessor. Housed in a green label PCGS holder.
From The Essex Palm Collection. (#9135)

Beautiful 1907 High Relief
Wire Rim Near-Gem Twenty

3782   1907 High Relief, Wire Rim MS64 PCGS. Jeff Garrett and Ron Guth, in their book *Encyclopedia of U.S. Gold Coins, 1795-1933*, in their writeup of the 1907 High Relief, write: "Aside from the handful of coins that show the Ultra High Relief, these represent the closest obtainable coin to Augustus Saint-Gaudens's conception of the design....Teddy Roosevelt demanded a change in our national coinage, and sought out one of the most talented artists of that era, Augustus Saint-Gaudens...(who)...rendered this magnificent design.

The wire rim shows around most of both sides of this radiantly lustrous example, though that on the obverse is partially obscured by the holder. The high relief motifs are powerfully executed, displaying bold definition on the fingers of both hands and on the toes, and on the eagle's plumage. Both sides are adorned with beautiful peach-gold color, and just a couple of trivial obverse marks preclude a higher grade.
From The RNB Collection. (#9135)

1907 High Relief, Wire Rim
Double Eagle MS64 PCGS

3783   1907 High Relief, Wire Rim MS64 PCGS. This early issue in the Saint-Gaudens double eagle series has proven to be one of the most enduringly popular and collectible coins in the history of American numismatics. Created from a modified design, after a small quantity of Ultra High Relief specimens had proven overly difficult to produce, the High Relief version still has a powerfully raised appearance on the devices that gives the coins a three-dimensional look. This near-Gem is bright, satiny, and smooth, with impressive striking detail and marvelously preserved surfaces. Under close examination with a magnifier, the coin reveals a tiny mark beneath Liberty's right (facing) elbow, and another on her right (facing) knee. The reverse is equally impressive, as a minor milling mark just above the eagle's head is the only mentionable flaw. Without a doubt, this is a lovely and conservatively graded example of America's most beautiful coinage design.
From The RNB Collection. (#9135)

Sharp Near-Gem Wire Rim
1907 High Relief Twenty

3784   1907 High Relief, Wire Rim MS64 NGC. In his succinct style, art critic Cornelius Vermeule, writing in his *Numismatic Art in America* (1971), says of the Saint-Gaudens design, "The double-Eagle is perhaps the most majestic coin ever to bear our national imprint. The Liberty striding forward is as grand in miniature as the Hellenistic Victory of Samothrace on a heroic scale." The marble statue of the winged goddess Victory (or Nike) stands in the Louvre in Paris. It was sculpted at the height of the Hellenistic period, perhaps as early as 288 B.C., to around 190 B.C., to commemorate a naval victory of Rhodes. The statue, nearly 11 feet tall, is considered one of the great surviving masterpieces of Hellenistic sculpture, although the figure is significantly damaged, missing its head and outstretched arms. Even though sculptor Augustus Saint-Gaudens died in August 1907 and President Roosevelt died in 1919, one likes to think they would take great pride at so noted a critic's assessment of their accomplishments.

The present example shows a trace of a wire rim around portions of each side. The well-struck, lustrous surfaces show no singular distractions and offer pleasing antique-gold color, deepening to tinges of lilac near the obverse rim. (#9135)

Lovely MS64 High Relief Double Eagle

3785   1907 High Relief, Wire Rim MS64 PCGS. In *Numismatic Art in America* Vermeule writes, "Although the authorities at the Mint flattened the [Saint-Gaudens double eagle] relief to facilitate striking and handling, this coin has remained a forceful demonstration that modern, mechanical coinage need in no way be pedestrian." Of course, the High Relief pieces demonstrate even more of that compelling design by Saint-Gaudens than the final modified circulation-strike design. Speaking of pedestrian, Charles Barber would not appreciate Vermeule's comment, "Both coins [the circulation-strike design, and the modified design with IN GOD WE TRUST added] seem as modern sixty years after they were conceived as any issues, American or otherwise, produced in the past generation; and compared with what had been tolerated heretofore in the United States both burst as artistic skyrockets in the horizons of our academic creativity."

Although the PCGS encapsulation makes it difficult to see, this lovely near-Gem appears to show more of a wire rim on the reverse than the obverse. The lustrous amber-gold surfaces show tinges of hazel in the protected areas, and singular distractions are expectedly nonexistent. (#9135)

Choice Mint State 1907
High Relief Double Eagle

3786   1907 High Relief, Wire Rim MS64 NGC. A satiny near-Gem, this lovely High Relief is struck in light greenish-gold. A few of the usual surface marks on each side keep it out of the Gem grade level. Like most, this piece has swirling die polish lines in the left and right obverse fields and others in the reverse fields. These are the same die polish lines that are seen on the proofs that were produced from this die pair. While it is unknown how many dies were created for the High Relief coinage, several were likely produced. A systematic mapping of the individual die polish lines seen on various examples might help to answer this question, but would require incredible patience. (#9135)

Brilliant Gem 1907
High Relief Twenty, Wire Rim

3787   1907 High Relief, Wire Rim MS65 PCGS. Volumes have been written about High Relief Double Eagles; perhaps the finest available embodiment of the vision of Augustus Saint-Gaudens for anyone not well-heeled enough to be able to acquire the Ultra High Relief piece such as the one also featured in this auction. When on display, this exquisite design stands out, quite literally, from the rest of the pack, and its reputation as a numismatic masterpiece is such that perhaps every serious collector of U.S coinage wants one. Heritage has the privilege of featuring several of these exquisite twenties in virtually all of our Signature Auctions, and recent results tell us that this piece's popularity shows no signs of abating.

This piece is an example of the Wire Rim variant, so-called because of the narrow ridge of metal that protrudes from the outer edges of the coin. Walter Breen referred to this as a Knife Rim, but whatever the nomenclature, it was unpopular with Mint officials in 1907 for practical reasons, and manufacturing methods were changed to minimize the feature, with some success. This particular coin shows its wire rim most prominently between 12 o'clock and 7 o'clock on the obverse. It is a brilliant, peach-gold Gem, blessed with a nearly uniform metallic sheen over its surfaces. Surface abrasions are few and unobtrusive, and detract neither from the coin's eye appeal nor from the magnificence of the design. (#9135)

Gem Quality 1907
High Relief Double Eagle

3788   1907 High Relief, Wire Rim MS65 PCGS. This satiny Gem Mint State piece has a remarkably sharp strike. Liberty's head and hands are fully detailed, and the Washington city scene is brought up nicely. The tail feathers on the reverse are sharply split to the border. While the surfaces have the usual tiny surface ticks that keep this piece out of the Superb Gem category, it is an excellent piece with wonderful eye appeal. Both sides are fully brilliant with light yellow-gold color.

This example appears to be from a different die pair than most High Relief double eagles. The typical example has swirling die polish lines in the obverse fields, especially among and above the rays to the left, and below Liberty's extended arm to the right. These die lines appear both on Mint State examples and those few that are certified as proofs. The Gem that is offered in this lot has finely visible die polishing lines, but in different locations. It also has a reverse die crack that we don't recall seeing on other pieces. This crack begins at the back of the eagle's mouth, up across the head just behind the eye, through the field, and across the leading edge of the top wing.

While it is doubtful that many collectors will consider collecting High Relief double eagles by die state, the presence of this die crack is important to the numismatic historian. It helps to document the number of dies actually used to produce these coins, and is clearly an aid in the authentication process. (#9135)

1907 $20 High Relief, Wire Rim MS69 PCGS

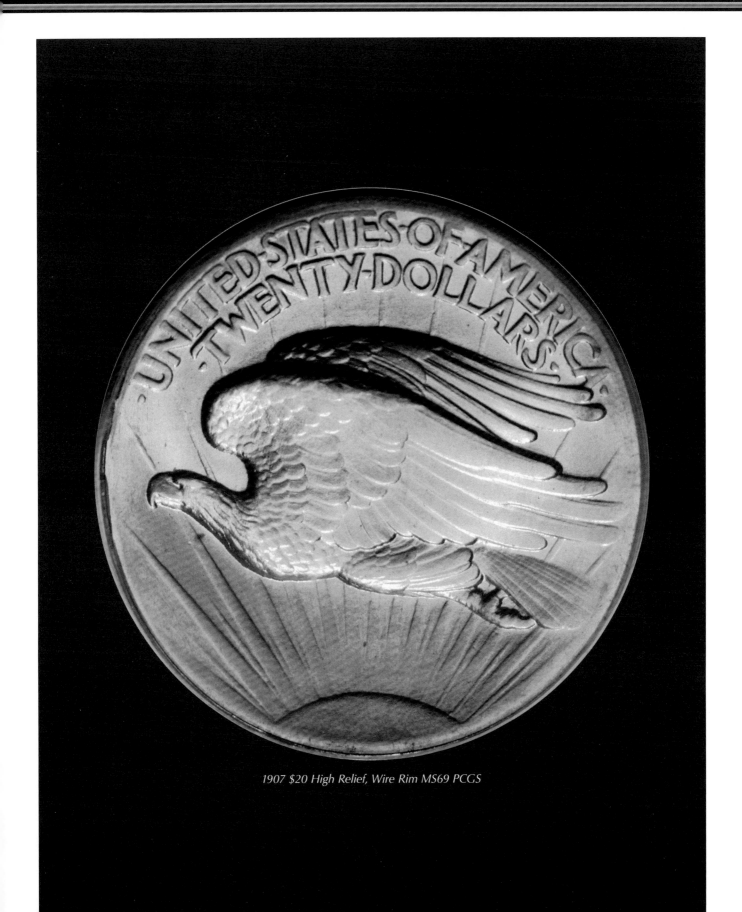

1907 $20 High Relief, Wire Rim MS69 PCGS

MS69 MCMVII Saint-Gaudens High Relief Twenty, Finest Known

3789   1907 High Relief, Wire Rim MS69 PCGS. Frank A. Leach was superintendent of the U.S. Mint in San Francisco from 1897 to 1907. He assumed the title of mint director in Washington in 1907 after the resignation of George E. Roberts from the post, and moved there in time to assume his new duties by Oct. 1, 1907. As the following excerpt shows, Leach was a crucial figure in the production of the Saint-Gaudens coinage. Leach wrote his memoirs titled *Recollections of a Newspaper Man—A Record of Life and Events in California,* published in 1917 by Samuel Levinson of San Francisco. Bowers and Merena Galleries republished a portion of that work in 1987 as *Recollections of a Mint Director.* Some excerpts from that text follow, dealing with the circumstances surrounding production of the High Relief issues:

> "Another very important matter was in hand in the bureau when I arrived at Washington, which was soon to cause me some anxiety, and that was the perfection of President Roosevelt's scheme for new designs for all the gold coins of our country. There were a number prominent people in the East, especially in New York and Boston, who some time before began an agitation for an improvement in appearance of all our coinage. The President quickly became the leading spirit of the movement. The prevalent idea in this undertaking was that the design and execution of our coinage were inferior and inartistic when compared with those of ancient Greece; and as the coins used by a nation are one of the most enduring records of the art and mechanical skill of its age, our government should make an issue of coinage that would leave to future generations and ages something that would more truthfully and correctly reflect the artistic taste and mechanical ability of our day than the coinage then in use, unchanged for so many years."

Leach then makes a surprising comment concerning what he considers to be the derivative nature of the Saint-Gaudens coinage—at least in their relief, if not in their design—and expresses his concerns with the practicability issues involved in producing the Ultra High Relief and High Relief designs:

> "The admiration for the ancient Greek coins unwittingly influenced those gentlemen to suggestions that were imitative rather than original. They wanted the designs for the proposed coinage to be brought out in high relief, or with medallic effect, like the designs on the ancient coins. The commercial use and requirements seemed to have been lost sight of in the enthusiasm of producing a highly artistic coin; but in all probability none of the leading spirits in the movement was familiar with the use of metallic money, and did not understand that the proposed high relief would make the face of the coins so uneven that the pieces would not 'stack,' which was a condition fatal to the practicability of the idea.
>
> "It was early in the year 1905 that President Roosevelt authorized the Director of the Mint to conclude a contract with the famous sculptor, Saint-Gaudens, to supply designs in high relief for the $20 and $10 gold coins. This was accomplished in July, but no designs were finally perfected that met the approval of the President until the early part of 1907. ... Dies from the model were made at the Philadelphia mint. On trial, the dies gave such a high relief to the figures on the design that all efforts to produce a perfect or satisfactory coin on the regular coining presses were ineffectual. A medal press was then resorted to, that the beauty of the design might be studied and preserved in the shape of a coin, but even by this process it required about twelve blows or impressions in the press for each piece, with an annealing process between each stroke of the process. ... Nineteen pieces only from this model were struck on the medal press, and these were subsequently given to mint and Washington officials connected with the work.
>
> "There were some who thought that by reducing the diameter of the piece to about the size of a 'checker,' with a corresponding increase in the thickness, the much desired high relief might be struck on the ordinary coin press; accordingly dies were made and several pieces struck, when it was discovered that the coinage act, passed in 1890, prohibited the change of the diameter of any coin. Thirteen pieces were struck from this small die for the thick or checker pieces, but with the exception of two coins placed in the cabinet or collection of coins at the Philadelphia mint, all of these pieces were melted and destroyed on account of the improper or illegal dimensions.
>
> "Saint-Gaudens then attempted to facilitate the work of coinage by supplying another or second set of models with the relief reduced to some extent, but satisfactory results were not obtained on the regular coinage presses. He then made a third model with still further and greater reduction of the high relief. The failure gave rise to considerable friction between the artist and the mint authorities. The President had become impatient and began to think that the mint officials were not showing a zeal in the work that promised results. It was at this stage of undertaking that I came into the office of Director. Before I had become familiar with my surroundings the President sent for me. In the interview that followed he told me what he wanted, and what the failures and his disappointments had been, and proceeded to advise me as to what I should do to accomplish the purpose determined upon in the way of new coinage. In this talk he suggested some details of action of a drastic character for my guidance, which he was positive were necessary to be adopted before success could be had. All this was delivered in his usual vigorous way, emphasizing many points by hammering on the desk with his fist. This was my first interview with the President, and it was somewhat embarrassing for me to oppose his views, but I felt that it was essential to my success that I should be untrammelled by any interference in the plans that I should adopt to secure the production of the new coinage. I determined then and there that if I could not have free rein in the matter

I would not attempt the work. In my reply to the President I finally made the wisdom of my position clear to him. I explained to him how I had not yet had time to look into the matter and locate the causes of failure, consequently could not say what was necessary to correct them. At any rate, I would have to insist that these were matters of details that should be left to my judgment.

" 'All you want, Mr. President,' I said, 'is the production of the coin with the new design, is it not?'

" 'Yes,' said he.

" 'Well, that I promise you.'

"He said he guessed I was right in my attitude in the matter, but I think he was not very confident of my getting results, for when a few days later I laid upon his desk a sample of beautifully executed double eagles of the Saint-Gaudens design, he was most enthusiastic in his expressions of pleasure and satisfaction. I certainly believed him when he declared he was 'delighted.' He warmly congratulated me on my success, and was most complimentary in his comments.

" 'Now,' he said, 'I want enough of these coins within thirty days to make a distribution throughout the country, that the people may see what they are like.' I replied that we would be able to meet with his desire, although I explained that the issue would have to be struck on medal presses from the second design model, but that in a few weeks later, we would have dies completed from model No. 3 with lower relief, so that the coins, when made, would meet the requirements of the bankers and business men in 'stacking,' etc., and these could be struck on the regular coin presses in the usual way. The pleasure of the President was manifested in the heartiness of his thanks. I had every medal press in the Philadelphia mint put into operation on these coins with an extra force of workmen, so that the presses were run night and day. The officers of the mint entered into the spirit of the work cut out for them, putting zest into the operations which assured me that the issue of the new double eagles, so greatly desired by the President, would be made on time. In fact, we delivered to the Treasurer of the United States 12,153 double eagles, representing $243,060, which was considerably more than asked of us, several days ahead of time."

As the fascinating and historic Leach account makes clear, the MCMVII Ultra High Relief coins were an instant rarity, and those coins today are all but unobtainable, as only 19 or 20 pieces were struck. In this way the Ultra High Relief coins are in the same class as other legendary rarities, say the 1894-S Barber dimes or the 1804 silver dollars. But the High Relief coins are in quite a different class. While retaining much of the original relief desired, the MCMVII High Relief coins are not particularly rare as a type, and nice specimens are within the means of many collectors. And while the Ultra High Reliefs are pattern pieces, the High Reliefs are regular-issue coinage. Mint Director Leach had the pieces struck to satisfy President Roosevelt's desires for high relief coinage that would emulate the Classical Greek coinage, all the while fully realizing that the de-

sign was still impractical for modern, one-blow circulation coinage. "Modern" circulating coinage of the era was produced on high-speed steam-powered coin presses, not the hydraulic medal presses used for the Ultra High Relief and High Relief coinage. The High Relief coins required only three blows of the medal press, not the seven or more blows required to fully articulate the Ultra High Relief design. Although the estimates for the number of pieces coined vary (and estimates for the number of blows required), Leach's documentation of more than 12,000 pieces appears essentially correct, according to modern research.

A so-called "Wire Rim" protruded around the outer extremity in the coins, which resulted from excessive metal flow between the die face and collar during the striking process. Unlike today's collectors who consider the Wire Rim to be a highly collectible variety, Mint officials considered it to be a striking deficiency. This "flaw" in the striking process was corrected around mid-December, and subsequent High Relief double eagles possessed what became known as a Flat Rim.

The High Relief Wire Rim example we offer in the present lot is a supremely preserved, satiny gem of this highly regarded Saint-Gaudens issue. The execution of this design in high relief has, to date, been the ultimate achievement of the coiner's art—a fact widely recognized and reflected in the price of these coins. The design elements on this coin are extremely well defined, indeed better that what might be expected for the issue. Despite multiple blows, the typical High Relief Wire Rim specimen may display weakness on the stars, on the Liberty and eagle motifs, and the on the tops of the letters. The present coin, formerly offered in the fabulous Phillip H. Morse Collection of Saint-Gaudens Coinage, reveals strong definition in most of those areas. Only small portions of the Capitol building and the eagle's wing feathers exhibit minor softness. A pleasing yellow-gold patina bathes each side, both of which have managed to escape any signs of post-striking impairments, and the radiant, satiny luster has a gleam that is unique to High Reliefs. The surfaces are unusual in that they are virtually mark-free, as expected for the grade. The overall effect is one of originality and three-dimensionality, giving this spectacular piece more the look of a medal than of a circulating coin. A minute alloy spot beneath the eagle's neck identifies the coin for future pedigree purposes. The Wire Rim feature is uncharacteristically present around virtually the entire obverse, and around a good portion of the reverse. Population: 1 in 69, 0 finer (11/06).

Ex: Trompeter Collection; Heritage private sale, 1999; The Phillip H. Morse Collection of Saint-Gaudens Coinage (Heritage, 11/05), lot 392, which realized $575,000. (#9135)

1907 High Relief Double Eagle
MS63, Flat Rim

3790 **1907 High Relief, Flat Rim MS63 PCGS.** This bright yellow-gold example is relatively free from abrasions and exhibits just a touch of contact on the highpoints of the portrait. The normal stacking friction is primarily found in the peripheral areas of the reverse. Just in case the viewer was just beamed down from another galaxy, the High Relief double eagle is one of the most popular and impressive of all American designs. The present example represents a logical compromise on this classic 20th century rarity between condition and affordability. (#9136)

Radiant 1907 High Relief Twenty
MS63, Flat Rim

3791 **1907 High Relief, Flat Rim MS63 PCGS.** Several times scarcer than its Wire Rim counterpart, the Flat Rim variant is not actually a conscious design change on the part of the Mint, but rather an answer to the problem of extruded metal on the earlier strikings of High Relief twenties. Based on the ratio of appearances between the two variants, it has been estimated that flat rims comprise fewer than 4,000 pieces of the total mintage of 11,250 high reliefs. A touch of reddish patina nicely accents this radiant yellow-gold example. Minor stacking friction on the reverse precludes a Choice rating. (#9136)

Choice High Relief MCMVII
Double Eagle with Flat Rim

3792   1907 High Relief, Flat Rim MS64 PCGS. A satiny near-Gem of this world-famous issue. The fully struck central devices rise in their high relief glory above the smooth and satiny fields. The right reverse border has a few tiny planchet flaws, and minor strike doubling is seen on the base of the LIBE in LIBERTY, but these mint-produced characteristics are of no consequence, and do not affect the significant eye appeal. As an issue, the High Relief is merely scarce, but by gold type standards, it is rare, and demand is furthered by its remarkable medallic appearance and undeniable historical importance. Its design came from America's foremost sculptor, and its production was compelled by Presidential order. (#9136)

Scarce Flat Rim 1907
High Relief Twenty MS64

3793   1907 High Relief, Flat Rim MS64 PCGS. Two varieties of the 1907 High Relief Saint-Gaudens double eagle were produced: the Wire Rim and the Flat Rim. A total of 11,250 pieces were minted of both varieties combined, with the Flat Rim coins being at least four to five times scarcer than their Wire Rim counterparts. This piece has beautiful, satin-like surfaces that show no obvious contact marks on either side. The luster is unimpeded, and the eye appeal is substantial, with lovely lime and peach coloration over sharply brought up design features. Although always available for a price, High Relief double eagles are coveted by numismatists for their historical importance, and because they represent the ultimate in artistic achievement for a product of the U.S. Mint. (#9136)

Exceptional Flat Rim
High Relief Twenty, MS65 NGC

3794   1907 High Relief, Flat Rim MS65 NGC. Scholarship in U.S. numismatics keeps growing at an ever-increasing pace. Just when it seems that there are no more unexplored areas, a new ground-breaking work is published. Recently, two books were published by Roger Burdette with the common title *Renaissance of American Coinage*. One volume covered the period from 1916-1921 and the other 1905-1908. In the latter book, he quotes from a letter from Mint Superintendent Landis to Director Leach dated December 6, 1907, concerning the "problem" of the wire rim or burr on the High Relief twenties.

> "I was exceedingly humiliated today to have the Secretary of the Treasury call attention to the excessive burr, or fin, on one of the new double eagle pieces now being distributed.
>
> "I was also surprised to find so many of these defective coins in a bag as I saw in the Treasurer's office here.
>
> "I gave explicit orders when in Philadelphia that such coins should not be delivered, and directed the man who seemed to have the coins in charge to see that the same should all be gone over and the bad ones laid aside.
>
> "I wish you to make [an] investigation and see why my instructions were not carried out, and if there was any negligence or carelessness, who is to blame."

Clearly, mint personnel at the highest levels saw the fin, burr, or as we know it today the "wire rim" as a minting flaw and sought to correct it. It was not seen as an aesthetic addition to the coin and was a source of "humiliation" as Landis indicated. In the hundred years since that time, attitudes of collectors have appreciably changed; and, in fact, it was not long after striking that collectors began to appreciate the difference between the Wire Rim and Flat Rim variants of these beautiful coins. While exact numbers are not known, it was not until December 20, toward the end of the production run for High Reliefs (in December), that Charles Barber and other members of the engraving staff completely eliminated the fin on High Reliefs.

This is a magnificent coin that has velvety surfaces with an even more pronounced satin finish than usually seen on High Relief twenties. The striking details are fully brought up in all areas with full separation between the reverse peripheral lettering and the rim. An exceptional High Relief, and part of a limited run of coins that have an interesting story behind it. *From The Freedom Collection.* (#9136)

Premium Gem 1907
High Relief Double Eagle

3795   1907 High Relief, Flat Rim MS66 NGC. This remarkably sharp example has many characteristics that are seen on examples certified as proof, although the details at the lower left part of the obverse lack just enough sharpness to qualify as a proof. This piece is fully brilliant with rich yellow-gold color and satiny luster. The surfaces are remarkable for their preservation, and the overall aesthetic appeal of this Premium Gem is second to none. As wonderful as this coin is, the accompanying paperwork tells of an interesting history. Two items are included with this coin, both pointing to an important provenance.

The first item is a somewhat tattered envelope imprinted "A. Raymond Raff, Builder, Philadelphia." A handwritten note, dated December 4, 1914, is on the outside of the envelope that obviously contained this coin for many years:

> To John, From Dady, Moral. Do not spend this coin. Keep it safely stored away. Today, it is worth $45.00. 20 years from today it will be worth $448.00. 30 years—$1,000.00. A good investment to hold inasmuch as it costs you nothing in the original investment."

Although the projected valuations were not entirely accurate, the note provides a fascinating glimpse into the numismatic scene during the early 20th century. Some twenty years after this note was written, the very same A. Raymond Raff was Superintendent of the Philadelphia Mint, as mentioned in a typed letter dated March 8, 1960, from then current Philadelphia Mint Superintendent (Mrs.) Rae V. Biester, addressed to Mr. James T. MacAllister:

> "In reply to your verbal inquiry, be advised Mr. A. Raymond Raff was appointed March 1, 1934—Superintendent of the Mint of the United States at Philadelphia, and resigned April 7, 1935." (#9136)

1907 $20 High Relief, Flat Rim MS68 PCGS

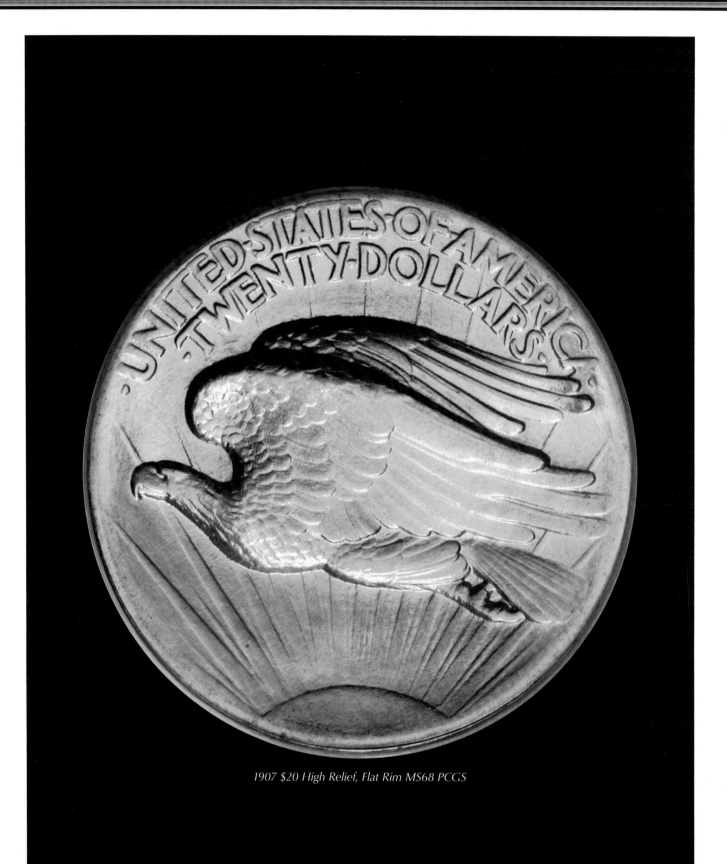

1907 $20 High Relief, Flat Rim MS68 PCGS

MS68 Flat Rim MCMVII High Relief
Among the Finest Known

3796   1907 High Relief, Flat Rim MS68 PCGS. The Flat Rim variant of the 1907 High Relief was produced to solve the problem of a wire rim. This "problem" was created by an extruded rim of metal, or "fin," caused by a tiny bit of gold that squeezed between the die and segmented collar from repeated blows of the 150-ton medal press employed to strike the coins. Most of the first two-thirds of High Relief double eagles suffered from the "fin," and mint officials considered it both an aesthetic defect and a legal difficulty: The fin quickly abraded off the coins, leaving an underweight gold piece. The "fin" was certainly not considered an aesthetic element, as commonly regarded by collectors today. The milling procedure and planchet size for the double eagle blanks were slightly modified to correct this small flaw about December 16, according to numismatic researcher Roger W. Burdette.

Flat Rim coins are several times scarcer than their Wire Rim counterparts, but they remain an underrated and largely underappreciated variant of the High Relief. Even though much of the original mintage was saved by collectors, after nearly 100 years most are in the lower to middle Mint State grades, or they show signs of circulation. Some were doubtless carried as pocket pieces.

After examining hundreds of High Relief twenties, we have observed that Wire Rim pieces do not necessarily have a complete wire rim, and conversely Flat Rim pieces may show traces of a localized wire rim. It is generally accepted that about 33% (the final 4,000 pieces or so out of the original mintage of more than 12,000 coins) of the High Reliefs minted were of the Flat Rim variety; however, their survival ratio is much lower, with probably no more than 20% to 25% of the Flat Rims known today. Another possibility for the lower survival rate is that perhaps the conventional wisdom's estimate is a bit off. It might be simply that the Flat Rim High Reliefs were released later, and thus were less of a novelty.

A strong strike is a given on High Relief double eagles, since they were struck with multiple blows with a hydraulic medal press. Even so, a few pieces still exhibit slight weakness on the figure of Liberty, the highest parts of the eagle's wing on the reverse, and the tops of the peripheral lettering. The dies were finished with myriad tiny lines and swirls that are particularly visible on early strikes. According to Q. David Bowers, "The surfaces are somewhat grainy or matte, rather than frosty or lustrous." High Reliefs do, however, usually show lovely satinlike luster that is usually a bright yellow-golden color.

This piece is no exception, boasting the usually seen satiny luster. The striking details, however, are exceptionally—and phenomenally—bold. The Capitol building, stars, olive branch, and the Liberty and eagle motifs display excellent definition. The surfaces are immaculately preserved over both sides, exhibiting no signs of mishandling. A barely discernible luster graze on the top rear of the eagle's left wing is mentioned for accuracy. As noted earlier, some Flat Rim pieces show traces of a localized Wire Rim. Such is the case with the present coin, where some wirelike remnants are noted along the right obverse rim. Another coin from the Morse Collection that is among the finest known. Population: 1 in 68, 0 finer (11/06).
Ex: The Phillip H. Morse Collection of Saint-Gaudens Coinage (Heritage, 10/05), lot 6527, which realized $264,500. (#9136)

Near-Gem Proof 1907 High Relief Twenty

3797   1907 High Relief PR64 NGC. Although the existence of proofs is controversial, Roger Burdette's monumental *Renaissance of American Coinage 1905-1908* provides valuable background concerning the numismatic atmosphere in which the 1907 double eagles were produced. In a December 17, 1907, letter to Charles Brewster (attorney for the recently widowed Augusta Saint-Gaudens), Mint Director Frank Leach wrote:

> "... There is a great demand for the coins [of Mr. Saint-Gaudens' design]. So far the medal press capacity at the mint at Philadelphia has been unable to satisfy it, and I am told the coins out there are all bringing a premium. I regret this, for I was in hopes that there would be sufficient struck to satisfy the wants of everybody. We shall continue running the medal presses as long as we can for this reason. We did not get the coin presses in operation on the double eagles of the new design as soon as expected. ... Of course, the coin from the coining press is not as fine a specimen of art as that struck on the medal press, yet, it seems to me, it is superior to anything any other country has produced. The relief is much higher than anything I have seen, and I think higher than that in existence on the gold coins of any country. ..."

Leach wrote this after the initial Ultra High Relief design was modified once to the High Relief design, then again to the final Low Relief, Arabic Numerals business strike style. Concerning potential proof coinage, what is known conclusively is that something less than two dozen "proofs," or specimen strikes, were made of the Ultra High Relief double eagle, those early in the year (February 1907). Several highly placed government officials—even the obstructionist Mint Engraver Charles Barber—received examples of that crowning glory of coinage art, as did, ultimately, Saint-Gaudens' widow. Those true patterns were made as early trials so that the various personages involved, from concept through commercialization, could see concrete examples. By a short time after, all involved had concluded that no coin with so high a relief could be mass-produced. But because of President Roosevelt's extreme fondness for his "pet project," he insisted on having coins to present to the public. The relief was modified a second time, to the High Relief design. Leach had 11,000 or 12,000 of the High Relief examples minted, turning what would have been a second pattern issue into circulating coinage. The relief was lowered a third time to the final coinage, capable of being struck with a single blow from the press. Given the demand for all examples of this issue, even the Low Relief coins, it would be extremely surprising, perhaps even shocking, if "proofs" or specimen strikings of the modified High Relief coins had *not* been produced. All available evidence points to the fact that specimen strikes were made, possibly at several different times, of the High Relief design, the best compromise between high artistry and wider availability. Much ado is made—probably overmuch—of the two variants found on the rims, as most examples show only a partial wire rim, sometimes only on one side.

The striking definition on this piece is truly exceptional, and that alone sets it apart from other High Relief twenties. All the pillars on the Capitol building are fully detailed, and the peripheral lettering is completely separated from the wire rim that encircles each side. Rich orange-gold coloration is seen over each side with a thin veneer of satiny mint luster. Simply outstanding quality of this important, experimental striking of the 1907 High Relief. (#9132)

Important Proof High Relief Twenty PR64 NGC

3798   1907 High Relief PR64 NGC. Chief Engraver Charles E. Barber reported that only five proof variants of the MCMVII High Relief Saint-Gaudens double eagle were originally produced. Breen, however, accounts for seven examples in his 1988 *Encyclopedia* that can be pedigreed to Barber, and he states that "others cannot be traced to him." We do not know exactly how many proof High Relief double eagles were originally produced, but they all display, in addition to a satin finish, the following diagnostics:

1. Sharp inner border on both sides.
2. All berries in the obverse olive branch are well rounded.
3. The Capitol building on the obverse is fully brought up with distinct pillars.
4. The eagle's tail feathers are distinct all the way up to the right reverse border.
5. The edge letters are bolder than those seen on business strikes, and there are horizontal striations between them.
6. No more than a trace of a wire rim is evident on either side.

Those features that we can examine on the present NGC-encapsulated specimen match those listed here, which we have taken from Breen (1988). What's more, the overall striking definition is appreciably sharper than that seen on the already carefully produced business strikes. Green-gold in color at indirect angles, the surfaces brighten to orange-gold shades as the coin rotates into the light. Both sides are expectantly blemish-free for the assigned grade with only a few tiny grazes and alloy spots toward the borders that seem to preclude a full Gem designation. This coin is certainly one of the most visually appealing proofs we have examined, especially at the PR64 level. *From The RNB Collection.* (#9132)

Compelling PR64 1907 High Relief Twenty

3799   1907 High Relief PR64 NGC. As of this writing (11/06), NGC recognizes proofs of the High Relief issue, while PCGS does not. Roger Burdette's monumental *Renaissance of American Coinage* does not support the theory of the existence of true proofs—coins that have been produced in a profoundly different manner than the regular issue pieces—but neither does it *disprove* their existence. These coins were, after all, a modified version of the Ultra High Relief coins. The Ultra High Reliefs were strictly pattern coins or specimen strikes, made early in 1907 in an indubitable proof format. Despite their best intentions to produce coins "worthy of the ancient Greeks," both President Roosevelt and Augustus Saint-Gaudens came to ultimately realize the exigencies of modern coinage (and banking) would not allow coins with as high a relief as the Ultras to be mass-produced on modern coining presses. Roosevelt's enthusiasm for coinage redesign led to some truly hilarious correspondences between him and Saint-Gaudens, who had had a "run-in" with the arch-conservative Mint Engraver Charles Barber in 1892 over the production of a medal for the upcoming World's Columbian Exposition. From then until 1905, Saint-Gaudens avoided contact with the Mint. Roosevelt to Saint-Gaudens, January 1906:

> ... Of course [Treasury Secretary Leslie Mortier Shaw] thinks I am a crack-brained lunatic on the subject, but he said with great kindness that there was always a certain number of gold coins that had to be stored up in vaults, and there was no earthly objection to having those coins as artistic as the Greeks could desire. ... I think it will seriously increase the mortality among the employees at the Mint at seeing such a desecration, but they will perish in a good cause!

Saint-Gaudens to Roosevelt, May 1906:

> ... Whatever I produce cannot be worse than the inanities now displayed on our coins, and we will at least have made an attempt in the right direction, and served the country by increasing the mortality at the Mint. There is one gentleman there, however, who, when he sees what is coming, may have the 'nervous prostitution,' as termed by a native here, but killed, no. He has been in that institution since the foundation of the government and will be found standing in its ruins.

The relief was modified a second time, to the High Relief design. Mint Director Frank Leach had 11,000 or 12,000 pieces of the High Relief examples minted, turning what would have been a second pattern issue into "business strike" coinage—but clearly one of a special nature. Leach is known to have expressed regret that the coins were bringing a premium, and apparently went to great lengths to satisfy the overwhelming demand (as well as to placate President Roosevelt). It may be that all of these coins were considered "proofs" in some sense, but that several, or even multiple, mintage occasions may have occasioned some pieces to have been struck with more care, higher pressure, or more blows from the press than at other times. This piece shows the proof diagnostics, as outlined in Walter Breen's *Proof Encyclopedia*: The berries in the obverse olive wreath are well rounded; there is only a slight suggestion of a wire rim; the pillars and other details in the Capitol building are boldly brought up; the eagle's tail feathers are sharp all the way to the rim; and the inner border is sharp on both sides. A couple of undistracting contact marks on each side are consistent with the grade. Census: 64 in 64, 58 finer (11/06). (#9132)

Beautiful PR66 High Relief Twenty

3800   1907 High Relief PR66 NGC. It is fairly well known that Augustus Saint-Gaudens, the "American Michelangelo," based his design for the double eagle on the winged goddess of Victory that forms part of the General William Tecumseh Sherman statue at the corner of Fifth Avenue and 59th Street in New York City. Sherman's horse treads on pine cones and fronds, fatefully representing Georgia, which Sherman had torched in his terrible 1864 March to the Sea. The equestrian figure of General Sherman received the Grand Prix at the 1900 Universal Exposition. The winged goddess of Victory leads Sherman's horse. She wears a headdress and strides purposefully forward, her right arm stretched out before her, giving the entire monument a rhythmic, driving propulsion. Her eyes are depthless blanks, her expression simultaneously tragic and inscrutable. Similar to the traditional olive sprig in Liberty's left hand on the coin, Victory holds a palm branch in her left hand.

One of Saint-Gaudens' great gifts—one that he shared with Michelangelo—was to be able to sculpt figures on a heroic scale, and yet imbue them with personality in the most human dimensions. It is perhaps less well known that Saint-Gaudens based the statue of Victory on that of his mistress, Davida Clark. The General Sherman Monument, commissioned by the New York Chamber of Commerce in 1892, was the last monumental work of Saint-Gaudens' cancer-shortened life. The final completed monument was installed in 1903. In the evolution from winged Victory to wingless Liberty, Saint-Gaudens managed to strip the nonessential from the female figure, while maintaining both her goddesslike grandeur and heroism as well as her powerfully human femininity. Removal of the wings and headdress allowed room for the *de rigueur* inscription above, while focusing more attention on the center of the coin, permitting her hair to blow freely in the wind, and making room beneath for the Capitol building.

This High Relief example clearly shows the diagnostics of NGC-acknowledged proofs. There is just a hint of a wire rim; the inner border is sharp; all the berries are well rounded; all the pillars of the Capitol are fully and distinctly brought up; and the tail feathers are fully distinct to the right rim. In addition, this beautiful realization of Saint-Gaudens' vision shows that ineluctable strength of definition throughout, with a purposeful strike and superb preservation that should remove any doubt as to its proof status in all but the most cynical. (#9132)

Impressive Gem Proof 1907 High Relief Double Eagle, PR66

3801   1907 High Relief PR66 NGC. Traces of a wire rim can be seen on each side of this magnificent Gem proof example, although it could be debated whether this example actually qualifies as a Wire Rim or Flat Rim variety. Similarly, a lively debate might take place about the status of these pieces as actual proofs. In fact, NGC certifies certain examples as proofs while PCGS does not certify any High Relief double eagles as proofs. The finish is satiny rather than mirrored, thus eliminating one of the clues to proof gold coinage. As the Mint experimented with special finishes from 1907 through 1915, proof gold coins took on an entirely new and different look from previous issues.

Various authors have commented on the proof pieces over many years. In his 1982 *Analysis of Auction Records,* David Akers noted: "There were no proofs officially struck for collectors, but a small number of pieces do exist that are undoubtedly proofs based on the fact that they were struck with the lettered edge collar used on the Extremely High Relief. They are also characterized by an unusually satiny surface and a myriad of raised die scratches and swirls in the fields." Walter Breen also believed in the existence of proof examples, and gave detailed descriptive notes in his *Proof Encyclopedia:* "True proofs do exist, though, and these appear to have received six or seven blows from the dies rather than the normal five. They do not have pronounced knife-rims; generally no trace of any, though rims are not as rounded as on normal impressions. Fields are most often satin finish, nearest to that on some proof 1909-10 Lincoln cents, but on one coin are sandblast type. Inner and outer edges of flat border sharp, relief details fully brought up, berries rounded, all Capitol pillars countable, clear ends to tail feathers; edge lettering much bolder than on normal strikings, with horizontal striae between edge letters. Charles E. Barber gave out the information that only five were struck on the medal press, but this was an outright lie as he owned seven or more himself. Proofs were evidently made on several occasions for presentation purposes, from more than one of the pairs of dies used for this issue, with two different edge collars, and in several different finishes." Breen continued to provide notes on a dozen different specimens.

Perhaps it is instructive to understand the criteria used by NGC to distinguish proofs from business strikes. These criteria were reported by Dr. Robert J. Loewinger in *Proof Gold Coinage of the United States:* "1) Extreme sharpness in all details, both at the centers and toward the peripheries. 2) The complete absence of die erosion or distortion. 3) Numerous, raised die-polishing lines on both sides. These appear in a random, swirling pattern. While also evident on currency strikes, these are particularly bold on proofs. 4) Uniformly satiny surfaces, without any of the radial flowlines that produce conventional mint luster. 5) A build-up of metal just inside both borders, though especially evident on the reverse. This appears as a slightly raised ridge forming a concentric circle within the coin's border. It probably resulted from the extreme compression to which the proofs were subjected by additional strikes."

In their *Significant Auction Records* reference, authors Jeff Garrett and John Dannreuther listed price records for both proofs and business strikes in a single section, explaining: "Many High Reliefs have been sold as proofs and are from proof dies, but do not have all the characteristics of true proofs. Therefore, proof High Relief listings are mingled with the Mint State flat edge coins. This is a very controversial area in which the few real High Relief proofs are obvious, while many other coins are not obvious as either proofs or business strikes. The price realized is a pretty good example of how the numismatic community views a particular proof offering, as the non-controversial proofs often bring multiples of questionable proofs."

The entire debate was summed up quite nicely by Dave Bowers in *A Guide Book of Double Eagle Gold Coins:* "This explanation [by Garrett and Dannreuther] gives the core of the puzzlement. It is seen that certain experts may avoid obvious non-proofs listed as proofs in auction catalogues, but this is not of much help to the vast majority of collectors who are not experts. At best, this is a tricky area, and I recommend that before buying one you enlist the help of a trustworthy gold coin expert to examine the coin and advise you."

This example, an amazing Premium Gem piece, meets all of the qualities defined by NGC for certification as a proof. It also meets the criteria noted by Walter Breen, including eight pillars in the Capitol. The edges are well defined, although the build-up of metal on the reverse as required by NGC tends to obscure the sharpness of the inner reverse border. Although we are not sure how Breen arrived at the count of six or seven blows by the press, this piece is clearly more sharply defined than most. It has bright yellow-gold color with only a few faint hairlines, and these are mostly hidden within the myriad die-polishing lines on both sides. Additional requirements [of this cataloger] are met by this example: all of the fingers on both hands are fully countable as are the toes, and Liberty's facial details are absolutely 100% fully defined. Census: 18 in 66, 15 finer (10/06). (#9132)

SAINT-GAUDENS DOUBLE EAGLES

Appealing Gem 1908 Motto Twenty

3802 1908 Motto MS65 PCGS. Ex: Park Avenue Collection. While the No Motto issue is widely available, the Motto coins of 1908 are rare in MS64, more so in Gem grade. An arm's-length, eye-appealing Gem, with brilliant luster cascading from the dual-toned greenish-gold and apricot-gold surfaces. The bold strike brings up the detail in both of Liberty's feet, in her head and hair, and on the olive branch, while on the reverse the eagle's wing feathers are well sculpted. An enormously eye-appealing example. Population: 30 in 65, 11 finer (12/06). (#9147)

Near-Gem 1909/8 Saint-Gaudens Double Eagle

3803 1909/8 MS64 PCGS. An important overdate variety within the series of U.S. gold coinage, the 1909/8 Saint-Gaudens double eagle is one entry among an extremely limited number of 20th century overdate coins. Unlike earlier overdate varieties, all of the 20th century overdates are sharp and clearly visible. These coins are doubled hub pieces, essentially doubled dies. It is believed that just one die was involved for the 1909/8 double eagles, This near-Gem specimen has satiny yellow-gold luster with sharp design definition, and pristine, nearly mark-free surfaces. Population: 77 in 64, 18 finer (11/06). (#9151)

Popular Near-Gem 1909/8
Overdate Twenty

3804   1909/8 MS64 PCGS. Ex: Park Avenue Collection. Current estimates place the number of survivors of the overdate compared with the nonoverdate variant at about 50:50, but that large number does not make the overdate—listed in the *Guide Book* and hugely popular as the only such variety in the popular Saint-Gaudens series—any less desirable. Created when a mismatch paired up a 1909 hub with an already-hubbed 1908-dated die between annealings, the overdate feature was born. Few specimens are found in MS64; most are MS63 or lower, and in the near-Gem grade the number of PCGS-certified examples drops to the double digits. This lustrous example offers beautiful orange-gold coloration and a few light, grade-consistent abrasions. Population: 77 in 64, 18 finer (12/06). (#9151)

Impressive Choice Mint State
1909-D Saint-Gaudens

3805   1909-D MS64 PCGS. It is little wonder that the '09-D Saint-Gaudens is a difficult coin to locate, even in circulated grades. Its original mintage of 52,500 pieces is the lowest for the type from the Denver Mint, and ensures the relative scarcity of this issue compared to most of the other dates in this immensely popular series. An impressive, Choice quality representative, this example displays a soft, frosty texture and warm golden-rose coloration. Both sides are typically clean for the grade and the striking details are generally unimpeachable; only Liberty's torch hand and the foliage near the lower right obverse border betray slight weakness. Once a great rarity, the number of available examples increased after a small hoard emerged from Central America in 1983. (#9152)

Outstanding 1909-D
Double Eagle MS65

3806   1909-D MS65 PCGS. After more than a million Saint-Gaudens double eagles of both No Motto and With Motto sub-types were produced at the Denver Mint in its initial year, the still relatively young facility delivered only 52,500 double eagles the following year. This limited mintage represents the lowest D-mint Saint production and the fourth lowest output in the entire series. As little as a quarter of a century ago, the 1909-D was regarded as a formidable rarity in Uncirculated grades, but the emergence of a sizeable Central American hoard in 1983 (the details of which are outlined in greater depth on the following MS66) has made the '09-D generally available in grades up to and including the MS63 level. As a quick glance at our auction archives illustrates, MS64 examples also appear with some regularity.

This high quality representative is typically satiny with a rich endowment of reddish-gold color blanketed over each side. Unlike the vast majority of Mint State survivors, there are few discernible marks over the generally placid fields and the major design elements show only minor evidence of contact upon close inspection. The only abrasion worthy of individual mention is a well concealed vertical cut hidden within the leg feathers. This desirable Gem possesses all the ingredients of a 20th century gold classic, an enticingly low mintage and undeniable rarity in top condition. Population: 19 in 65, 5 finer (12/06). (#9152)

Radiant, Unimprovable Superb Gem 1911 Double Eagle

3807   1911 MS67 NGC. Most of the Philadelphia Mint double eagle issues from 1908 to 1915 are fairly scarce, and the 1911 is a bit more so due to its lower original mintage of 197,350 pieces. By comparison, the 1910 issue was produced to the extent of 482,167 examples, and the 1912 saw an emission of 149,284 coins. While examples of the 1911 are obtainable up to about MS64, pieces in Gem and higher grades are quite rare and elusive. In the Superb Gem MS67 grade, this is one of only two pieces so graded at NGC, with none at PCGS. To give a better idea of the rarity of this date, the Smithsonian Institution's finest example is an AU58!

Fortunately for collectors, most examples of the issue are well struck, although luster varies greatly from coin to coin. This example is near the top echelons not only in terms of technical merit, but also in terms of aesthetics and overall eye appeal. The radiant greenish-gold surfaces appear to be almost completely unencumbered by even the most minuscule impairments. Particularly on Liberty's head, thighs, and torso—areas often prone to unsightly abrasions—this piece is remarkably free of distracting ticks and contact evidence. The surfaces fairly glow with cartwheel luster that is more reminiscent of a Morgan dollar than a Saint-Gaudens double eagle. Blessed by a sharp strike that brings up the minute details of the eagle's breast and wing feathers, as well as the fine detail on Liberty's face, torch, gown, and the Capitol building, this piece stands head and shoulders above the examples typically encountered of this difficult issue. Simply unimprovable! Census: 2 in 67, 0 finer. (#9157)

Superb Gem 1916-S
Saint-Gaudens Twenty

3808 **1916-S MS67 NGC.** Among S-mint Saint-Gaudens issues, few dates are as obtainable as the 1916-S in grades up to and including Gem condition. Indeed, population figures indicate that the number of MS64 and finer survivors totals several thousand coins. The appearance of a Superb example, however, is a vastly different story. The only other MS67 we have ever offered (and one of just three pieces certified by both major services) was the outstanding Philip H. Morse specimen that realized just over $25,000 just over a year ago. This satin-like representative boasts peerless fields and lovely, delicate orange accents. Trivial contact in the vicinity of Liberty's knee is the only noticeable disturbance on the silky-smooth surfaces. Census: 3 in 67, 0 finer (11/06). (#9169)

Rare, Key Date 1920-S
Saint-Gaudens Twenty, MS61 PCGS

3809   1920-S MS61 PCGS. The 1920-S is one of the keys to the series of Saint-Gaudens twenties, and it is a prized find in any grade. A previous estimate by Breen (1988) of "Probably 8-12 survive" is woefully inadequate; nevertheless, most collectors have never seen, much less owned a 1920-S. A more realistic estimate is somewhere around 55-60 examples are extant today in the various grades of Uncirculated. This estimate underscores the unavailability of this issue from the usual hoards from Europe or South America. Apparently the 1920-S was struck, a number were released into circulation, most were set aside in government vaults, apparently none were exported, and what was not distributed or sold in the early 1920s appears to have been melted in the mid-1930s.

This is an attractive example, especially for the grade. Numerous small to mid-sized abrasions seem to be the primary deterrent to a higher grade. The surfaces display pleasing, although somewhat muted mint frost. Both sides also possess rich reddish-golden coloration—a deeper hue than the often-seen orange-gold color, and certainly different from the green-gold pieces that are known. The strike on this coin is somewhat atypical, as the Capitol building, Liberty's toes, and the breast feathers on the eagle are all strongly defined. Only the nose of Liberty shows any weakness.

This coin represents the opportunity for the collector of Saint-Gaudens twenties to acquire this key issue in solid Uncirculated condition. (#9171)

Elusive Premium Gem 1922 Twenty Dollar

3810   1922 MS66 NGC. A bold striking with peerless, satiny surfaces that radiate outstanding luster from both obverse and reverse. Even close inspection reveals only the slightest luster grazes. Delicate orange patina combines with subtle pink highlights to provide equally impressive color. While hardly a scarcity in grades up to and including MS64, a considerably smaller number of Gems survive and Premium Gems such as this provide an extraordinary challenge for the quality conscious buyer of Saint-Gaudens twenties. Census: 9 in 66, 0 finer (11/06). (#9173)

Outstanding 1922-S
Double Eagle MS66

3811   1922-S MS66 PCGS. Despite the large quantities of this issue that have made a return trip to this country after years in overseas bank vaults, Gem quality examples are still exceedingly rare, and in Premium Gem grade, they are essentially non-existent. Prior to the 1950s, this issue was considered one of the major rarities in the series. In the 1950 catalog of the Jerome Kern sale, for example, B. Max Mehl stated his belief that only 12 examples were known to exist. Such a limited population placed this date on par with such major rarities as the 1804 silver dollar, the 1838-O half dollar, and the 1876-CC twenty-cent piece. No longer can it be considered such a rarity, as examples are generally available in all grades through MS64. Any finer, however, and it remains that this is extremely rare.

This radiant Gem has brilliant yellow luster with frosty surfaces and hints of pinkish toning highlights. The surfaces are remarkably well-preserved, with only a few of the tiniest imperfections. Unlike most examples of this issue, there are no unsightly copper spots, save for a tiny one below the right curve of U in UNITED, and this is an excellent pedigree marker. The bottoms of ERT in LIBERTY are weakly defined, as often seen. Similar weakness is visible on the dome of the Capitol building. The rims are beveled as almost always seen. The remaining design elements on both sides are crisply defined.

This example is tied with one other coin for the finest example of this issue to be certified by PCGS. We have handled many remarkable Saint-Gaudens double eagles in recent sales, but have not recently handled so fine an example of this date. In fact, the best example in the amazing Phillip H. Morse Collection was just MS65. Population: 2 in 66, 0 finer (11/06). (#9174)

Scarce Choice 1924-D Twenty Dollar

3812   1924-D MS64 PCGS. Ex: Brahin. Aside from the 1923-D, which must have been distributed in a different manner, all branch mint double eagles from the 1920s and 1930s are rare. Philadelphia dates between 1922 and 1928 survived the 1933 gold recall in sufficient quantities for today's collectors, but the 1924-D did not, despite a production of more than 3 million pieces. Apparently, bags of the 1924-D remained at the Treasury, although any collector could have obtained an example for face value, or close to it, prior to 1933. Most 1924-D twenties were melted, and among those that remain, the majority are in AU58 to MS63 grades. MS64 is the highest collectible grade, since PCGS has certified just seven pieces finer (11/06). This lustrous apricot and green-gold near-Gem has a well preserved obverse, and the reverse is also pleasing despite a couple of minor marks on the front wing. A splendid opportunity for the rare date gold specialist. (#9178)

Satiny 1924-S Double Eagle, MS64

3813   1924-S MS64 PCGS. The 1924-S is a median scarcity in the Saint-Gaudens series and is very similar in both overall population and condition rarity to the 1924-D, also a heavily melted branch mint issue of comparable mintage. This satiny representative is notable for its soft, frosted sheen and blatant originality. Tinges of pale orange and green-gold patina highlight each side. Abrasions are well scattered and generally shallow, a few of the more noticeable marks being found near the base of Liberty's torch. The quantity of MS64s in this sale aside, a difficult issue in Choice condition. (#9179)

Choice Mint State 1924-S Double Eagle

3814 1924-S MS64 NGC. Golden-rose, pastel-blue, and deeper orange-gold colors alternate as the coin rotates into and out of the light. The uncommonly sharp strike is praiseworthy, as are the surfaces, which do not reveal any abrasions that are out of context with the assigned grade. A satiny textured example destined for an advanced gold collection. The 1924-S double eagle is a condition rarity that is virtually unobtainable any finer than this piece. It is only due to European holdings of gold that this date is not extinct. Nearly all examples that were not exported in the late 1920s and early 1930s were melted during the gold recall of 1933. (#9179)

Challenging 1924-S Double Eagle MS64

3815 1924-S MS64 PCGS. Another high quality survivor of this once-rare San Francisco issue. Nearly all of the 1924-S Saints that remained in the United States until the following decade fell victim to the mass melting of the 1930s. Only those that made it across the Atlantic Ocean prior to that time slipped past the recall. This boldly struck example is satiny with a soft, frosted finish on the devices. A thin veil of mottled patina is limited to the obverse while appealing lemon-yellow accents are most noticeable on the reverse. Extremely scarce any finer. (#9179)

Vivacious Near-Gem
1925-D Double Eagle

3816   1925-D MS64 PCGS. Ex: Brahin. The *Guide Book* states that 2,938,500 double eagles were struck at Denver in 1925. But one might as well run a magic marker across the mintage figure, since third party population data suggests that only a few hundred pieces have survived, nearly all in AU58 and higher grades. MS64 is the highest collectible grade of the issue, and there are insufficient examples at that level to satisfy the many date and mintmark collectors of the popular series. This lustrous representative features rich peach and green-gold patina. The strike is assertive, despite slight softness on the raised knee and on the Capitol dome. Small marks can be located beneath a glass, but none distract. Those who aspire to own key date double eagles should note the present opportunity. Population: 74 in 64, 5 finer (10/06). (#9181)

Lustrous 1925-S Double Eagle MS62

3817   1925-S MS62 PCGS. One of several Mint State examples of this deceivingly scarce, heavily melted Saint-Gaudens issue offered in this year's FUN sale, including no less than four different Uncirculated grades. Survivors of this challenging S-mint are more apt to be lightly circulated than other branch mints from the era, as can be quickly confirmed by number of AU55 and AU58 pieces certified by both PCGS and NGC. This bright yellow-gold example is hardly wanting for luster, but is kept from a Select or finer rating by numerous light field marks on the obverse and noticeable stacking friction at the borders. (#9182)

Elusive 1925-S Saint-Gaudens MS63

3818   1925-S MS63 NGC. The 1925-S is one of the elusive mint-marked Saint-Gaudens issues from the mid-1920s forward that saw extensive melting in the following decade. Unlike other mass-melted issues, quite a few of the survivors are circulated to some degree, usually in the AU50 to AU58 grade range. This bright, satiny example is one of only a couple hundred pieces that managed to survive in Uncirculated condition (out of an enormous mintage of 3,776,500 pieces). The rose-gold surfaces are imbued with greenish accents, creating a wonderfully variegated appearance. Both sides are boldly detailed and show only a few minor marks, none of which are cause for individual concern. Census: 29 in 63, 14 finer (11/06). (#9182)

High-End, Appealing Near-Gem
1925-S Double Eagle

3819   1925-S MS64 PCGS. Ex: Brahin. Aside from the sole exception of the 1923-D, mintmarked Saint-Gaudens double eagles from the 1920s are quite elusive in Mint State. Of this issue, Q. David Bowers' *Guide Book of Double Eagle Gold Coins* says, "The 1925-S is a sleeper. The large mintage belies the rarity of this coin. The population of 1925-S double eagles is about evenly divided between high grade worn pieces and lower level Mint State examples, although some notable Gems exist, some of which appeared in the market in the late 1980s." Of course, there are many Saint-Gaudens issues whose mintage belies their rarity. Perhaps "sleeper" is a bit of a stretch; it looks as though the issue has awakened! The current PCGS online price guide lists the 1925-S in MS64 at $55,000 (with a three-fold increase to $165,000 in MS65), while the current (11/06) Greysheet Bid price is $44,000 ($67,500 in MS65). PCGS has graded only 19 pieces in MS64, with two coins in MS65, and one piece each in MS66, MS67, and MS68. NGC, meanwhile, has certified 11 examples in MS64, with three finer.

Most of this issue, again like many others, was later melted after the 1933 gold recall. The few survivors emanate from European bank holdings, or from the few American collectors who managed to put away an example. The present example offers minimally abraded surfaces, with pleasing orange-gold coloration, excellent luster, and a generous strike. A few small ticks on Liberty's torso prevent a Gem grade, but the eye appeal is extremely high-end. Numerous small radial die cracks are seen on the left-side obverse, through LIBERTY, the upper-right quadrant, and Liberty's rock. (#9182)

Lovely MS64 1925-S
Saint-Gaudens Twenty

3820   1925-S MS64 PCGS. The heavily melted 1925-S Saint-Gaudens was originally minted in comparatively large numbers, well over 3.7 million pieces, and is one of the few branch mint issues from the decade of the 1920s that circulated to any appreciable degree. Unlike many of the D and S-mint Saint-Gaudens issues that follow, even marginal quality Uncirculated pieces are seen with no greater frequency that than their AU55 and AU58 counterparts. In Uncirculated grades, dozens of marginal quality pieces are available in MS60-63 condition. However, the real drop-off in availability occurs between MS63 and MS64. In MS63, the two major services have certified a total of 87 pieces. In MS64, only 25 coins have been seen (14 at PCGS and 11 at NGC). This general lack of availability of the 1925-S in high grades accounts for the enduring popularity of this issue.

This issue has a couple of striking peculiarities of note. As with several S-mints from the mid-1920s, the 1925-S is usually encountered with "beveled" rims. Also, this issue is usually seen with a weaker impression on the 5 in the date. Both of these features are seen on this coin. As with most examples seen, this piece is well defined overall. The surfaces are lightly abraded with the only noticeable marks clustered between the head of Liberty and the olive branch. The coin has lovely reddish tinged surfaces and the luster is softly frosted. An important and highly collectible example of this semi-key issue in the Saint-Gaudens series. (#9182)

Lustrous 1926-D Double Eagle MS61

3821   1926-D MS61 PCGS. Decades ago, the 1926-D was a prized rarity within the series of Saint-Gaudens double eagles. Since the 1970s when a steady stream of gold coins formerly held in European bank vaults found their way back to the United States, rarity rankings have been dramatically adjusted. As a result, this once elite issue is now somewhat underappreciated when compared to other former rarities. Both the strike and luster on this dazzling reddish-gold example are the equal of much higher graded examples, but a deep, lengthy vertical abrasion along the right obverse border necessitates a more conservative rating. Population: 16 in 61, 92 finer (11/06). (#9184)

Scarce 1926-S Twenty Dollar MS64

3822   1926-S MS64 PCGS. A highly lustrous example that is generally lighter yellow in color with considerable honey-gold toning in the protected areas of each side. A few light surface marks are evident on each side, strictly consistent with the grade, and a small, curly-cued fragment connects to the 2 in the date. The 1926-S is one of many mass-melted branch mint issues from the 1920s and a prized rarity any finer. (#9185)

Appealing Gem 1926-S Saint-Gaudens

3823   1926-S MS65 PCGS. One of the more attractive 1926-S Saints we can recall handling, being especially vibrant and bold with distinctive pinkish-orange highlights. Under close scrutiny, a few modest luster grazes can be detected in the left obverse field, but overall the texture and smoothness of the fields is simply outstanding. The difficulty in acquiring a Gem example of this heavily melted San Francisco twenty is understandably skewed by the presence of several high quality examples in tonight's Platinum session. We doubt that any of the few Gems certified could surpass the eye appeal of this example. (#9185)

Challenging 1927-S Double Eagle MS62

3824   1927-S MS62 PCGS. The 1927-S was once regarded as the fourth rarest issue in the Saint-Gaudens double eagle series. In recent decades, however, enough examples have been repatriated from Europe to lower the overall rarity ranking of this issue. However it should be noted that, like the 1926-D double eagle, no sizeable hoards of this issue were ever uncovered and that the 1927-S is still a daunting scarcity within the popular Saint-Gaudens series.

This piece displays rich, yellow-gold surfaces and flashy mint frost, with eye appeal that would do justice to a considerably higher grade. There are a few light abrasions on both sides, but even these are miniscule in number for the grade. In sum, this is a premium quality example of this desirable S-mint twenty that deserves a carefully considered bid. (#9188)

Lustrous Near-Gem 1927-S Double Eagle

3825   1927-S MS64 PCGS. The Saint-Gaudens double eagle gold piece has the best of both worlds, when one stops to consider. Not only are its surfaces graced by what is generally considered to be America's most beautiful coin design, but it also makes a real *statement,* with its large size and heft. Somehow, four gold half eagles fail (some might say miserably) to make the same impact as one of these weighty gold double eagles. Perhaps that is why so many collectors pursue rare-date gold, or gold type coins, when they would never consider "lesser" series. The keys and semikeys to the Saint-Gaudens series, like the present near-Gem 1927-S double eagle, are a "badge of accomplishment" for their owners, as Bowers' double eagle *Guide Book* so aptly puts it.

Although the 1927-S double eagle had one of the highest mintage totals among mintmarked Saint-Gaudens issues, nearly the entire emission was apparently melted in the 1930s gold recalls, leaving precious few choice examples for posterity. As of this writing (11/06), NGC has certified 111 pieces in all grades, with a few in circulated condition. The average grade of those pieces is 61.3. PCGS has graded 124 pieces, also including a few lightly circulated coins, with an average grade of exactly 60. Although a couple of pieces have been certified as high as MS67, most pieces cluster around the lower Mint State levels. When seen, pieces typically have a beveled edge and satiny luster. The present piece offers rich, lustrous orange-gold surfaces with deeper reddish patina around the peripheries, and few mentionable distractions, save for a couple of small, grade-limiting ticks on Liberty's right (facing) calf. Some strike weakness is seen on the lower obverse, also typical for the issue, but the eye appeal is high. Astute aficionados of rare-date gold or the Saint-Gaudens series will need no further prompting. Population: 5 in 64, 9 finer (11/06). (#9188)

Coveted Near-Gem 1927-S
Double Eagle

3826   1927-S MS64 PCGS. During the 1940s, specialists in United States gold assigned an extremely high rarity ranking to the 1927-S, behind only the 1924-S, 1926-D, and 1926-S. Of course, why the 1927-D was not included among the top four Saint-Gaudens issues is a bit perplexing. Shipments of gold coins that returned to the United States from Europe since the 1950s have substantially reordered the rarity scale among later issues in this series. Despite the emergence of a few examples of this issue, numismatists generally believe that there are no more than 80-100 Mint State specimens extant today. While the majority of these pieces are marred by unsightly carbon spots and/or heavy bagmarks, this lovely near-Gem is certainly among the more attractive representatives of its issue. In fact, a small, shallow lamination within the left obverse field and the characteristic circular die crack that joins LIBERTY to the date are the only disruptions worthy of note on the otherwise smooth faces. The strike is noteworthy for its strength with abundant frosty brilliance over both the fields and the devices. The obverse of this specimen displays vibrant orange-gold toning with soft undertones of green-gold coloration. The reverse, on the other hand, carries a warm blanket of copper-gold patination that recedes slightly to yellow-gold in the field about the eagle's head. Population: 5 in 64, 9 finer (11/06). (#9188)

1927-S $20 MS66 NGC

1927-S $20 MS66 NGC

Important Premium Gem 1927-S
Saint-Gaudens Double Eagle

3827   1927-S MS66 NGC. Long regarded as a legendary rarity within the series of Saint-Gaudens double eagles, the 1927-S has properly maintained its high profile status to this day. It would be unfair to judge the issue with anything less than ultimate respect in spite of several appearances in tonight's Platinum Night session. Only in the memorable Philip Morse Collection Sale held in November, 2005 have two Premium Gem or finer examples crossed the auction block.

The wonderfully preserved example offered in this lot possesses an attractive mix of apricot and yellow-gold patination, and exhibits characteristically vibrant luster. The design elements are exceptionally well struck, with the Capitol showing excellent definition. Two lengthy die cracks that nearly connect in the right obverse field are not an uncommon feature on 1927-S Saints. It is devoid of significant marks, save for an inoffensive shallow linear abrasion on Liberty's chest. A slightly curved scrape is noted on the sun. As it runs parallel to the rim, we believe this is probably some sort of mint made flaw, possibly having to do with ejection from the die. Perhaps the parent die was over polished in this area. This same mint-caused "scrape" was also noticed on the amazing specimen from the Connecticut Public Library that currently resides in a PCGS MS67 holder and realized an impressive $345,000 in the Phillip Morse Collection Sale.

While not quite on the scale as that Superb, record-breaking representative, the extraordinary eye appeal of this lovely Premium Gem and the ever-increasing degree of interest in 20th century gold rarities is sure to generate an unprecedented amount of bidder interest. Census: 4 in 66, 2 finer (11/06). (#9188)

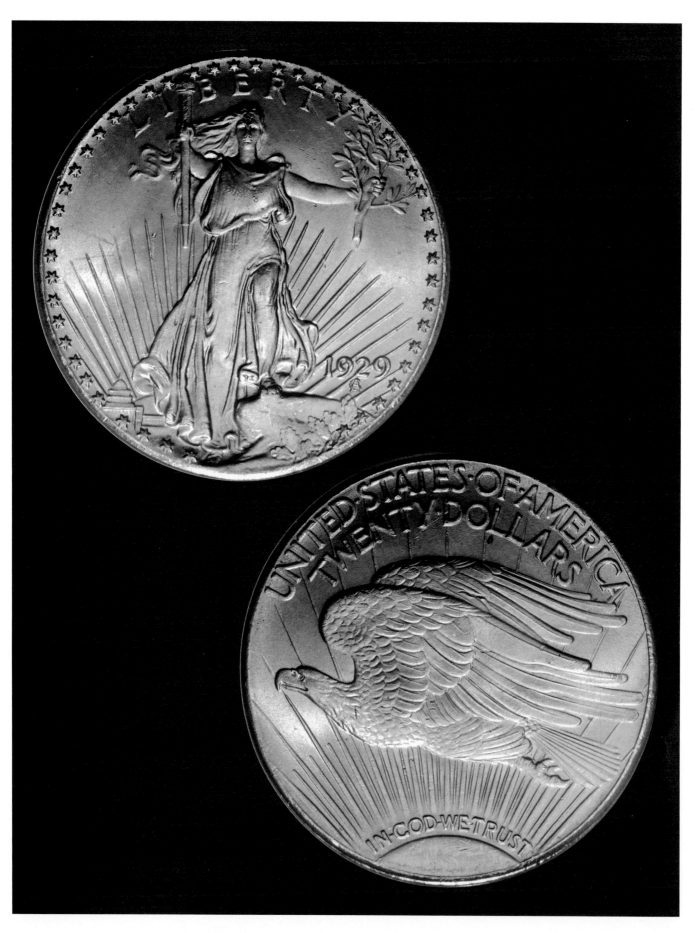

Impressive Premium Gem 1929
Double Eagle Rarity, MS66 PCGS

3828   1929 MS66 PCGS. Various experts have different opinions regarding the number of 1929 double eagles that still exist. While the original mintage was 1,779,750 coins, most remained in the hands of the Treasury and were melted after gold was recalled in 1933. Jeff Garrett and Ron Guth wrote: "The last readily obtainable Saint-Gaudens double eagle is the 1928 issue. Beginning with the 1929 double eagle and continuing through the 1933 issue, any collector who undertakes obtaining these issues does so with extreme care and financial fortitude. As seen on earlier mintmarked issues, the 1929 double eagle was summarily rounded up and melted down in the 1930s. Few examples of this issue had left the country at this time, as the world economies sunk into a deepening depression, which started in mid-1929 with contracting trade and was loudly announced by the American stock market crash on October 29, 1929." Actual opinions of the experts regarding the number of known pieces ranges from 60 to 1,750. Only 293 pieces have been certified by NGC and PCGS (11/06), suggesting that the estimate that 1,750 coins still exist is exceptionally high.

What is not open to debate is the number of coins that survive in Gem or finer grades. For example, PCGS has certified just 20 pieces in MS65 and five more in MS66, for a total of 25 coins. At the same time, NGC has graded exactly four Gem MS65 grade coins and only one MS66 piece.

As we wrote in our Phillip Morse catalog: "The astute collector, with patience and the concomitant finances, should be able to acquire a better Mint State 1929. Furthermore, such a coin is likely to exude considerable eye appeal. According to Akers (1988) and Bowers, the typical 1929 is nearly always very sharply struck, is fully frosty, and very lustrous. Most specimens are a medium to rich greenish-gold or yellow-gold color, sometimes with faint rose or orange overtones." This Premium Gem seems to match the description from our Morse catalog in terms of individual appearance with extremely sharp design elements, highly lustrous and fully brilliant frosty surfaces, and exceptional yellow-gold color. It is also finer than either of the Morse coins, which graded MS65 and MS64. (#9190)

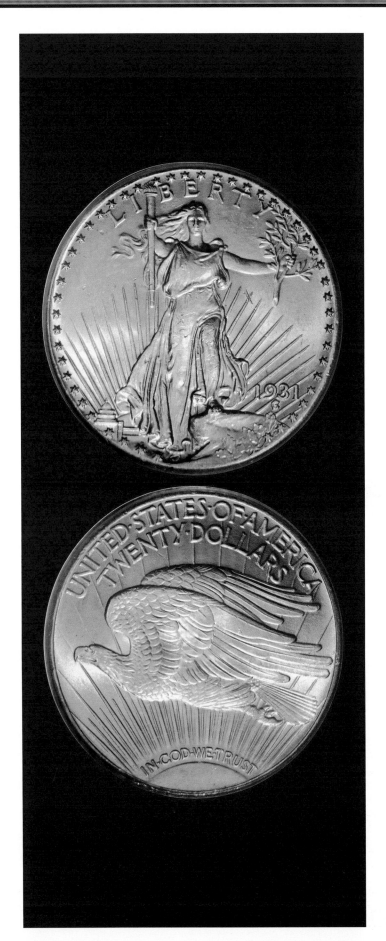

Elusive 1931 Saint-Gaudens Double Eagle MS63

3829   1931 MS63 PCGS. Opinions vary regarding the rarity of the 1931 relative to the 1929, 1930-S, and 1931-D. We can definitely say that, in an absolute sense, the 1931 is more difficult to locate than the 1929. Some experts feel that, in terms of total number of coins known, it is also scarcer than the 1931-D and 1932. As a Gem, the 1931 appears to be more plentiful than the 1929, 1930-S, and 1931-D, but less available than the 1932. Such debates, however, are purely academic because there can be no doubt that the 1931 is among the keys to the 20th century U.S. gold series.

This is a sharply struck issue, and the present representative is no exception. Liberty's portrait, the eagle's feathers, and the peripheral devices are all crisply defined. The surfaces show lovely rich coloration and a pleasing satiny sheen. The reverse is nearly immaculate, and free of the die crack that bisects the eagle's beak on most 1931 double eagles. There are a few minor marks on the obverse, the most noticeable of which resides in the right field area, below Liberty's elbow. While copper stains are common on this issue, the present example has entirely avoided this unsightly tendency, one of the reasons that this Select representative boasts a level of visual appeal that definitely seems exceptional, for the MS63 grade level. An exciting opportunity for the high quality gold specialist. (#9192)

Desirable Gem Uncirculated
1931 Saint-Gaudens

3830   1931 MS65 PCGS. Since it was struck only two years before the gold recall and is almost exclusively found in Mint State, it is obvious that the 1931 Saint-Gaudens double eagle was never released for general circulation. Most of the 2,938,250 pieces originally struck were melted in the Mint and today the '31 has been reduced to such modest numbers that it is comparable in overall rarity to the highly respected 1932. Gem or better survivors probably number fewer than three dozen coins, allowing for a moderate number of resubmissions at the grading services.

The desirable Gem offered here not only boasts wonderful eye appeal, but it is an equally well preserved example whose surfaces show smooth champagne-gold color and frosty texture. The reverse is free of the die crack that bisects the eagle's beak on many 1931 double eagles and there are no bothersome post-production distractions. High-end quality for the assigned grade and a definite find for the discriminating gold specialist. Population: 25 in 65, 10 finer (11/06). (#9192)

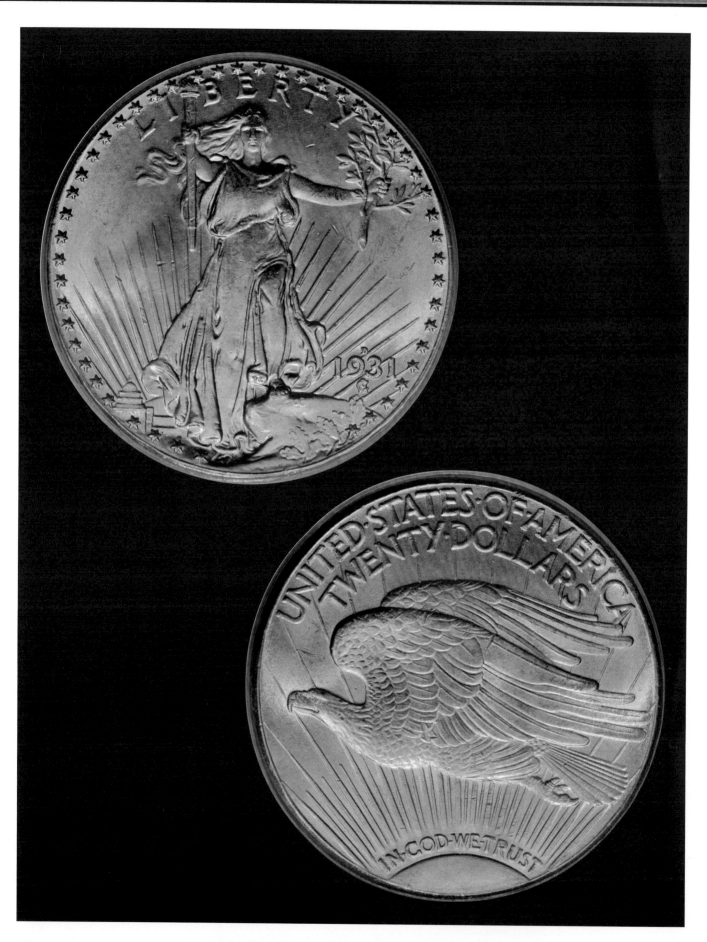

Subtly Toned, Elusive MS65 1931-D Twenty

3831   1931-D MS65 PCGS. Wholesale meltings of this date, which was issued during the Depression only to be melted a few years later after President Franklin D. Roosevelt's gold recall, succeeded in further decimating an already-skimpy mintage, numbered at 106,500 pieces. Gems are rare, and pieces grading finer than MS65 are seldom obtainable—even though Heritage is fortunate enough to also be offering an MS66 specimen in the current sale.

NGC and PCGS combined, as of this writing (11/06), have certified only 23 specimens in Gem condition, with five MS66 pieces finer. The Garrett-Guth *Gold Encyclopedia* comments concerning the rarity and desirability of this issue: "The 1931-D has survived in similar numbers to the 1931 Philadelphia issue; however, the Denver issue is more elusive in Gem MS-65 grades. The finest known examples are a pair that PCGS graded MS-66, and one of each [is] in the collections of the American Numismatic Society and the Smithsonian. Obviously the entire mintage was virtually wiped out, but a handful survived here and there. These range from frosty to satiny, and are typically well struck. Author Jeff Garrett handled a group of eight examples in late 1908 [sic-1998]. Most of these would grade MS-63 by today's standards." At one time the 1931-D was considered to be among the rarest Saint-Gaudens issues save but a handful, but subsequent repatriations of small groupings of coins have made this still-elusive issue considerably more available in recent years than in the 1940s and 1950s. A search of our internal auction archives reveals that only six times previously in our 13-year history of maintaining auction records have we offered this issue in Gem condition.

Regarding specifics of the 1931-D double eagle, Bowers' *Guide Book of Double Eagle Gold Coins* notes that "Today not many over 100 or so exist, but most of those are lustrous, beautiful, and range from choice to gem preservation." The present Gem specimen certainly fits that characterization. The surfaces are pinkish-gold with lilac accents around the margins. Brilliant and beautiful cartwheel luster emanates from each side. Extensive scrutiny fails to reveal any singularly mentionable distractions or impairments of any kind, although a few minuscule ticks, completely consistent with a Gem grade, are noted on Liberty's face and torso. A bold strike has articulated the pillars in the Capitol building, the heart-shaped sandal ornament and Liberty's toes, the foliage on the rock nearby, and the small details on the eagle's wing feathers. A single small tick is noted on the upper edge of the eagle's left wing. Lastly, for that most elusive and essential of coin-grading criteria, *eye appeal,* this charming, awe-inspiring key-date Saint-Gaudens gold piece has it in spades. Specialists in this largest and most impressive U.S. coin series will not hesitate. Acquisition of a Gem 1931-D Saint-Gaudens is not an opportunity that comes by frequently, and only the boldest, most forthright bidder will capture this prize. Population: 17 in 66, 2 finer (11/06). (#9193)

1907 $20, Large Edge Lettering PR64 NGC

1907 $20, Large Edge Lettering PR64 NGC

Unique 1907 Matte Proof Arabic Numerals
With Large Edge Lettering, Ex: Trompeter

3832   1907 Large Edge Lettering PR64 NGC. Arabic Numerals. The year 1907 was one of great experimentation in the Mint. Great diversity is seen in the double eagle series. In that single year, the Mint struck coins as MCMVII Ultra High Reliefs; proof MCMVII High Reliefs; regular MCMVII High Reliefs with a wire rim; regular MCMVII High Reliefs with a flat rim; lowered relief Arabic Numerals proofs from both Collar I (Large Edge Letters) and Collar II (Small Edge Letters; and low relief Arabic Numerals business strikes.

This coin is *apparently unique, but it is neither an MCMVII Ultra High Relief nor an MCMVII High Relief coin. It is an Arabic Numerals matte proof in the low relief business strike style, one struck with the same edge-lettering collar used for the standard High Relief double eagles.*

The Barber-modified 1907 twenty dollar Saint-Gaudens gold coins were issued in proof format with Large Edge Letters (the High Relief edge) and with Small Edge Letters (the standard edge). **NGC has obligingly encapsulated this unique matte proof in a special plastic slab that holds the coin by four tabs, enabling the viewer to see the edge lettering details around the circumference of the coin.**

The standard High Relief double eagles were produced in a lettered edge collar, a three-part innovation that enabled the Mint to do two things simultaneously. First and foremost, it imparted the desired edge lettering and devices to the "third side" of the coin. Second, and most ingeniously, it *enabled this to be done while the other two sides were being struck.* After the three sides were stamped, the collar "broke apart" into three segment, enabling the struck coin to be removed without damaging the lettering on the edge. In the two edge diagrams that follow, a vertical line (actually visible on the edge of the coin) shows where the break occurred.

Interestingly, as of this writing, the Mint is well on its way to producing the first regular-issue coinage with edge lettering—the Presidential one dollar coins slated to begin production in 2007—since the Saint-Gaudens coinage with edge lettering. We qualify the statement with "regular-issue" because the 1992-D Olympic silver dollars with a baseball pitcher on the obverse have the phrase XXV OLYMPIAD impressed four times around the edge, alternately inverted and on a reeded background.

Along with the Small Letters, Arabic Numerals low relief proofs, the Large Letters, Arabic Numerals twenty matte proof is technically a pattern, although unrecognized as such in the literature. There is no record of production of any 1907 proof double eagles with the low relief design. This is an extremely powerful statement in support of these coins as pattern issues, for it was required that all standard coinage production quantities had to be recorded. In the early and mid-19th century, production of proof coinage was unrecorded, but beginning in 1858 all silver and gold proof coinages were recorded annually.

LARGE EDGE LETTERS COLLAR

SMALL EDGE LETTERS COLLAR

The Ultra High Reliefs had the largest edge lettering in the series, followed by the regular issue High Reliefs with Collars I and II. Collar I was either used in error or experimentally on this matte proof and only one coin was produced. Coins with the Large Edge Letters Collar I read: | * * * * * * * E * | P L U R I B U S | * U N U M * * * *. The coins struck from Collar II, the Small Edge Letters collar, read | * * * * * * * E * | P L U R I B U S * | U N U M * * * * *. Note that the Large Edge Letters variant has only the word PLURIBUS on a single section, and one star before and four stars after UNUM, while the Small Edge Letters variant has a single star on the segment with PLURIBUS, and five stars after UNUM, none before.

A passage from Roger W. Burdette's *Renaissance of American Coinage 1905-1908* shows the difficulties that mint personnel faced in producing the High Relief coins with edge letters:

> The mint had three hydraulic medal presses capable of producing up to three hundred tons of pressure per square inch. The presses were designed to "squeeze" the planchet between the dies rather than "strike" it with a very quick blow as on the automatic production coin presses. Typical tempered steel coinage dies of the era could withstand little more than one hundred fifty tons of pressure before they would collapse or crack. The coiner wanted to use the minimum pressure necessary to bring up the design since this would reduce wear on the dies and make them last longer.
>
> High relief double eagles presented unusual problems for the mint's mechanics. The coins had high relief obverse and reverse designs, plus an edge with raised lettering instead of the normal vertical reeding. (Plain edge examples are probably production errors.) The relief took three blows of the press to bring up the obverse and reverse designs, but the edge lettering of the motto E PLURIBUS UNUM could only be imparted by an edge collar with recessed lettering. When the coin was struck, the metal flowed into the face designs as well as the raised edge lettering. Obviously, the collar had to be able to open or the newly struck coin would be locked inside the collar.
>
> For the first five hundred high relief coins made in August and September 1907, a plain retaining collar was placed in the press and the planchet given two blows with the coin removed and annealed between blows. The plain collar was then replaced with the lettered edge collar consisting of three segments. This was surrounded by a second, solid retaining collar. The planchet was placed back on the press, aligned with the anvil die, and given one or two more blows with the edge collar in place. After striking, the mechanic running the press had to lift off the retaining collar and pull the segmented collar away from the coin. This process was slow and resulted in much lower productivity than was achieved beginning in November. It was also partially responsible for a pronounced die fin on many of the coins. The first batch of five hundred double eagles took 105 hours (about twelve minutes each) to make; by late November the medal presses were turning out approximately four hundred eighty coins per day. Productivity continued to improve until 995 high relief double eagles were made during the day's work on December 30. The improvement was due to experience gained in striking the earlier batch of coins, and from a change in the way the segmented collar was used.

Further distinguishing this coin from its Small Letters sibling, the Collar I coins show the bases of M in UNUM level, but on Collar II coins they are slanted. We believe this unique Large Letters Arabic Numerals proof was produced after the Small Letters proof striking(s). We base this belief on the presence of an area of die polishing seen around 9 o'clock on the obverse rim. Such an area of die polish would surely have been present and visible on an earlier striking, and it is for this reason that we conclude that this piece was struck after the Small Letters proof(s). Also, this piece shows complete definition on the Capitol building, indicating mint personnel had a better grasp of how many tons of pressure to apply to strike this coin than the Small Letters piece, which displays obvious softness on the Capitol. This particular coin is most easily identifiable by a shallow, horizontal planchet flake to the left of the branch stem held in Liberty's right (facing) hand. There are minor planchet imperfections around the eagle's beak. The coin is lightly hairlined in the fields, but it is quite pleasing, with brighter surfaces than seen on matte proofs struck the following year, more closely resembling the "Roman Gold" finish of 1909-1910 in overall appearance. Medium orange-gold coloration is seen over each side of this impressive and unique proof striking.

Ex: The Captain North cased set; New England Rare Coin Galleries; Ken Goldman; Hatie Collection (Bowers), lot 2855; Trompeter Collection; Heritage private sale, 1999; The Phillip H. Morse Collection of Saint-Gaudens Coinage (Heritage, 11/05), lot 392, which realized $230,000. (#9198)

1910 $20 PR66 NGC

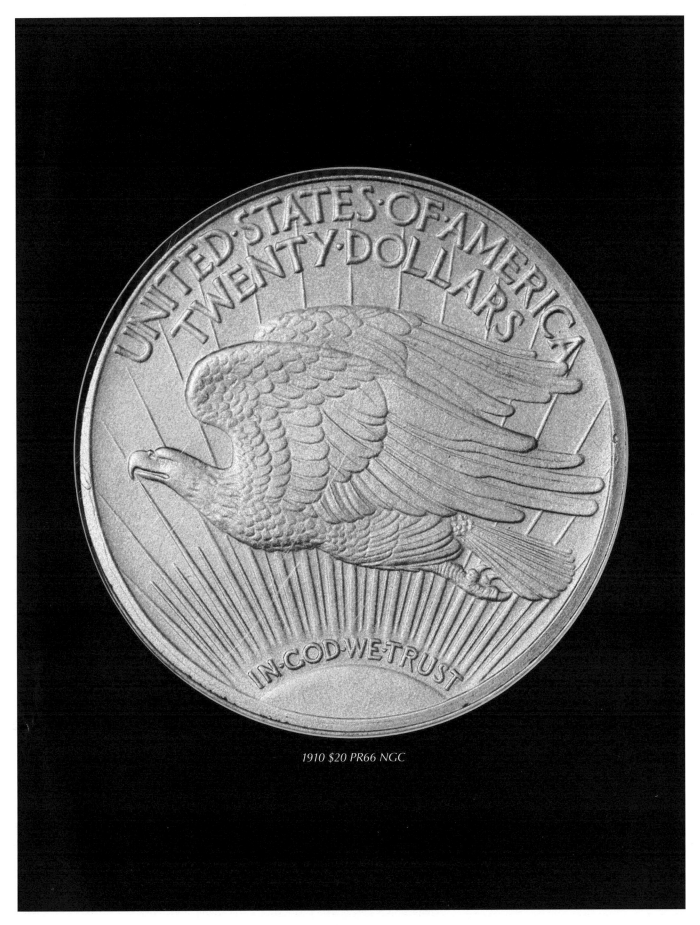

1910 $20 PR66 NGC

Unique Matte Proof 1910 Double Eagle, PR66

3833   1910 PR66 NGC. Matte. The Garrett-Guth *Encyclopedia of U.S. Gold Coins* notes that "One Proof example exists of this date in matte finish. It was last seen in 1908 [sic-likely 1998]— that coin is graded NGC PF-66. It is part of a unique 1910 matte Proof gold set." This piece is from the set that Jeff Garrett and Ron Guth wrote about, although the set is no longer intact. The quarter eagle and half eagle from that set were offered in our November 2006 sale. Walter Breen wrote about the existence of 1910 matte proof quarter eagles and half eagles in his *Proof Encyclopedia,* but made no mention of similar eagles and double eagles.

After production of Matte Finish proof gold coins in 1908 was met with extreme collector dissatisfaction, the Mint tried an alternative finish in 1909 and 1910, usually called the Roman Finish but also described as Satin Finish. The Roman Finish proof gold pieces have surfaces that display a watery or wavy appearance, sometimes described as an orange-peel texture, much the same as the watery appearance of earlier brilliant proof gold pieces, only without the mirrored fields. Breen discussed coins of this finish in his *Proof Encyclopedia:* "So-called 'Roman Gold' finish, so designated since the early 1940s (I have been unable to find the actual source for the term). Surfaces light in color, midway between satiny and mirrorlike, entirely without the granularity of matte or sandblast. Wayte Raymond used to call them 'brilliant matte proofs.' "

The surfaces of this 1910 matte proof double eagle have lovely light yellow color, similar to the Roman Finish proofs, but the texture is entirely different. In fact, the appearance of this piece is quite similar to the matte proof 1911 double eagle that we sold in November 2005 as part of the Phillip H. Morse Collection: "This piece shows thousands of tiny sparkling facets under magnification and the basic mustard color is overlaid by a thin veneer of olive-green." The existence of the "tiny sparkling facets" is the universal description for nearly all matte proof gold pieces, and it is these tiny facets that provide the sandblast appearance of such coins. In different years, the matte proof gold coins exhibit a wide range of colors, from the light yellow or orange-gold of this piece, to certain issues that had an extremely dark brown color.

The surfaces of this piece are pristine with no disturbances that we can locate, suggesting that future pedigree identification will be nearly impossible. Both sides have full and crisp design details in all areas. The reverse border has a small raised lump at 9 o'clock and a tiny depression at 3 o'clock. (#9207)

Superb Matte Proof 1912
Twenty Dollar

3834   1912 PR67 NGC. When we cataloged the 1994 ANA Sale, we were fortunate to have complete set of matte proof gold consigned. This was an opportunity for study, and it was also an opportunity to reassess the rarity of these coins. Previous estimates had been based on Breen (1988) and Akers (1988). Both authors had understated the number of survivors in all series. Jim Halperin used his many years of experience and revised the numbers believed extant before the catalog went to press. The result were write-ups and estimates of the number of survivors that has proved to be more in line with the number of coins certified by the major services. For instance, it was previously believed that the 1912 proof twenty had only 10-12 proofs surviving (Breen, 1988), or 20 to 25 pieces according to Akers (1988). However, we believe the actual number of survivors out of the original mintage of 74 coins to be somewhere in the range of 25 to 35 pieces.

The surfaces of matte proof gold vary from year to year because of the method of manufacture. Sometimes a finer grain finish was used, sometimes a coarser grain. The 1912 shows a fine-grain finish with darker color. The color is certainly not as dark as the 1908 coins, but significantly deeper than other years, especially the 1911. There is also a slight variation in hue on this piece, with the center of the obverse showing a slightly reddish cast. The surfaces are nearly perfect, as indicated by the Superb grade. The only vaguely noticeable surface flaw is a shiny spot on the knee of Liberty. Census: 11 in 67, 1 finer (12/06). (#9209)

Pristine, Phenomenal PR68 1913 Twenty
Among the Finest for the Issue and the Type

3835   1913 PR68 NGC. An incredible example of early 20th century coinage art, this breathtaking specimen proof is not only among the finest coins of the issue, it is certainly *among the Condition Census for the entire Saint-Gaudens type.* As of this writing (11/06), NGC has yet to ever assign a PR69 grade to any Saint-Gaudens double eagle. In PR68, that service has recognized a total of 14 coins with the PR68 grade, along with a single PR68 ★ example, the latter a 1912-dated piece. This coin is tied with another PR68 piece as the finest for the issue at NGC. The highest-graded proof examples for the entire type at PCGS, excepting the Ultra High Relief pieces, are six PR67 coins, a total that includes no 1913-dated examples.

The U.S. Mint was prone to what today looks like almost continuous experimentation with the surfaces of proof gold coins during the pre-World War I era from 1907 to 1915, and sometimes several different proof finishes were produced within a single year, varying from deep, dark matte or sandblast finishes to satiny "Roman gold" surfaces, as well as in differing degrees of color and fineness of granulation for the sandblast proofs. After experimenting with Roman or satin finish proof double eagles in 1909 and 1910, the Philadelphia Mint reverted from 1911 through 1915 to the matte proof surfaces, similar to the 1908 With Motto matte proof pieces. The matte proof coins, lacking brilliance and, to many, basic eye appeal, were popular in European mints of the time, but they were highly unpopular with many collectors. Today, with the separation of nearly a hundred years, it is difficult to entirely divorce the aesthetic appeal, or lack thereof, from these coins' undoubted rarity, desirability—and marketability. However, it is fair to say that history and today's aesthetic sensibilities are also much kinder to these pieces, and many collectors find them quite lovely and appealing. The recorded proof mintages peaked in 1910 at 167 pieces, dwindling to 100 for the 1911 matte proofs, to 74 in 1912, and to 58 for the 1913 matte proof examples. The only issue with a lower proof mintage is the last-year 1915, with a proof emission of but 50 pieces.

The present piece has wonderfully consistent, fine-grained matte surfaces on both sides that are a light olive-gold color. The strike is essentially full, with no apparent weakness on any part of the Capitol building, Liberty's head, or any other small detail. Perusal with a strong lens reveals a short, straight line well-hidden in the short feathers at the rear of the eagle's wing that is likely mint-produced, as the matte surface continues uninterrupted through it. This is mentioned strictly as a future pedigree identifier, as it is completely undistracting and invisible without magnification.

As mentioned previously, the present PR68 example is tied with another 1913 coin for finest of the issue, and *in toto* there are a bit more than a dozen PR68 examples certified for the entire Saint-Gaudens type at NGC, a figure that likely includes duplications. Step back for a moment from the statistics, and consider what that means in aesthetic terms. Proof gold coins are generally recognized as the most appealing form of gold coinage. The Saint-Gaudens design is usually acknowledged to be the most beautiful—or at least among the most beautiful—U.S. coinage designs. Finally, *here we have a coin that is officially recognized to be among the most beautiful and aesthetically flawless examples available in the numismatic marketplace.* One can almost hear the generations of legendary collectors— Garrett, Eliasberg, Norweb, Pittman, Bass— who would be figuratively chomping at the bit to obtain so pristine and phenomenal an example as the present piece. It goes without saying that this piece, perfectly suited for the finest Registry or type set, will instantly become the centerpiece, the *pièce de résistance* in the collection of anyone sufficiently fortunate to acquire it. (#9210)

Rare Choice Matte Proof 1915
Saint-Gaudens Double Eagle

3836   1915 PR64 PCGS. Despite a tiny production of just 50 pieces, there doesn't appear to be an appreciable drop-off in the number of proof twenties extant from the previous seven years. Our best estimate places the number of survivors in the vicinity of 30 coins. By 1915 officials at the United States Mint were no doubt keenly aware that the European-inspired matte proofing process had been a dismal failure in the eyes of collectors and the practice was discontinued after this year. This Choice specimen displays the coarse finish and olive-gold color that is characteristic of the issue. There is a pinpoint alloy stain on the left side of Liberty's robe, but even close inspection yields no obvious hairlines or shiny spots. An important opportunity for the 20th century gold specialist. Population: 8 in 64, 1 finer (11/06). (#9212)

Premium Gem 1903
Louisiana Purchase/Jefferson

3837   1903 Louisiana Purchase/Jefferson MS66 NGC. A shimmering, fully defined little jewel with an even coating of reddish patina over both sides. Even by the normal high standards of the Louisiana Purchase/Jefferson gold dollar, a particularly attractive representative of the type. *From The Prinzi Trust Collection.* (#7443)

Splendid Premium Gem 1903 McKinley Gold Dollar

3838   1903 Louisiana Purchase/McKinley MS66 PCGS. According to Swiatek and Breen (1990): "Originally the gold dollars were only to portray Jefferson as the president in charge when the territory was sold to the United States. In the meantime, President McKinley, who had signed the Exposition into law as of March 3, 1901, was assassinated at another Exposition in September 1901. Through some unrecorded agreement, a new obverse die portraying McKinley was struck." Beautifully deep red-gold, orange, and mint-green toning adorns the shimmering, frosty surfaces of this splendid Premium Gem. The surfaces are virtually pristine, except for a few faint, mint-made die lines and lint marks.
From The Prinzi Trust Collection. (#7444)

Radiant 1904 Lewis & Clark Gold Dollar MS66 Star

3839   1904 Lewis and Clark MS66 ★ NGC. The Lewis and Clark Centennial Exposition, held in Portland, Oregon in 1905 and the 1904 Louisiana Purchase Exposition in St. Louis were the first two occasions for the issuance of commemorative gold dollars. Interestingly, both of these gold commemoratives were sold on the fairgrounds of their respective expos by Farran Zerbe, a fellow with a lot of pull at the United States Mint who was also present at the 1915 Panama-Pacific Exposition with a variety of gold tokens and coins. Not only this is a wonderfully preserved Lewis and Clark, but as can be deduced from the star designation, the eye appeal of this Premium Gem is nothing short of extraordinary. Radiant, almost mark-free surfaces are cloaked in beautiful orange patina. Census: 4 in 66 Star, 1 finer (12/06).
From The Prinzi Trust Collection. (#7447)

Sublime 1904
Lewis and Clark Dollar, MS67

3840   1904 Lewis and Clark MS67 NGC. So...which of the dashing (but unlabeled) portraits represents Lewis, and which is Clark? As Swiatek-Breen put it succinctly: "In this, our nation's only two-headed coin, the obverse is legally the date side, and this side portrays—after a fashion—Captain Meriwether Lewis, who had been Thomas Jefferson's secretary despite his appallingly poor spelling. The side with ONE DOLLAR supposedly portrays Captain William Clark." With that bit of confusion out of the way, this lovely Superb Gem is among the best-preserved survivors of this century-old commemorative. Both wheat-gold sides display strong luster, and the portraits have above-average detail. Only a few tiny marks appear in the fields, and none of these are individually distracting. A great choice for a high-end set of commemorative gold. Census: 19 in 67, 1 finer (11/06). (#7447)

Lustrous Gem 1905 Lewis & Clark Dollar

3841   1905 Lewis and Clark MS65 PCGS. Although the vast majority of Lewis and Clark dollars are found in mint state grades, those attaining the Gem level are much scarcer than those collectors wishing to own such a piece. Indeed, the 1905 must be considered considerably scarcer in high grades than its 1904 predecessor, since although the number of pieces certified in MS65 is similar for the two dates, less than half as many 1905s have been certified finer by the two major services. This little beauty is blessed with a minimum of distracting surface marks, with orange and just a hint of high point olive color overlying lustrous surfaces that hint at reflectivity. (#7448)

Pristine Gem 1905
Lewis and Clark Gold Dollar

3842   1905 Lewis and Clark MS65 NGC. The early U.S. gold commemoratives never seem to flag in popularity, especially in these days of strong gold prices. The recent upsurge in Lewis and Clark materials, aided by the new Jefferson nickel designs related to the Lewis and Clark expedition and the 2004 Lewis and Clark bicentennial silver dollars, has also increased interest for the 1904- and 1905-dated issues. Although both issues show similar mintages around 10,000 pieces, the 1905 is considerably rarer in Gem condition. The present piece offers lustrous green-gold surfaces with a pleasing halo or aura around both figures. Even under a lens, the surfaces appear distraction-free. (#7448)

Sparkling 1905 Lewis and Clark
Gold Dollar, MS66

3843   1905 Lewis and Clark MS66 NGC. The large-scale meltings and rapid price depreciation of the Louisiana Purchase gold dollars made collectors wary of the new Lewis and Clark commemoratives, and after the relative failure of the issues of 1904 and 1905, it would be another decade before any commemorative coinage, gold or silver, would be struck in the United States. This example from 1905, generally considered to be the scarcer of the two dates, has highly lustrous yellow-gold surfaces, though without the prooflike surfaces often seen on higher-grade pieces. The portraits have suitable detail, and hardly any marks are visible to the unaided eye. With only two finer examples certified by NGC, it is hard to come across a better example for a high-grade set of commemorative gold (11/06).
From The RNB Collection. (#7448)

Outstanding Premium Gem
1905 Lewis and Clark Dollar

3844   1905 Lewis and Clark MS66 NGC. Many numismatists accept the assertion of Q. David Bowers that Charles Barber copied the portraits for the Lewis and Clark dollars from a pair of paintings by Charles Wilson Peale. The transition from two dimensions to three did not turn out well, and in his *Numismatic Art in America,* Cornelius Vermeule savaged the design. Nonetheless, collectors have come to view the 1904 and 1905 issues as treasures.

Radiant with a pleasing semi-prooflike finish, this gorgeous survivor displays lemon-gold color that brightens as the surfaces dip into the light. There is not a single distracting abrasion to report, and the strike is sharp for the type. The only pedigree marker of note is a small mint-made mark in the lower right reverse field, below the final A in AMERICA. Interestingly, a loupe also reveals numerous tiny planchet voids (also as struck), though these are neither unsightly nor grade-limiting. An important opportunity to acquire one of the finest known examples of this popular early commemorative. (#7448)

Beautiful Premium Gem 1905
Lewis & Clark Dollar

3845   1905 Lewis and Clark MS66 NGC. Our offerings of Premium Gem '05 Lewis and Clark gold dollars have been few and far between. After all, NGC reports just 37 examples of this key date at the MS66 level, with a mere two MS67 representatives finer (12/06). Radiant with a dazzling, satiny finish, this beautiful piece displays deep red-gold color that yields to lime-green near the centers. There is not a single distracting abrasion to report, and the strike is sharp for the type. A coin that represents an important bidding opportunity for the Commemorative gold specialist who will accept nothing but the finest quality.

From The Prinzi Trust Collection. (#7448)

Appealing Superb Gem 1915-S
Pan-Pac Gold Dollar

3846 1915-S Panama-Pacific Gold Dollar MS67 NGC. Ex: Prinzi Collection. This piece is among the finest few dozen of this popular and historic gold commemorative issue. Interestingly, as of this writing (11/06), both NGC and PCGS have each certified 45 pieces (including duplicates), with none finer. Both sides of this Superb Gem are distraction-free and as struck. The worker's cheek and hat area, a magnet for abrasions on lower grade examples, are especially clean on this piece, and the beautiful luster and orange-gold coloration complete the appeal. The reverse shows a couple of dark-amber toning areas.
From The Prinzi Trust Collection. (#7449)

Magnificent Superb Gem 1915-S
Pan-Pac Quarter Eagle

3847 1915-S Panama-Pacific Quarter Eagle MS67 NGC. A magnificent example of this scarce commemorative gold coin, from a net mintage of 6,749, after 10,000 were produced and 3,251 were melted as unsold. Designed by Charles Barber and George Morgan. The mostly green-gold surfaces also display lovely accents of peach-rose, especially near the borders. Close examination shows myriad die polishing lines on each side, but post-striking defects are limited to a couple of wispy marks on the neck of the hippocampus. Superior overall quality.
From The Prinzi Trust Collection. (#7450)

Classic Near-Mint 1915-S
Panama-Pacific Fifty Dollar Round

3848   1915-S Panama-Pacific 50 Dollar Round AU58 NGC. With a net mintage of only 483 pieces, the round version of the grand Panama-Pacific fifty dollar gold piece is the single most elusive of the classic commemoratives, gold or silver, and has a mintage less than half of the 1848 "CAL." quarter eagle to boot. Presumably, a significant number of well-heeled purchasers found the octagonal version intriguing enough to own, but were unwilling to spend the money for a five-coin or ten-coin set, the source of the vast majority of this issue. Modern collectors recognize that the round-format examples are comparatively scarce and offer a premium for them over their eight-sided counterparts.

A large number of the fifty dollar Panama-Pacific commemoratives of both varieties were kept as pocket pieces, or else removed from sets and mishandled. Cleaned, worn, and otherwise significantly impaired examples appear on the market, and many collectors who believe that this issue is out of reach otherwise will settle for one of them. A patient numismatist, however, who seeks a lightly rubbed but otherwise untroubled example can find a much more attractive piece for only slightly more outlay. A coin such as this represents a real bargain for such a collector. Minor but distinct friction affects the high-points, and a number of small handling marks affect the fields. Yet the luster remains strong, and the suitably struck devices are unaffected by unsightly abrasions. The yellow-orange surfaces have a touch of olive near the rims, appropriate given the figure on the obverse. An appealing representative that would fit well in an otherwise Mint State collection of commemorative gold. *From The Twin Hollows Collection.* (#7451)

1915-S Panama-Pacific 50 Dollar Round MS64 PCGS

Exceptional Panama-Pacific Fifty Dollar Round, MS64

3849　**1915-S Panama-Pacific 50 Dollar Round MS64 PCGS.** One of the most magnificent gold coins ever struck, by any country, emanated from the first-ever world's fair held on the American west coast, the Panama-Pacific International Exposition held in San Francisco, which opened on February 20, 1915. The fair celebrated dual events: the historic and commercially vital opening of the Panama Canal (linking the Atlantic and Pacific Oceans) in August 1914, as well as the 400th anniversary of the discovery of the Pacific Ocean by the Spanish explorer Vasco Núñez de Balboa (he claimed it for Spain in 1513). This mammoth exposition was a showcase for mankind's achievements, including the first-ever use of nighttime lighting at a fair, enjoyed and visited by some 18 million people from all over the world. For 257 days, the PPIE hosted pavilions of exhibits, reproductions of classical buildings, luxurious gardens, carnivals, visits by celebrities, even nighttime fireworks—all the wonders of the world (the official brochure proclaimed) displayed on the 635 beautifully landscaped acres alongside San Francisco Bay. In many ways it commemorated the best of the new and the old—not just the canal and Balboa's discovery, but also man's greatest ideas and inventions, both classical and modern. As such, the expo promoted itself as a festival that linked the 19th and 20th centuries. And numerous mementoes came from it, most of them ephemeral (ribbons that frayed, badges that rusted, paper products that aged).

Among the mementoes that will always survive are the silver and gold commemorative coins. The Art Deco styled half dollar coin (jointly engraved by Barber and Morgan) saw the largest mintage, but many were spoiled in fair-goers' pockets. The gold dollar (by Charles Keck) is starkly simple but shares its dolphins with the huge octagonal gold fifty dollar piece; the little gold dollar is the least rare of the PPIE coins. The elegant quarter eagle (again by Barber and Morgan) is very scarce, and once again a sea-theme is depicted on its obverse. As lovely as those coins are, the rarities and the most beautiful coins of this world's fair are the two varieties of gold fifties—which were called "quintuple eagles" on the printed inserts that accompanied the coins that were sold within the copper frames that housed the rare sets. Each fifty sold for $100 or double face-value at the time; remembering that approximately $1,250 was the average American's annual income in 1915, it is no wonder that the U.S. Mint's authorized mintage of 1,500 piece each of these fifty dollar gold pieces was never sold. But what a captivating memento each of these was! The rarer of the two types today is the round version, of which a mere 483 pieces were sold, many of which have never appeared on the numismatic market. The size and shape are said to have been inspired by the Wass, Molitor fifties of the Gold Rush era. Robert Aitken's deft engraving depicts on the obverse the Greek goddess Athena (symbol of wisdom and invention, of the arts and of warfare) wearing a plumed helmet, while the date 1915 appears as MCMXV (with "round stops") in Roman numerals on the top edge of a shield held in front of her torso. This could so easily be seen as an image of Liberty! The reverse shows yet another allusion to antiquity, the owl of Minerva (the Roman name for Athena), but this is a decidedly modern bird of prey, vigilantly seated upon a branch surrounded by pinecones of the native California Ponderosa tree—a wise "watch bird" for the Republic. As befits its unveiling at the Panama-Pacific fair, this coin is the very best in Neo-Classical art.

This is a truly exceptional specimen that has the usual soft, satiny mint luster. The surfaces are reddish-gold with the slightest accent of lilac on each side. Conservatively graded, only a couple of tiny marks on each side (magnification required) preclude an even higher grade.
From The Freedom Collection. (#7451)

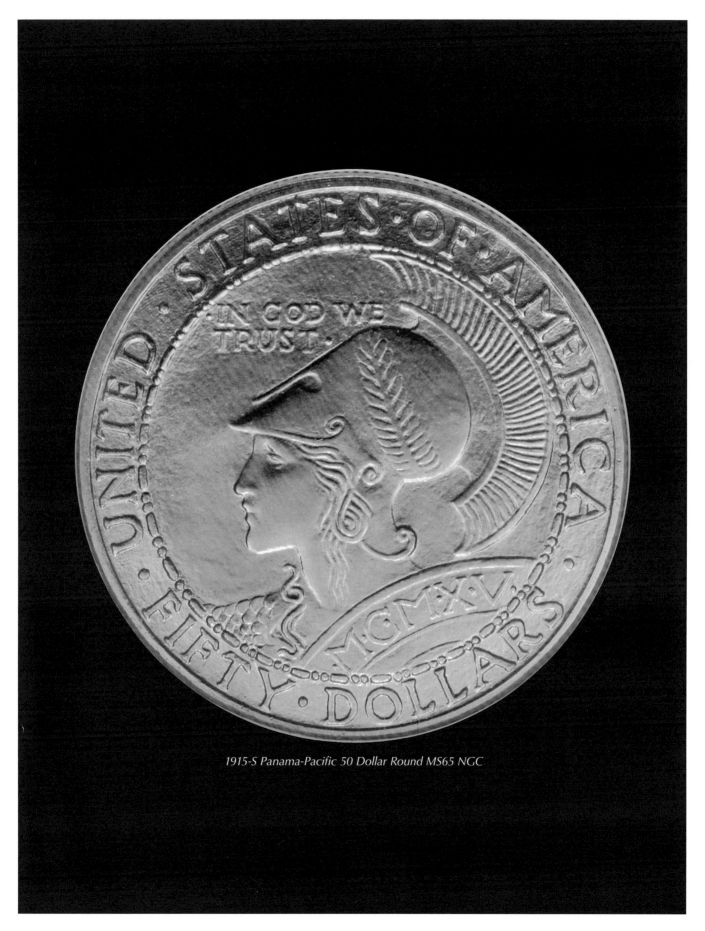

1915-S Panama-Pacific 50 Dollar Round MS65 NGC

1915-S Panama-Pacific Fifty Dollar Round MS65 NGC

Amazing Gem 1915-S Round Panama-Pacific Fifty Dollar

3850   1915-S Panama-Pacific 50 Dollar Round MS65 NGC. Ex: Prinzi Collection. Public celebrations are an age-old phenomenon. Two thousand years ago, in ancient Rome, contests of strength and gladiator combat at the Colosseum (then known as the Flavian Amphitheater) and chariot races at the Circus Maximus served not merely as entertainment, but typically occurred as part of a period of celebration declared by the emperor to mark special events. The reason might be the successful conclusion of a war, an unusually fine harvest, or especially the beginning of the reign of a new Caesar. Centuries earlier, the Greeks called the public to contests of physical abilities at various sports, of which the games at Olympia are the best remembered but were not unique at the time. No doubt there were gatherings to celebrate events even before history recorded them.

It took a modern humanity, however, to create festivals called "world's fairs"—huge expositions of mankind's achievements intended to draw public attention to a particular site but celebrating works and staging entertainments, contributed by countries far and wide.

Energy was gathering across the American nation at the turn of the 19th century to hold another gigantic fair. Within memory of most adults living at the time, there had been world's fairs. Philadelphia had hosted the Centennial Exhibition of 1876, marking our first century as the United States and held where patriots first declared their liberty. Chicago had mounted an even grander World's Columbian Exposition in 1892-93, a celebration of the 400th discovery of America which, in its physical dimensions, became a colossal complex of streets and canals and buildings that simulated a city. In 1889 and again in 1900 there had been the Paris Exposition. St Louis, Missouri, put on its own world's fair in 1904, to celebrate the centennial of the Louisiana Purchase. Largest in scope of all fairs to date, it had featured a complex of grand, neo-classical exhibition palaces, as had the Columbian Exposition. Its formal name was The Louisiana Purchase Exposition; among its numerous attractions it hosted the 1904 Summer Olympic Games, the first Olympics ever held in the United States (the ancient sporting games were revived in Athens as the modern Olympics in 1896). All of these fairs had been largely commercial enterprises, generating capital for the host cities and for the organizing committees, but proceeds were commonly used for some public good. The idea for a new world's fair was taking root.

The U.S. mint was also involved in this new world's fair. Four new designs were spread over five coins. The most impressive were undoubtedly the round and octagonal fifty dollar gold pieces designed by Robert Aitken. A helmeted Greek goddess Athena (symbol of wisdom and of warfare, as well as of the practical arts) occupies the obverse of each. Her helmet is that seen on a number of classical coins, but this time it is plumed, with the date 1915 in Roman numerals on the top edge of a shield held in front of her torso. She could easily also be seen as an image of Liberty. On the reverse is another allusion to antiquity, the owl of Minerva seen on other classical Greek coins, but this owl is decidedly modern, seemingly alive and patiently seated upon a branch supposedly surrounded by Ponderosa pine cones, native to California. Here indeed is Neo-Classical art at its finest! These two coins were so massive that a medals press was needed to coin them. They are medallion-like. Their beauty is undeniable. So is their symbolism. The 483 round fifties that exist today comprise the lowest mintage of any U.S. commemorative coin. At the fair, they were sold either individually or framed as a set with the other commemoratives. So few of these sets, in copper frames, were sold that the exact number of sets in existence is not known.

This is a magnificent Gem that is a perfect companion piece to the Gem octagonal also from the Prinzi Collection. The surfaces are essentially flawless and suggestive of an even higher grade. The bright, satiny luster shows even orange-gold color. An amazingly well-preserved example of this rare 20th century gold coin. *From The Prinzi Trust Collection.* (#7451)

Five-Piece 1915-S Panama-Pacific Set With Original Holder

3851   1915-S Panama-Pacific Half Dollar—Obverse Improperly Cleaned—NCS. Deep sea-green and golden-brown patina embraces this glossy example. Glossy and lightly hairlined, but aesthetically pleasing nonetheless. The mintmark is lightly repunched north. (#7451)

3852   1915-S Panama-Pacific Gold Dollar MS65 PCGS. Booming luster and essentially immaculate lemon-gold surfaces ensure the eye appeal of this sharply struck Gem. The dolphins, depicted on the reverse, are a mariner's symbol for good luck. Dolphins also appear on the 1915-S Panama-Pacific Octagonal fifty dollar variety. (#7451)

3853   1915-S Panama-Pacific Quarter Eagle—Reverse Improperly Cleaned—NCS. A satiny yellow-gold quarter eagle with a bold strike and pleasing eye appeal despite its mild impairment. A few hairlines are visible on the upper right reverse, but these can only be seen beneath a loupe while patiently rotating the piece beneath a light. (#7451)

3854   1915-S Panama-Pacific 50 Dollar Round—Bent—NCS. Unc. Details. While the designs of Robert Aitken, sculptor of the Panama-Pacific fifty dollar gold pieces and two later silver commemoratives, have attracted considerable attention from numismatists, the artist himself has not received the same treatment. In fact, few numismatists knew more than fragments about his life prior to Q. David Bowers' biographical sketch in the appendix of *Commemorative Coins of the United States*. As a native son of San Francisco, Mr. Aitken was a natural choice to design a coin with such close ties to San Francisco, though by the time he received the commission, Mr. Aitken had maintained a studio in New York City for eight years. His sculpture was well-represented elsewhere at the Panama-Pacific Exposition, particularly his renditions of the four classical elements, and generations of schoolchildren, lawyers, and scholars have viewed his work in Washington, D.C., which includes the West Pediment of the United States Supreme Court Building and the South Pennsylvania Avenue entrance to the National Archives.

This piece has rich orange-gold color and essentially contact-free surfaces. The mint luster is a bit thin, as indicated by the net grade. NCS has called this piece "Bent" and it does look that way when one views the left obverse field. But just from the sheer size and weight of this coin, it would seem unlikely. We leave it to viewers to make up their own minds when viewing this coin. (#7451)

3855   1915-S Panama-Pacific 50 Dollar Octagonal—Spot Removed—NCS. Unc Details. The technical specifications for most commemoratives are fairly obvious. Typically, the law stipulates a weight and fineness identical to that of the existing denomination. Sometimes, however, there is no such precedent. The bimetallic Library of Congress ten dollar commemorative of 2000 is a modern example, but the coins of interest for classic commemorative collectors are the round and octagonal Panama-Pacific fifty dollar pieces of 1915. The fineness is identical to that of circulating coinage of the era, that is, .900 fine, alloyed with copper. These mammoth pieces stretch a full 1.74 inches (44.2 centimeters) from tip to tip on the octagonal, with a diameter of the same size for the round. They weigh 83.55 grams apiece, logical enough, given how close the value is to two-and-a-half times the weight of a double eagle. At the given fineness, this translates to more than 2.4 ounces of pure gold. The "slugs" of Augustus Humbert were 60 years in the past. These grand commemoratives were unlike anything most people had ever seen, but whether they recognized it or not these octagonal pieces were a numismatic tribute to the "slugs" from the Gold Rush days.

The surfaces of this coin are an interesting study in themselves. It appears that there were several streaks of copper alloy on

the obverse that eventually turned green. Someone saw these as a defect and tried to remove them. Unfortunately, it was not done with the greatest care. As a result, each green streak still remains but is now overlaid with noticeable (with a magnifier) hairlines. A few small contact marks are also located in the centers, but the coin appears quite pleasing at arm's length. (#7451)

3856   1915-S Panama-Pacific Five-Piece Holder. An attractive box that is far above average for Pan-Pac boxes. There is no gold imprint on the top or bottom, and the top is not buckled as most are. Even matte black finish on the outside with a fully working clasp. The interior is pristine and unfaded.

1915-S Octagonal Panama-Pacific 50 Dollar Gold Uncirculated Details

3857   1915-S Panama-Pacific 50 Dollar Octagonal—Scratched—NCS. Unc Details. A lengthy scratch on the reverse extends from the lower rim, through the A in SAN, the owl's wing, and over MA in PANAMA. A pair of tiny contact marks are also noted in the upper right reverse field. The obverse shows the typical satin-like luster and undisturbed surfaces of a Mint State example. Both sides display lovely, even green-gold coloration.

From *The Encyclopedia of United States Silver & Gold Commemorative Coins (1990)*: "The Panama-Pacific International Exposition, celebrating the opening of the Panama Canal (by the *S.S. Ancon,* August 15, 1914), was set up late in 1914 through early 1915 on a 635-acre site near the Marina in San Francisco: some of Bernard Maybeck's buildings erected for it still survive, notably the colonnade at the Exploratorium at the foot of Lyon Street." The Panama-Pacific Exposition was the most expensive event of its type ever held in the United States, up to that time. Breen reported that the total cost was in excess of fifty million dollars. Fortunately for its organizers, the Exposition drew 19 million visitors. Some of those people attended the June 15, 1915 ceremony where the first octagonal fifty-dollar pieces were struck on the fairgrounds themselves. Various dignitaries, including a Congressman, San Francisco's mayor, and numismatist Farran Zerbe participated in the event.

From The Lanterman's Mill Collection. (#7452)

Gleaming 1915-S Panama-Pacific Fifty Dollar Octagonal, MS62

3858   1915-S Panama-Pacific 50 Dollar Octagonal MS62 NGC. Compilations of certified coin populations are among the most useful tools available to the modern numismatists, yet they have their limits. If one combines the populations from the NGC *Census* and the PCGS *Population Report* for the octagonal variant of the Panama-Pacific "half union" commemorative, the sum is 784 pieces, a number that has to reflect resubmissions, since the net mintage was only 645 coins! A similar situation exists for the round version as well, and to a lesser extent for other low-mintage issues, such as 19th century proof gold.

That said, most numismatists recognize that some of the 645 eight-sided commemoratives have been lost to attrition, and still other survivors exhibit some form of impairment. The outsized pieces have heft and a broad surface area that attracts nicks and marks, particularly at the rim and on the broad devices. The present example is far better preserved in this respect than the grade would suggest. A number of minor flaws appear at the upper and lower rims, and a handful of small ticks are present on the cheek, but the fields have hardly any such marks. Evidence of a soft strike is present on the reverse, especially at the eagle's lower legs and on the dolphins, whose tails and fins blend into the rims. Still, this is a highly lustrous and appealing example of this important and popular gold commemorative, one of the most dramatic pieces ever coined by the United States and a suitable celebration of the Exposition. *From The Twin Hollows Collection.* (#7452)

Impressive MS63 1915-S
Octagonal Fifty Dollar

3859   1915-S Panama-Pacific 50 Dollar Octagonal MS63 PCGS. This heaviest of all U.S. gold coins shares its design with the round fifty also issued at the exposition in San Francisco that celebrated the opening of the Panama Canal and Balboa's discovery of the Pacific Ocean some four centuries earlier. What makes this piece unique among U.S. Mint issues is its shape, of eight sides. The designs of the round gold fifty dollar piece are replicated, although slightly reduced to fit within the broad octagonal borders. The major design difference is the appearance on each side of eight swimming dolphins, filling in what would otherwise be blanks between the inner round circle and the outer octagonal edge. These, of course, were intended not merely to be fillers but also to be emblematic—to represent the flowing waterway provided for sea-to-sea navigation of ships traversing the canal. They are also symbols of the sailor's guardians, to be seen in the open sea on each side of the canal. Much has been written about the Neo-Classical designs of the Pan-Pac fifties. So too has it been suggested that the Mint selected this shape as an obeisance to the most famous coins of the California Gold Rush, the "gold slugs" struck by Augustus Humbert from 1851-53 at the facility that shortly became the U.S. Mint at San Francisco.

The circumstances of this coin's creation, however, make for just as interesting reading and only add to its allure. In fact, so prohibitive was its price at issue that the PPIE's Coin and Medal Department (headed by leading dealer Farran Zerbe) sent a letter to bankers offering unsold pieces some six months after the expo closed. Zerbe suggested they might make exceptional publicity displays and even offered to ship them to banks without prior payment. This final effort evidently produced few sales. Engraver Robert Aitken, a native of San Francisco, might have been disappointed at the public's reception of his magnificent gold fifties, but in truth it was not his design that put the sales so low. It was the cost, at $100 each. The result was a total mintage for the fifties that created a rarity: in all, only 483 Rounds and 645 Octagonals were sold or kept for mint records. Most contemporaries would never appreciate the skill that went into their design, nor the effort required to produce them by the hydraulic coin press that weighed 14 tons and was shipped from the Philadelphia Mint to the exposition for the express purpose of coining them. In fact, most of the authorized 3,000 specimens were never even struck. After the fair ended, the nation suffered through World War I and then the Great Depression. Aitken's precious fifties lay largely forgotten for decades, mostly in the possession of their original purchasers. Interest in commemorative coinage was renewed in the late 1930s but then another world war displaced public awareness. It was not until half a century after they were created that their significance began to be understood by a new generation of numismatists. And, in the last 40 years, these splendid creations of a United States just coming to international prominence have gained legendary stature in our hobby.

This beautiful specimen is from the same collection as the Round MS64 a few lots back. The coins have a similar overall appearance and look like pieces that have been in the same environment for decades. The rich orange-gold color of this coin is also accented with pale lilac. A few tiny marks and one small depression on the cheek of Minerva account for the grade of this lovely commemorative gold coin of unique design.

From The Freedom Collection. (#7452)

Choice 1915-S Octagonal
Panama-Pacific Fifty

3860 1915-S Panama-Pacific 50 Dollar Octagonal MS64 NGC. Octagonal fifty dollar slugs were struck by the U.S. Assay Office of Gold in the years preceding the San Francisco Mint. However, there is only one octagonal issue from the U.S. Mint. That is the octagonal variety of the Panama-Pacific gold fifty dollar commemorative. A round fifty dollar variety was also struck, and its mintage of 483 pieces makes it even more rare than the octagonal version, which has a tiny production of 645 pieces. The designs for the two issues are similar. Both show Minerva, a.k.a. Athena, adorned with an Athenian helmet and shield. The shield bears the date in Roman numerals, MCMXV. This classical but alert military pose was suitable, considering World War I was raging in Europe and could bring in the United States at any time. The reverse features Athena's owl, symbolic of wisdom. The octagonal variety shows these motifs in slightly reduced scale, relative to the round issue. The octagonal variety adds eight dolphins across both peripheries. Dolphins are symbols of good luck, and often accompanied vessels on their way through the Panama Canal.

The present near-Gem has full satin luster and seamless canary-gold toning. The strike is complete. The unaided eye can locate only a single thin mark, located on the reverse field just left of the owl. Once a glass is used, patient observation finds a wispy pinscratch on the obverse above the G in GOD. These two imperfections are of little relevance, particularly given the large diameter of this hefty gold commemorative. The eye appeal is significant. The fifty dollar gold Panama-Pacific varieties are the two keys of the entire U.S. commemorative series, and the present near-Gem is a worthy representative that would highlight any collection. (#7452)

Lot 3861: 1915-S Panama-Pacific 50 Dollar Octagonal MS65 NGC

Exceptional Gem 1915-S Octagonal Panama-Pacific Fifty

3861   1915-S Panama-Pacific 50 Dollar Octagonal MS65 NGC. In 1915, San Francisco was far to the west of any American city where a major fair had yet been held. In that city, a leading citizen named James Phelan headed up a group that had ambitions to turn their city into a world-class town. In 1904, inspired by recent fairs, and particularly those hosted by Chicago and St Louis, they approached Daniel Burnham, an architect involved in the building of both the Chicago World's Fair and San Francisco's Chronicle Building and Merchant's Exchange. He possessed precisely the vision this group shared. He had been quoted in print as saying that "Beauty in the public work of a city has always paid." This was exactly the spirit Phelan and his friends desired—a neat blending of pleasing aesthetics and commercialism that would pay off, producing a showcase for the many qualities of their city as host to a world gathering. They also insisted that it was high time for such a fair to be held on the West Coast.

The Burnham Plan was presented to and endorsed by the San Francisco Board of Supervisors in 1905. Architects were chosen for the project. Sketches of planned monuments, buildings, streets, and parks were all readied by the spring of 1906. All were lost when the great earthquake of that year almost destroyed the city. The plans burned with City Hall. Enthusiasm for rebuilding San Francisco was almost immediate, and Phelan's group hoped it included their plan for the world's fair. But such was not to be. Financing the rebuilding of the city proved daunting, and many citizens felt that a celebration was not yet appropriate. Thus, for a few years the idea of staging a fair at this locale faded.

Elsewhere, others had plans of their own. Momentum built particularly in New Orleans for the next American exposition. Within a mere five years of the earthquake, however, San Franciscans had gathered enough spiritual steam to launch an advertising and lobbying campaign. In 1911, they achieved their goal when, following Congressional debates, President Taft declared that San Francisco would be host to the next American world's fair. This inspired a funding campaign. Almost all of the required money was given by Californians, who hoped to showcase San Francisco's resurrection. Their campaign succeeded largely because it had two spearheads that New Orleans could not equal. They proposed an exposition that would honor the 400th anniversary of Vasco Núñez de Balboa's historic discovery of the Pacific Ocean as well as the upcoming completion of the Panama Canal, which in 1911 was seen as a new world wonder. New Orleans was a great shipping center that would benefit from the opening of the canal, but the Pacific Ocean was far away.

San Francisco set to work. Before the Panama Canal officially opened to sea traffic in August 1914, an army of architects, designers, inventors, contractors, and builders descended on the city by the bay. It had taken 50 years to plan and construct the canal, but the expo city seemed almost to grow organically. The fair site would be huge, and would even feature a detailed reproduction of the Panama Canal covering five acres! But it would not be a real city. Much would be fantasy. The stage would be real enough, but the buildings that would look so substantial were actually constructed almost entirely of temporary materials intended to last approximately one year. Most of the building material was called "staff," an odd combination of burlap fibers and plaster which could be painted and decorated to look like concrete or marble. It had been used in building the Chicago fair in 1892 and tended to disintegrate slowly; it was not intended to last more than the duration of the exposition.

It took three years to put up this new city for the fair. It was located at the northern end of San Francisco on the bay, where land space was too short. This was alleviated by filling in the mud flats there, the site of today's Marina District. The fairgrounds eventually occupied 635 acres, stretching between the Presidio and Van Ness, bordered on the south by Chestnut Street and on the north by the bay. When the exposition officially opened on February 20, 1915, all of the anticipation and years of planning and building proved worth the wait. Over the next 257 days, more than 18 million visitors passed through the turnstiles of the entrance to wander through the modern and classical wonders displayed on the 635 acres.

The octagonal fifty dollar gold pieces that were produced at the fair are said to have been a tribute to the Gold Rush era, the famous "gold slugs" struck by Augustus Humbert from 1851-53. Humbert's work had led directly to the establishment of the U.S. Mint at San Francisco. However, mint officials may not have been as acutely aware of this history as we suppose. It is entirely possible that the two types of gold fifties were intended to reflect the dual nature of the events being celebrated—one for the Canal, and one for the anniversary of the discovery of the Pacific. No one has looked deeply enough into the archives to see if such an idea was postulated.

This stunning orange-gold example has a lovely overlay of satiny mint luster. The surfaces are as clean as one would expect from a Gem. In fact, the only mark we see is a tiny horizontal mark across the highpoint of the cheek of Athena. An outstanding example of this unique gold commemorative. (#7452)

Lot 3862: 1915-S Panama-Pacific 50 Dollar Octagonal MS65 NGC

Magnificent MS65 NGC Panama-Pacific Octagonal Fifty Dollar

3862   1915-S Panama-Pacific 50 Dollar Octagonal MS65 NGC.
Ex: Prinzi Collection. Landscape architecture, statuesque buildings, ornate gardens, art of many kinds, clever inventions, countless displays of wares and products, sports, and entertainment—the Panama-Pacific Exposition showed the throngs of visitors what the world looked like in 1915. Other fairs had done the same, some to almost the same degree, but the Panama-Pacific International Exposition was called the first truly modern world's fair, if for only one phenomenal reason. It was lit up at night by a fanfare of electric lights!

Electricity was not entirely novel. It had come to America in the 1880s, but seldom had the public been treated to such a circus-like atmosphere of innovative and captivating illumination. Now the expo city could be seen and enjoyed night and day. It was a phenomenon.

The General Electric Company, a novelty in itself in 1915, provided indirect lighting of all the fairgrounds, including something that the company called the "Scintillator," which was described as a battery of searchlights housed on a barge in the bay. It projected numerous beams of light—given any of seven colors by a gigantic fan made of colored rays—across the famous fog banks, and if no fog accommodated the moment then a locomotive's steam engine would be used to generate some artificial fog. A company of U.S. marines manipulated this fan using military drill precision, to enormous effect. It was said that this illumination was at its best on misty nights when the foggy air's moisture "provided a screen to catch the colored lights and create the effect of an aurora overhead." A visit to the fair was the first sight of electric lights for many people. General Electric impressed an awed public with its new technology.

Yet old technology could be just as impressive, and in truth the fair was a celebration of both venerated imagination and novelty. Many said that the Tower of Jewels was the focal point for all who visited the exposition. It stood more than 40 stories high and was festooned by a riot of cut-glass made with handmade precision. Some 102,000 pieces of Austrian crystal, in total weighing 20,000 pounds, hung from hooks all over the structure. Each reflector had a small mirror behind it. These crystals came in five colors—white, ruby, emerald, aquamarine, and "canary" yellow. These would swing in the breeze and reflect the sunlight by day. The effect was never less than dazzling.

Indirect lighting, another novelty at the time, included concealed colored lights that glinted through the many fountains, and reflectors inside otherwise unlit buildings which bounced the beams of colored strings of lights into the night sky. These contrasted with the stark white lighting of the courtyards of some of the buildings, while others were lit a uniform red or green "aura" which shone from powerful arc lamps. Visiting the fair at night was like being in a fairyland.

The buildings themselves were a marvel. Flags, shields and banners adorned replicas of palaces and courtyards, of familiar state buildings and of "exotic" architecture shown on buildings of foreign lands. Travel abroad was not commonplace in America in 1915, and for many visitors the mere glance at a "Moroccan palace" (its replica) was thrilling.

Some idea of the awe inspired by the fair may be gotten from the language used in guidebooks published at the time. The Union Pacific Railroad issued one. But the official exposition brochure waxed ecstatic. It proclaimed proudly that the location was "a natural amphitheater, fronting on the wonderful island-dotted Bay of San Francisco, just inside the famous Golden Gate" and yet convenient, "within fifteen minutes' street car ride from the City Hall." It continued as follows: "With this wonderful scene as a background, the architects, artists and landscape gardeners of the Exposition have planned and erected a city straight out of a beautiful dream." ..."Through the portals of the Golden Gate the nations of the earth can bring their richest offerings to the very gates of the Exposition, avoiding a long continental haul and consequent damage from re-shipping."... "Carnivals, maneuvers by the fleets of all nations, international yacht racing, motor boat racing, exhibitions by submarines and hydroplanes" could all be seen, along with an "aviation field, race track, and live stock exhibit, terminating in the grounds of a great military reservation, the Presidio, where ... army maneuvers will take place." Surrounding the Tower of Jewels there were eight exhibit "palaces"—called Education, Liberal Arts, Manufactures, Varied Industries, Agriculture, Food Products, Transportation and Mines, and Metallurgy.

The coinage from the exposition was no less spectacular than the grounds themselves. The fifty dollar gold pieces were struck in two variants, round and octagonal. The octagonal version reduces the image on each side slightly, but adds a border of swimming dolphins on each side, which Breen neatly summarizes as being "friendly companions of boats throughout the continuous water route completed by the Canal." The mint was authorized to strike 1,500 examples of each. The price was double face value, or $100 per coin. If anyone bought either one, or one of each, he or she would get, at no extra charge, one each of the three smaller coins. As tempting as this might seem to today's numismatists, it was a daunting price for all but the wealthy in 1915, when the average annual income was $1,267. The result was not surprising: only 645 octagonal fifties were sold (more popular than the round version, probablybecause it was so unusual in shape), and a mere 483 were not melted of the round fifties.

But how elegant these coins are! In 1915, America was on the verge of entering the first major war outside its borders, the world war in Europe. Athena shows us ready but wise enough to wait. On the octagonals, the dolphins are emblematic of the sailor's guardians, to be seen in the open seas on each side of the Canal, but also of the continuous water route it provided. The Panama Canal eliminated the long and dangerous sea-route for commercial shipping around Cape Horn, the southernmost headland of Chile, taking ships from the Atlantic to the Pacific Oceans, or vice-versa, easily and quickly for the first time in history. The dolphins symbolize this flow as well.

This piece shows rich orange-gold color and thick, satiny mint luster. Magnification reveals a couple of minor abrasions on the obverse, but they are so minor they do not merit individual mention.

A true masterpiece of the coinage art was created in 1915 at the world's fair in San Francisco, and it comes in two distinctive versions. With the possible exception of the High Relief 1907 Saint-Gaudens double eagle (with its date in distinctive Roman numerals), there is no other American coin of such luminous beauty—or so finely conceived or so clearly representative of a significant event in our cultural history.
From The Prinzi Trust Collection. (#7452)

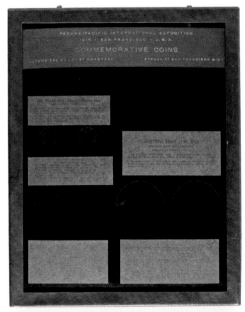

Historic Shreve & Co. Panama-Pacific Double Set Frame

3863 **Original Panama-Pacific Double Set Frame.** Perhaps the second most ornate packaging for a set of United States commemorative coins, after the 32-slot cherrywood caddy crafted for the 1995-1996 Olympic issues. The copper frames, which supplemented existing leatherette-and-velvet holders, were created by Shreve & Co., a noted San Francisco jeweler that operates under that name to this day. While the copper frames for the five-coin and ten-coin sets are identical, the interiors are different, and the former is far more common than the latter.

The frame, glass, and interior labels are in Excellent condition. At the top, the left screw protrudes slightly, and the interior velvet is frayed in a spot at the upper right, revealing the surface beneath. Minor crushing of the velvet is visible in the quarter eagle slots as well. On the back, the leatherette is worn at the edges, most notably at the upper corners, though this is minor in context, and the prop and ring are intact. This is a great opportunity to acquire an important numismatic artifact.

Impeccable 1916 McKinley Gold Dollar MS67

3864 **1916 McKinley MS67 PCGS.** Satiny and well frosted with a few delicate speckles of coppery patina on the obverse. Faint olive highlights are also noted about the peripheral lettering and borders. The shimmering fields are almost totally undisturbed and only the most insignificant evidence of contact can be detected on the portrait of the slain president. Two well-known engravers by the names of Barber and Morgan are responsible for this two-year commemorative gold design. Census: 49 in 67, 0 finer (12/06).
From The Prinzi Trust Collection. (#7454)

Pleasing MS67 1917 McKinley Dollar

3865 **1917 McKinley MS67 NGC.** Ex: Prinzi Collection. The mintage of the 1917 final-year McKinley gold dollar was half that of the 1916 issue, and sales were sluggish, even though proceeds of the issue were earmarked for a memorial to the assassinated president. Eventually Fort Worth, Texas, dealer B. Max Mehl obtained 10,000 examples of the 1916 and 1917 issues for sale, offering them at $2.50 each. Orange-gold centers meld into green-gold near the peripheral lettering. Both sides are essentially pristine, pleasing, and attractive. NGC has certified 46 examples in MS67, with none finer (11/06).
From The Prinzi Trust Collection. (#7455)

Attractive 1922 MS67 Grant No Star Gold Dollar

3866 **1922 Grant no Star MS67 NGC.** Ex: Prinzi Collection. Unlike many other commemorative gold issues, the Grant No Star pieces are usually encountered in highly choice condition and are a boon to collectors of commemoratives and/or gold. The present Superb Gem is no exception, offering mellow apricot-gold coloration on each side with tinges of hazel on the highpoints. The reverse is especially attractive and shows no sign of the die cracks through the trees sometimes encountered on this issue. This piece is one of a few dozen MS67 pieces at both services, with a single NGC piece finer (11/06).
From The Prinzi Trust Collection. (#7458)

Gorgeous 1922 With Star Grant Gold Dollar MS67

3867   1922 Grant with Star MS67 NGC. Struck with pinpoint sharpness and displaying a touch of reddish patina over impeccable satiny surfaces. From both a technical and aesthetic perspective, nearly unsurpassable quality. Unlike their half dollar counterparts, an almost equal number of Star and No Star gold dollars were produced, this variety being just 5,016 pieces. The reason for the inclusion of the star appears to be unknown, but some have conjectured that it's emblematic of Ulysses Grant's status as a general during the Civil War.

From The Prinzi Trust Collection. (#7459)

Impressive Premium Gem 1926 Sesquicentennial Quarter Eagle

3868   1926 Sesquicentennial MS66 NGC. The 1926 Sesquicentennial Exposition nearly added a new denomination to the list coined by the United States, one with a value of one and a half dollars (or 150 cents), but that proposal fell by the wayside, and the more prosaic quarter eagle was authorized instead.

Seasoned commemorative collectors know the difficulty of acquiring a pleasing example of either Sesquicentennial issue, but this beauty should meet every expectation. The strike is more than adequate, and the gold-orange surfaces have pretty luster and delicate apricot accents. The usual marks on Liberty and her scroll that bar the way to a Gem grade are absent, and only a handful of tiny marks are visible on Liberty's lower gown. NGC has certified three coins finer, and PCGS has graded none (11/06).

From The RNB Collection. (#7466)

Stunning Superb Gem 1926 Sesquicentennial Quarter Eagle

3869   1926 Sesquicentennial MS67 NGC. The National Sesquicentennial Commission, the organization responsible for the Sesquicentennial Exposition, optimistically ordered the full authorized mintage of 1,000,000 half dollars and 200,000 quarter eagles, plus the assay pieces required by law. Like most of the commemorative coin vendors up to that time, the Commission's grandiose dreams floundered on the reefs of reality, and a total of only 45,793 quarter eagles found buyers. The net mintage most often given for this final classic gold commemorative is either the preceding number, the *Guide Book*'s total, 46,019 pieces, or something in between, depending on the ultimate fate of the 226 assay pieces.

As one may derive from the grade, this is a simply exceptional example. The apricot-gold surfaces, laced with peach and emerald, have strong, frosty luster that is a far cry from all but the finest representatives. Liberty's fingers and toes, as well as the building's door and windows, display uncharacteristic, practically pinpoint detail. Only a handful of minuscule marks affect each side, though a small mint-made flaw below the R in AMERICA is noted as a pedigree marker. This is only the fourth Superb Gem of this exceptionally tricky issue ever offered by Heritage. The two most recent pieces were housed in NGC holders, while the earliest was PCGS-graded, though this example likely crossed over to NGC, since no such piece appears in the *Population Report*. Census: 3 in 67, 0 finer (11/06).
From The Prinzi Trust Collection. (#7466)

TERRITORIAL GOLD

Noteworthy Mint State 1852
Assay Office Ten

3870   1852 Assay Office Ten Dollar MS61 NGC. K-12a(2), R.5. An attractive yellow-gold representative of this early U.S. Assay Office of Gold variety. The eagle's breast feathers are well defined, and luster dominates all legends and devices. A few moderate obverse marks emerge beneath a strong lens, characteristic of the MS61 grade. Most Assay Office gold coins are circulated or impaired. Mint State pieces are subject to formidable demand from Territorial specialists. K-12a(2) is the "Faint Beads" subvariety of K-12a. The reverse dentils or beads are indistinct, a feature presumably caused by die wear. Slender die cracks are present throughout the lower obverse border, and also across the left reverse legends. Listed on page 351 of the 2007 *Guide Book*.
From The Jones Beach Collection. (#10001)

Desirable MS62 1853 Assay Office Twenty

3871   1853 Assay Office Twenty Dollar, 900 Thous. MS62 NGC. K-18, R.2. This straw-gold example is crisply struck and exhibits impressive cartwheel luster, particularly on the reverse. Minor obverse marks are present, but fewer than expected for the grade. Regarding K-18, Kagin (1981) states, "2 1/2 million pieces were minted from 3/53 to 10/30/53, from some 30 different dies destroyed in the fire of 1906." These dies were hubbed, since there are positional differences on either the obverse or reverse. Individual dies do have their peculiar characteristics, however. The present piece lacks crossbars on the A's in AMERICA. An upper right serif on the M in AMERICA is missing, while the neighboring E has an upper left serif. The Kagin plate coin is the opposite, with serifs on the M and an absent serif on the E. A comprehensive study of these die varieties and their comparable rarity has yet to be performed. Census: 48 in 62, 40 finer (10/06).
From The Jones Beach Collection. (#10013)

Appealing 1853 Assay Office
Twenty Dollar MS62

3872   1853 Assay Office Twenty Dollar, 900 Thous. MS62 NGC. K-18, R.2. Assay twenties, although routinely listed under the category of private or territorial gold coins and private partners (Curtis, Ward, and Perry) were contracted to produce them, neither is technically correct. More than 2 million pieces were struck under authorization from the United Assay Office of Gold and they soon became the workhorse gold coins in Gold Rush San Francisco. This uncommonly well preserved example is only minimally abraded and is notable for appealing reddish accents. Listed on page 352 of the 2007 *Guide Book*. (#10013)

Select Mint State 1853 Assay
Office Twenty Dollar

3873   1853 Assay Office Twenty Dollar, 900 Thous. MS63 NGC. K-18, R.2. Flashy and bright, both sides exhibit lovely green-gold and peach coloration. A few small abrasions are noticeable, mostly near the reverse center, but the surfaces are remarkably clean for a Territorial gold coin of this size and weight. A couple of minor rim nicks are also noted along the right side of the reverse. The generally powerful strike is only incomplete near the center of the obverse, where the eagle's arrows and fletchings are flat. This coin clearly represents an important bidding opportunity for advanced collectors. Listed on page 352 of the 2007 *Guide Book*. (#10013)

Important Near-Gem 1853 Assay Office Twenty, K-18

3874   1853 Assay Office Twenty Dollar, 900 Thous. MS64 PCGS. K-18, R.2. The surfaces of this coin have a bright yellow-gold color with greenish peripheral accents, and the features are uncommonly well struck with sharp, clear definition on the arrows and top of the shield. A few small field marks are noted on the obverse as well as a moderate blemish below ME in AMERICA; the reverse is quite smooth and shows just one mentionable mark beneath and above the C in CALIFORNIA. The fields of this piece show a slight bit of metal flow that gives the coin a mild granularity and seems to add thousands of facets of individual sparkle to the surfaces, similar to a matte proof gold coin. Listed on page 352 of the 2007 *Guide Book.* (#10013)

Condition Census
1853 U.S. Assay Office
Twenty Dollar Gold, MS65

3875   1853 Assay Office Twenty Dollar, 900 Thous. MS65 PCGS. K-18, R.2. The U.S. Assay Office gold pieces are normally included in the Territorial and private mint gold coinage of the early West, but in reality the pieces are neither Territorial nor private. The U.S. Assay Office was the forerunner of what would become, in 1854, the San Francisco Mint, which began producing quarter eagles, half eagles, eagles, and double eagles in that year. When legislation was passed that required all Assay Office coinage to conform to the Mint Act of 1837, the effect was to have the older dies, with a listed fineness of 880 THOUS, repunched with 900 over the 880. All the pieces made by the U.S. Assay Office are of the 900 over 880 variety, but the undertype 880 fades over time. The 900 fine pieces were coined from March 1 to Oct. 30, 1853, with a total production of about 2.5 million pieces. Those dies, perhaps 30 in all, were destroyed in the San Francisco Great Earthquake and Fire of 1906, which ironically left the San Francisco Mint standing amid the rubble of hundreds of other nearby buildings.

This piece shows considerable evidence remaining of the 88. While the 9 shows an unrecognizable jumble at the top left loop, the first 0 shows prominent "horns" atop it, from the left and right sides of the underlying 8's top loop, which fail to join at the apex of their respective arcs. Both sides are highly lustrous, with deep golden-orange color and a complete absence of singular distractions. This delightful specimen of Territorial gold stands squarely atop the Condition Census of known examples of this available variety. It is one of five pieces graded in Gem condition at PCGS, with none finer, while NGC has graded an additional four pieces in MS65, again with none finer (11/06). (#10013)

MS62 R.5 K-10 C. Bechtler Quarter Eagle Tied for Finest Certified

3876 (1837-42) **C. Bechtler Quarter Eagle, 67G. 21C. MS62 NGC.** K-10, R.5. Similar to the Kagin-9 variety, but with 67.G./21 in the center, and a period after CARATS. This rare Bechtler piece shows a somewhat dished appearance, with slight bulging that shows toward the center of the reverse (denomination) side. That side is rotated about 90 degrees counterclockwise from its expected location. This piece has considerable luster remaining on the green-gold surfaces, with tinges of copper color on the reverse. Only a few light scrapes and abrasions are noted, consistent with the MS62 grade. This piece is tied with a half-dozen or so other pieces at both services for the finest certified of this elusive issue. Listed on page 345 of the 2007 *Guide Book*.
From The Stone 1837 Collection. (#10067)

Rare K-13 C. Bechtler Quarter Eagle AU58

3877 (1837-42) **C. Bechtler Quarter Eagle, 70G. 20C. AU58 NGC.** K-13, R.6. Plain Edge. This rare issue was struck using South Carolina gold. Interestingly, the engraver used an inverted V for the letter A on the reverse die. The Bechtlers' coinage earned great respect during this period as the coins were of the true weight and fineness stated, and the gold value was actually worth slightly more than face value. The Bechtlers also coined the first gold dollars in the United States, and the Philadelphia Mint followed with their own gold dollars some 18 years later. Remarkably, the Bechtler coining press still survives in the American Numismatic Society's Museum. NGC has graded two examples this high with three coins seen finer (the finest MS62). The coin is sharply and evenly struck throughout, and the green-gold surfaces are lightly abraded with the only notable distractions being a series of faint pinscratches below 250 on the reverse. Listed on page 345 of the 2007 *Guide Book*. (#10070)

Scarce Bechtler Five Dollar
Gold AU50, K-23

3878   (1837-42) C. Bechtler Five Dollar, 128G. 22C. AU50 PCGS. K-23, High R.6. This piece is a clean, problem-free example with just a few noticeable marks on each side, along with numerous trivial nicks and a small number of wispy hairlines. The striking details are excellent, and highpoint wear is minimal. The surfaces have taken on a rich, deep olive-gold color in the fields with contrasting copper-red luster around the devices. A pleasing AU example of this scarce Bechtler variety. Listed on Page 346 of the 2007 *Guide Book*. Population: 2 in 50, 8 finer (11/06). (#10103)

Lustrous, Attractive MS62
1860 Clark, Gruber Five

3879   1860 Clark, Gruber & Co. Five Dollar MS62 NGC. K-2, R.4. The lustrous yellow-gold surfaces complement deeper pinkish-gold and copper hues at the rims on each side. The peripheral stars are well struck and show central details, although the highpoint hair on Liberty is a trifle weak. On the reverse a bit of weakness shows on the left and upper shield borders, but there are few distractions otherwise. The few light, unbothersome field hits noted on the reverse side are characteristic of most Territorial gold pieces. Lustrous and attractive. (#10136)

Important 1860 Clark, Gruber & Co. Five Dollar MS64

3880   1860 Clark, Gruber & Co. Five Dollar MS64 PCGS. K-2, R.4. The predecessor to the Denver Mint began several decades earlier when Austin M. Clark, Milton Edward Clark, and Emmanuel H. Gruber formed the firm of Clark, Gruber & Company and began a banking business in Leavenworth, Kansas. The Clark brothers were originally grocers who profited from selling their merchandise and goods to prospective miners. With all the news of gold discoveries around Denver City, a banking office was soon opened there and attention eventually turned to converting the gold dust they purchased from their new venture into coin. The firm erected a two-story brick building at (present-day) 16th and Market Streets, about one mile from the current site of the Denver Mint and a private mint was opened in 1860. While having a lasting impact on the fledgling territory, coinage operations lasted for just two years.

The central motifs of the Clark, Gruber & Co. five dollar are similar to the federal design except that Clark & Co. replaces LIBERTY on her headband. In addition to the denomination, the legend PIKES PEAK GOLD DENVER appears on the reverse. Only a handful of Choice and finer examples are believed to survive of the first year half eagle. Struck from native ore, these 1860 issues tended to become easily abraded, but such is not the case with this outstanding example. Only the normal weakness is seen over the central devices and a thin veil of reddish-orange patina accents each side. Population: 2 in 64, 2 finer (11/06). Listed on page 362 of the 2007 *Guide Book*. (#10136)

Attractive 1860 Clark, Gruber Ten Dollar, AU55

3881   1860 Clark, Gruber & Co. Ten Dollar AU55 PCGS. K-3, R.5. The start of the Colorado Gold Rush followed that of California by almost exactly ten years. The stage was set for a local mint in Denver, and there to fill the void was Clark, Gruber, & Co. Coinage totaled approximately $120,000 between July and October of 1860. In 1863, the federal government purchased the facility, which served as a U.S. Assay Office prior to the erection of a Federal Mint in 1906.

1860 Clark, Gruber ten dollar pieces are rare in any grade. On the present example, the highpoints show only a trace of wear. A few scattered marks are present on each side, but none are individually distracting. The green-gold surfaces are clean, and retain ample luster. The "Pike's Peak" motif, and the fictitious rendering of the mountain, have made this piece popular among collectors for decades. This attractive example should inspire bidders, and will be a highly valued historic relic and numismatic treasure to its next owner. Listed on page 362 of the 2007 *Guide Book*.
From The Jones Beach Collection. (#10137)

Choice AU 1860 Clark, Gruber & Co Ten, K-3

3882   1860 Clark, Gruber & Co. Ten Dollar AU55 PCGS. K-3, R.5. Well struck, save for minor weakness to the dentils on the lower right quadrant of obverse and reverse; with even green-gold coloration and a slight shimmer to the surfaces from bits of remaining mint luster. Modest highpoint wear is seen on both sides, along with a few scattered, small abrasions. The 6 in the date is noticeably repunched. Clark, Gruber & Co. was a private minting firm that struck gold coinage in Denver in 1860 and 1861. Approximately 125 pieces have been certified by NGC and PCGS combined, with AU55 examples falling near the middle of the grade range overall. Population: 20 in 55, 19 finer (11/06). (#10137)

Scarce 1860 Clark, Gruber & Co. Ten Dollar MS60, K-3

3883 1860 Clark, Gruber & Co. Ten Dollar MS60 NGC. K-3, R.5. The Clark, Gruber gold coinage was produced in 1860 and 1861. Six out of eight issues were patterned after the federal gold coins, with a Liberty Head, 13 stars, and the date on the obverse, and with an eagle, denomination, and legend on the reverse. The other two issues, the 1860 $10 and $20 coins, had a triangular mountain on the obverse, said to be Pikes Peak but obviously not familiar to the engraver, who must have been from the East.

This is a pleasing Mint State piece with bright green-gold color and lighter yellow luster near the borders. The obverse has a raised ridge of metal from the D of GOLD, through the right base of the mountain, and down toward the rim at 5 o'clock. It is apparently a minor planchet lamination, but may have an associated die crack. Listed on page 362 of the 2007 *Guide Book*. Census: 6 in 60, 11 finer (11/06). (#10137)

MS63 Gilt 1861 Clark, Gruber Copper $5 Dies Trial

3884 1861 Clark, Gruber $5 Copper Dies Trial MS63 Gilt NGC. K-10c, R.7. Struck in copper with a reeded edge, later gilt. Well struck, unlike most gold 1861 Clark, Gruber five dollar pieces, which tend to be softly defined in the centers. Tiny center dots appear on Liberty's ear lobe and on the lowest horizontal shield stripe. These are rarely visible on gold examples. The glossy straw-gold surfaces are splendidly smooth. 1861 was the final date for the Clark, Gruber & Co. coined private gold coins. In 1862, the firm began to produce rectangular ingots instead. The assets of the company were purchased by the Federal government in 1863, which opened an assay office, and decades later, a branch mint. From the same dies as the gold variety, K-6, listed on page 363 of the 2007 *Guide Book*. *From The Jones Beach Collection.* (#10151)

Extremely Rare Copper
1861 Clark, Gruber Twenty Dollar
Dies Trial, K-12b

3885   1861 Clark, Gruber $20 Copper Dies Trial MS64 Brown NGC. K-12b, High R.7. A rare dies trial from the final year of true private gold coinage. Jewelers continued to produce small denomination gold pieces for sale as souvenirs, but these fall into a different category than the 1861 Clark, Gruber & Co. issues, which were intended for circulation due to a shortage of Federal coin in Colorado territory. Kagin-12b uses the same reverse die as the issued 1861 Clark, Gruber twenty dollar piece. This reverse die is identified by the V in DENVER, which appears to be recut over the letter N. However, the obverse die for K-12b was apparently never used to strike gold coins. Unlike the issued twenty dollar piece (K-8), PIKES PEAK is centered on the coronet, and star 7 is left of the coronet. Presumably, the K-8 obverse die lasted longer than anticipated, and never required replacement by the obverse die used to strike the K-12b dies trial. Copper dies trials were also struck for the K-8 dies, and are listed in the standard Kagin reference under K-12c.

This K-12b example is attractively toned light chocolate-brown, with sky-blue shades near the margins. The fields show good reflectivity, which suggests that both the planchets and dies were polished prior to the strike. Denticles are only faintly evident, since the piece was broadstruck, without the restraint of a collar die. The strike is sharper than seen on the gold examples struck for circulation (compare against the 2007 *Guide Book* photo on page 363), particularly on the horizontal shield lines. The obverse stars and occasional portions of the hair lack a complete impression. Post-strike imperfections are limited to faint obverse hairlines, which are only visible at certain angles and under strong magnification. As of (10/06), NGC has certified only one example of K-12b, the current lot, and many years may pass before another opportunity for acquisition comes along.

From The Jones Beach Collection. (#10153)

Choice Proof 1861 Clark, Gruber
Two and a Half Copper Dies Trial

3886   1861 Clark, Gruber & Co. Quarter Eagle Copper Dies Trial PR64 Red and Brown PCGS. K-9, High R.7. Lovely orange, ruby-red, and gunmetal-blue toning enrich this pleasing near-Gem. The fields are moderately mirrored and are void of remotely mentionable marks. The strike is exquisite, unlike the issued gold two and a half dollar pieces, which are typically soft in the centers. Each side has a partial knife rim, from 9 to 2 o'clock on the obverse and from 12 to 6 o'clock on the reverse. K-9 is from the same dies as the regular issue gold pieces, K-5a. As of (10/06), PCGS has certified two dies trial pieces as proof and an additional seven dies trial pieces as Mint State. The present example is the finest certified among the two proof pieces, and is housed in a green label holder.
From The Jones Beach Collection. (#10159)

Mint State 1852 Humbert
Ten Dollar, K-10a

3887   1852 Humbert Ten Dollar MS60 PCGS. K-10a, R.5. The IINITED variety, caused by a heavy die crack along the bases of UNITED. An unusually high grade for this popular issue, one of the last produced by the U.S. Assay Office prior to the departure of John Moffat from the firm. This honey-gold piece displays full detail on the eagle's breast, although the fletchings show slight incompleteness. Die rust causes a pebbled texture to the obverse, as made, but conspicuous marks are absent. Luster is particularly abundant across the reverse, which exhibits the engine-turned design attributed to Humbert's prior experience as a watchmaker. Listed on page 350 of the 2007 *Guide Book.* Population: 2 in 60, 5 finer (10/06).
From The Jones Beach Collection. (#10187)

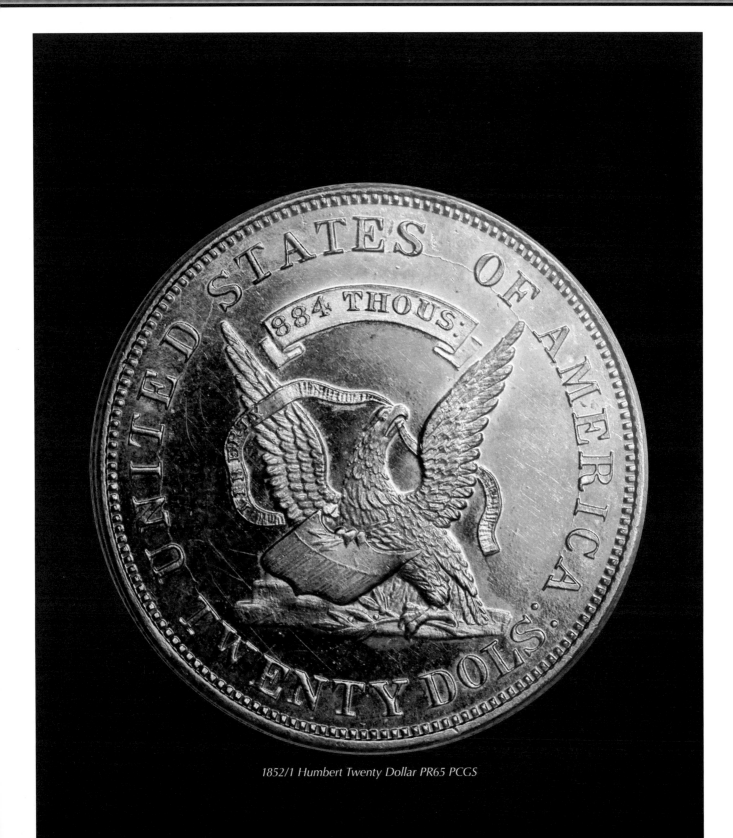

1852/1 Humbert Twenty Dollar PR65 PCGS

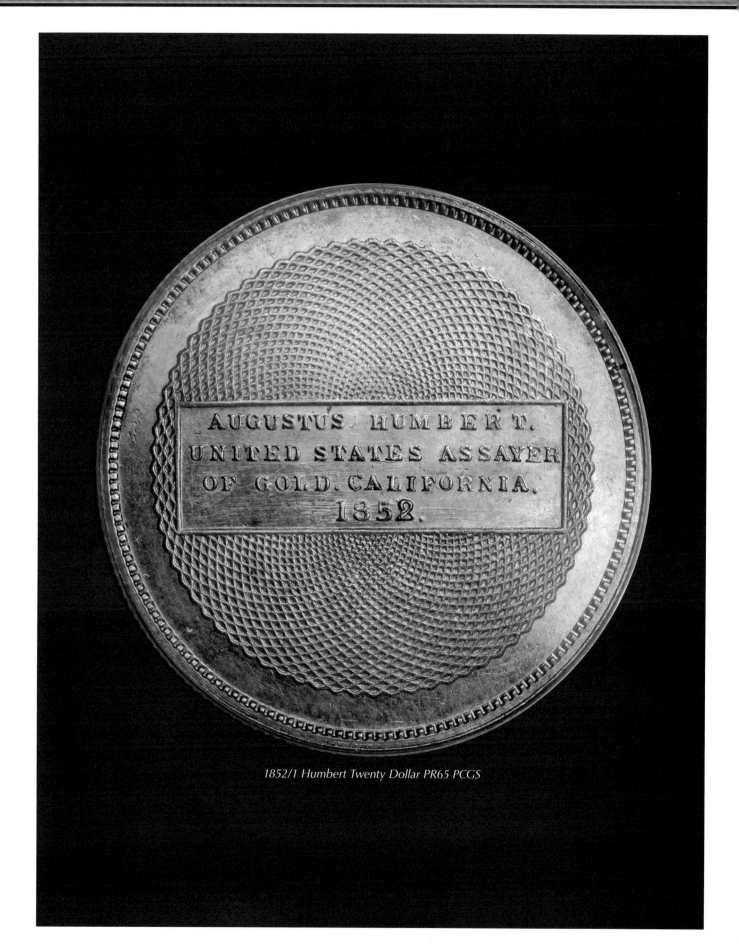

1852/1 Humbert Twenty Dollar PR65 PCGS

Exceptionally Rare Gem Proof 1852/1 Humbert Twenty
The Personal Specimen of John Glover Kellogg

3888 **1852/1 Humbert Twenty Dollar PR65 PCGS.** The 1851 opening of the U.S. Assay Office was a boon to the San Francisco gold rush economy. Miners and merchants could deposit gold dust and receive fair value in the form of $50 gold pieces, which were also accepted at par by the U.S. Customs Office.

The Assay Office pieces effectively removed private gold coins from circulation. In 1849 and 1850, numerous private California mints such as Baldwin and the Miner's Bank produced gold pieces. These were proven underweight, and merchants and bankers refused to accept them except at a steep (and profitable) discount. The bankers then took the disparaged private gold coins to the Assay Office, which melted them into market-acceptable $50 "slugs."

By late 1851, these $50 pieces dominated commerce. Due to their high face value and the absence of lower denomination coins, business had to be conducted using round amounts. Change for the cumbersome slugs largely consisted of a potpourri of foreign coins, which traded above their bullion value.

The Assay Office was well aware of this untenable situation, and repeatedly requested the Federal government back East to allow the production of $10 and $20 ingots. Dies dated 1851 for these two denominations were prepared in anticipation of approval. Permission to strike $10 and $20 pieces was finally received in early 1852. The dies were overdated to 1852/1, and coinage began. The $10 pieces are relatively plentiful, by the difficult standards of territorial gold. The $20 pieces are significantly rarer.

The John Glover Kellogg Specimen

The present Gem proof 1852/1 Humbert $20 piece was the personal coin of John Glover Kellogg , cashier for Moffat & Co., which struck the 1852/1 $20 "ingots" under the authority of the U.S. Assay Office of Gold. Kellogg later was a partner in Kellogg & Richter, which struck Kellogg $20 pieces in 1854 and 1855, along with a few 1855 $50 proofs. Kellogg began a partnership with former U.S. Assayer Augustus Humbert in 1855, and many of their stamped large gold ingots were cargo on the famous 1857 S.S. Central America shipwreck.

Kellogg died in 1886, and several high grade territorial gold pieces passed down from Kellogg were included in the October 27, 1916 Thomas L. Elder auction. This proof 1852/1 Humbert $20 was cataloged as lot 742.

Chicago beer baron and legendary coin accumulator Virgil Brand (1862-1926) was likely the winning bidder. Upon Brand's death, his brothers Armin and Horace inherited the massive collection, which contained over 350,000 items. Beginning in 1932, the collection was slowly dispersed. Prominent numismatic dealer Burdette G. Johnson (1885-1947) helped appraise the Brand estate, and sold pieces consigned by Armin Brand.

Johnson sold the proof 1852/1 Humbert $20 to Chicago collector Jacob F. Shapero. Shapero's noteworthy collection was auctioned in three parts, by Stack's in 1944, Abe Kosoff in 1948, and RARCOA in 1963. The Kellogg specimen of the proof 1852/1 Humbert $20 appeared as lot 1058 in Stack's December 1944 auction, and sold for $850 to Major Alfred Walter.

In 1944, the 1852/1 Humbert $20 in proof format was believed to be unique. It was understandable, then, that the Stack's catalogers mistakenly pedigreed it as the Humbert specimen. In 1968, John J. Ford, Jr. wrote "In the Bell catalogue this coin was described as, 'The original Augustus Humbert piece sold to Capt. Zabriski (sic) then to Col. Green and to Mr. J.F. Bell. This piece is absolutely unique in this condition.' Unfortunately, that information is totally erroneous. The Zabriskie coin is another example ... and is now in the J.W. Garrett collection at Johns Hopkins with at least one other different Humbert coined proof.."

The "other different Humbert coined proof" referred to by Ford was a proof 1851 Humbert $50, Kagin-6, which became lot 897 in the Bowers & Ruddy March 1980 auction of the second part of the Garrett Collection.

Major Alfred Walter purchased the present piece from its appearance in the 1944 J.F. Bell auction. Walter's own collection appeared in New Netherland's 60th public auction, held December 1968, and his proof 1851 Humbert $20 was lot 574. It sold for $3,200.

The present 1852/1 Humbert $20 is one of two or three known in proof format. For its appearance in a December 1968 New Netherlands auction, John J. Ford, Jr. described the piece as "Mostly brilliant proof. Struck from the regular dies after they had cracked, rusted, been worked on, and partially polished (as has the other specimen known to us). The flan is minutely granular, spotted, and defective. Pristine save for a few microscopic handling marks, the most apparent of which can be found on the obv. Border and the rev. rim. Of unquestioned authenticity."

The piece emerged in two different Superior auctions, first as lot 2328 in an October 1990 sale, then as lot 1737 in the October 1992 auction of the Clark E. Adams & Duncan MacMillan collections. The prices realized for the 1990 auction state that lot 2328 was sold for $434,500.

The Augustus Humbert Specimen

Augustus Humbert was the United States Assayer of Gold in California, and his name appeared on the U.S. Assay Office "ingots" produced in 1851 and early 1852. After the Assay Office closed in favor of a new branch mint at San Francisco, Humbert became a partner with Kellogg at his private mint and assay facility. Humbert was one of the few individuals at the time who appreciated the numismatic importance of the various issues of the Assay Office and Kellogg & Co., and was responsible for several extremely rare proofor specimen strikings.

Best known among these are the proof 1855 Kellogg $50 pieces, but Humbert also owned proof or specimen examples of a Reeded Edge, 887 Thous. 1851 Humbert $50, an 1852 Moffat $10, an 1852/1 Humbert $20, and an 1854 Kellogg $20.

Humbert died in 1873, and his proof territorial gold pieces were inherited by his brother, Pierre. Pierre died in 1901, and his numismatic holdings were acquired by Samuel Hudson and Henry Chapman. Several pieces appeared in their May 1902 auction, Collections of United States Coins of William R. Weeks, Esq. And the late Augustus Humbert. The proof 1852/1 Humbert $20 was not among them, however, since it was sold privately to Andrew C. Zabriskie prior to the 1902 auction.

Zabriskie's collection was auctioned by the Chapman brothers in June 1909. The proof 1852/1 Humbert $20 was lot 356, and realized $360. Col. James W. Ellsworth was the buyer, under the name "Deem."

Ellsworth sold his collection intact to Wayte Raymond for $100,000 in 1923. This purchase was partly funded by John Work Garrett, who had first pick from Ellsworth's magnificent holdings. Among Garrett's selections was a Brasher doubloon, and the proof 1852/1 Humbert $20.

Garrett donated his collection to John Hopkins University, which deaccessioned it through a series of auctions between 1976 and 1981. The proof 1852/1 Humbert $20 appeared as lot 890 in Bowers and Ruddy's March 1980 Garrett II auction, and realized $325,000.

The Sept. 22, 1989 issue of *Coin World* reported the private sale of the Humbert specimen for a whopping $1.3 million dollars, said to be the first single coin transaction to exceed a million dollars. To put this amount in perspective, the Norweb Gem-quality 1861 Paquet $20, the finest of only two examples known, sold at auction for $660,000 in November 1988. This unprecedented private sale undoubtedly motivated the Kellogg specimen owner to consign that piece to an October 1990 Superior auction.

Humbert's proof 1852/1 $20 surfaced again in the May 1992 Superior auction of the Dr. Jack Adams collection as lot 3111. It sold for $374,000.

Business strikes of the 1852/1 Humbert $20 are very rare. The 1981 reference *Private Gold Coins and Patterns of the United States* by Donald H. Kagin is the standard text for the territorial gold series, and lists the issue (K-9) as R.6. This rarity level has held up since, given its paucity of auction appearances. Heritage is the largest rare coin auctioneer, yet in the present decade only two examples of the issue have appeared in Heritage auctions, a VF Details, Damaged piece in our July 2005 San Francisco ANA Signature, and an AU Details, Tooled example in last year's January FUN Signature. Despite their problems, these two coins realized $6,325 and $7,475, which demonstrates the rarity of any 1852/1 Humbert $20.

The present Gem is exceptionally struck for an Assay Office product. Only a couple of vertical shield lines lack pinpoint definition. Only a few trivial obverse hairlines and minuscule alloy spots preclude perfection. It is the personal specimen of Assay Office cashier John Kellogg, and is one of only two proofs known for the issue. It is worthy of the finest territorial gold collection, and the opportunity for acquisition may not arrive again for decades.

Ex: John Glover Kellogg; Kellogg Collection (Thomas L. Elder, 10/16, lot 742); J.F. Bell Collection (Stack's, 12/44), lot 1058; Maj. Alfred Walter; New Netherlands 60th Sale, 12/68, lot 574; Superior, 10/90, lot 2328; Superior, 10/92, lot 1737. (#10194)

Near-Mint 1851 Lettered Edge $50 Slug

3889   1851 Humbert Fifty Dollar, 880 Thous. AU58 NGC.
Lettered Edge, No 50 on Reverse K-2, R.5. This piece has a small target at the center of the reverse. The denomination appears at the bottom of the obverse, where the number 50 is punched into the surface of the coin just left of a raised D. When the dies were made, the letters D and C where included below the eagle, with the blanks left so that the appropriate number of dollars and cents could be punched into the piece to indicate its actual value. While production was limited to pieces of the 50 dollar size, the original intention was to produce large examples and others of odd value. How exciting it would be for collectors today if Augustus Humbert had stuck to the original plan, producing pieces of various and unusual denominations.

The 1851 date does not appear on either the obverse or the reverse, but rather, is included as part of the edge lettering. Each individual segment of the edge was lettered, reading AUGUSTUS / HUMBERT / UNITED / STATES / ASSAYER / OF GOLD / CALIFORNIA / 1851. This example is a lovely green-gold representative with considerable luster. Delicate orange toning has formed around certain devices, adding to the overall eye appeal and desirability of this large gold piece. A few small surface marks are visible on each side, consistent with the grade. *From The Twin Hollows Collection.* (#10196)

Important Mint State 1851 Humbert Fifty Dollar, Kagin-4

3890   1851 Humbert Fifty Dollar, 887 Thous. 50 Rev. MS60 NGC. Kagin-4, High R.5. This is an important example of California Gold Rush history. Although usually called a "slug," and occasionally a "quintuple eagle," the official name for these large gold pieces was "ingot." On September 30, 1850, a bill was passed creating an assay office in California, sanctioned by Congress and serving as a branch of the United States Government. The United States Assay Office of Gold was authorized to produce ingots no smaller than 50 dollars and no larger than 10,000 dollars.

New York watchmaker Augustus Humbert arrived in San Francisco on January 30, 1851. In his possession were master dies bearing the design created by Charles Cushing Wright for the obverse, and by Humbert himself for the reverse. The first ingots were struck by Humbert the very next day. The obverse features the defiant eagle design below a scroll inscribed 887 THOUS in incuse numerals. In the eagle's mouth is a ribbon inscribed LIBERTY. The legend UNITED STATES OF AMERICA around the outside is surrounded by a wide border on this massive octagonal gold coin. Below the eagle are the raised letters D and C, preceded by another incuse 50 punched into the surface. On the reverse is the famous engine-turned design with an incuse 50 at the center. One of the most fascinating features of this slug is the edge, although it is only partially visible inside the NGC holder.

This is a pleasing example with fully brilliant greenish yellow-gold color and substantial luster. The obverse striking details are impressive, with every design element boldly rendered. On the ribbon, the 887 is incuse, and has replaced a previous 880 that was also hand-punched into the coin's surface. The surfaces display a number of moderate marks, mostly on the obverse. This important territorial issue is listed on page 349 of the 2007 *Guide Book*. (#10208)

1851 Humbert 880 THOUS Fifty Dollar, XF40

3891   1851 Humbert Fifty Dollar, 880 Thous. XF40 PCGS. K-5, Low R.5. The former facilities of Moffat & Co. were used when newly appointed U.S. Assayer Augustus Humbert began production of $50 slugs in 1851. This issue represents the lesser of two finenesses used to strike the reeded edge, target reverse variety. Offered here is a bright yellow-gold example with typically weak definition at the center of the obverse, but generous luster still adhering to the devices. A few small edge knocks are more-or-less expected for the grade. Listed on page 349 of the 2007 *Guide Book*.
From The Freedom Collection. (#10211)

Lightly Circulated 1851 Humbert Fifty Dollar, AU50, K-6

3892   1851 Humbert Fifty Dollar, 887 Thous. AU50 NGC. K-6, R.4. A lightly circulated example of this large format Territorial gold coin. The Assay Office in San Francisco actually did very little in 1851 to help alleviate California's need for a circulating medium. What they did under Humbert's leadership was to convert the raw gold dust that had previously been used as currency into these large, so-called $50 "slugs." This piece is moderately abraded on the obverse, and lightly marked on the reverse. The often weak central details are typically soft on this example, and the coloration is a pleasing, uniform, light green-gold.
From The Twin Hollows Collection. (#10214)

1855 Kellogg & Co. Fifty Dollar PR64 PCGS

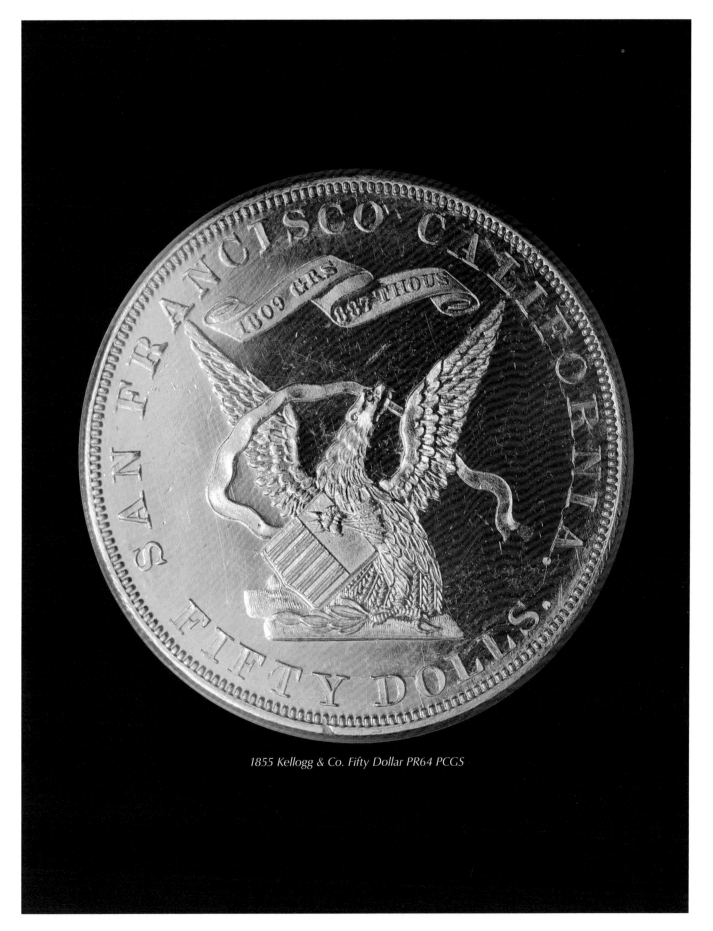

1855 Kellogg & Co. Fifty Dollar PR64 PCGS

Majestic 1855 Kellogg & Co. Fifty Dollar Gold
Tied For Finest Known

3893   1855 Kellogg & Co. Fifty Dollar PR64 PCGS. K-4, Breen-7921, High R.6. This is a remarkable example with extraordinary greenish-gold surfaces. Both sides have deeply mirrored fields with hints of satiny mint frost on the devices. All of the design elements on each side are especially sharp, including the hair details and stars on the obverse, and the feather and claw details on the reverse. A few faint hairlines and tiny contact marks are evident on each side, keeping this specimen out of the Gem grade level. A tiny planchet flake next to the right center of the final 5 in the date provides pedigree identification. Of all 13 pieces currently recorded, this example and the Garrett specimen have each been certified as PR64 by PCGS, **and these two coins are the finest known examples.**

The obverse features a central motif of Liberty wearing a coronet, virtually identical to the U.S. double eagles of the time, except the coronet is inscribed KELLOGG & CO. rather than LIBERTY as on the federal issues. Around the circumference are placed 13 evenly spaced six-point stars, with 1855 below the bust. Frederick Gruner prepared the dies and he signed the obverse F. GRUNER on Liberty's bust truncation. The first 5 in the date is recut, as are stars 4, 6, and 10. Each of the 13 individual stars on the obverse were made by repeated punches from a single diamond-shaped punch. Not only is proof surface seen between the individual elements, but that space is on the same plane as the surrounding field. Equally important, the amount of field space between each element is variable from one star to the next.

The reverse design has an eagle and shield motif at the center, with a blank ribbon in its beak. The claws grasp a branch and three arrows, supporting a shield. The eagle is standing on a base that appears to be a field of grass. In the field above the eagle is a scroll-inscribed 1309 GRS 887 THOUS. Along the border is the lettering SAN FRANCISCO CALIFORNIA and FIFTY DOLLS. The reverse has several fine die cracks, mostly through the peripheral field, yet rather surprising for a coin of such limited production. At first glance, the weight as shown on the coin appears as 1809 grains. However, a simple calculation will show that 1309 is the correct figure, as the higher 1809 grains would equal nearly four ounces!

In the early 19th century, gold mining efforts in the U.S. were concentrated in the Southeastern part of the country, specifically Western North Carolina and Northern Georgia. During the 1830s and 1840s, the Bechtler family operated a private coinage practice in that part of the country, the first large scale producer of private gold coinage. Gold was discovered in California a few years later, and a number of individuals and firms operated assay offices that produced ingots and private gold coins. Among these was the operation of John Glover Kellogg. For more than a decade, Kellogg operated with various partners, including G.F. Richter, J. Hewston, and Augustus Humbert.

The most plentiful issues of the earlier gold rush years were produced by the United States Assay Office operated by Augustus Humbert as assayer. Eventually, a branch of the U.S. Mint was authorized in San Francisco, and began operations in 1854. In that year, a limited coinage commenced, although the earliest San Francisco Mint coinage was sporadic and hardly met local business needs. Area merchants urged Kellogg to produce gold coinage to help meet demand, and the firm minted large quantities of $20 pieces, under the auspices of Kellogg & Richter.

There is no doubt that Kellogg also intended to produce a $50 gold piece for commerce, as evidenced by the dozen known examples of this variety. But why did production stop with a few proof examples? Perhaps a larger coinage was contemplated, but the private enterprise may have been preempted by larger government production. In *Private Gold Coins and Patterns of the United States,* author Donald H. Kagin noted:

> "There are several significant differences between this series [1852-1856] of private gold coins and the previous one. All private gold issuances during this series were the direct result of petitions from the community. This series of private coinage is also characterized by the minters' scrupulous avoidance of any debasement of their products. They also ceased their coinage when the need that precipitated the petitions had been fulfilled."

The following roster derives from a variety of sources, expanded from the listing in Walter Breen's *Complete Encyclopedia of U.S. and Colonial Coins,* and updated through the courtesy of Dr. Donald H. Kagin, a specialist in private gold coinage whose assistance is most appreciated. It is believed that just 12 or 13 examples of this famous rarity are known. The numbers assigned to each specimen rank them according to grade, with the associated number from Walter Breen's roster included. At one time or another, most of the known examples have been described as the finest known.

1. **PR64 PCGS. The specimen offered here.** Breen #11. British private collection; Stack's (5/1984), lot 784; Robert Hughes; Bowers and Merena (8/1995), lot 498. In their 1984 catalog, Stack's noted: "From information conveyed to us, this coin has recently come from England along with a few less important Territorial and Federal gold coins."

2. **PR64 PCGS.** Breen #1. Augustus Humbert; Capt. Andrew C. Zabriskie; Col. James W. Ellsworth; John Work Garrett; Johns Hopkins University (Bowers and Ruddy, 3/1980), lot 910; Kagin's; Paul Padget; Donald Kagin and Stuart Levine; private collection. In the Garrett catalog, it was noted: "It is believed to be the finest known example of its kind." However, that catalog was written several years before the present example became known to the numismatic community.

Note: Walter Breen recorded the Garrett piece as later appearing in Auction '85. However, the coin in that auction was the unique 1854 Kellogg $20 proof from the Garrett Collection.

3. **PR63 PCGS.** Not in Breen. Smith & Son (3/1941); Frank Heim (6/2000); Don Kagin; Q. David Bowers; Don Kagin; Superior (1/2005), lot 953; Western collector.

4. **Choice Proof.** Not in Breen. Superior (5/1987), lot 3140. This piece appears to be a new example that does not match any of the others, and was not listed in the Breen Census.

5. **PR62 PCGS.** Breen #3. George W. Rice; DeWitt Smith; Virgil M. Brand; William F. Dunham (B. Max Mehl, 6/1941), lot 2369; W.D. Waltman Collection (B. Max Mehl, 6/1945), lot 37; Amon Carter Collection (Stack's, 1/1984), lot 1149; Harlan White; Heritage (8/1997), lot 7898; Donald Kagin; Craig Smith; Bowers and Merena (6/2000), lot 1053; Bowers and Merena (1/2002), lot 857; Midwest collection.

6. **PR62 NGC.** Breen #7. N.M. Kaufman Collection (RARCOA, 8/1978), lot 66; Auction '80 (Paramount, 8/1980), lot 982; Auction '84 (RARCOA, 7/1984), lot 2000; Heritage (8/1992), lot 2583; RARCOA; Donald Kagin; private collection.

7. **PR62.** Breen #9. John Story Jenks; Reuting Collection; Arthur C. Nygren (B. Max Mehl, 11/1914), lot 82; George Alfred Lawrence (Thomas Elder, 6/1929), lot 1365; John H. Clapp; Louis E. Eliasberg, Sr.; Eliasberg Estate (Bowers and Merena, 5/1996), lot 366; East Coast collection.

8. **PR62.** Breen #4. Fred Huddart; George H. Earle; Judge C.W. Slack (B. Max Mehl, 5/1925), lot 29; Col. E.H.R. Green; Josiah Lilly Collection; Smithsonian Institution. Walter Breen recorded this specimen as once the property of Amon Carter, Sr. and Jr., although such a listing is doubtful. Additional intermediaries handled this coin on a consignment basis. Both Smithsonian pieces have recently been examined and graded by Jeff Garrett and Ron Guth.

9. **PR62.** Breen #5. H.O Granberg; William H. Woodin; Waldo C. Newcomer; Willis duPont; Smithsonian Institution. This piece was stolen from duPont in October 1967 and recovered in July or August 1978, as reported in *Coin World,* August 9, 1978. Illustrated at http://americanhistory.si.edu.

10. **PR58 PCGS.** Breen #2. Kellogg family; "J.F. Bell;" Memorable Collection (Numismatic Gallery, 3/1948), lot 967; Don Keefer; F.K. Saab; Gibson Sale (Stack's, 11/1974), lot 189; Stack's (Auction '79), lot 996; Stack's (10/1983), lot 239; Stack's (10/2003), lot 2292. In the earlier sales, Stack's described this piece as a "Brilliant Proof," upgrading the description to "Gem Brilliant Proof" in their 2003 catalog, although it was later certified as PR58.

11. **PR53 PCGS.** Breen #10. J.W. Schmandt (Stack's, 1954); Dan Brown; John H. Murrell; Henry H. Clifford; Kagin's (1983 ANA Sale), lot 3630; Superior (Auction '88), lot 491; Superior (Auction '90), lot 1406; Superior (8/1992); private collection.

12. **Impaired Proof.** Breen #6. John A. Beck, part I (Quality Sales, 1/1975), lot 729; Dr. Ketterman; Arnold and Romisa Collections (Bowers and Merena, 9/1984), lot 330; Bowers and Merena (6/1985), lot 24; Christies (3/1994), lot 375; Stack's (3/2005), lot 1320; Donald Kagin; private collection. Described as a "Brilliant Proof with some hairlines and minor friction."

13. **XF Details NCS.** Breen #8. C.W. Cowell (B. Max Mehl, 1911); Waldo Newcomer; Amon Carter, Sr.; 1962 N.Y. Metropolitan Sale (Stack's, 4/1962), lot 2814; John Rowe; Abner Kreisberg (1968); Quality Sales Corp. (11/1972), lot 1410A; Jack Klauson; 1973 ANA Sale (Jess Peters), lot 1030; Pine Tree (3/1974), lot 455; West Coast collection; Christies (3/1990); Stack's (3/2005), lot 1321; Donald Kagin; private collection. In 1972, Abner Kreisberg and Jerry Cohen commented: "The usual surface abrasions and scratches have all been removed and quite a bit of luster is still adhering. Extremely Fine."
    Listed on page 359 of the 2007 *Guide Book.* (#10228)

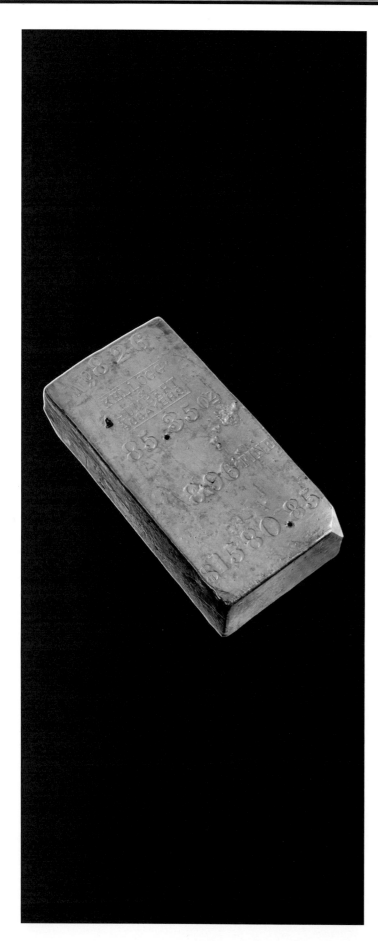

85.35 Ounce
Kellogg & Humbert Gold Ingot

3894 **Kellogg & Humbert Gold Ingot.** The firm of Kellogg & Humbert was well known among the California private concerns that produced coins and assayed the raw gold bullion that was discovered in the American River region beginning in 1848. The partnership of Kellogg and Humbert was formed in April of 1855, just 17 months before the massive transport of bullion went to the bottom of the North Atlantic. The loss was catastrophic, not only in terms of the number of lives lost but also the monetary value that sank to the bottom of the ocean. One hundred thirty-one years later the wreckage of the *S.S. Central America* was discovered and salvage operations began. In October 1988, Tommy Thompson and the salvage crew saw images from the remote underwater explorer *Nemo* of a color they had not seen before: gold. In *America's Lost Treasure*, Thompson relates that moment of discovery:

> "Because *Nemo's* dives are precise, we knew exactly where on the shipwreck site the underwater robot had taken the pictures and where the next dive would take place. Within hours, the submersible was back on the bottom. As we flew the ROV toward the location of the photographs, Milt set the lights. At first we thought we were looking at bricks, but as the beams were adjusted, the color came out. Suddenly, the same monitors that had revealed nothing but colorless ocean terrain for weeks now appeared to be painted a brilliant gold.
>
> "These weren't bricks, but ingots, ingots everywhere ... stacked on the bottom like brownies ... stacked like loaves of bread ... spectacular gold bridges of gold ingots piled on top of timbers and spread over the ocean floor. Then, a little farther along, we found piles of coins, heaped in towers and seemingly spilling into frozen waterfalls. The coins in this part of the shipwreck, which we named the "Garden of Gold," were spread amid the wreckage, stretching beyond *Nemo's* lights into the blackness of the sea."

This was one of the "loaves of bread" the crew saw that October morning 19 years ago. This medium to large-sized ingot is impressed on the top side: No 826 / company imprint / 85.35 Oz / 896 FINE / $1580.85. The back side has a repeat of the individual ingot number, 826. Two assay cuts are out of opposing corners. The ingot is bright yellow-gold, except for deep red patina in the center of the back side. An important ingot from this highly respected California firm.

Elusive XF40 1849 Mormon Gold Five Dollar

3895   1849 Mormon Five Dollar XF40 PCGS. K-2, R.5. The Mormon coinage was an important development in the history of private gold coinage, as related by Donald Kagin: "Of all the fascinating tales of pioneer numismatic history, few can compare with the Mormons and the development of their coinage. Under the guidance of one of the major leaders in American history, Brigham Young, the Mormons significantly influenced the entire history of the West. Among their numismatically related accomplishments was the discovery of gold at Sutter's Mill, the public announcement of that discovery and the subsequent promotion of the gold mining industry in California, the issuance of the first American $20 gold piece, and, finally, the introduction of an entirely new alphabet and its use on a coin."

Despite widespread acceptance within the Mormon community, these "Valley Coins" were unpopular outside Utah. Contemporary assays, especially those conducted at the New Orleans and Philadelphia mints, showed that the value of these coins ranged from 10% to 20% below face value. The five dollar pieces, for example, were valued at about $4.30 each. These coins were made from native California gold, despite the inscription G.S.L.C.P.G. (Great Salt Lake City Pure Gold). Territorial bankers would only accept these coins at a 25% discount, and most were eventually melted. Today, all of these coins are rare, and the five dollar denomination is a bit more plentiful than the other denominations.

This example, exhibiting light green-gold color, was struck on a defective planchet with a crack from the obverse at 2 o'clock to the center, crossing the three-pointed crown. This planchet crack can also be seen on the reverse. Both sides have minor hairlines and other small abrasions. Listed on page 361 of the 2007 *Guide Book*. (#10262)

Choice XF 1849 Mormon Five Dollar

3896   1849 Mormon Five Dollar XF45 PCGS. K-2, R.5. Issued by the Deseret Assay Office under authority of the Mormon Church in Utah, the Mormon gold pieces were issued in 1849 in denominations of two and a half, five, ten, and twenty dollars. The twenty dollar gold coins were the first such coins issued in the United States, preceding the regular-issue Federal double eagles by a few months. In 1850 an assay of the Mormon gold pieces—which due to a lack of parting acids were produced from unrefined California gold dust that contained only the native silver alloy—show them to be underweight in terms of their face value, averaging 866 thousandths fineness. If they circulated at all, they were taken at a considerable discount, and it is quite likely that many of the small mintages were later melted. All examples of Mormon coinage are quite rare. The present example shows about half of its remaining original luster over green-gold surfaces. A couple of light scrapes beneath the 1849 date are barely worthy of singular mention. Population: 21 in 45, 27 finer (11/06).
From The Twin Hollows Collection. (#10262)

Important 1849 Mormon
Five Dollar AU58

3897   1849 Mormon Five Dollar AU58 NGC. A sharply struck example of this famous issue, since the fingers of the clasped hands show greater definition than usually seen. It is possible that the piece was struck twice by the dies, given the quality of the strike and the slight doubling on LORD and the D in DOLLAR. The light green-gold surfaces retain considerable luster, particularly across the peripheral legends. As expected from a piece with a brief stint in commerce, the fields show a few faint marks, but none are of any individual consequence. 1849 was the only Mormon gold date with more than one denomination struck. The Mormons struck two and a half dollar, five dollar, ten dollar, and twenty dollar pieces in 1849, but only five dollar pieces in 1850 and 1860. Listed on page 361 of the 2007 *Guide Book.* Census: 6 in 58, 5 finer (10/06).
From The Jones Beach Collection. (#10262)

Rare 1849 Norris, Gregg, & Norris Five Dollar, AU53

3898   1849 Norris, Gregg, & Norris Five Dollar, P.E. AU53 PCGS. K-2, R.5. This rare variety has the period after ALLOY, appearing as two periods (with the nearby dot between ALLOY and GOLD). In fact, according to the Kagin gold reference, this is the rarest five dollar Territorial gold issue after the R.6 reeded edge, No Period variety. This example is well struck (with medallic alignment), although the eagle shows typical mushiness, and there are a few light abrasions on the obverse and a couple of small puncture marks in the reverse fields. The coloration is a variegated combination of green-gold and red. Listed on page 347 of the 2007 *Guide Book*. Population: 4 in 53, 16 finer (11/06). (#10279)

1849 Norris, Gregg, & Norris Five Dollar AU58

3899   1849 Norris, Gregg, & Norris Five Dollar R.E. AU58 PCGS. K-3, R.6. The Reeded Edge subvariety without a period after ALLOY. Norris, Gregg, & Norris holds a footnote in numismatic history as the first California private gold coiner, although their monopoly ended once Moffat & Co. began production of gold coins in late July 1849. Presumably, the firm was unable to compete with Moffat, and relocated to Stockton, since a single 1850-dated N. G. & N. half eagle is known with the reverse inscription STOCKTON instead of SAN FRANCISCO. This bright canary-gold piece shows only light wear on the shield, and the fields lack detrimental marks. The reverse field at 6 o'clock has a slight change in color and texture. Listed on page 347 of the 2007 *Guide Book*. Population: 5 in 58, 4 finer (10/06).
From The Jones Beach Collection. (#10282)

Appealing AU53 Oregon Exchange Company Five Dollar

3900   1849 Oregon Exchange Co. Five Dollar AU53 NGC. K-1, R.5. The news of the discovery of gold in California reached the Oregon Territory in late July 1848. That news was confirmed in Oregon City, seat of Clackamas County, on August 9 of that year, when the brig *Henry* docked with gold dust, arriving from San Francisco, and by October more than two-thirds of the men in Oregon had departed to seek treasure in the gold fields of California. The *Oregon Spectator,* founded in 1846, one of the first newspapers west of the Mississippi River, was forced to stop publishing in 1848 "because its printer, with 3,000 officers, lawyers, physicians, farmers and mechanics were leaving for the gold fields." (Kagin, *Private Gold Coins and Patterns of the United States.*) By spring of the following year, gold dust had almost entirely replaced beaver and other fur pelts as the primary medium of exchange, although it traded at a substantial discount to silver coins (when available) and to its value at the Philadelphia Mint. Miners were losing money.

Against this backdrop, the Oregon Exchange Company was formed, with the express purpose of weighing and stamping gold. Although Oregon was officially declared a territory of the United States on March 3, 1849—rendering any plan to coin gold clearly unconstitutional—several prominent residents determined to proceed with the plan. The surnames of those residents were Kilborn, Magruder, Taylor, Abernethy, Willson, Rector, (Gill) Campbell, and Smith. Their initials K. M. T. A. W. R. G. S. appear around the rim of the five dollar gold pieces, which also picture a beaver on a log and a laurel wreath. In error, the initials T.O. (rather than O.T., for Oregon Territory) were stamped on the obverse. The five dollar contains the reverse legend OREGON EXCHANGE COMPANY around the periphery, with 130 G. / NATIVE GOLD. / 5 D. in the center. The initials of two men were omitted from the ten dollar pieces struck later, and the T.O. was corrected to O.T.

The gold coinage was unalloyed with silver or copper, and succeeded in raising the price of gold dust from $12 to $16 as the pieces circulated. Alloy was purposely omitted to ensure that the pieces would be accepted regardless of variances in the purity of gold dust, but their inherent softness caused them to suffer in contact with the harder alloyed gold coinage from California—and their higher intrinsic value caused them to soon be melted.

The fives were struck to the extent of 6,000 pieces, along with 2,850 of the tens. The present example shows light rub and strike softness on the beaver and his log, along with miscellaneous small abrasions and surface nicks characteristic of a soft, unalloyed gold. A bit of softness is also visible around the N's in OREGON and NATIVE. Much luster remains, however, and the surfaces are enormously appealing. Census: 3 in 53, 3 finer (11/06). Listed on page 360 of the 2007 *Guide Book.* (#10288)

Rare 1855 Wass Molitor Ten Dollar AU53

3901   1855 Wass Molitor Ten Dollar AU53 PCGS. Ex: *S.S. Central America*. K-6, High R.5. All 1855 Wass Molitor tens display a "plug" around the final 5 in the date, a feature that suggests modification of this obverse die from an 1852-dated die. As is characteristic, this still-lustrous example is reasonably sharp on the portrait, but star detail ranges from strong to virtually nonexistent. A general mushiness prevails on the reverse. An old scratch between the C and A in CALIFORNIA should help pedigree this scarce territorial. Listed on page 357 of the 2007 *Guide Book*. (#10354)

Tied for Finest Certified 1855 Wass Molitor Ten, AU58 PCGS

3902   1855 Wass Molitor Ten Dollar AU58 PCGS. K-6, High R.5. It is the method of manufacture that gives this piece its appearance, with sharper central details and weak peripheral details. A few of the stars on the obverse are nearly invisible, but this has nothing to do with circulation. Indeed, this coin exhibits virtually full frosty luster with only a trace of wear on the highest points. A small nick on the forehead is the only mark of any consequence on this beautiful piece. This is an impressive coin that probably qualifies for the overall Condition Census of the variety, and it is tied with one other coin for the finest that PCGS has certified (11/06). Listed on page 357 of the 2007 *Guide Book*. (#10354)

Scarce 1855 Wass Molitor Twenty, AU50 Details

3903   1855 Wass Molitor Twenty Dollar, Small Head—Tooled, Cleaned—ANACS. AU50 Details. K-7, R.6. Well struck on the obverse, especially on the rims and dentils, with just the final three of the peripheral stars showing weakness. The reverse is likewise well defined around the edges, but the eagle shows typical mushiness. A few abrasions and numerous small planchet flaws and laminations are noted on each side, along with a few die lumps and nicks along the rim. Faint tooling marks are evident in the left obverse field. This is a scarce issue from the final year of the Wass Molitor company, which was the last private mint still operating in San Francisco after the establishment there of the Western U.S. branch mint. Listed on page 358 of the 2007 *Guide Book*. (#10357)

Wass Molitor Fifty Dollar, XF Details

3904   1855 Wass Molitor Fifty Dollar—Repaired, Polished—NCS. XF Details. K-9, R.5. Samuel Wass and Agoston Molitor had both been active in their native Hungary's war for independence. They emigrated to California in 1850 and 1851 respectively, traveling via London. The two established an assaying office in October 1851. Wass had wide-ranging knowledge of mining, chemistry, and mineralogy, while Molitor was an assayer. The pair established one of the most respected private mints in the San Francisco area. The few coins that remain today of this successful partnership are among the most avidly sought-after of all territorial issues. This fifty dollar piece has bright green-gold color and few of the abrasions one would associate with a coin of this size. The surfaces have obviously been smoothed as indicated by the NCS disclaimer, and both sides are bright from polishing. Still, this represents a rare opportunity to acquire a large-size Wass Molitor, and should be seriously considered by the territorial specialist.

From The Twin Hollows Collection. (#10363)

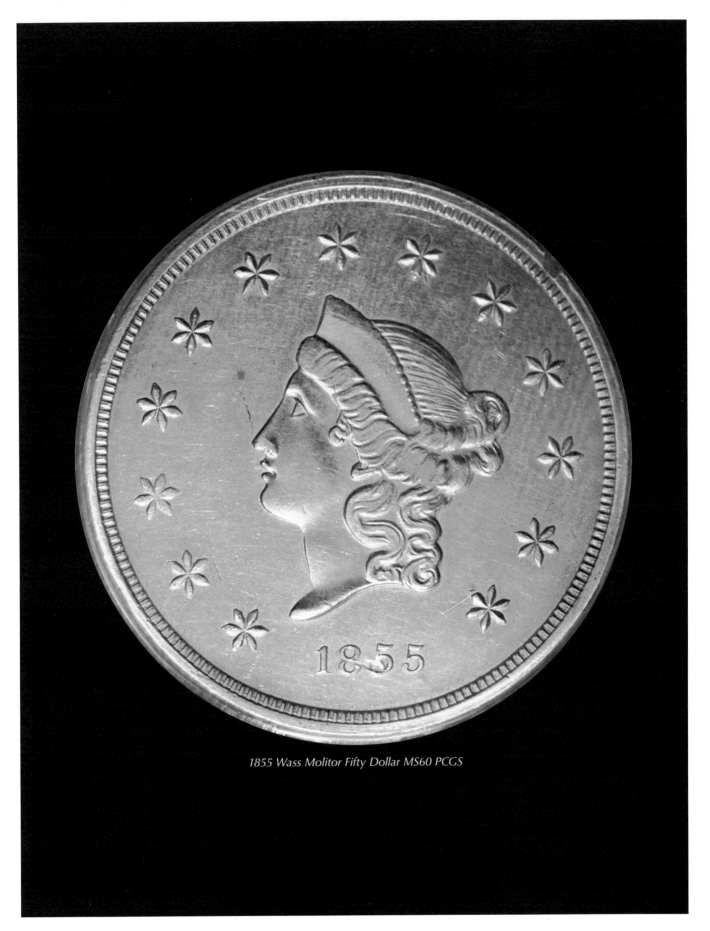

1855 Wass Molitor Fifty Dollar MS60 PCGS

1855 Wass Molitor Fifty Dollar MS60 PCGS

1855 Wass Molitor Fifty Dollar MS60 PCGS, Kagin-9

3905   1855 Wass Molitor Fifty Dollar MS60 PCGS. K-9, R.5. According to Donald Kagin (1981), Hungarian expatriates Count Samuel Wass and Agoston Molitor had operated a well-respected private mint in 1852, coining five and ten-dollar gold pieces for local consumption. They ceased their operation with the impending opening of the San Francisco Mint, but resumed production of larger denomination gold coins during 1855, when the Mint was forced to close periodically for lack of proper acids to refine gold dust and copper alloy. The fifty dollar pieces proved eminently acceptable, even if not beautiful in appearance. Questions about the new coins' true value had arisen, and Wass requested that an assay be done by the San Francisco Mint, which concluded that they were of true value within the provisions of the then current coinage laws. The only round fifty dollar gold coins issued in California, they found acceptance in other areas of the United States as well. The Wass Molitor pieces had the highest intrinsic value of any of the private coiners in California. As a result, a small number were saved rather than being melted, as were the less reputable private minters' coins. A surviving population of seventy to eighty examples has been proposed, and seems like a reasonable estimate, based upon third-party grading service reports.

This coin has a commanding and impressive appearance. The small head of Liberty leaves much open field space on the obverse, even with the oversized stars at the periphery. The reverse is well designed, with a well executed wreath around the bottom, and the other design elements nicely positioned throughout that side. This piece displays deep green-gold color and there are several small abrasions on each side, a trait characteristic of virtually all large denomination territorial gold coins. The overall striking quality seems particularly impressive for the product of a small, private mint. The denticles and other devices are very sharply rendered. The fields show faintly prooflike tendencies, and just a few scattered hairlines that restrict the grade. Currently, the combined population reports of NGC and PCGS show that just nine examples of this scarce issue have been certified in Mint State grades, making this a rare opportunity for the territorial gold collector. Listed on page 358 of the 2007 *Guide Book*. PCGS Population: 1 in 60, 1 finer (10/06). (#10363)

EXPOSITIONS AND FAIRS

1962 Seattle World's Fair Gold Medal Set

3906   Set of 1962 Seattle World's Fair Gold Medals. This set consists of one large (64 mm.) medal, eight medium (38 mm.) medals, and one small (33.5 mm.) medal, each struck in 14K gold. The large and small medals were struck by the U.S. Mint while the eight medium size medals were struck by the Metal Arts Company of Rochester, N.Y. The two medals produced by the U.S. Mint were designed by George Tsutakawa. It is believed that just four of these sets were produced in gold, with one set reportedly held by the Smithsonian Institution.

Each of the eight medium medals have a common reverse design featuring the Century 21 Exposition logo and the inscription SEATTLE WORLD'S FAIR OFFICIAL MEDAL with the 1962 date.

$1,000,000 Display. MS66 NGC. Inscribed 30 TONS OF SILVER DOLLARS PRESENTED BY BEHLEN OF COLUMBUS, NEBRASKA.

World of Century 21. MS67 NGC. Inscribed WORKING, LIVING, PLAYING, TRAVELING, LEARNING IN CENTURY 21.

Century 21 Exposition. MS64 NGC. 64 mm. The obverse is dated 1962 and inscribed CENTURY 21 EXPOSITION SEATTLE WASHINGTON U.S.A. and depicts the Space needle. The reverse is inscribed UNITED STATES COMMEMORATIVE MEDAL SPACE AGE WORLD'S FAIR with an image representing space.

Commerce & Industry. MS66 NGC. Inscribed WORLD OF COMMERCE AND INDUSTRY. THE GATEWAY TO TOMORROW'S LIVING PREVIEWED TODAY.

Space Needle. MS65 NGC. Inscribed SPACE NEEDLE. WORLD'S LARGEST REVOLVING RESTAURANT 600 FEET IN THE SKY.

World of Entertainment. MS65 NGC. Inscribed THE MERRY GO ROUND OF FUN AND LAUGHTER PAST, PRESENT & FUTURE.

Monorail. MS65 NGC. Inscribed MONORAIL. THE WORLD'S FIRST HIGH-SPEED MASS TRANSIT MONORAIL.

Century 21 Science. MS67 NGC. Inscribed WORLD OF SCIENCE. USE DEVELOPMENT SPACEARIUM METHODS & HORIZONS OF SCIENCE.

World of Art. MS66 NGC. Inscribed WORLD OF ART. MUSEUM MASTERPIECES, PAINTINGS & SCULPTURE SINCE 1950. NORTH-WEST COAST INDIAN ART.

Century 21 Exposition. MS64 NGC. 33.5 mm. The obverse and reverse are identical to the large 64 mm. medal.

(Total: 10 medals).

End of Session Eight

A WORLD OF COLLECTIBLES